"Amazingly easy to use. Very portable, very complete."

—*Booklist*

♦

"Complete, concise, and filled with useful information."

—*New York Daily News*

♦

"Hotel information is close to encyclopedic."

—*Des Moines Sunday Register*

♦

"The only mainstream guide to list specific prices. The Walter Cronkite of guidebooks—with all that implies."

—*Travel & Leisure*

# Frommer's®

2nd Edition

# Budapest &
# the Best of
# Hungary

## Joseph S. Lieber & Christina Shea

### with Erzsébet Barát

Macmillan • USA

## ABOUT THE AUTHORS

All four of **Joseph S. Lieber**'s grandparents emigrated from Eastern Europe at the turn of the century, settling in New York City, where he was born and raised. Mr. Lieber lived in Hungary in the early 1990s, teaching English and researching the first edition of this book. He has also worked as a curator, taxi driver, ski bum, and encyclopedia writer, and is presently practicing law in Boston.

**Christina Shea** attended Kenyon College and received her MFA in creative writing from the University of Michigan. Ms. Shea served as a Peace Corps volunteer in Hungary. Subsequently, she directed Peace Corps language-training programs in Lithuania and Kyrghyzstan. Her first novel is forthcoming in the fall of 1998 (St. Martin's Press).

**Erzsébet Barát** was born in Kunhegyes, a small town in the Great Hungarian Plain. She currently lives in Szeged, where she is an associate professor of English at Attila József University. She is working toward her Ph.D. in Linguistics at Lancaster University, in England. Her dissertation concerns Hungarian womens' oral histories.

## ACKNOWLEDGMENTS

The authors wish to thank **Tamás Tóth** and **Marta Totis**, without whom everything would have been far more difficult. We also thank the Bereczki family, our longtime hosts and friends in Pécs. And finally, we thank **Aryeh T. Lieber** for being such a curious and bright-eyed traveler on his first trip to Hungary.

# MACMILLAN TRAVEL

A Simon & Schuster Macmillan Company
1633 Broadway
New York, NY 10019

Find us online at **www.frommers.com**.

ISBN 0-02-862082-8
ISSN 1042-8399

Editor: Neil E. Schlecht
Production Editor: Tony McDonald
Design by Michele Laseau
Digital Cartography by Jim Moore & Ortelius Design
Maps copyright © by Simon & Schuster, Inc.

## SPECIAL SALES

Bulk purchases (10+ copies) of Frommer's and selected Macmillan travel guides are available to corporations, organizations, mail-order catalogs, institutions, and charities at special discounts, and can be customized to suit individual needs. For more information write to Special Sales, Macmillan General Reference, 1633 Broadway, New York, NY 10019.

Manufactured in the United States of America

# Contents

## 5   Where to Dine in Budapest   81

## 6   Exploring Budapest   102

# List of Maps

## AN INVITATION TO THE READER

In researching this book, we discovered many wonderful places—hotels, restaurants, shops, and more. We're sure you'll find others. Please tell us about them, so we can share the information with your fellow travelers in upcoming editions. If you were disappointed with a recommendation, we'd love to know that, too. Please write to:

*Frommer's Budapest & the Best of Hungary,* 2nd Edition
Macmillan Travel
1633 Broadway
New York, NY 10019

## AN ADDITIONAL NOTE

Please be advised that travel information is subject to change at any time—and this is especially true of prices. We therefore suggest that you write or call ahead for confirmation when making your travel plans. The authors, editors, and publisher cannot be held responsible for the experiences of readers while traveling. Your safety is important to us, however, so we encourage you to stay alert and be aware of your surroundings. Keep a close eye on cameras, purses, and wallets, all favorite targets of thieves and pickpockets.

## WHAT THE SYMBOLS MEAN

### ❂ Frommer's Favorites

Our favorite places and experiences—outstanding for quality, value, or both.

The following abbreviations are used for credit cards:

| | | | |
|---|---|---|---|
| AE | American Express | EURO | Eurocard |
| CB | Carte Blanche | JCB | Japan Credit Bank |
| DC | Diners Club | MC | MasterCard |
| DISC | Discover | V | Visa |

## FIND FROMMER'S ONLINE

Arthur Frommer's Outspoken Encyclopedia of Travel (www.frommers.com) offers more than 6,000 pages of up-to-the-minute travel information—including the latest bargains and candid, personal articles updated daily by Arthur Frommer himself. No other website offers such comprehensive and timely coverage of the world of travel.

# Budapest, the Heart of Hungary

For much of the 20th century, Budapest languished in relative obscurity, off the itinerary and out of the minds of most European and North American travelers. The dramatic political changes of 1989 irreversibly altered the state of the Hungarian capital, however. Budapest, awakened after its long slumber behind the Iron Curtain, now ranks as one of Europe's hottest travel destinations. One of the great cities of Central Europe, Budapest embodies all the elements of the region's peculiar and rich cultural legacy. Poised between East and West, both geographically and culturally, Budapest stands proudly at the center of the region's cultural rebirth.

Budapest came of age as a city in the 19th century. In the early 1800s, the two towns of Buda and Pest were little more than provincial outposts on the Danube. The dawning of a modern Hungarian identity spawned the neoclassical development of the city, from which period several monuments survive, foremost among them the National Museum. Later in the century, the rise of the eclectic style coincided with the great post-1867 boom, creating most of the historic inner city. Indeed, Budapest, despite its Roman ruins and reconstructed medieval castle district, is very much a *fin-de-siècle* city, its characteristic coffeehouse and music-hall culture attesting to this. Unfortunately, the decades after World War I were not kind to Hungary's charming capital, and Budapest's turn-of-the-century glory seemed irretrievably lost. How fitting it is, then, that Budapest's post–Cold War renaissance comes when it does: The city will once again attract visitors from far and wide as a new century turns.

Despite the collapse of the Iron Curtain, Budapest retains an exotic feeling seldom experienced in the "better known" capital cities of Europe. This is partly due to the complex and unusual language of the Hungarians. *Magyar* originated on the eastern side of the Ural Mountains: Along with Finnish and Estonian, it's one of Europe's few representatives of the Finno-Ugric family of languages. As you listen to people conversing on the bus and you attempt to read the labels in the grocery store, you'll indeed know that you've arrived in a different and new place. While Budapest is well on its way to integrating itself into Europe, the Hungarian language will always be a mystery to the great majority of those outside its borders. This has long been one of the country's greatest obstacles; nevertheless, the Hungarian people are intensely proud of their language and its charms.

Budapest's extraordinary ambience can be felt throughout the city. Take a turn off any of the main boulevards one morning and quickly find yourself in a quiet residential neighborhood. The scent of a hearty *gulyás* wafts from a kitchen window. A woman with a brightly colored kerchief tied about her head sweeps the sidewalk with a homemade broom. Cigarette smoke fogs the cavelike entryway of the corner pub and the sign on the door states that beer is served up as early as 7am. Rows of salamis hang in the window of the grocery store next door. In the little park across the way, men play chess in the shade of chestnut trees, young lovers kiss on a bench, and the famed Hungarian pedigree dog, the *vizsla*, can be glimpsed darting through the trees. Budapest's residential streets are truly enchanting, but it is inside the courtyards of the apartment buildings that the city's greatest secret is told: Budapesters are villagers at heart. Fruit trees and flower gardens flourish, cats lounge in the sun, and jars of pickled vegetables line the window ledges.

From the old women selling boxes of raspberries in the heart of downtown Pest, cars careening by on all sides, to the young boys playing soccer in the green foothills of Buda, where the air is fresh and clean, this city and its people take you in and hold you tight. Budapest is a remarkable and yet wholly unpretentious place.

And from Budapest, venture out into Hungary. A great part of this nation's allure lies in the countryside and villages. The most distant outposts are no more than 4 or 5 hours away by train, fewer still by car. In Hungary, a land of rivers and plains, you'll discover sunburnt hillside vineyards and deep verdant valleys, lush cherry orchards, and endless fields of dusty sunflowers. You'll also encounter more Hungarian history, as the towns and cities are filled with statues and monuments to a glorious distant past. Explore the string of small riverside towns along the Danube Bend for a day. Or take several days to visit national parks, the famous caves in Aggletek, or well-preserved villages. Travel into the hills of northern Hungary or the Great Plain in the southeast or relax along the shores of Lake Balaton. Have a spontaneous picnic, a midday swim, a hike in the hills, or a shopping trip in a village market.

# 1 Frommer's Favorite Experiences in Budapest & Hungary

- **Attending the Opera.** The Opera House is one of Budapest's most spectacular buildings. For the price of a baseball ticket back home, you can sit in the royal box, once the preserve of Habsburg monarchs.
- **Taking a Leisurely Walk in the Buda Hills.** It's hard to believe that such an expanse of hilly forest land is right here within the capital city. There are trails aplenty; every Budapest native has a favorite hiking trail.
- **Shopping for Produce and Salami at the Market Halls.** Built at the turn of the century, Budapest's vintage market halls continue to be home to lively commerce in fruits and vegetables. Even if the vendors seem oblivious to the great halls they work in, you'll marvel at their size and dignity.
- **Stopping for Coffee and Pastry at the New York Kávéház.** One of the city's finest art nouveau interiors, the New York Coffeehouse has been serving coffee and pastries since the turn of the century, when it was *the* place for artists, writers, and actors.
- **Dipping into the Thermal Baths.** No Central European could imagine a trip to Budapest without at least one session in the city's fabled thermal waters. The art nouveau Hotel Gellért is the most glorious of the many bathhouses—others are 16th-century Turkish baths.

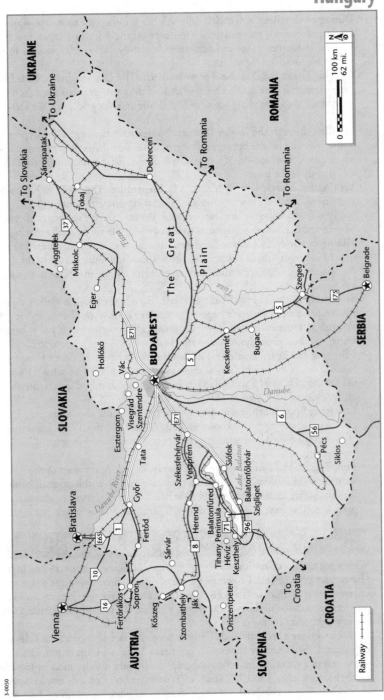

Railway +++++

3-0050

3

- **Dining in Grandeur at Gundel.** Although this is Budapest's most expensive and fanciest restaurant, you can get a meal here for the price of a casual lunch in Vienna. The owner is George Lang, whose book *The Cuisine of Hungary* is an authoritative source on the subject.
- **Cruising Down the Danube.** The wide stretch of the Danube divides Buda from Pest; a boat ride affords you a view of most of the city's great buildings. You can go by boat to the charming towns of Szentendre and Visegrád along the Danube Bend.
- **Strolling through the Jewish District.** Budapest has the largest Jewish population of any city on the European continent (outside Russia). Pest's historic Jewish neighborhood, run-down but relatively unchanged, resonates with the magic and tragedy of the past.
- **Visiting the Margit Kovács Museum in Szentendre.** The works of Hungary's best-known ceramic artist are displayed in this expansive museum in a lovely, if tourist-infested, village of the Danube Bend. Kovács's unique sculptures of elderly women and her folk-art–influenced friezes of village life are especially moving.
- **Hiking in the Hills outside Szigliget.** You can hike up to the fantastic ruins of a 13th-century castle that remain above this scenic little village in the Lake Balaton region, or go a few miles farther north and hike up into hills covered with vineyards.
- **Swimming in the Thermal Lake at Héviz.** Even in the bitterest spell of winter, the temperature in Europe's largest thermal lake seldom dips below 85° to 90° Fahrenheit. Hungarians swim here year-round, and you can, too! If you're here in winter, it'll be a great photo op and travel tale.
- **Climbing the Eger Minaret.** This beautiful, small city in northern Hungary is home to one of the country's most impressive Turkish ruins: a 14-sided, 110-foot-tall minaret. Those who succeed in climbing the steep, cramped spiral staircase are justly rewarded with a spectacular view.
- **Exploring Pécs.** When you wander around this delightful city in southern Hungary, you'll discover why it's known as the 2,000-year-old city. Pécs is home to one of Hungary's most pleasing central squares and some great examples of Turkish architecture.
- **Sampling the Fruit and Vegetable Market in Szeged.** At the main open-air market behind the bus station, in this town near the Serbian and Romanian borders, the vendors are local farmers selling their bounty: peaches, apricots, cherries, and pears, as well as fresh flowers, and of course, dried paprika wreathes.

## 2 The City Today

With a population of approximately 2.1 million, Budapest is home to one in five Hungarians. Few capitals so dominate the life of their country: Compared to the capital, every other Hungarian city is no more than a provincial town. Present-day Hungary has a population of about 10.5 million, while some 3 million ethnic Hungarians live in neighboring countries.

Hungarians are a predominantly Catholic people; in fact, along with the Poles and Lithuanians, they represent the eastern frontier of European Catholicism. Once the junior seat of a sprawling multinational empire, Hungary is today more or less ethnically homogeneous. The 1920 Treaty of Trianon, imposed on a defeated Hungary after World War I, delegated most minorities to neighboring countries. Scarcely a generation later, the destruction of Hungarian Jewry in World War II and the departure of thousands of ethnic Germans after the war further homogenized the population. Hungary's 500,000 Gypsies comprise the country's largest minority today, while other minority populations include ethnic Germans, Slovaks, Serbs, Croats, Jews (Budapest is home to the largest Jewish population of any European city outside Russia), and Romanians. The capital city reflects this ethnic mix.

Budapest is in every way Hungary's cultural and economic center—as well as, more or less, its geographical center. All major Hungarian highways and rail lines emanate from Budapest like spokes from the hub of a wheel. The city encompasses 525 square kilometers (203 square miles), of which just over two-thirds lies on the right bank in predominantly flat Pest. Buda, on the other hand, is distinguished by its hills—its highest is 529m (1,735-foot) János Hill—and wooded areas.

Oddly enough, this capital of a landlocked country is defined by water. The Danube River cuts a wide swath between its constituent parts, Buda and Pest, while over 100 natural hot springs bubble beneath the city. The river flows through the city at an average width of 400 meters (1,312 feet), and its 28-kilometer (17.4-mile) stretch at Budapest represents almost 1% of its total length. Several Danube islands are considered part of the city, the largest of which is Csepel Island. To the north of Budapest, the Danube alters its west-east course sharply in a series of curves at the celebrated Danube Bend, an area famous for its historic towns and lovely scenery.

Among Hungarian cities, Budapest is the clear leader in the rapid Westernization process. For example, Budapest's fast-food market, as recently as 1991 cornered by McDonald's, is now crowded with outlets of Burger King, Kentucky Fried Chicken, Dunkin Donuts, Pizza Hut, and Wendy's. Most consumer products are now available in the Hungarian capital, but some things do not change so fast. Salaries, for example, have not kept pace with inflation, and as a result many citizens can only look longingly through shop windows at these new goods. A certain amount of bitterness has thus accompanied the rapid development, as Hungarians begin to understand the drawbacks of a consumer society.

Still, Hungary is wasting little time in trying to undo four decades of stunted economic development and cultural orthodoxy. The first act was symbolic: Hundreds of streets reverted back to their prewar names, shedding appellations like "Red Army Square," "Road of the People's Republic," and "Lenin Boulevard." Western visitors are also pleased to see new standards of efficiency, service, and cleanliness in Hungary. Tourists are flocking to Budapest in numbers no one could have imagined even a few years ago.

In 1997, Hungary, along with Poland and the Czech Republic, was invited to join NATO. Membership in that Western military alliance now appears imminent, as does eventual membership in the European Union. Troubled by inflation, unemployment, and the fast pace of privatization, however, a significant number of Hungarians fear the darker side of their country's transition to a Western-style free-market economy. The Socialist Party, the most successful party in the 1994 elections and the lead party in the governing coalition, remains firmly entrenched in power, even as the prime minister, Gyula Horn, fends off criticism of his ignominious, though minor, role in suppressing the 1956 anti-Communist uprising. In the midst of all these changes, Hungary in 1996 found the time and energy to celebrate the 1,100th anniversary of the Magyar Conquest. Most Hungarians, it seems, can look back more than a thousand years with a clear gaze, but few pretend to know what tomorrow has in store for them.

# 3 A Look at the Past

## Dateline

- **3rd century B.C.** Celtic tribes establish settlements in the area around Budapest.
- **1st to 5th century A.D.** Roman Empire extends to the Danube; Aquincum (present-day Óbuda) chosen as capital of Roman province of Pannonia.
- **5th century** Huns take over Pannonia, soon to be replaced by migratory tribes.
- **6th to 9th century** Avars control Hungary.
- **896** Magyar (Hungarian) conquest of Carpathian Basin.
- **1000** Stephen I becomes Hungary's first Christian king; the House of Árpád is established; the capital is first at Esztergom, and later at Visegrád and Székesfehérvár.
- **12th century** Buda and Pest develop as trading towns.
- **1241–42** Mongol armies under Batu Khan overrun Hungary, leaving it in ashes when they suddenly depart.
- **1242–70** King Béla IV rebuilds the country; a fortress is built in Buda.
- **14th century** Royal court is moved to Buda; late in the century King Sigismund of Luxembourg builds a great Gothic palace at Buda.
- **1458–90** Reign of King Matthias Corvinus, who initiates Golden Age of Buda and introduces ideas and culture of the Renaissance.

*continues*

**THE ROMANS & THEIR SUCCESSORS** Although Celtic tribes established themselves in the area around Buda in the 3rd century B.C., the Romans built the first extensive settlements. After conquering present-day western Hungary (Transdanubia), the Romans extended their empire east to the Danube and occupied the Celtic settlement of Ak-Ink (Abundant Waters), renaming it Aquincum. The military camp of Aquincum was near where the Árpád Bridge now stands, while the civilian town was farther north; ruins of both can be seen today. By the early 2nd century, Aquincum had become the capital of the Roman province of Lower Pannonia. It was the seat of the imperial governor; the future emperor Hadrian was the first to fill the position in this Roman outpost. The Romans ruled Transdanubia for four centuries, building impressive fortifications along the Danube's west bank. They were the first to develop the thermal waters of Buda, building a number of bathhouses. At its height, Aquincum had a population of 50,000 people. As the empire waned, however, the garrisons on the Danube were increasingly subject to attacks from "barbarians" from the east, and Rome evacuated Aquincum in the early 5th century.

**THE AGE OF MIGRATIONS** The Huns succeeded the Romans, but their rule here was brief. After the death of their great leader Attila in 453, the Hun empire crumbled and present-day Hungary became the domain of a succession of mostly Teutonic tribes. A conquering tribe from central Asia, the Avars, moved into the area in the 6th century. Under their sponsorship, commerce-oriented Slavic tribes settled in the area of present-day Budapest.

**THE MAGYAR CONQUEST** Led by Prince Árpád, whose family line (the House of Árpád) would rule Hungary until 1301, the seven allied Magyar tribes took the entire Carpathian Basin (a natural geological formation incorporating parts of present-day Romania, Serbia, Croatia, Slovenia, Austria, Slovakia, and Ukraine) in 896. Legend has it that the tribes fanned out, each taking control of a different part of the country. Árpád and his tribe are believed to have settled on Csepel Island in present-day Budapest, and another tribe settled in Óbuda, refortifying the Roman town. Once established, the Magyars engaged in a series of successful 10th-century raids on Western Europe, penetrating as far west as the Pyrenees. During these raids they earned their lasting reputation as skilled horsemen; the tricky "feigned withdrawal" was their most famous ploy. The raids ended with a decisive defeat at Augsburg in southwest Germany in 955.

## THE DEVELOPMENT OF THE STATE   A feudal state was forged under Hungary's first Christian king, István (Stephen) I (later Saint Stephen), who was crowned by the pope in 1000. The forced conversion of the Magyars was not without its darker side: Those who preferred to maintain their traditional ways were treated with the utmost cruelty. Nevertheless, Stephen succeeded in organizing a feudal state apparatus, without which the fledgling Hungarian kingdom certainly would not have survived. After Stephen's death, there was renewed strife between the Christians and the pagans. The iron-fisted Bishop Gellért, who had served Stephen for many years, was killed in 1046 when he was rolled in a barrel into the Danube from the hill in Buda that now bears his name. Despite this, and a number of succession crises in the following centuries, the feudal Christian state remained intact.

In this period, Esztergom, then Székesfehérvár, and briefly Visegrád had served as Hungary's capital. Not until the 12th century did Buda and Pest begin to develop into major towns, populated in large part by German, French, and Walloon settlers. But in 1241 disaster struck: Rampaging out of Asia, the Mongols overran Hungary. Pest was destroyed, and after crossing the frozen Danube in the winter of 1241–42, the Mongols conquered Buda and all of Transdanubia beyond, burning and looting everything in their path. King Béla IV was forced to flee the country. During his brief exile he vowed his daughter would become a nun if he could return to rebuild Hungary. The Mongols retreated in 1242, and Princess Margit was duly sent to the convent on "Rabbit Island": This island in the Danube, now Budapest's most popular park, bears Margit's name today.

Because only hilltop fortresses had withstood the Mongol onslaught, King Béla had a series of new ones built around the country. Buda was one of the spots chosen; in addition to the fortification of Castle Hill, a royal palace was constructed (though it was not Béla's primary residence). German settlers were invited to replace the Hungarians who

- **1541** 150-year Turkish occupation of Buda and Pest begins.
- **1686** United Christian armies drive Turks from Buda, but the city is destroyed in the liberation; Habsburg occupation of Hungary commences.
- **1703–11** Ferenc Rákóczi II's rebellions against Austria defeated.
- **Late 18th century** Buda and Pest begin to undergo rapid growth; in 1777, the University of Nagyszombat moves to Buda and then to Pest in 1784.
- **1825–48** Age of Reform; rise of neoclassical style in Budapest; building of National Theater (1837) and National Museum (1848).
- **1838** Great Danube flood destroys much of Pest.
- **1848–49** Hungarian Revolution defeated by Austrians, with critical aid from tsarist Russia; plans to unite Buda, Pest, and Óbuda into one city are not realized.
- **1849** The first permanent bridge across the Danube, the Chain Bridge, is opened.
- **1867** Austro-Hungarian empire established; Franz Joseph crowned king of Hungary in Matthias Church.
- **1873** Pest, Buda, and Óbuda are united into one city—Budapest.
- **1873–1914** Pest's Golden Age: City Park, Andrássy út, the ring boulevards, Opera House, the continent's first metro, and Parliament are built.
- **1896** Millennial of Magyar Conquest; city is site of great celebrations.

*continues*

- **1914–18** Austria-Hungary is on losing side of World War I; the Habsburg monarchy disintegrates.
- **1918–19** Country in chaos; Hungarian Republic established; Béla Kun forms a short-lived Communist government, which is succeeded by the reactionary regime of Admiral Miklós Horthy.
- **1920** Treaty of Trianon codifies the enormous territorial losses suffered by Hungary in the aftermath of World War I.
- **1941** Hungary, obsessed with revision of Trianon treaty, enters World War II, joining Germany's unprovoked attack on Yugoslavia.
- **1944–45** Nazis occupy Hungary; Budapest Jews are forced into a walled ghetto; bitter Soviet-German fighting leaves Budapest in ruins; Soviets liberate—and occupy—the country.
- **1945–56** Brief parliamentary democracy is followed by the establishment of a Stalinist state.
- **1956** Hungarian Uprising, led by Imre Nagy and centered in Budapest, is crushed by Soviet troops; János Kádár installed as new Communist leader.
- **1968** Period of internal Communist reform is capped by the New Economic Mechanism, which decentralizes the economy and allows limited private enterprise.
- **1988–89** Kádár ousted by party reformers and Hungary begins transition to multiparty government; Eastern European communism collapses in summer and fall 1989.

*continues*

had been wiped out by invasion. These Germans gave the name *Ofen* (oven) to the town on the Danube's right bank, probably because of the presence there of a lime kiln industry. The Slavic name *Pest*, also meaning oven, is believed to derive from this time. In 1255, Castle Hill was made a city, usurping the name Buda from the former Buda to its immediate north, which was henceforth known as *Óbuda* (Old Buda). Buda became the residence of an increasing number of aristocrats and burghers, while the medieval walled city of Pest continued to develop across the river. In 1301, the male line of the House of Árpád died out; Hungary would be ruled henceforth by a mixed succession of foreign-born and Hungarian kings.

**THE GOLDEN AGE OF BUDA**   King Charles Robert (1308–42), of the House of Anjou, moved his court from Visegrád to Buda, and his son Louis the Great (1342–82) expanded the palace. The town began to blossom at the turn of the 15th century under the rule of King Sigismund of Luxembourg (who was also the Holy Roman Emperor), who had a glorious Gothic palace built on Castle Hill. But it was King Matthias Corvinus (1458–90), influenced by the Italian Renaissance, who oversaw the Golden Age of Buda. Matthias's palace was expanded in Renaissance style by Italian architects and decorated with the finest European art, while his court became a center of European culture and learning. He amassed an enormous and fabled library, filled with the famous Corvinae manuscripts. The András Hess Press, one of Europe's earliest, was operating in Buda at this time as well. Called "Matthias the Just," the king remains one of the best-loved figures of Hungarian history, and the largest church of the Castle District bears his name.

**THE TURKISH PERIOD**   After Matthias's death, a divided nobility and the bloody suppression of a peasant revolt severely weakened Hungary. The Ottoman armies swept north up the Danube, and in 1526 routed the Hungarians at the Battle of Mohács. The fortified city of Buda fell in 1541. The 150-year Turkish period that followed is rued by Hungarians as one of stagnation and decay. Little new building, aside from fortification of existing walls and bathhouse construction, was undertaken. Everywhere churches were converted into mosques, and Buda's skyline filled with minarets.

## THE HABSBURG PERIOD: LIBERATION BY FIRE

The wry joke "the operation was successful, but the patient died" might describe the liberation of Buda and Pest by the united Christian armies in 1686. The two towns were utterly destroyed, with only a few thousand people remaining alive inside the walls by the time the Turks were vanquished. Having survived the Turkish period intact, the royal palace was destroyed in the siege.

Resettlement and rebuilding were gradual, and formerly Gothic Buda took on a decidedly baroque appearance during the process. Though it would never again be a royal seat, the palace was rebuilt and expanded over the years.

Hungary was to be ruled by the victorious House of Habsburg until the collapse of the Habsburg empire in World War I. Relations with the new Viennese rulers were strained from the outset, flaring into open conflict for the first time when the Transylvanian prince Ferenc Rákóczi II led a series of valiant, but ultimately unsuccessful, rebellions between 1703 and 1711. The beginnings of modern Hungarian nationalism, which would explode into revolution in 1848, can be detected in this period.

Budapest's population grew steadily throughout the 18th century, while the university was moved from Nagyszombat (now Trnava, Slovakia) first to Buda, in 1777, and subsequently to Pest, in 1784. Pest expanded beyond its medieval city walls in the late 18th century with the development of Lipótváros (Leopold Town, now considered part of the Inner City).

- **1990** First free elections since 1945 bring center-right Hungarian Democratic Forum to power.
- **1991** Last Soviet troops leave country; Pope John Paul II visits.
- **1994** Socialist Party prevails in election; forms coalition government.
- **1997** Hungary invited to join the North Atlantic Treaty Organization (NATO).

## THE 19TH CENTURY: REFORM, REVOLUTION & COMPROMISE

By the early 19th century, Pest and Buda had become the centers of political, economic, and cultural life in Hungary. Habsburg Archduke Joseph, longtime palatine of Hungary (1796–1847), was a leading force in Pest's development in the early part of the century. The great Danube Flood of 1838 would destroy much of Pest, but it also provided an opportunity for the town to be rebuilt along more contemporary and progressive lines. For the first time, Pest began to surpass Buda as the center of commerce and industry, a role it has never relinquished. Jews played a major part in the early development of Pest and continued to do so until World War II.

The second quarter of the century is known as the Age of Reform in Hungary. Concomitant with the development of modern nationalism, this period saw the construction of many important and grand buildings; first among them are the National Theater (1837) and the National Museum (1848). Emblematic of the era was the construction of the first permanent bridge across the Danube, the Chain Bridge (1839–49). Like the Academy of Sciences, founded in 1825, this project was the brainchild of Count István Széchenyi. One of the period's leading figures, Széchenyi argued for increased Hungarian independence within the Habsburg empire and was the first to call for the union of Buda and Pest. His more radical rival, and the other giant figure of the mid-19th century, was Lajos Kossuth, a lawyer of Slovak ethnic origins, who demanded full independence from Austria in addition to the abolition of Hungary's feudal structure.

Hungary's nationalistic and anti-Habsburg sentiments culminated in the revolutionary events of 1848. Legend has it that the poet Sándor Petőfi rallied the radical forces of Pest by reciting his incendiary "National Song" from the steps of the

*In the city of Buda, which is extraordinarily high, lies the king's palace, which reaches to the sky.*

—Dzhelalshade Mustapha, Turkish chronicler, 16th century

National Museum. Students seized the university and City Hall. A revolutionary body, the Budapest Committee of Public Safety, was formed. Weakened by revolts spreading throughout their empire, the Austrians initially agreed to Hungarian independence, but as they consolidated power in the summer it became increasingly clear that Hungary would have to defend its independence militarily. Despite Lajos Kossuth's passionate leadership, the defeat of the revolution was eventually ensured by the defection of most minorities living within Hungary—who saw that their own national aspirations had no future in an independent, ultranationalist Hungary—and the willingness of the Russian tsar to aid the Habsburgs. The tragic heroes of the day—Kossuth, who spent his remaining years in exile; Széchenyi, who went mad; the prime minister Lajos Batthyány, who was executed by his captors; and the poet Petőfi, who was killed in battle—remain among the most revered figures in the land.

A brief but painful period of absolutism followed, during which the Citadel on Gellért Hill was built as an overt symbol of Austrian supremacy. The 1867 Compromise, engineered by Ferenc Deák, established the dual Austro-Hungarian monarchy and brought a lasting peace and a measure of independence to Hungary. Following the coronation of the Habsburg emperor Franz Joseph, the union of the three cities—Buda, Pest, and Óbuda—became a reality in 1873.

**PEST'S GOLDEN AGE: 1873–1914**   The most intense period of development in the city's history was now under way. The national railway system was developed, with all lines converging in the capital. The distinctive ring boulevards of Pest were designed, as well as the radial road, now called Andrássy út, on which the lovely State Opera House opened in 1884. The City Park was laid out, with Heroes' Square as its entrance, and more bridges were built over the Danube. The first metro on the continent was built underneath Andrássy út; this antique line, renovated in 1996, is still functioning today. Much of this development culminated in the 1896 Hungarian millennial celebration, the greatest expression to date of Hungarian national pride. The predominantly neo-Gothic Parliament building, modeled on London's, was completed in 1902, although only once prior to 1990 did a democratically elected legislature convene in its great hall (in 1945).

A strident Hungarian nationalism fueled this period of frenetic expansion. Under the policy of "Magyarization," ethnic assimilation was encouraged—indeed, coerced—throughout the country. The use of the Hungarian language by ethnic minorities became more widespread; Jews, adopting it for the first time as their mother tongue, continued to play a leading role in the city's rapid expansion.

Population growth in the combined cities reflects the magnitude of Budapest's expansion: In 1867, the city had 270,000 residents; by 1890, there were 500,000 people living in the now unified city; and only 20 years later, in 1910, there were almost 900,000.

If King Matthias Corvinus's day was Buda's Golden Age, the turn of the century was certainly Pest's. The distinctive eclectic and art nouveau buildings that still define the city today date from this brief period when some of the country's greatest architects labored to create a singular Hungarian style. Cafe society was at its peak, rivaling that of Vienna. In the first heady days of the new century, Budapest seemed poised to take its place among Europe's great capitals. But as Matthias introduced the Italian Renaissance to a city in the path of the Turkish armies, so, too, did the burgeoning of Pest occur under the gathering clouds of World War I.

**THE WORLD WARS: DESTRUCTION, DESOLATION & LOSS**   The advent of war in 1914 and Hungary's alliance with the Central Powers was greeted with great shows of patriotism in the capital. Almost from the outset, however, the civilian population suffered great hardships. Under the pressures of wartime production, the nascent workers' movement gained new ground in Hungary.

After Emperor Franz Joseph's death in 1916, the last Habsburg emperor, Charles IV, was crowned in Matthias Church. Juxtaposed against the steadily deteriorating war situation and desperate shortages of food and fuel in the city, the coronation was the last gasp of a dying empire. The winter of 1917–18 was a particularly difficult one for the Hungarians, both on the battlefield and at home. Antiwar protests, usually met by police repression, increased, and opposition forces rallied around Count Mihály Károlyi, a vocal opponent of the war.

The total defeat of the Central Powers in 1918 led to the collapse of the Austro-Hungarian empire, and the new Hungarian Republic was declared on November 16 of that year. Károlyi was elected president, but his position was untenable from the start. Chief among his domestic problems was the increasingly radical position of the labor movement, inspired by the recent Russian Revolution. His unwillingness to enact a land reform program caused unrest in the countryside. The international situation was even grimmer. The victorious powers insisted on treating Hungary as a vanquished nation, much to the delight of the other newly formed successor states (particularly Romania, Czechoslovakia, and Yugoslavia) that were competing with Hungary for disputed territory. Hungary suffered enormous territorial losses (later codified by the Treaty of Trianon) during these postwar days as the country's new leaders stood by helplessly. Károlyi's fall was ultimately caused by the French demand that Hungarian troops withdraw a further 50 kilometers (30 miles) from the Romanian border, in order to create a "neutral zone." Unwilling to comply, he resigned.

In 1919, the Hungarian Communist Party leader Béla Kun formed a new government and declared a "Republic of Councils." Allied with Bolshevik Russia, the Kun administration initially enjoyed some measure of popular support in Hungary. Industry was nationalized, and the leading figures of Hungarian culture were enlisted to champion the regime. Much of the initial enthusiasm waned with the advent of a Red Terror on the Bolshevik model, and the rural population turned against Kun when it became clear that collectivization was his version of land reform.

In reality, the experiment was a generation, or a world war, too early. The Western powers, alarmed at the developments in Russia, were certainly not prepared to permit another Bolshevik government to remain in power in a country over which they exerted some measure of control; and Lenin's infant regime, fighting desperately for its own survival, was in no position to lend fraternal assistance. Kun was banking on the outbreak of a general proletarian revolution in Europe, a dream which, in the ashes of World War I, inspired no small number of radicals. Such a revolution would not only

**Impressions**

*And when day dawned mournfully on a sea swarming with the remains of a ruined city and hundreds and hundreds of the drowned, the carcasses of cows and horses floated in the pale rays of the rising sun.*
                                        —Miklós Wesselényi, hero of the 1838 Danube flood

solve the otherwise intractable nationalities problem in Central and Eastern Europe, he believed, but would sweep away the hated Western powers as well. But it was not to be: With tacit French approval, Romania attacked Hungary on April 16, followed by an April 27 Czech incursion. The Hungarian Red Army scored some initial victories, but Kun also had to contend with counterrevolutionary struggle within the country. The counterrevolution was centered in the town of Szeged, from which Admiral Miklós Horthy launched a "White Terror" of his own, massacring leftists and Jews. In June, a rightist coup was attempted in Budapest, but was defeated. In the end, the Romanian army, entering the city on August 3, overwhelmed the short-lived Republic of Councils; after this brief flirtation with radicalism, Hungary was to be ruled throughout the interwar period by the reactionary Horthy, who was "elected" Regent in 1920 by a rubber-stamp parliament.

As Hungary drifted inexorably to the right in the interwar period, many of the country's greatest minds would seek their fortunes elsewhere. At the same time, the interwar period was one of enormous, uncontrolled growth for Budapest, its numbers swelled by refugees from the lost territories and the countryside. While the city expanded in all directions, it also suffered the effects of the worldwide recession: Social problems ballooned, hand in hand with increasing poverty.

The 1920 Treaty of Trianon confirmed the massive territorial losses of the past few years: 70% of the former Hungary was ceded to its neighbors, while 60% of the population found itself living beyond Hungary's new borders. Hungarians across all class and political lines were united in considering the treaty unjustly punitive, and every Hungarian government of the interwar period was concerned chiefly with reversing it. This national obsession had the unfortunate consequence of inducing Hungary to ally itself in the 1930s with Nazi Germany, which, in its own zeal to redraw the map of Europe, endorsed Hungary's revisionist claims. It was a reckless path, and one about which the Hungarian people remain deeply troubled to this day.

As the war progressed, Horthy began to have second thoughts about the alliance with Germany. The Nazis, unwilling to accept anything other than total commitment to the war effort, occupied Hungary in March 1944. Adolf Eichmann arrived with the Nazi forces and immediately set up a ghetto for the Budapest's Jews in the historic Erzsébetváros district. While relatively few Hungarian Jews outside the capital survived the deportations (most perished in Auschwitz in the war's last year), at least half of Budapest's Jews were saved, many through the intervention of the Swedish diplomat Raoul Wallenberg, who at great personal risk issued thousands of false passports and established dozens of "safe houses."

In October, the Horthy regime, caught red-handed by the Germans in a clumsy attempt to negotiate a separate peace with the Allies, was replaced by Hungary's fascist Arrow Cross Party. The next four months saw bizarre and wanton acts of cruelty in Budapest, as the city was plunged to a level of barbarism unseen since the Middle Ages. Heavily armed Arrow Cross gangs wandered the scarred city, and hundreds of Jews were taken to the Danube that winter to be shot on its bank or thrown alive into its icy waters.

Meanwhile, the Red Army had penetrated eastern Hungary by late summer, and by Christmas had surrounded the capital. The war all but over, Germany itself breached by Allied forces, the Nazis stubbornly refused an invitation to quit the city honorably. Pest fell to the Russians on January 18, ensuring the survival of those who remained alive in the Jewish ghetto. Retreating to Buda, the Nazis blew up all the Danube bridges and retrenched on Castle Hill. In one of the most bitter sieges of World War II, Soviet artillery pounded the Castle District from the top of Gellért Hill until the Germans were finally driven from the capital on February 13. Budapest

**Impressions**

*Bandits are skulking around the city beating, looting, and shooting people. Among my staff, I have already had forty cases of people being carried off and abused. . . . We hear the thundering cannons of the approaching Russians day and night.*

—Raoul Wallenberg, Swedish diplomat, in a letter to his mother

was again in ruins; three-quarters of its buildings (including the Royal Palace and most of the Castle District) were damaged or destroyed in the war.

**THE STALINIST ERA**   After the war, reconstruction was the primary task facing Budapest and the country. In the absence of clear central authority, a civic spirit characterized the immediate postwar period, as newly formed local organizations assumed control of rebuilding projects, chief among them the reconstruction of the Danube bridges. The postwar days also saw Hungary suffering the most dramatic inflation in world history: Between January and July 1946, for instance, the price of a standard postage stamp soared from 100 pengó to 100,000 quadrillion pengó! The introduction of a new currency, the forint, halted the runaway inflation.

Soviet forces remained in the country as an occupation army. The Allied Powers at Yalta relegated Hungary to the Soviet sphere of influence, and by 1949 a Stalinist state was in place. A "cult of personality" surrounded Communist Party leader Mátyás Rákosi, now known as Stalin's "wise Hungarian disciple." The next few years would be an oppressive period of secret police activity and party infighting. In 1950, the first Soviet-style Five-Year Plan was introduced, emphasizing heavy industry and massive construction projects. Peasants, forced onto collective farms, became bitter opponents of the regime.

In Hungary, as elsewhere in the East Bloc, Stalin's death in 1953 led to pronounced swings between reform and retrenchment. Rákosi continued to play a major role, although the popularity of reformist Imre Nagy also rose. Following Khrushchev's "Secret Speech" at the 20th Party Congress in February 1956 denouncing Stalin's crimes, the stage was set for political and social upheaval throughout the disenchanted Bloc.

**1956–89: REVOLUTION, REACTION & REFORM**   Almost all the key events of the 1956 Hungarian Uprising occurred in Budapest. The spark that lit the fire was an October 23 student demonstration in support of reforms unfolding in Poland. Tens of thousands marched from Petőfi Square in Pest to Bem Square in Buda. Spontaneously, the students decided to march on Parliament, where they lit torches and called for the reinstatement of the increasingly popular Nagy as prime minister (a post he had held briefly in the aftermath of Stalin's death). Another smaller group collected in front of the Budapest radio station, near the National Museum, and were fired upon by the secret police. Shortly thereafter, outraged crowds toppled the enormous Stalin statue near the City Park and paraded through the darkened streets with the fallen dictator in tow. Army units, called out to protect key buildings, turned their weapons over to the rebels.

The events of the next 13 days would capture headlines around the world, though the simultaneous outbreak of war in the Middle East, at the Suez Canal, significantly detracted attention from Central Europe. In the end, the lack of Western assistance to the Hungarians gave unmistakable notice that the West, in the grip of the Cold War, essentially accepted the division of Europe as defined by Yalta.

Reappointed prime minister on October 24, Nagy found events moving beyond his control. The revolt was no longer aimed at reforming the system, but at overthrowing it. On October 25, the police again fired on unarmed demonstrators, this time at the

Parliament. Two days later, a beleaguered Nagy announced the formation of his new government with most of the hard-line Stalinists excluded. Nagy announced the removal of Soviet military units from Budapest, the dissolution of the secret police, and his desire to negotiate with the Soviet Union regarding full military withdrawal from Hungary. In his boldest act, Nagy announced Hungary's unilateral withdrawal from the Warsaw Pact and pleaded for assistance from the West.

There was optimism in the capital as Nagy formed yet another new government. But by November 4, a Soviet invasion was in full swing. Facing little resistance, the Soviets crushed what they were now calling a "counterrevolution." Budapest was heavily damaged by the fighting, and altogether about 2,000 Hungarians died in the uprising while another 200,000 fled the country. Nagy and several of his associates were eventually executed.

János Kádár was placed in control of the government, a position he would maintain for 30 years. A short period of hard-line repression was used to break the spirit of the uprising, but during his long rule Kádár, who was initially despised for his treacherous role in 1956, was able to achieve a level of public popularity enjoyed by few East Bloc leaders. Because of the many reforms Kádár carried out, Hungary earned the nickname of "the happiest barracks" in Eastern Europe. His easygoing slogan "those who are not against us are with us" was the reverse of the menacing Stalinist catchphrase. By and large, Hungarians accepted the "goulash communism" Kádár practiced, but no longer required to express their support, most people withdrew into political apathy.

Kádár's best-known reform, the 1968 New Economic Mechanism (NEM), encouraged limited private enterprise and partially decentralized the economy. Ironically, while the NEM foreshadowed "perestroika" a generation before Gorbachev, Hungarian troops were sent in the same year to join the Warsaw Pact forces in crushing the Prague Spring. Nevertheless, Hungary soon became known as the most liberal country of the Bloc, and Budapest became a magnet for East Bloc youth. Western tourists, too, found Budapest to be a hospitable place in comparison to other Eastern European cities, and its proximity to Vienna increased its accessibility.

Despite economic difficulties caused by inflation and foreign debt, Hungary continued throughout the 1970s and 1980s to lead a sluggish Eastern Europe in gradual reforms. The advent of Gorbachev in the Soviet Union emboldened the most radical elements within the Communist Party; while the world's eyes were turned to Moscow and Warsaw in early 1989, Hungary was quietly playing a key role in the drama. In May 1989, six months before the opening of the Berlin Wall, Hungary began dismantling portions of the barbed-wire frontier with Austria, becoming the first country to open a hole in the "Iron Curtain." The reburial of Imre Nagy in June attracted as many as 250,000 to Budapest's Heroes' Square, and helped heal the psychic wounds left by the failed uprising. By September, thousands of East Germans

## Impressions

*From the rooftop of my flat in Buda I saw the silent crowds sweeping across the city, torches flashing in every hand. . . . By the tens of thousands they congregated in Kossuth Square, milling about beneath the glistening red star atop the dome of the Hungarian Parliament. . . . I huddled in the damp October air, aware of the momentousness of what I was witnessing, giddy and exhilarated, but also apart from it and somehow unable to share in the ominous jubilation of Budapest's long-suffering thousands.*
—Peshoj Eberli, Albanian journalist, 1956

had gathered in Hungary, hoping for permission to flee to the West; when permission was finally granted, more than 50,000 crossed over to Austria. The year, of course, would conclude with the toppling of the East German, Czechoslovak, and Romanian Communist systems. As for the collapse of Communism in Hungary itself, it was far less dramatic, more gradual, and unaccompanied by violence.

**POST-COMMUNIST BUDAPEST**   Hungary's first free elections since 1945 were held in 1990, marking the end of nearly half a century of Communist rule. The new center-right coalition government was led by the late József Antall's Hungarian Democratic Forum (MDF), a party that used overtly nationalist themes in its campaign. The last Soviet troops left the country in 1991, and Pope John Paul II visited Hungary in the same year.

The Treaty of Trianon still strikes a deep chord of resentment and discontent in Hungarian society. The twin questions of national borders and Hungarian ethnic minorities abroad dominate relations with nearly all neighboring states. The false rhetoric of communism clumsily attempted to bury Eastern and Central Europe's nationality problems, just as Trianon had vainly endeavored to solve them in one fell swoop: Now, civil war has ravaged the former Yugoslavia; the Balkans remain an ethnic tinderbox; and throughout the region, few countries trust their neighbors. Hungary's relations with Romania remain bitter; regarding former Yugoslavia, Hungarian concern is over the very survival of Serbia's Hungarian minority; and relations with the aggressively nationalistic regime in Slovakia are strained at best. The neofascist right, though small, has deep roots in this land and remains the country's most disturbing manifestation of chauvinistic nationalism.

## 4  Famous Budapesters

**Béla Bartók** (1881–1945)   The giant figure of 20th-century Hungarian music, Bartók's greatest achievement was the systematic collecting and cataloguing—along with his colleague Zoltán Kodály—of Hungarian folk music. For this project, he is considered a founder of Hungarian ethnomusicology. A composer and teacher of international fame, Bartók drew creative inspiration from the folk music he so laboriously studied. A refugee from fascism, he died in New York.

**Matthias Corvinus** (1443–90)   Crowned king of Hungary as a teenager, Matthias (born Mátyás Hunyadi) oversaw Buda's Golden Age. His Renaissance court flourished as a center of European arts and culture, and his famed Biblioteca Corvinae was one of the continent's finest libraries. "Matthias the Just" was twice married in Buda's Church of Our Lady, which has since been known as the Matthias Church.

**Theodore Herzl** (1860–1904)   Widely considered the founder of modern Zionism, Herzl was born in Budapest, but spent most of his life in Vienna. The Zionist movement that his writings helped to inspire did not, incidentally, find fertile ground in his native Hungary, where a deeply assimilated Jewry resisted the pull of a separate homeland.

**Attila József** (1905–37)   A revolutionary poet, and one of the country's best-loved authors, József was born in Budapest and grew up in extreme poverty, abandoned by his father. A brilliant but intensely lonely man, he committed suicide by jumping under a train near Lake Balaton. The university in Szeged from which he was expelled now bears his name.

**János Kádár** (1912–89)   One of Eastern Europe's longest-standing Communist rulers, Kádár was installed by the Soviets after the 1956 Hungarian Uprising was crushed; he ruled the country until 1988. At first despised as a Hungarian quisling, he soon demonstrated his eagerness for genuine reform, evolving into one of the region's more popular leaders. He was ousted shortly before the collapse of communism in Eastern Europe.

**Zoltán Kodály** (1882–1967)   Along with Béla Bartók, Kodály traveled the country collecting and cataloguing a vast amount of Hungarian folk music, becoming in the process one of the founders of Hungarian ethnomusicology. Like Bartók, he was inspired by Hungarian folk music, whose influence can be seen in his own compositions. Internationally, Kodály is best known as the developer of the Kodály Method, a widely used system of musical education for children.

**Lajos Kossuth** (1802–94)   Lawyer, politician, and journalist, Kossuth was perhaps the best-known leader of the 1848–49 Revolution. He spent the second half of his long life wandering in exile, alone among his associates in resolutely refusing to accept the compromise with the Habsburgs. A giant statue of him graces Kossuth Square, site of the Hungarian Parliament.

**Ödön Lechner** (1845–1914)   One of Hungary's most influential architects, Lechner used colorful Zsolnay tiles and unusual Eastern motifs to create a uniquely Hungarian variant of the art nouveau style popular in Europe at the turn of the century. His most impressive buildings in Budapest are the Applied Arts Museum, the Geological Institute, and the Postal Savings Bank.

**Ferenc (Franz) Liszt** (1811–86)   A towering figure of 19th-century classical music, Liszt, though he lived most of his life abroad, was born in Hungary and spent his later years living in Budapest. There he was a founder and the first president of the Academy of Music. A virtuoso performer as well as a world-renowned composer, Liszt was the founder of the symphonic poem. His *Hungarian Rhapsodies* and *Coronation* Mass are among the best-known pieces of Hungarian classical music.

**György Lukács** (1885–1971)   A Marxist theorist who managed from 1918 until his death to survive all the byzantine twists and turns of the party line, Lukács enjoyed a level of respect and renown in the West which few Communist philosophers could boast of. He played a major role in Béla Kun's 1918 Communist regime, and was again prominent in the first post–World War II Communist regime. After 1956, though, he no longer took part in governmental affairs, though he remained influential until his death.

**Imre Nagy** (1896–1958)   A lifelong Communist, Nagy was a member of the postwar Stalinist regime that terrorized Hungary in the late 1940s and early 1950s. He achieved his lasting international fame, however, when he (somewhat reluctantly) emerged as one of the chief leaders of the 1956 Hungarian Uprising. After the defeat of the uprising, Nagy was tricked into leaving his sanctuary in the Yugolsav Embassy. Two years later he was executed.

**Sándor Petőfi** (1823–49)   A radical poet whose "National Song," supposedly recited on the steps of Pest's National Museum, helped inspire the 1848 Revolution, Petőfi is presumed to have died at the battle of Segesvár in 1849, though his body was never identified. Interestingly, this great Hungarian nationalist was of Slovakian descent, serving as a reminder of the complicated ethnic history of Hungary and the surrounding region.

**Ignác Semmelweis** (1818–65)   A Buda native, Semmelweis is hailed as the "savior of mothers" for his role in identifying the cause of puerperal fever and preventing it by asepsis. His ideas, opposed by a leading English physician of the time, only gained acknowledgment at the turn of the century.

**István Széchenyi** (1791–1860)   Revered today as "the Greatest Hungarian," Széchenyi was a nobleman at the center of Hungarian intellectual life during the Age of Reform. He founded Hungary's Academy of Sciences (1825) and personally financed the building of Budapest's famous Chain Bridge (completed in 1848), which is named for him. An influential writer on subjects ranging from economics to horse breeding, he sought reform within the Habsburg monarchic system and viewed the outbreak of revolution in 1848 with mixed emotions. After it ended in failure and destruction, he went mad.

**Raoul Wallenberg** (1912–?)   The only non-Hungarian listed here, Wallenberg achieved his fame as a Swedish diplomat stationed in Budapest during World War II. At great personal risk, he saved the lives of thousands of Hungarian Jews during the Nazi occupation. Shortly after the Red Army liberated Budapest, Wallenberg was arrested, disappearing into the vast system of Soviet prison camps. His arrest has never been properly explained by the Russians, nor has his death been confirmed. There is a statue of him on Szilágyi Erzsébet fasor in Buda, and a street named for him in Pest.

**Miklós Ybl** (1814–91)   Ybl was one of the greatest figures of Hungarian architecture during the eclectic period of the late 19th century. Among his many buildings in Budapest, the State Opera House, the Main Customs House, and St. Stephen's Basilica stand out. He also extended the Royal Palace in Buda, though his work was destroyed in World War II.

## 5  Architecture 101

Budapest's present architectural landscape has been shaped by its periodic destruction in war and conquest. Because of this unfortunate history, the architectural legacy of present-day Budapest is peculiarly and wonderfully 19th century. Medieval Budapest, or what remains of it, certainly cannot compare with other Central European cities like Prague or Cracow, but few cities in Central Europe or elsewhere can boast of a comparable wealth of 19th-century and *fin-de-siècle* architecture. Many of the city's finest buildings are in a state of woeful disrepair, reminders of a vanished age of imperial grandeur; this particular charm, however, is fleeting, as one by one the great buildings are restored.

Examples of Roman architecture remain in present-day Óbuda, the result of excavation and reconstruction. The best ruins are the two amphitheaters and the buildings of the civilian town.

Supplanting the Romanesque style of the 11th and 12th centuries (of which nothing remains in Budapest), the Gothic style appeared in Buda in the late 13th century, becoming dominant during the 14th century. Little survives in an unreconstructed state from this period. The Matthias Church on Castle Hill was originally initiated at this time, as was the Royal Palace; both have since undergone many changes and reconstructions. A number of Gothic residences have been reconstructed in the Castle District, while in some predominantly baroque Castle District residences a few Gothic elements remain, including "niches" of unknown purpose built into the walls of entryways.

King Matthias Corvinus (1458–90), a great patron of the Renaissance, invited Italian architects to Hungary. Renaissance elements—mainly rounded arches and symmetrical composition—were incorporated into many gothic structures, including the expanded royal palaces in Buda and Visegrád.

In architectural terms, the period of Turkish rule (1541–1686) was one primarily of structural decay. The Turks did little new building, aside from the construction of bath houses, several of which—the Király and the Rudas—survive to the present day. Most of the city's churches were converted into mosques; elements of this conversion, later reversed by the Christian reconquest, can still be seen in the Inner City Parish Church, with its prayer niche, and in the Capuchin Church, with its Turkish door and window frames. A Turkish mausoleum, that of the dervish Gül Baba, still survives in Buda as well.

After the establishment of Habsburg rule the city came under German and Austrian influence. The major construction and reconstruction projects reflected the prevailing baroque style, with its characteristic use of decoration, color, and sculpture. The reconstruction of the Royal Palace was undertaken at this time, but its present stylistic hodgepodge results from postwar reconstruction. A number of baroque churches were built in the 17th and 18th centuries, the best examples being Pest's University Church and Buda's St. Anne's Church. The current City Hall of Pest, designed as a hospital by Anton Martinelli, is the outstanding example of nonecclesiastical baroque in the city. In addition, baroque houses, mostly in reconstructed form, remain in the Castle District.

By the early 19th century, neoclassicism, characterized by buildings of monumental scale that are restrained in ornamentation, was on the rise, reflecting the Hungarians' ballooning sense of historical purpose. The ascendancy of neoclassicism coincided with the first boom in Pest's development and with the rise of a middle class intent on commissioning buildings of a secular nature. Neoclassicism was further advanced by the advent of the Age of Reform (1825–48), during which people like Count István Széchenyi sponsored the construction of public buildings and academies. The leading architects of this style in Hungary were József Hild and Mihály Pollack, the latter's National Museum in Pest being one of the country's foremost examples of neoclassicism.

Their country's national aspirations crushed by the defeat of the 1848–49 revolution, Hungarian architects turned away from the strictness of neoclassical style in search of a specifically Hungarian form. This search first expressed itself in the Romantic style, characterized by Frigyes Feszl's Pesti Vigadó (Concert Hall). Another fine example of romanticism in Pest, though designed by the Viennese architect Otto Forster, is the Dohány Synagogue, which incorporates Eastern motifs as well.

After the 1867 Compromise establishing a joint Austro-Hungarian monarchy, the development of Pest proceeded at a rapid pace with the laying out of the ring boulevards and the great radial boulevard known today as Andrássy út. In this period, the city took on the eclectic appearance for which it is now treasured. Eclecticism (sometimes known as historicism) is defined as the combining in architecture of two or more historical styles; this definition gives little hint of the richness and diversity of Pest's eclectic architecture. Most of the city's architecturally significant public buildings date from this short but explosively creative period. Miklós Ybl is considered the leading architect of the time; his works include the Opera House, the expansion of the Royal Palace, and work on St. Stephen's Basilica. Ignác Alpár was another celebrated architect. His two most important buildings, both on Szabadság Square, are the National Bank and the former Stock Exchange (now headquarters of Hungarian Television). The crowning accomplishment of the era, however, is undoubtedly Imre Steindl's predominantly neo-Gothic Parliament, dramatically capped by a Renaissance-style dome. This building, probably more than any other, has come to symbolize the ambitions and verve of *fin-de-siècle* Pest.

Art nouveau (also known as *Jugendstil*), an exuberant, colorful, free-flowing style of art and architecture initiated in Paris and Brussels, was much in vogue in turn-of-the-century Budapest. Many of Budapest's art nouveau buildings, however, borrow heavily from the language of eclecticism (Zsigmund Quittner's Gresham Palace and the Gellért Hotel, for example), suggesting that Hungarian architects were reluctant to break completely with the latter. Ödön Lechner was the exception; along with his colleague, Gyula Pártos, he strived to create a uniquely Hungarian form of art nouveau. Lechner experimented with incorporating not just Hungarian folk-art elements, but also elements of Asian architecture. His fanciful buildings, many with roofs covered by colorful majolica tiles from the famous Zsolnay factory in Pécs, are instantly recognizable. The best examples in Budapest are the Museum of Applied Arts, the former Post Office Savings Bank, and the Geological Institute.

The Rózsavölgyi House in Szervita Square, designed by Béla Lajta, is widely cited as the building that—with its bold combination of retail, office, and living quarters—best bridges the gap between art nouveau and modernism in Budapest. But the advent of World War I and subsequent years of cultural conservatism stunted development in Hungary. The post–World War I period has seen little architectural development of note. Monolithic Stalinist forms were favored in the 1950s, while the subsequent decades saw the tentative introduction of largely uninspiring international trends. Perhaps the most notable architectural development of post–World War II Budapest was the painstaking reconstruction of Castle Hill and the medieval village called the Castle District; many wonderful examples of past glories were excavated and rebuilt.

## 6  The Art of Hungary

Hungary has produced several artists whose works measure up to the highest international standards, even if their names are hardly known outside of art circles. Many of their finest paintings (including most of those mentioned below) can be seen in the Hungarian National Gallery in Budapest. Smaller museums around the country focus on the works of individual artists, usually in their home towns.

Until the 19th century, Hungarian art was essentially ecclesiastical, heavily under the influence of Austrian and Italian styles. Not until the advent of modern Hungarian nationalism in the 19th century did a uniquely Hungarian art begin to emerge. Even then, however, Hungarian artists almost without exception followed—rather than established—international trends. Indeed, many of the country's best artists lived abroad, usually in Paris, Munich, or Vienna. Thus, despite the creative flowering of Hungarian artists in the 19th century, it remains difficult to pinpoint a specifically Hungarian art.

Hungarian nationalism in the 19th century manifested itself in the arts most forcefully in the development of the historicist genre, whose best-known practitioners were **Viktor Madarász** (1830–1917), **Bertalan Székely** (1835–1910), and **Gyula Benczúr** (1844–1920). Their paintings, usually based on events from Hungary's past, tended to be very large yet detailed. Madarász is perhaps best known for his *Mourning of László Hunyadi,* which, in depicting the unjustly executed 15th-century nobleman, evokes the tragic nature of Hungarian history. Székely's *Women of Eger* celebrates the heroic women who, alongside their husbands, defended Eger Fortress against the 16th-century Turkish siege. Benczúr's *Baptism of Vajk* (Stephen I) celebrates Christianity's beginnings in Hungary.

The artist **Károly Lotz** (1833–1904) is best known as a fresco painter. Among his most famous works are the ceiling frescoes of the Opera House and the wall frescoes of the National Museum.

**Pál Szinyei Merse** (1845–1920), a contemporary of the French impressionists, is the outstanding figure of the Hungarian plein-air school. He lived in Munich, not

Paris. His *Picnic in May* is widely considered one of the finest Hungarian paintings of the century.

**Mihály Munkácsy** (1844–1900), who lived in Paris, was a contemporary of Szinyei Merse. Munkácsy, heavily influenced by Courbet, was the unrivaled master of the Hungarian folk genre and enjoyed an international reputation unequaled by any of his countrymen. Among his finest paintings, on view at the National Gallery on Castle Hill, are *The Condemned Cell, Woman Churning Butter, Woman Carrying Wood,* and *The Lint Makers.* All show a profound empathy with the common folk who were the subjects of most of his paintings.

Advancing beyond studio-painted art, many of the best Hungarian plein-air painters gathered at Nagybánya (now in Romania) after 1896, where they established a thriving colony ("the Hungarian Barbizon"). **Simon Hollósy** (1857–1918) and **Károly Ferenczy** (1862–1917) were the colony's leading figures; many of Ferenczy's finest paintings can be seen in the Ferenczy Museum, near Budapest at Szentendre.

One of Hungary's most unusual and cherished artists was the post-impressionist **Tivadar Csontváry Kosztka** (1853–1919), whose mystical landscapes and portraits reflect a unique personal vision. He was little known in his own lifetime, but by the mid-20th century even Picasso was calling him a genius.

"The Eight," a group that included **Dezso Cigány** (1883–1931) and **Lajos Tihany** (1855–1939), was formed in Budapest in the early 1900s. Hungary's first avant-garde school, the Eight looked to cubism and the German expressionists for inspiration. The journal *Ma (Today),* edited by the painter and writer **Lajos Kassák** (1887–1967), became the movement's mouthpiece. Other important 20th-century artists include **László Moholy-Nagy** (1895–1946), Hungary's leading Bauhaus artist and a photographer of considerable renown; **Victor Vasarely** (1908–1997), the founder and leading figure of op-art, who fled the country in 1919; and the expressionist **Gyula Derkovits** (1894–1934).

Another leading 20th-century figure in Hungarian art is the ceramic artist **Margit Kovács** (1902–77), whose unique works combined Hungarian folk themes with elements of modern art. She represents one of the most successful in a long series of Hungarian artists—including writers, musicians, and architects—who drew inspiration from the richness of Hungarian folk life and customs. A museum dedicated to her work is in Szentendre, near Budapest (see "Szentendre," in chapter 10). Finally, **Imre Varga** (b. 1923) is Hungary's leading contemporary sculptor. His works are on display throughout Budapest (most notably his new statue of Imre Nagy outside Parliament), as well as in a small museum in Óbuda (see "More Museums & Sights in Pest, Buda & Óbuda," in chapter 6 and "Leopold Town & Theresa Town" in chapter 7).

## 7  Paprika, Pastry & Pálinka: Hungarian Cuisine

Hungary's cuisine reflects the rich and varied flavors of four major geographic regions. From Transdanubia, west of the River Danube, come rich mushroom sauces, sorrel soups, cottage cheese and onion dumplings, and high-quality goose liver. A host of excellent wild-game dishes come from forested northern Hungary. Bucolic Erdély (Transylvania) introduces spices such as tarragon, summer savory, and fresh dill to the palate. The region is also known for its lamb dishes and sheep's cheese. And, finally, from the Great Hungarian Plain, the home of Hungary's renowned paprika, come hearty fish, bean, and meat stews all spiced with the red powder ground from different varieties of peppers ranging from sweet *(édes)* to hot *(csípós).*

Lunch, the main meal of the day, begins with soup. *Gyümölcs leves,* a cold fruit soup, is excellent when in season. *Sóskakrém leves,* cream of sorrel soup, is another good seasonal choice. *Babgulyás,* a hearty bean soup, and *halaszle,* a fish soup popular at river and lakeside eateries, constitute meals in themselves.

The main course is generally a meat dish. Try the *paprikás csirke,* chicken cooked in a savory paprika sauce. It's especially good with *galuska,* a pasta dumpling. *Pulykamell,* turkey breast baked with plums or served in a mushroom gravy, is also delicious. *Pörkölt* is a stewed meat dish, which comes in many varieties. *Töltött káposzta,* whole cabbage leaves stuffed with rice, meat, and spices, is another favorite.

Vegetarianism is gradually gaining acceptance in Hungarian restaurants; many establishments now offer a vegetable plate entree, usually consisting of steamed and grilled vegetables in season. Otherwise, vegetarians would do well to order *lecsó tojással* (eggs scrambled in a thick tomato-onion-paprika sauce), *rántott sajt* (batter-fried cheese with tartar sauce), or *túros csusza tepertó nélkul* (a macaroni-and-cheese dish). The kitchen should be able to prepare any of these dishes to order, even if they don't appear on the menu.

Snack foods include *lángos,* a slab of deep-fried bread served with your choice of toppings: sugar and whipped cream, or garlic sauce and cheese. *Palacsinta,* a paper-thin crêpe stuffed with cheese or draped in hot chocolate sauce, is another excellent light bite. *Kalács,* a hollow, tubular honey-cake, made so by wrapping the dough around a bottle, is an old-fashioned treat sometimes available in metro stations or at outdoor markets. *Fagylalt,* ice cream, is the national street food; even early in the morning you'll see people standing in line for cones. Scoops are small, so order more than one. Fruit flavors are produced seasonally: In the spring, try strawberry (*eper*) and sour cherry (*meggy*); in the fall, plum (*szilva*) and pear *(körte).* A summer regular is delicious cinnamon *(fahéj).*

Hungarian pastries are scrumptious and cost a fraction of what they do in Vienna, so indulge. The light, flaky *rétes* are filled with fruit or cheese. *Csoki torta* is a decadent chocolate layer cake, and a *Dobos torta* is topped with a shiny caramel crust. *Mákos* pastry, made with poppy seeds, is a Hungarian specialty. *Gesztenye,* chestnuts, are another popular ingredient in desserts.

Picnickers should pick up a loaf of Hungarian bread and sample any of Hungary's world-famous salamis. A number of tasty cheeses are produced in Hungary as well: *Karaván füstölt* (a smoked cheese), *Edami, márvány* (similar to bleu cheese), and *jutúró* (a soft, spreadable sheep's cheese similar in flavor to feta). In season, fresh produce is delightfully cheap and high quality. You won't find much fresh fruit or vegetables in the winter or in traditional dishes served in restaurants, but at the wonderful markets you'll be amazed at the abundance and variety. Sour cherries (*meggy*) in July are out of this world.

**BEER, WINE & SPIRITS**   Unlike its Austrian, Czech, and Slovak neighbors, Hungary does not have a beer culture; as a result its beer is unexceptional. A number of European beers are now produced under license in Hungary. Among them are German beers (Holsten and Hofbrau Munchen), Austrian beers (Gösser, Steffl, Schwechater, Gold Fassl, and Kaiser), a Danish beer (Tuborg), a Dutch beer (Amstel), and a Belgian beer (Stella Artois). Even Pennsylvania's Rolling Rock is produced in Hungary now! To our taste, however, all these beers tend to be inferior to those under whose license they are sold and only marginally better than the best Hungarian beer—Dreher. Your best bet in Hungary is clearly Czech beer, such as Budvar, Staropramen, or Pilsner Urquell. Czech beers are not produced in Hungary under license; they are the real thing.

Hungarian wines, on the other hand, are excellent. The most renowned red wines come from the region around Villány, a town to the south of Pécs by the Croatian border. As a result of the aggressive marketing strategy of the former Communist regime, many foreigners are familiar with the red wines from Eger, especially *Egri Bikavér* (Eger Bull's Blood). Eger wines, though rich and fruity, are markedly inferior to Villányi reds. The country's best white wines are generally believed to be those from the Lake Balaton region, though some Hungarians insist that white wines from the Sopron region (by the Austrian border) are better. *Tokaj* wines—*száraz* (dry) or *édes* (sweet)—are popular as apéritifs and dessert wines. Travelers seeking advice on Hungarian wines are encouraged to visit La Boutique des Vins, a full-service wine store in Budapest (see chapter 8).

*Unicom,* the richly aromatic bitter that some call "Hungary's national drink," is a taste worth acquiring. *Pálinka* is another variety of Hungarian "fire water," which is often brewed at home from apricots, plums, or pears; in folk wisdom, it's acclaimed for its medicinal value.

**COFFEE & TEA**  Hungarians drink coffee *(kávé)* throughout the day, either at stand-up coffee bars or in elegant coffeehouses. Until recently, Hungarian coffee drinking borrowed from the Turkish tradition: Alarmingly strong, unfiltered espresso was served straight up, generally without cream or sugar. These days, coffee drinking has expanded to include milder and more refined tastes. In general, though, when ordering coffee in Hungary, you are still ordering espresso. If you ask for coffee with milk *(kávé tejjel)*, you are served espresso with cream on the side. Cappuccino (and its variant *cappuciner,* with chocolate shavings on top) is now available in most coffeehouses, as is decaffeinated coffee *(koffein mentes)*. *Tejeskávé,* a Hungarian version of café au lait, is another option.

Tea drinkers will have a difficult time in restaurants; if tea is available at all, it's generally of the strong black variety. For more variety and a peek at Hungary's burgeoning world of herbal medicine, look for teas in any of the numerous shops: *gyógynövény, herbárium,* or *gyógytea.*

**WATER**  While tap water *(csapvíz)* is safe to drink in Budapest, it isn't generally offered in restaurants, and few Hungarians request it. Instead they drink *ásványvíz,* a carbonated mineral water, or *szóda víz,* carbonated tap water. Purified bottled water *(szénsav mentes)* is now available at fancier restaurants as well as at delicatessens and grocery stores in tourist areas.

## 8  Recommended Books & Films

### BOOKS

A good number of the best books on Hungary are now out of print. If you can't find a given book in a bookstore, your best bet is to check in a university library. A small bookstore in New York City called **Puski Corvin,** 251 E. 81st St., New York, NY 10028 (☎ 212/879-8893), specializes in Hungary. Many books published by Corvina, a Budapest-based English-language press, are recommended below. They can be purchased at English-language bookstores in Budapest, or you can write for a free catalog: **Corvina kiadó,** P.O. Box 108, Budapest H-1364, Hungary.

**HISTORY & POLITICS**  For a general history of Hungary, there's still nothing better than C. A. McCartney's *Hungary: A Short History* (Aldine, 1962), which is unfortunately out of print and difficult to find. *A History of Hungary* (Indiana University Press, 1990), edited by Peter Sugar, is an anthology with a number of good essays. *The Habsburg Monarchy, 1809–1918* (London: Hamish Hamilton, 1948), by A. J. P. Taylor, is a readable analysis of the final century of the Austro-Hungarian empire.

Two memoirs of early 20th-century Budapest deserve mention: *Apprentice in Budapest: Memories of a World That Is No More* (University of Utah Press, 1988) by the anthropologist Raphael Patai; and *Budapest 1900* (Weidenfeld & Nicolson, 1989), by John Lukacs, which captures the feeling of a lively but doomed imperial city at the turn of the century.

*The Holocaust in Hungary: An Anthology of Jewish Response* (University of Alabama Press, 1982), edited and translated by Andrew Handler, is notable for the editor's excellent introduction. Elenore Lister's *Wallenberg: The Man in the Iron Web* (Prentice Hall, 1982) recounts the heroic life of Raoul Wallenberg, written against the chilling backdrop of Nazi-occupied Budapest.

Joseph Rothschild has written two excellent surveys of 20th-century Eastern European history, both with large sections on Hungary. They are *East Central Europe Between the Two World Wars* (University of Washington Press, 1974) and *Return to Diversity: A Political History of East Central Europe Since World War II* (Oxford University Press, 1989).

**CULTURE**   *The Cuisine of Hungary* (Bonanza Books, 1971), by the famous Hungarian-born restaurateur George Lang, contains all you need to know about the subject. Tekla Domotor's *Hungarian Folk Beliefs* (Corvina and Indiana University Press, 1981) covers witches, werewolves, giants, and gnomes. Zsuzsanna Ardó's *How to Be a European: Go Hungarian* (Biográf, 1994) is a witty little guidebook to Hungarian culture, etiquette, and social life.

Julia Szabó's *Painting in Nineteenth Century Hungary* (Corvina, 1985) contains a fine introductory essay and over 300 plates. In our opinion, the best tourist-oriented coffee-table book available in Budapest is *Budapest Art and History* (Flow East, 1992), by Delia Meth-Cohn.

Architecture buffs should try to find Tamás K. Pintér's *Századeleji Házak Budapesten* (Magyar Építomuvészek Szövetsége, 1987), a wonderful guidebook to turn-of-the-century architecture in Budapest. Available at Litea Bookstore (see chapter 8), this book, written in Hungarian, has an English-language introduction and lists the addresses of all buildings pictured. Another fine architectural guide to Budapest is *Budapest 20th Century Architecture Guide,* also available at Litea. Other architecture-oriented guidebooks more generally available in Budapest include András Török's *Budapest: A Critical Guide* (Park Books), notable for its walking tours, and István Wellner's *Budapest: A Complete Guide* (Corvina). Make sure you get the third edition (1997) of András Török's book; out-of-date editions are still floating around.

**FICTION**   Not all the best examples of Hungarian literature are available in translation, but look for the following: Gyula Illyés's *The People of the Puszta* (Corvina, 1979), an unabashedly honest look at peasant life in the early 20th century; György Konrád's *The Case Worker* (Penguin, 1987), a portrayal of a political system in disrepair; Péter Esterházy's *Helping Verbs of the Heart* (Weidenfeld & Nicolson, 1991), a gripping story of grief following a parent's death; István Örkény's *The Toth Family and the Flower Show* (New Directions, 1966), the first an allegorical story about fear and authority, the second a fable about different types of reality in modern life; Zsolt Csalog's *Lajos M., Aged 45* (Budapest: Maecenas, 1989), an extraordinary memoir of life in a Soviet labor camp; Kálmán Mikszáth's *St. Peter's Umbrella* (Corvina, 1962); and Zsigmond Móricz's *Seven Pennies* (Corvina, 1988), a collection of short stories by one of Hungary's most celebrated authors.

Corvina publishes three good anthologies of modern Hungarian short stories and poetry: *Present Continuous: Contemporary Hungarian Writing* (1985), edited by István Bart; *Nothing's Lost: Twenty-Five Hungarian Short Stories* (1988), edited by Lajos Illyés; and *Today: An Anthology of Contemporary Hungarian Literature* (1987), edited by Éva Tóth. Another good anthology is *Ocean at the Window: Hungarian Prose and Poetry Since 1945* (University of Minnesota Press, 1980), edited by Albert Telzsa. For poetry, look for *Modern Hungarian Poetry* (Columbia University Press/Corvina, 1977), edited by Miklós Vajda.

# FILMS

Several Hungarian-born directors, working abroad, had a tremendous impact on the development of cinema: Alexander Korda, George Cukor, and Michael Kertész (a.k.a. Michael Curtiz) are giant names in film history. And Hungarian-born actors like Tony Curtis and the Gabor sisters achieved international fame on the silver screen.

But not all the best talent emigrated. Some Hungarian directors whose films are worth looking for include (in rough chronological order) Zoltán Fábri, whose *Merry Go-Round* is a recognized masterpiece of socialist realism; Péter Bacsó, whose classic *The Witness* is a well-loved parody of Stalinist-era terror; Miklós Jancsó, whose most famous film is *Confrontation,* about the first post–World War II generation; Péter Gothar, whose *Time Stands Still,* a dark vision of alienated youth in post-1956 Budapest, is a cult classic in Hungary; and the contemporary filmmaker István Szabó, whose most internationally acclaimed films have been *Mephisto* (1981), filmed in Berlin; and *Meeting Venus* (1991), the story of a conductor and the diva with whom he falls in love.

One Hollywood film, *Music Box* (1989, starring Jessica Lange and Armin Mueller-Stahl), should be mentioned. It is a haunting tale of a daughter's dawning awareness of her father's past identity as a Hungarian fascist; it includes some interesting Budapest footage.

# 2

# Planning a Trip to Budapest

**N**ow that you've decided to travel to Budapest, you must have dozens of questions. Do I need a visa? What currency is used in Hungary, and can I get my hands on some at home? Will any festivals take place during my trip? What's the best route to get there? This chapter is devoted to providing answers to these and other questions.

## 1 Visitor Information & Entry Requirements

### VISITOR INFORMATION

For general country information and a variety of pamphlets and maps before you leave, contact the government-sponsored **Hungarian National Tourist Office,** 150 E. 58th St., New York, NY 10155 (☎ **212/355-0240**). You might also take advantage of **"Virtual Hungary,"** a comprehensive online reference guide to the country. Visit their homepage at www.datanet.hu/virtual/index.htm.

### ENTRY REQUIREMENTS

**DOCUMENTS** Citizens of the United States, Canada, the Republic of Ireland, and the United Kingdom need only a valid passport to enter Hungary. Citizens of Australia and New Zealand need a visa as well as a passport; contact the nearest Hungarian embassy for details and requirements concerning visas.

**CUSTOMS** You're allowed to bring duty-free into Hungary 250 cigarettes, 2 liters of wine, and 1 liter of spirits. There's no limit to the amount of currency you may bring in, but import or export of more than 300,000 Hungarian forints ($1,500)—in bank notes no greater than 1,000 Ft ($5)—is forbidden.

## 2 Money

### CURRENCY

The basic unit of currency in Hungary is the **forint (Ft).** There are 100 **fillérs** (almost worthless and soon to be taken out of circulation) in a forint. Coins come in denominations of 50 fillérs (smaller denominations are already out of circulation); and 1, 2, 5, 10, 20, 100, and 200 Ft. Two different kinds of 100 Ft coins are in use. The 200 Ft coins are almost never used. Banknotes come in denominations of 100, 500, 1,000, 5,000, and 10,000 Ft.

In 1997, the forint was devalued by 14%, while inflation stood at 18%. At the same time, the U.S. dollar gained considerably against foreign currencies. The result, at least in late 1997, was a U.S. dollar that went further in Hungary than it had the year before. A trustworthy Hungarian economist tells us that 1998 should see approximately a 10.5% currency devaluation and 14% inflation. Depending on the strength of the dollar, the economic reality faced by tourists in 1997 may repeat itself. Regardless of the exact numbers and rates, Hungary continues to be considerably less expensive for travelers than most Western countries. Labor-intensive services, such as picture framing, tailoring, shoe and watch repair, and the like, are particularly inexpensive.

You are allowed to reexchange up to half the amount of forints you originally purchased, so be circumspect converting dollars.

As of this writing, the rate of exchange is $1 = 200 Ft, and this is the rate used to calculate all the U.S. dollar prices in this book. Of course, exchange rates will fluctuate over time.

## CHANGING MONEY

The best official rates for both cash and traveler's checks are obtained at banks. Exchange booths are also located throughout the city center, in train stations, and in most luxury hotels. The exchange booths generally offer lower rates than banks. This is particularly true of one chain of exchange booths called Inter Change, which offers a rate up to 20% lower than the going bank rate, depending on the amount you exchange. ATM machines are found in front of banks throughout the city. You may withdraw forints at the daily exchange rate from your home account through the CIRRUS and PLUS networks.

**BLACK MARKET**   The black market no longer serves a useful purpose for tourists. The bands of money changers that were once a permanent fixture of Keleti Station (by the entrance of the international ticket office) can still be found in reduced numbers, offering an exchange rate just 2% to 3% higher than the official rate. You are unlikely to be cheated by the money changers in Keleti Station, though you have little to gain by trading with them. However, you should regard with extreme suspicion anyone who accosts you on the street wanting to change money, especially someone offering you a rate more than 2% to 3% better than the official rate. Such a person is certainly out to cheat you. There is simply no money to be made on a rate beyond the 2% to 3% pillow; the money changers are limited by the difference between the official buying rate and official selling rate.

## HARD CURRENCY

It makes sense to have some cash on hand. At certain banks and at all exchange booths you will get a better rate when exchanging cash. Dollars might also come in handy at flea markets.

## TRAVELER'S CHECKS

Traveler's checks are accepted for exchange at most banks and exchange offices, including the American Express office between Vörösmarty tér and Deák tér in central Pest, at V. Deák Ferenc u. 10, 1052 Budapest (☎ **1/266-8680;** fax 1/267-2028 or 1/267-2029). Many hotels (but not stores) also accept them as payment. You are likely to get a slightly lower exchange rate with traveler's checks than with cash, especially at exchange booths. If you wish to cash in your traveler's checks for dollars at the American Express office, you will end up losing 7% since first they exchange the checks for forints and then buy the forints back for dollars.

## (They'll) Take the Money and Run

As large numbers of Western tourists pour into Budapest, money-changing scams appear to be on the rise. In August 1997, a Korean tourist and I were walking in a neighborhood near the New York Kávéház when we were approached by a man who asked if we could exchange his deutsche marks. We declined and continued on our way, but he followed us down the street. I insisted that we neither wanted nor needed to exchange money, as we had done so at a bank. Still, he produced a fistful of marks and began waving it in our faces when—right on cue—out from an alleyway rushed a gruff older man flashing some sort of picture badge and identifying himself as "Hungarian police." Claiming "there was too much false money on the street," he demanded our passports and foreign currency "as evidence of false bills." "Dollars. I want to see your yen," he barked.

Smelling a scam, but still curious, I showed him two Hungarian forint notes worth no more than $1. In a grand bit of impromptu theater, he held the bills up against the street lamp and scratched them with his thumbnail to check, I suppose, their authenticity. He asked for my dollars; I told him that I had left them in the hotel safe and he would have to escort me either to the police station or my embassy if he wished to pursue the matter. Frustrated, he turned to the Korean woman, who likewise refused to turn over any hard currency and began to scream: "Take me to my embassy!"

Hungarian friends later told us the obvious: Had we been naïve enough to show him any dollars or "yen," he would have pronounced the bills false, claimed them as "evidence" and disappeared into the alleyway with our money. Fortunately, this fake cop tired of pursuing our false money and, pronouncing us "safe," retreated with the young man he claimed would be placed under arrest. As we turned our heads, we saw the partners in heated debate, no doubt refining their failed plan for the next potential victim.

—Neil E. Schlecht

## GETTING CASH WHILE YOU'RE THERE

There are now numerous ATM machines in Budapest that access the PLUS or CIR-RUS networks, as well as credit card accounts. Look for them at the airport or on the street in front of banks. You may withdraw money from your account *in Hungarian forints only*. The exchange rate is the official daily rate. Inquire at your bank before departure to find out if there is a commission charged or if there is an ATM fee. The addresses of a few centrally located ATM machines are as follows: V. Szabadság tér 7-8; V. Deák F. u. 5-7; V. Vörösmarty tér 1; II. Moszkva tér 11; VI. Nyugati tér 1-2.

## CREDIT & CHARGE CARDS

Credit and charge cards are widely accepted. All first- and second-class hotels, many pensions, and all of the more expensive restaurants in Budapest accept at least one major card. Many—but not all—boutiques, art galleries, antiques stores, crystal and china stores, and trendy shops in the city center also accept credit and charge cards. Inexpensive restaurants and shops that cater more to locals than tourists generally do not.

## The Hungarian Forint

**For American Readers**    At this writing $1 = approximately 200 Ft (or 100 Ft = 50¢), and this was the rate of exchange used to calculate the dollar values given in this chapter.

**For British Readers**    At this writing £1 = approximately 320 Ft (or 100 Ft = 31 p), and this was the rate of exchange used to calculate the pound values in the table below.

*Note:* The rates given here fluctuate from time to time and may not be the same when you travel to Hungary. Therefore this table should be used only as a guide:

| Ft | U.S.$ | U.K.£ | Ft | U.S.$ | U.K.£ |
|----|-------|-------|-----|-------|-------|
| 5 | .03 | .02 | 3,000 | 15.00 | 9.30 |
| 10 | .05 | .03 | 4,000 | 32.00 | 12.40 |
| 25 | .13 | .08 | 5,000 | 25.00 | 15.50 |
| 50 | .25 | .16 | 6,000 | 30.00 | 18.60 |
| 75 | .38 | .23 | 7,000 | 35.00 | 21.70 |
| 100 | .50 | .31 | 8,000 | 40.00 | 24.80 |
| 200 | 1.00 | .62 | 9,000 | 45.00 | 27.90 |
| 300 | 1.50 | .93 | 10,000 | 50.00 | 31.00 |
| 400 | 2.00 | 1.24 | 15,000 | 75.00 | 46.50 |
| 500 | 2.50 | 1.55 | 20,000 | 100.00 | 62.00 |
| 750 | 3.75 | 2.33 | 25,000 | 125.00 | 77.50 |
| 1,000 | 5.00 | 3.10 | 30,000 | 150.00 | 93.00 |
| 1,500 | 7.50 | 4.65 | 40,000 | 200.00 | 124.00 |
| 2,000 | 10.00 | 6.20 | 50,000 | 250.00 | 155.00 |

## 3  When to Go

### THE CLIMATE

Budapest has a relatively mild climate—the annual mean temperature in Hungary is 50°F. Nevertheless, summer temperatures often exceed 80° to 85°F, and sweltering hot, humid days are typical in July. January is the coldest month, averaging 30°F, though temperatures can dip well below that on any given day. Be prepared for damp and chilly weather in winter. Spring is usually mild and, especially in May and June, wet, and autumn is usually quite pleasant with mild cooler weather through October.

**Budapest's Average Daily Temperatures**

|  | Jan | Feb | Mar | Apr | May | June | July | Aug | Sept | Oct | Nov | Dec |
|--|-----|-----|-----|-----|-----|------|------|-----|------|-----|-----|-----|
| Temp. (°F) | 30 | 34 | 38 | 53 | 62 | 68 | 72 | 71 | 63 | 52 | 42 | 35 |
| Temp. (°C) | –1 | 1 | 3 | 12 | 17 | 20 | 22 | 22 | 17 | 11 | 6 | 2 |

### HOLIDAYS

Hungarian holidays are: January 1 (New Year's Day), March 15 (National Holiday), Easter Sunday and Easter Monday, May 1 (May Day), Whitmonday, August 20 (St. Stephen's Day), October 23 (Republic Day), and December 25–26 (Christmas). Shops, museums, and banks are closed on all holidays.

| What Things Cost in Budapest | U.S. $ |
| --- | --- |
| Taxi from Ferihegy I airport to the city center | 15.00–20.00 |
| Metro from Nyugati Station to Deák tér | .30 |
| Local telephone call | .10 |
| Double room at the Hilton (Very Expensive) | 208.00–302.00 |
| Double room at the Hotel Victoria (Expensive) | 111.00 |
| Double room at Hotel Queen Mary (Moderate) | 68.00 |
| Double room at Hotel MEDOSZ (Inexpensive) | 46.00 |
| Dinner for one, without wine, at Kis Buda Gyöngye (Expensive) | 11.00 |
| Dinner for one, without wine, at Horgásztanya Vendéglő (Moderate) | 7.00 |
| Dinner for one, without wine, at Makkhetes Vendéglő (Inexpensive) | 5.00 |
| Half liter of beer | 1.40 |
| Coca-Cola | .60 |
| Cup of coffee | .60 |
| Roll of ASA 100 Kodacolor film, 36 exposures | 6.00 |
| Admission to the Hungarian National Museum | 1.25 |
| Movie ticket | 1.25 |
| Opera ticket | 1.50–22.50 |

## HUNGARY CALENDAR OF EVENTS

With a little luck, your trip to Budapest will coincide with one or more of the city's cultural events. Keep in mind, though, that during some of them, particularly the Spring Festival and the Formula One Grand Prix in mid-August, hotel rooms are particularly hard to come by. All inquiries about ticket availability and location of events should be directed to Budapest's main tourist information office, **Tourinform,** at Süto u. 2, 1052 Budapest (☎ 1/117-9800, 118-8718, or 117-8992; fax 1/117-9578). It's open daily from 8am to 8pm (to 3pm on weekends in winter).

March

✪ **Budapest Spring Festival.** For 2 weeks in mid- to late March, performances of everything from opera to ballet, from classical music to drama, are held at all the major halls and theaters of Budapest. Simultaneously, temporary exhibitions open in many of Budapest's museums. Tickets are available at the Festival Ticket Service, V. 1081 Rákóczi út 65 (☎ 1/210-2795, 133-2337) and at the individual venues.

• **Hollókő's Easter Festival.** During Easter in this charming small town in north-eastern Hungary, villagers wear national costumes and participate in a folklife festival. Traditional song, dance, and foods are featured.

May or June

• **Book Fair.** During the last week of May or first week of June, publishers set up kiosks throughout central Pest to display the year's newly released titles. Most books are in Hungarian, of course, but there are always beautiful books on art, architecture, and other subjects.

June

• **Open-air Theater Programs.** A rich variety of open-air performances are given throughout Budapest from June to August. Highlights include opera and ballet at the Margaret Island Open Air Theater, folklore and dance at the Buda Park Theater, musicals in Városmajor Theater, and classical music recitals in the Dominican Courtyard at the Hilton Hotel.

- **Organ Concerts.** Concerts are given in the Matthias Church, in the lovely Castle District of Buda, June to August.

July–August

- **Organ Concerts.** Budapest's largest church, St. Stephen's Basilica, hosts organ concerts, July through August.
- ✪ **Summer Opera and Ballet Festival.** Except for this 10-day festival, which falls either in July or August, the wonderful Hungarian State Opera House in Budapest has no summer performances. Tickets are available at the Opera House box office at VI. Andrássy út 22 (☎ 1/332-7914) or at the National Philharmonic Ticket Office, V. Vörösmarty tér 1 (☎ 1/118-0281).
- **International Palace Tournament, in Visegrád.** Each summer on the second weekend in July, this town on the Danube hosts an authentic medieval festival replete with dueling knights on horseback, early music, and dance.

August

- **Formula One Grand Prix,** at the HungaroRing. One of the European racing circuit's most important annual events is held the second weekend in August.
- **St. Stephen's Day.** On August 20, Hungary's patron saint is celebrated with folk dancing and cultural events and a dramatic display of fireworks over the Danube.
- **Student Island (Diáksziget),** on Óbuda Island in the Danube. Established in 1994 as Hungary's very own Woodstock, Diáksziget is a weeklong music festival that draws young people from all over the region. The event that usually begins in the third week of August features foreign and local rock, folk, and jazz groups on 10 different stages playing each day from early afternoon to the wee hours of the morning. Pick up a program schedule at Tourinform.
- **International Guitar Festival in Esztergom.** During the first week of August, this elegant town hosts the guitar festival, which features performers from around the world. Classical concerts are performed in the Basilica.
- **Szeged Summer Festival.** Szeged, the proud capital of the Great Plain, is home to a summer-long series of cultural events (ballet, opera, open-air theater). If you find that many of the concert halls and theaters in Budapest are closed (as is often the case in the summer months), board a southbound train.

September

- **Budapest International Fair,** at HungExpo. For 10 days in mid-September, the HungExpo grounds are filled with Europe's latest consumer goods.

September–October

- **Budapest Art Weeks.** In celebration of the opening of the season, special classical music and dance performances are held for three weeks in all the city's major halls. The festival's traditional start is September 25, the day of Béla Bartók's death.
- **Contemporary Music Weeks.** Held in conjunction with the Budapest Art Weeks, this 3-week festival also features performances in all the capital's major halls.

# 4  Health & Insurance

**STAYING HEALTHY**   No shots or inoculations are required for entry to Hungary. Hungarian pharmacies are generally not well stocked, so try to bring enough of any medication you may need. In case you do run out, take along a copy of all prescriptions.

Sunscreen is available in Budapest but tends to be more expensive than in the United States; the same is true of other toiletries, so bring what you need with you.

**INSURANCE**   Emergency medical treatment is provided free of charge in Hungary, but you'll have to pay for prescription medications and for nonemergency care. Check with your insurance company before leaving home to see if you're covered for foreign travel. If not, it might be a good idea to take out a special short-term travel policy. Some homeowner's insurance policies cover items like cameras even when you're traveling abroad.

## 5  Tips for Travelers with Special Needs

**FOR TRAVELERS WITH DISABILITIES**   Buses and metros in Budapest are not equipped for people with disabilities, and places, such as hotels, restaurants, or museums, are generally not accessible to wheelchairs. However, Hungarians are accustomed to helping people with disabilities get on and off buses, up and down stairs, etc.

Many agencies provide information for travelers with disabilities. The **Travel Information Service,** at the MossRehab Hospital in Philadelphia (☎ **215/456-9603**), answers questions by telephone only; call for assistance. For names and addresses of organizations offering tours for travelers with disabilities, contact the **Society for the Advancement of Travel for the Handicapped,** 347 Fifth Ave., Suite 610, New York, NY 10016 (☎ **212/447-7284;** fax 212/725-8253); send a self-addressed stamped envelope. Yearly membership in this society is $45 ($25 for senior citizens and students).

For travelers who are blind or visually impaired, the best source is the **American Foundation for the Blind,** 15 W. 16th St., New York, NY 10011 (☎ **800/232-5463** or 212/620-2147).

**FOR SENIORS**   The best U.S. organization for seniors is the **American Association of Retired Persons (AARP),** 601 E St. NW, Washington, DC 20049 (☎ **202/434-AARP**). Members are offered discounts on car rentals and hotels.

Information is also available from the nonprofit **National Council of Senior Citizens,** 1331 F St. NW, Washington, DC 20005 (☎ **202/347-8800**). For $12 per person or couple, you receive a monthly newsletter partly devoted to travel tips and discounts on hotels and auto rentals.

**FOR STUDENTS**   **Express,** the former state-run student travel agency, remains a valuable resource for students. In addition to selling the International Student Identity Cards (ISIC) and IYHF cards (bring a photo; the nearest photo booths are at V. Október 6 u. 22 and at Nyugati railway station), they offer discount travel fares for students and youths under 26. They also sell the FIYTO card and teacher's card. The main office of Express is located at V. Szabadság tér 16 (☎ **1/131-7777** or 1/131-6393); it's open on Monday, Wednesday, and Thursday from 8am to 4:30pm, on Tuesday from 8am to 6pm, and on Friday from 8am to 2:30pm.

**Council Travel** (a subsidiary of the Council on International Educational Exchange) is America's largest student, youth, and budget travel group, with more than 60 offices worldwide. The main office is at 205 E. 42nd St., New York, NY 10017 (☎ **212/661-1450**). Council Travel's London Centre is located at 28A Poland St., London W1V 3DB, just off Oxford Circus (☎ **0171/287-3337** for European destinations, 0171/437-7767 for other destinations). International Student Identity Cards, issuable to all bona fide students for $16, entitle holders to generous travel and other discounts. Discounted international and domestic air tickets are available. Eurotrain rail passes, YHA passes, weekend packages, and hostel/hotel accommodations are also bookable.

To keep down costs, membership in the **International Youth Hostel Federation (IYHF)** is recommended. Many countries have branch offices, including **American Youth Hostels (AYH)/Hostelling International,** 733 15th St. NW, Suite 840, Washington, DC 20005 (☎ **202/783-6161**). Membership costs $25 annually, though those under 18 pay $10 and those over 54 pay $15.

**British students** can purchase the IYHA card from the youth hostel store at 14 Southampton St., London (☎ **0171/836-4739**) or Campus Travel (☎ **0171/730-3402**).

**FOR WOMEN    NANE,** an organization to help women in the case of rape and/or domestic abuse, operates a hot line in Hungarian and English; call ☎ 1/267-4900. Leave a message if necessary. **La Leche League,** a support group for breast-feeding moms, can be contacted at ☎ 1/202-2157.

**OTHER    Alcoholics Anonymous** (AA) meetings in English are held in Budapest, although the location is not fixed. Call ☎ 1/341-3741.

# 6  Getting There

## BY PLANE

The flying time to Budapest from New York is just over 9 hours; from London, approximately 2¹/₂ hours.

You may want to consider flying to Vienna to keep down your travel costs. You can easily get a train from Vienna to Budapest, so you won't have to spend a night in the wallet-busting Austrian capital if you don't want to.

### THE MAJOR AIRLINES

**Delta Air Lines** (☎ 800/241-4141, 800/361-9783 from eastern Canada, 0800/414-767 in London) and **Malév** (☎ 800/223-6884), the former Hungarian state airline, now partially owned by Alitalia, offer nonstop service between North America and Budapest. Other leading carriers include **Lufthansa** (☎ 800/645-3880), **British Airways** (☎ 800/247-9297), and **Austrian Air** (☎ 800/843-0002).

### BUDAPEST'S AIRPORTS

Budapest's two airports, **Ferihegy I** (☎ 1/296-6000) and **Ferihegy II** (☎ 1/296-8000 arrival information, 1/157-7000 departure information), are adjacent to each other in the XVIII district in southeastern Pest. Malév and Lufthansa flights land at Ferihegy II; all other flights land at Ferihegy I.

Both airports are quite small, and each has only one exit from Customs (there's no domestic air service in Hungary, so all arriving flights are international). Ferihegy II has been modernized recently, while Ferihegy I is a bit antiquated and run-down (although plans are supposedly afoot for renovation). Both airports also have a number of accommodation offices, rental-car agencies, shops, and exchange booths. Exchange rates are generally less favorable than in the city, so you may not want to change very much money at the airport.

The easiest and most reliable way into the city is the **Airport Minibus** (☎ 1/296-8555), a public service of the LRI (Budapest Airport Authority). The minibus, which leaves every 10 or 15 minutes throughout the day, takes you directly to any address in the city. From either airport, it costs 1,200 Ft ($6); the price includes luggage transport. To go between Ferihegy I and II, it costs 500 Ft ($2.50). In both airports the Airport Minibus desk is easily found in the main hall. Minibuses also provide the same efficient service returning to the airports; arrange for your pickup *one full day in advance.* The minibus will pick up passengers virtually anywhere in the

Budapest area, and the trip takes from 30 minutes to an hour, depending on how many stops are made before one's own stop.

LRI also runs an **Airport-Centrum** shuttle bus, which leaves every half hour (5am to 9pm) from both airports. Passengers are dropped off at Pest's Erzsébet tér bus station, just off Deák tér, where all three metro lines converge. The price is 500 Ft ($2.50). You can also take the LRI Airport-Centrum bus to return to the airports; pickup is at the Erzsébet tér bus station. Tickets are sold aboard the bus. The trip takes between 30 and 40 minutes, depending on which airport you're going to.

The private **taxi** drivers who hang out at the airport are notoriously overpriced. Foreigners have been charged as much as $50 for a ride that would cost a third of this in a reliable fleet taxi. However, for three or more people traveling together, an honest taxi to the city will be cheaper than the combined minibus fares. A Fő Taxi, which we recommend, costs about 2,500 to 3,000 Ft ($12.50 to $15); an Airport Taxi costs about 3,000 Ft ($15); and a dishonest or expensive private taxi might cost anywhere from 5,000 to 12,000 Ft. ($25 to $60). Our advice is to take only taxis of the recommended fleets (see "Getting Around," in chapter 3). If you don't see any taxis from these reliable outfits, call for one. The Hertz desk in the main arrivals hall will call a Fő Taxi for you. You can also dial **Fő Taxi** yourself (☎ 1/222-222); it rarely takes more than 5 minutes for the cab to arrive. A taxi from airport to downtown takes about 20 to 30 minutes.

It's also possible to get to the city by public transportation; the bus-to-metro trip takes about 1 hour. From either airport, take the red-lettered **bus no. 93** to the last stop, Kőbánya-Kispest. From there, the Blue metro line runs to the Inner City of Pest. The cost is two transit tickets, which is 120 Ft (60¢); tickets can be bought from any newsstand in the airport.

## BY TRAIN

Countless trains arrive in Budapest from most corners of Europe. Many connect through Vienna, where 11 daily trains depart for Budapest from either the Westbahnhof or Sudbahnhof station. Six daily trains connect Prague and Budapest, while one connects Berlin with Budapest and two connect Warsaw with Budapest.

### TRAIN PASSES

Almost all the countries represented in this guide offer individual rail passes or discounts; regional passes, such as European East Pass (for Austria, Hungary, the Czech Republic, and Poland), are also available. Some passes include senior discounts, and some can be purchased only in the United States. Most can be booked through travel agents.

If you plan to visit only one European country or region, keep in mind that a country or regional pass will cost less than a Eurailpass.

Since you cannot replace a pass, even if it's lost or stolen, guard it carefully. And if you're planning a trip of more than 2 hours' duration, always make a reservation, even if it's not required by the railroad of a particular country. European trains are popular and can fill up quickly, so don't be left standing.

The **European East Pass** is good for first-class unlimited rail access in Austria, the Czech Republic, Hungary, Poland, and Slovakia. You must purchase the pass from a travel agent or **Rail Europe** (see contact information below) before you leave for Europe. A pass for any 5 days of unlimited train travel in a 15-day period costs $185 for adults, $93 for children ages 4 to 11. A pass for any 10 days of unlimited train travel in a 1-month period costs $299 for adults, $150 for children ages 4 to 11.

**OTHER PASSES AVAILABLE IN NORTH AMERICA**   For American travelers, the most extensive (and popular) passes remain Eurail, and information about them is provided below, with 1997 prices that are expected to remain unchanged in 1998. Note that for the Eurailpass, Eurail Saverpass, and Eurail Flexipass, children 11 and under travel for half the adult fare and those under 4 travel free. For additional Eurail information, contact **Rail Europe,** 2100 Central Ave., Suite 200, Boulder, CO 80301 (☎ **800/438-7245;** fax 303/444-4587).

- **Eurailpass:** 15 days, $522; 21 days, $678; 1 month, $838; 2 months, $1,188; 3 months, $1,468. Accepted in Austria, Belgium, Denmark, Finland, France, Germany, Greece, Hungary, Ireland, Italy, Luxembourg, the Netherlands, Norway, Portugal, Spain, Sweden, and Switzerland. First class only, with access to many ferries, steamers, and buses free or at a discount.
- **Eurail Saverpass:** For two or more people traveling together: 15 days, $444 per person; 21 days, $576; 1 month, $712; 2 months, $1,010; 3 months, $1,248. Same privileges as the Eurailpass. First class only.
- **Eurail Flexipass:** Any 10 days within 2 months, $616; any 15 days within 2 months, $812. Same privileges as Eurailpass. First class only.
- **Eurail Saver Flexipass:** Any 10 days within 2 months, $524; any 15 days within 2 months, $690.
- **Eurail Youthpass:** 15 days, $365; 21 days, $475; 1 month, $587; 2 months, $832; 3 months, $1,028. For travelers 26 and under. Same benefits as Eurailpass. Second class only.
- **Eurail Youth Flexipass:** Any 10 days within 2 months, $431; any 15 days within 2 months, $568.
- **Europass Youth:** About 35% discount off Europass fares. Second class only; no discount for second traveler.
- **EurailDrive Pass:** Any 7 days (4 for rail, 3 for car) for use within 2 months, $345 with economy car, $375 with compact, $395 with medium-size. Extra rail days available for $55 and extra car days from $55 to $85, depending on size of car.

Children under 12 travel for half fare, and under 4 for free, when with a parent with a Eurailpass, Eurail Saverpass, and Eurail Flexipass.

These passes can be purchased from Rail Europe; call ☎ 800/4-EURAIL for tickets, information, or brochures.

In Hungary, you must have your pass validated at the **MÁV Service Office** (☎ **1/322-9035**) prior to train travel; otherwise pay $50 for validation aboard the train. Dates of travel should also be filled in.

Thomas Cook's International Timetable has the most complete schedule information. The Eurail and InterRail timetables are also helpful.

The train trip between Vienna and Budapest (7 trains daily) takes about $3^1/2$ hours and costs approximately $50 one way for first class, $33 one way in second class. For more information on Vienna trains, contact the Austrian National Tourist Board: 500 Fifth Ave., Suite 800, New York, NY 10110 (☎ 212/944-6885); 11601 Wilshire Blvd., Suite 2480, Los Angeles, CA 90025 (☎ 310/477-3332); 30 St. George St., London W1R 0AL (☎ 0171/629-0461); 2 Bloor St. E., Suite 3330, Toronto, ON M4W 1A8 (☎ 416/967-3381); or 1010 Sherbrooke St. W., Suite 1410, Montréal, PQ H3A 2R7 (☎ 514/849-3708).

For British travelers, many different rail passes are available in the U.K. for travel in Europe. Stop in at the **International Rail Centre,** Victoria Station, London SW1V 1JY (☎ **0171/834-2345**); or **Wasteels,** 121 Wilton Rd., London SW1V 1JZ (☎ **0171/834-7066**).

## BUDAPEST'S TRAIN STATIONS

Budapest has three major train stations: Keleti pályaudvar (Eastern Station), Nyugati pályaudvar (Western Station), and Déli pályaudvar (Southern Station). The stations' names, curiously, correspond neither to their geographical location in the city nor to the origins or destinations of trains serving them. Each has a metro station beneath it and an array of accommodation offices, currency-exchange booths, and other services.

Most international trains pull into bustling **Keleti Station** (☎ 1/113-6835), located in Pest's Baross tér, beyond the Outer Ring on the border of the VII and VIII districts. Tourists are met here by various hustlers offering rooms, youth hostels, and taxis. The Red line of the metro is below the station; numerous bus, tram, and trolleybus lines serve Baross tér as well.

Some international trains arrive at **Nyugati Station** (☎ 1/149-0115), a gem of a station designed by the Eiffel company and built between 1874 and 1877. It's located on the Outer Ring, at the border of the V, VI, and XIII districts. A station for the Blue line of the metro is beneath Nyugati, and numerous tram and bus lines serve busy Nyugati tér (formerly Marx tér).

Few international trains arrive at **Déli Station** (☎ 1/175-6293), an ugly modern building in central Buda; the terminus of the Red metro line is beneath the train station.

The individual train station telephone numbers are good between the hours of 8pm and 6am. During the day, obtain **local train information** over the phone by dialing 1/322-7860 and international train information at 1/342-9150. Purchase **tickets** at train station ticket offices or from the MÁV Service Office, VI. Andrássy út 35 (☎ 1/322-9035).

MÁV now operates a minibus that will take you from the station to any point in the city for 900 Ft ($4.50) per person, or between stations for 600 Ft ($3) per person. To order the minibus, call ☎1/153-2722. Often, however, a taxi fare will be cheaper, especially for groups of two or more travelers.

## BY BUS

International buses arrive at the **Erzsébet tér bus station** (☎ 1/117-2345) just off Deák tér in central Pest. All three metro lines converge on Deák tér. Inland and international bus services depart from three terminals. For destinations west of the Danube and Western Europe, the **Erzsébet tér bus station.** For destinations east of the Danube and to other countries of Eastern Europe, the **Népstadion bus station** (☎ 1/252-4496 local information and 1/252-2896 international information). Take the red line metro to Népstadion. For destinations along the Danube bend, **Árpád híd bus station** (☎ 1/129-1450). Take the blue line metro to Árpád híd.

## BY CAR

Several major highways link Hungary to nearby European capitals. The **E60** (or M1) connects Budapest with Vienna and points west; this highway was recently expanded into a multilane motorway, and is now a toll road from the Austrian border to the city of Győr. The **E65** connects Budapest with Prague and points north.

The **border crossings** from Austria and Slovakia (from which countries most Westerners enter Hungary) are hassle-free. In addition to your passport, you may be requested to present your driver's license, vehicle registration, and proof of insurance (the number plate and symbol indicating country of origin are acceptable proof). A green card is required of vehicles arriving from Bulgaria, France, the former USSR, Greece, Poland, Italy, Romania, and Israel. Hungary no longer requires the International Driver's License. Cars entering Hungary are required to have a decal indicating country of registration, a first-aid kit, and an emergency triangle. If you seek to travel to Ukraine by car from Hungary, be prepared for confusing and lengthy waits of up to 8 hours as you fill out documents prepared only in the Cyrillic alphabet. For traffic regulations, see "Getting Around," in chapter 3.

Driving distances are: from Vienna, 248 kilometers (154 miles); from Prague, 560 kilometers (347 miles); from Frankfurt, 952 kilometers (590 miles); and from Rome, 1,294 kilometers (802 miles).

## BY HYDROFOIL

The Hungarian state shipping company **MAHART** operates hydrofoils on the Danube between Vienna and Budapest in the spring and summer months. It's an extremely popular route, so you should book your tickets well in advance. In North America or Britain, contact the Austrian National Tourist Board (see "By Train," above). In Vienna, contact MAHART, Handelskai 265 (☎ **1/729-2161;** fax 1/729-2163).

From April 11 through July 3 the MAHART hydrofoil departs Vienna at 9am daily, arriving in Budapest at 2:30pm, with a stop in Bratislava when necessary (passengers getting on or off). From July 4 to August 30 an additional hydrofoil makes the daily passage, departing Vienna at 1pm, arriving in Budapest at 6:30pm. From August 31 to November 2, the schedule returns to one hydrofoil daily. The one-way fare is 750 AS ($60) and round-trip fare is 1,100 AS ($88). Children 5 and under not requiring seats ride free; children between 6 and 14 are charged half price. Eurailpass holders also receive a discount, as long as they buy the ticket before boarding. ISIC holders also receive a discount. The Budapest office of **MAHART** is at V. Belgrád rakpart (☎ **1/118-1704,** 1/118-1953, and 1/118-1586). Boats and hydrofoils from Vienna arrive at the **Belgrád rakpart,** which is on the Pest side of the Danube, between the Szabadság and Erzsébet bridges.

If you enjoy traveling by hydrofoil, but can't get reservations or find the price a bit too stiff, you can always take an inexpensive hydrofoil excursion up the Danube from Budapest to Esztergom, taking in the glories of the Danube Bend, Hungary's most scenic stretch of the river, along the way. For details, see chapter 10.

## PACKAGE TOURS

A number of companies offer package tours to Hungary and Central Europe. Among the more reputable are the following.

**Hungarian Air Tours Limited,** Kent House, 87 Regent St., London W1R 7HF (☎ **071/437-9405;** fax 071/287-7505).

**Blue Danube Holidays,** 80 Richmond St. W., Suite 1502, Toronto, Ontario, Canada M5H 2A4 (☎ **416/362-5000** or 800/268-4155; fax 416/362-8024) (specializing in spa packages). **Allegro Holidays,** at the same address and telephone number as Blue Danube Holidays, specializes in music tours.

**Tradesco Tours,** 6033 West Century Blvd., Suite 670, Los Angeles CA 90045 (☎ **310-649-5808;** fax 310-649-5852)

**Wingshooting Adventures,** 0-1845 West Leonard, Grand Rapids, MI 49544 (☎ **616/677-1980;** fax 616/677-1986) (hunting tours).

# Getting to Know Budapest

In this chapter you'll find a host of practical information you will need during your stay in Budapest—everything from neighborhood orientation to listings of the cheapest rental-car agencies, how to use a pay phone to how to avoid taxi hustlers. Glance through this chapter before your arrival, and consult it during your stay.

## 1 Orientation

### VISITOR INFORMATION

Since Budapest is undergoing rapid change, published tourist information is often out of date. The best information source in the city is **Tourinform** (☎ **1/117-9800** or 1/117-8992), the office of the Hungarian Tourist Board. Centrally located at V. Sütő u. 2, just off Deák tér (reached by all three metro lines) in Pest, the office is open every day of the year from 8am to 8pm. The staff all speak English and dispense advice on all tourist-related subjects, from concert tickets to pension rooms, and train schedules to horseback riding. Of the many free pamphlets, the most useful are the monthly "Programme in Hungary" and "Budapest Panorama." These contain information on scheduled cultural events.

You can also access information through the "Touch Info" user-friendly computer terminals located at both airports, Déli railway station, Astoria metro station, and in the market hall at Fővám tér.

*The Budapest Sun,* an English-language weekly newspaper, has extensive listings for concerts, theater, dance, movies, and other events; it's available at most hotels and many newsstands.

### CITY LAYOUT

You'll follow this section much better with a map in hand. The city of Budapest came into being in 1873, the result of a union of three separate cities: **Buda, Pest,** and **Óbuda.** Budapest, like Hungary itself, is defined by the **River Danube (Duna).** The stretch of the Danube flowing through the capital is fairly wide (the average width is 400m/1,325 ft.), and most of the city's historic sites are on or near the river. Eight bridges connect the two banks, including five in the city center. The Széchenyi Chain Bridge (Lánchíd), built in 1849, was the first permanent bridge across the Danube. Although blown up by the Nazis, it was rebuilt after the war.

# Budapest at a Glance

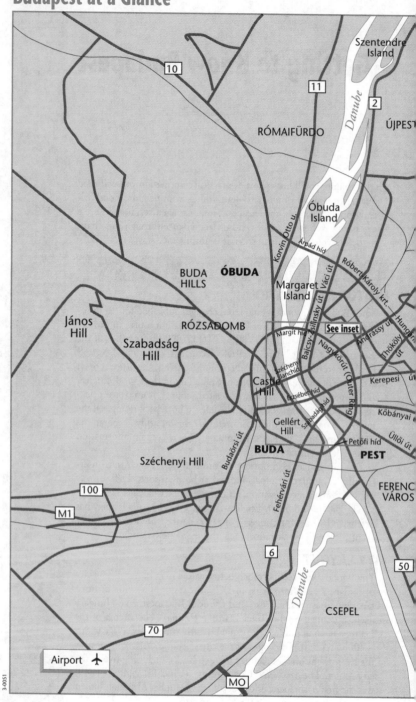

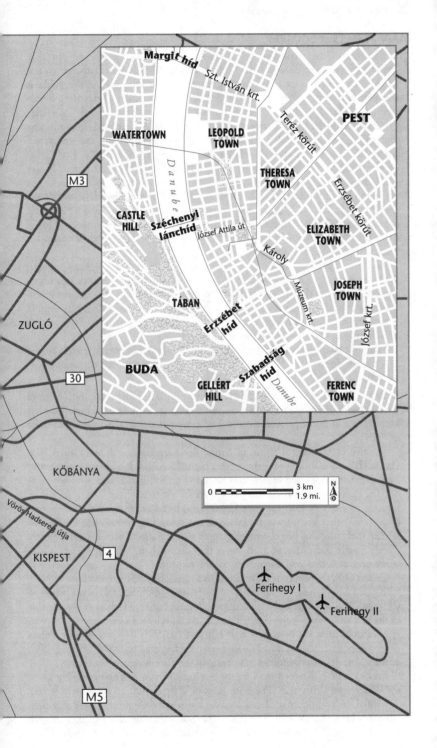

## MAIN STREETS & SQUARES

**PEST**   On the right bank of the Danube lies Pest, flat as a *palacsinta* (pancake), spreading far into the distance. Pest is the commercial and administrative center not just of the capital, but of all Hungary. Central Pest, the term used in this guide, is that part of the city between the Danube and the semicircular **Outer Ring** boulevard (Nagykörút), stretches of which are called by the names of former monarchs: Ferenc körút, József körút, Erzsébet körút, Teréz körút, and Szent István körút. The Outer Ring begins at the Pest side of the Petőfi Bridge in the south and wraps itself around the center, ending at the Margit Bridge in the north. Several of Pest's busiest squares are found along the Outer Ring, and Pest's major east-west avenues bissect it at these squares.

Central Pest is further defined by the **Inner Ring** (Kiskörút), which lies within the Outer Ring. It starts at Szabadság híd (Freedom Bridge) in the south and is alternately named Vámház körút, Múzeum körút, Károly körút, Bajcsy-Zsilinszky út, and József Attila utca before ending at the Chain Bridge. Inside this ring is the **Belváros,** the historic Inner City of Pest.

**Váci utca** (distinct from Váci út) is a popular pedestrian shopping street between the Inner Ring and the Danube. It spills into **Vörösmarty tér,** one of the area's best-known squares and site of Gerbeaud's coffeehouse. The **Dunakorzó** (Danube Promenade), a popular evening strolling place, runs along the river in Pest, between the Chain Bridge and the Erzsébet Bridge. The historic Jewish district of Pest is in the **Erzsébetváros,** between the two ring boulevards.

**Margaret Island** (Margit-sziget) is in the middle of the Danube. Accessible via the Margaret Bridge or Árpád Bridge, it's an enormously popular park without vehicular traffic.

**BUDA & ÓBUDA**   On the left bank of the Danube is Buda; to its north, beyond the city center, lies Óbuda. Buda is as hilly as Pest is flat; Óbuda is somewhat less hilly. Streets in Buda, particularly in the hills, are not as logically arranged as those in Pest.

The two most dramatic points in central Buda are Castle Hill and Gellért Hill. **Castle Hill** is widely considered the most beautiful part of Budapest. A number of steep paths, staircases, and small streets go up to Castle Hill, although no major roads do. The easiest access is from Clark Ádám tér (at the head of the Chain Bridge) by funicular or from Várfok utca (near Moszkva tér) by foot or bus. Castle Hill consists of the royal palace itself, home to numerous museums, and the so-called **Castle District,** a lovely medieval neighborhood of small, winding streets, centered around Holy Trinity Square (Szentháromság tér), site of the Gothic Matthias Church. There's little traffic on Castle Hill, and the only industry is tourism.

**Gellért Hill,** to the south of Castle Hill, is named after the martyred Italian bishop who aided King István I (Stephen I) in his conversion of the Hungarian nation to Christianity in the 10th and 11th centuries. A giant statue of Gellért sits on the side of the hill, and on top is the Citadella, a fortress built by the Austrians.

An area of parks lies between Castle Hill and Gellért Hill, in the historic **Tabán** neighborhood, an impoverished quarter razed for hygienic reasons in the early 20th century. A few Tabán buildings still stand, on the eastern edge of the quarter.

Below Castle Hill, along the Danube is a long, narrow neighborhood known as the **Watertown** (Víziváros). The main street of Watertown is Fő utca (Main Street).

Central Buda, the term used in this guide, is a collection of mostly low-lying neighborhoods below Castle Hill. The main square of central Buda is Moszkva tér, just north of Castle Hill. Beyond Central Buda, mainly to the east, are the Buda Hills.

## Hungarian Address Terms

Navigating in Budapest will be easier if you are familiar with the following words (none of which are capitalized in Hungarian):

| | |
|---|---|
| *utca* (abbreviated as u.) | street |
| *út* | road |
| *útja* | road of |
| *körút* (abbreviated as krt.) | boulevard |
| *tér* | square |
| *tere* | square of |
| *köz* | alley or lane |
| *liget* | park |
| *sziget* | island |
| *híd* | bridge |
| *sor* | row |
| *part* | riverbank |
| *pályaudvar* (abbreviated as pu.) | railway station |
| *állomás* | station |

Óbuda is on the left bank of the Danube, north of Buda. Although the greater part of Óbuda is modern and drab, it boasts both a beautiful old city center and the impressive Roman ruins of Aquincum. Unfortunately, the road coming off the Árpád Bridge slices the old city center in half, destroying its integrity. The historic center of the old city is Fő tér (Main Square), a square as lovely as any in Hungary. Óbuda Island (Óbudai-sziget) is home to a huge, and underused, park.

### FINDING AN ADDRESS

Locating addresses in Budapest can be daunting at first, largely because of the strangeness of the Hungarian language. However, with a little practice and a good map, you should meet with success.

Budapest is divided into 22 districts, called *kerülets* (abbreviated as *ker.*). A Roman numeral followed by a period precedes every written address in Budapest, signifying the kerület; for example, XII. Csörsz utca 9 is in the 12th kerület. Because many street names are repeated in different parts of the city it's very important to know which kerület a certain address is in. If the address you seek doesn't have a Roman numeral preceding it, you can also tell the kerület from the four-digit postal code. The middle two digits represent the kerület; thus, Csörsz utca 9, 1123 Budapest will be in district XII.

A common mistake made by visitors is to confuse Váci út, the uninteresting road that goes from Nyugati Station toward the city of Vác, with Váci utca, the shopping street in the Inner City. Similarly, visitors sometimes mistake Vörösmarty utca, a station on the Yellow metro line, with Vörösmarty tér, the terminus of the same Yellow metro line. Read signs carefully—Hungarian is a language with a fine sense of detail. Refer to the "Hungarian Address Terms" box above.

Street signs are posted on buildings and give the name of the street or square, the kerület, and the building numbers found on that block. Even- and odd-numbered buildings are on opposite sides of the street. Numbers are seldom skipped; often you'll end up walking longer than you expected to reach a given number.

Many street names have been changed since 1990, reverting for the most part back to their pre-World War II names, though on some central streets with politically evocative former names, like Lenin körút (now Teréz körút) and Népköztársaság út ("People's Republic Road," now Andrássy út), the old signs have been left up alongside the new, with red slashes through them. But the great majority of streets offer no such hint to the foreigner that the names have been changed.

Floors in buildings are numbered European style, meaning that the first floor is one flight up from the ground floor *(földszint),* and so on. Addresses are usually written with the floor number in Roman numerals and the apartment number in Arabic numerals. For example, XII. Csörsz utca 9, IV/3 is on the fourth floor, Apartment 3.

## STREET MAPS

A good map can save you much frustration in Budapest. Western-made maps are sold throughout Budapest, but **Cartografia,** a Hungarian company, makes two maps that are substantially cheaper and cover Budapest in great detail. The Cartografia fold-out map is fine, but if you find its size awkward you should pick up the Cartografia *Budapest Atlas.* Both maps are available throughout central Pest at kiosks and bookstores. Public transportation lines are shown on the maps, but in places the map is too crowded to make the lines out clearly. The ***BKV térkép*** (Budapest Transportation Authority map), available from metro ticket windows, is therefore recommended as a complement (see "Getting Around," later in this chapter). If you plan on any hiking excursions in the Buda Hills, you should pick up the *A Budai Hegység* map, no. 6 of the *Cartografia Turistatérképe* (Touring Map) series.

Our favorite **map stores** in Pest, where you can buy maps of other cities in Hungary, the Budapest-by-Bike map, as well as maps of other countries are: **Globe Map Shop,** at VI. Bajcsy-Zsilinszky út 37 (☎ **1/312-6001**), open Monday through Friday from 9am to 5pm (the closest metro station is Arany János utca on the Blue line) and the map store at VII. Nyár u. 1 (☎ **1/322-0438**), open Monday through Friday from 9:30am to 5:30pm (the closest metro station is Blaha Lujza tér on the Red line). You can also find maps in most bookstores recommended in chapter 8.

# NEIGHBORHOODS IN BRIEF

## PEST

**Inner City (Belváros)**    The historic center of Pest, the Belváros is the area inside the Inner Ring, bounded by the Danube to the west. Many of Pest's historic buildings are found in the Belváros, as well as the city's showcase luxury hotels and most of its best-known shopping streets.

**Leopold Town (Lipótváros)**    Just to the north of the Belváros, Lipótváros is considered a part of central Pest. Development began here at the end of the 18th century; it soon emerged as a center of Pest business and government. Parliament, plus a number of government ministries, courthouses, banks, and the former stock exchange, are all found here. Before the war it was considered a neighborhood of the "high bourgeoisie."

**Theresa Town (Terézváros)**    The character of Terézváros is defined by the great boulevard running the length of it, Andrássy út, formerly the best address in Budapest, now the center of the embassy district. The Teréz körút section of the Outer Ring cuts through Terézváros; Oktogon is its major square. The area around Nagymező utca is the city's theater district.

**Elizabeth Town (Erzsébetváros)**   Directly to the southeast of Terézváros, Erzsébetváros is the historic Jewish neighborhood of Pest. During the German occupation of 1944–45, a ghetto was constructed here. This district is still the center of Budapest Jewish life, though it is exceedingly run-down and is by no means as vibrant a place as it once was.

**Joseph Town (Józsefváros)**   One of the largest central Pest neighborhoods, Józsefváros is to the southeast of Erzsébetváros. It has long had a reputation of being the seediest part of Pest, and for all appearances this reputation is a deserved one. József körút, the neighborhood's segment of the Outer Ring, is a center of prostitution and pornography.

## BUDA

**Castle District (Várnegyed)**   The city's most beautiful and historic district dates to the 13th century. On a plateau above the surrounding neighborhoods and the Danube beyond, the Castle District is defined by its medieval walls. The immense Buda Palace and its grounds fill the district's southern end. The northern end is home to small winding streets, as well as Matthias Church, the Fisherman's Bastion, and the Hilton Hotel.

**Watertown (Víziváros)**   The long, narrow neighborhood wedged between the Castle District and the Danube, the Víziváros is historically a quarter where fishermen and small artisans reside. Built on the steep slope of Castle Hill, it has narrow alleys and stairs instead of roads in many places. Its main street, Fő utca, runs the north-south length of the Víziváros, parallel to and a block away from the river.

**Buda Hills**   The Buda Hills are numerous remote neighborhoods that feel as if they're nowhere near, let alone within, a capital city. By and large, the hills are considered a classy place to live. Neighborhoods are generally known by the name of the hill on which they stand.

**Rose Hill (Rózsadomb)**   This is the part of the Buda Hills closest to the city center and one of the city's most fashionable neighborhoods.

## ÓBUDA

Óbuda is a mostly residential area now, its long Danube coastline once a favorite spot for workers' resorts under the old regime. Most facilities have been privatized by now, explaining the large number of hotels found here. The extensive Roman ruins of **Aquincum** are Óbuda's chief claim to fame.

## 2  Getting Around

### BY PUBLIC TRANSPORTATION

Budapest has an extensive, efficient, and inexpensive public transportation system. If you have some patience and enjoy reading maps, you can easily learn the system well enough to use it wisely. The system, however, is not without its drawbacks. The biggest disadvantage is that except for 17 well-traveled bus and tram routes, all forms of transport shut down for the night at around 11:30pm (see "Night Service," below). Certain areas of the city, most notably the Buda Hills, are beyond the reach of this night service, and taxis are thus required for late-night journeys. Another problem with the system is that travel can be quite slow, especially during rush hour. A third disadvantage, pertinent mostly to tourists, is that Castle Hill can be reached in only three ways by public transportation, all of which are crowded in busy tourist seasons. Finally, and perhaps most important, crowded public transport is the place where you are most likely to be targeted by Budapest's professional pickpockets (see "Fast Facts: Safety," below ).

**FARES**    All forms of public transportation in Budapest require the self-validation of prepurchased tickets (*vonaljegy*), which cost 60 Ft (30¢) each; they can be bought at metro ticket windows, newspaper kiosks, and the occasional tobacco shop. There are also automatic machines (requiring exact change) in most metro stations and at major transportation hubs, but these are not always reliable. On weekends and at night it can be rather difficult to find an open ticket window, so buy enough to avoid the trouble of constantly having to replenish your stock. For 540 Ft ($2.70) you can get a 10-pack (*tizes csomag*), and for 1,000 Ft ($5), you can get a 20-pack (*huszos csomag*).

This standard ticket is valid on the metro, but three new types of metro tickets were also introduced in 1997, making ticket-choice all the more complicated. A "metro section ticket" (*metrószakaszjegy*) costs 40 Ft (20¢) and is valid for a single metro trip of three stations or less. A "metro transfer ticket" (*metróátszállójegy*) costs 100 Ft (50¢) and allows you to transfer from one metro line to another on the same ticket, without any limit to the number of stations you may travel. And a "metro section transfer ticket" (*metró-szakaszátszállójegy*), costing 65 Ft (33¢), allows you to transfer from one metro line to another but only for a trip totaling five or fewer stops.

For the sake of simplicity, we recommend that you purchase a day pass or multiday pass while in Budapest. Passes are inexpensive and they save you the hassle of having to validate a ticket every time you board. They might actually save you a bit of money, too, as you are likely to be getting on and off public transportation all day long. Day passes (*napijegy*) cost 500 Ft ($2.50) and are valid until midnight of the day of purchase. Buy them from metro ticket windows; the clerk validates the pass at the time of purchase. A 3-day *turistajegy* costs 1,000 Ft ($5), a 7-day pass (*hétibérlet*) costs 1,230 Ft ($6.15), and a 2-week pass (*kéthétibérlet*) costs 1,640 Ft ($8.20); these have the same validation procedure as the day pass. For longer stays in Budapest, you can buy either a monthly pass (*havibérlet*) or a 30-day pass (*30 napos bérlet*) for 2,460 Ft ($12.30). Such passes are available only at major metro stations, and you need a regulation passport photo. Students and seniors receive a substantial discount on the monthly pass. Children under 6 travel free.

Inspectors frequently come around checking for valid tickets, particularly in the metro stations. On-the-spot fines (800 Ft/$4) are assessed to fare dodgers; pleading ignorance generally doesn't work. Given how inexpensive public transport is, risking a time-consuming altercation with metro inspectors is probably not worth it.

You are likely to see advertised something called the Budapest Card for 2,900 Ft ($14.50), which combines a 3-day *turistajegy* with free entry to 55 of the city's museums. Given the low price of museum entry in the city, the Budapest Card seems more a gimmick than a bargain.

**SCHEDULES & MAPS**    All public transport operates on rough schedules, posted at bus and tram shelters and in metro stations. The schedules are a little confusing at first, but you'll get used to them. The important thing to note is when the last ride of the night departs: Many a luckless tourist has waited late at night for a bus that won't be coming until 6am!

The transportation map produced by the Budapest Transport Authority (*BKV térkép*) is available at most metro ticket windows for 200 Ft ($1). Since transportation routes are extremely difficult to read on most city maps, we suggest that you buy one of these handy maps. In addition, on the map's reverse side is a full listing of routes, including the all-important night-bus routes.

**NIGHT SERVICE**    Most of the Budapest transportation system closes down between 11:30pm or midnight and 5am. There are, however, 17 night routes (13 bus and 4 tram), and they're generally quite safe. The number 78 night bus follows the route of the Red metro line, while the number 182 night bus follows the route of the Blue metro line. Though night buses often share the same number as daytime routes (with an *É* suffix, meaning *észak,* or night), they may actually run different routes. A full listing appears on the BKV transportation map. Night buses require the standard, self-validated ticket. Skipping stops is prevalent on night buses, so pay attention.

**UNDERPASSES**   Underpasses are found beneath most major boulevards in Budapest. Underpasses are often crowded with vendors, shops, and the like, and many of them have as many as five or six different exits, each letting you out onto a different part of the square or street. Signs direct you to bus, tram, trolleybus, and metro stops, often using the word *fele,* meaning "toward." (Note that although Budapest is a very safe city, especially when compared to American cities of comparable size, underpasses tend to be among the more menacing places late at night; varied lowlifes enjoy hanging out in these subterranean confines.)

Directions given throughout this book use a metro station as a starting point whenever possible. In cases where that's simply impossible, other major transportation hubs, such as Móricz Zsigmond körtér in southern Buda, are used as starting points.

## BY METRO

You'll no doubt spend a lot of time in the Budapest metro. The system is clean and efficient, with trains running every 3 to 5 minutes from about 4:30am until about 11:30pm. The only problem is that there are just three lines, only one of which crosses under the Danube to Buda. The three lines are universally known by color—Yellow, Red, and Blue. Officially they have numbers as well (1, 2, and 3 respectively), but all Hungarians refer to them by color and all signs are color coded. All three lines converge at **Deák tér,** the only point where any meet.

The **Yellow (1) line** is the oldest metro on the European continent. Built in 1894 as part of the Hungarian millennial celebration, it was recently refurbished and restored to its original splendor. Signs for the Yellow line, lacking the distinctive colored M, are harder to spot than signs for the Blue and Red lines. Look for signs saying **földalatti** ("underground"). Each station has two entrances, one for each direction. The Yellow line runs from Vörösmarty tér, site of Gerbeaud's Cukrászda in the heart of central Pest, out the length of Andrássy út, past the Városliget (City Park), ending at Mexikói út, in a part of Pest known as Zugló. So, depending on the direction you're heading, enter either the side marked IRÁNY MEXIKÓI ÚT or IRÁNY VÖRÖSMARTY TÉR. Incidentally, somewhere in the middle of the line is a stop called Vörösmarty utca; this is a small street running off Andrássy út and should not be confused with the terminus, Vörösmarty tér. Tickets for the Yellow line are self-validated on the train itself. It's worth taking a ride on this line, which seems little changed since the 19th century.

The **Red (2) and Blue (3) lines** are modern metros and to reach them you descend long, steep escalators. The Red line runs from Örs vezér tere in eastern Pest, through the center, and across the Danube to Batthyány tér, Moszkva tér, and finally Déli Station. Keleti Station is also along the Red line. The Blue line runs from Kóbánya-Kispest, in southeastern Pest, through the center, and out to Újpest-Központ in northern Pest. Nyugati Station is along the Blue line.

On the street above stations of both the Red and Blue lines are distinctive colored M signs. Tickets should be validated at automatic boxes before you descend the escalator. When changing lines at Deák tér, you're required to validate another ticket (unless you have a special "metro transfer ticket"). The orange validating machines are in the hallways between lines, but are easy to miss, particularly if there are big crowds. Metro tickets are good for one hour for any distance along the line you're riding. You may get off and reboard with the same ticket within this time period.

## BY BUS

There are about 200 different bus (*busz*) lines in greater Budapest. Many parts of the city, most notably the Buda Hills, are best accessed by bus. Although buses are the most difficult to use of Budapest's transportation choices, with patience (and a BKV map) you'll be able to get around in no time. With the exception of night buses, most lines are in service from about 4:30am to about 11:30pm. Some bus lines run far less frequently (or not at all) on weekends, while others run far more frequently (or only) on weekends. This information is both on the reverse of the BKV transportation map and on the schedules posted at every bus stop.

Budapest's buses are blue. Black-numbered local buses constitute the majority of the city's lines. Red-numbered buses are express; generally, but not always, the express buses follow the same routes as local buses with the same number, simply skipping some stops along the way. If the red number on the bus is followed by an *E* the bus runs nonstop between terminals (whereas an *É*—with an accent mark—signifies *észak,* meaning night). Depending on your destination, an express bus may be a much faster way of traveling. A few buses are labeled by something other than a number; one you'll probably use is the *Várbusz* (Palace Bus), a minibus that runs between Várfok utca, off Buda's Moszkva tér, and the Castle District.

Bus tickets are self-validated on board by the mechanical red box found by each door. Unlike metro tickets, bus tickets are valid not for the line, but for the individual bus; you're not allowed to get off and reboard another bus going in the same direction without a new ticket. Tickets cannot be purchased from the driver. You can board the bus by any door.

The biggest problem for bus-riding tourists is the drivers' practice of skipping stops when no one is waiting to get on and no one has signaled to get off. To signal your intention to get off at the next stop, press the button above the door (beware—some drivers open only the doors that have been signaled). Most stops don't have their names posted; a list of stops is posted inside all buses, but if stops are skipped you may lose track. Chances are, though, that the Hungarians riding a given bus will know exactly where your stop is, and people are generally enthusiastic about helping foreigners on buses. You can also ask the driver to let you know when he has reached your stop.

Avoid buses in central areas during rush hours, since traffic tends to be quite bad. It pays to go a bit out of your way to use a metro or tram at these times instead.

## BY TRAM

You'll find Budapest's 34 bright-yellow trams (known as *villamos* in Hungarian) very useful, particularly the nos. 4 and 6, which travel along the Outer Ring (Nagykörút).

Tickets are self-validated on board. As with buses, tickets are valid for one ride, not for the line itself. Trams stop at every station, and all doors open, regardless of whether anyone is waiting to get on. The buttons near the tram doors are for emergency stops, not stop requests.

When a tram line is closed for maintenance (a frequent occurrence) replacement buses ply the tram route. They go by the same number as the tram, with a *V* (for *villamos*) preceding the number.

## BY TROLLEYBUS

Red trolleybuses are electric buses that receive power from a cable above the street. There are only 14 trolleybus lines in Budapest, all in Pest. Of particular interest to

# Budapest Metro

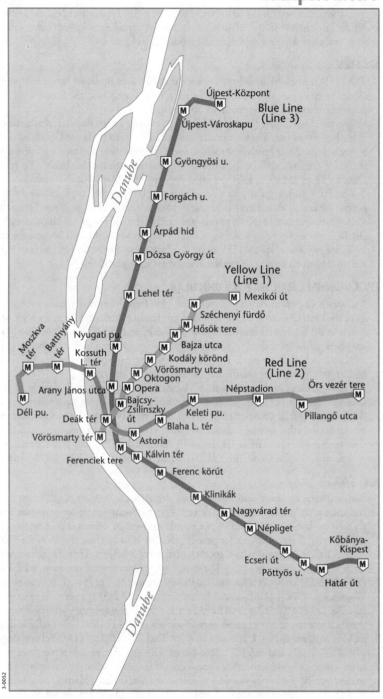

Újpest-Központ

**Blue Line
(Line 3)**

Újpest-Városkapu

Gyöngyösi u.

Forgách u.

Árpád hid

Dózsa György út

**Yellow Line
(Line 1)**

Lehel tér

Mexikói út

Széchenyi fürdő

Hősök tere

Nyugati pu.

Bajza utca

Kossuth
L. tér

Kodály körönd

**Red Line
(Line 2)**

Moszkva
tér

Batthyány
tér

Vörösmarty utca

Oktogon

Arany János utca

Opera

Népstadion

Örs vezér tere

Déli pu.

Bajcsy-
Zsilinszky
út

Keleti pu.

Pillangő utca

Deák tér

Blaha L. tér

Vörösmarty tér

Astoria

Ferenciek tere

Kálvin tér

Ferenc körút

Klinikák

Nagyvárad tér

Népliget

Kőbánya-
Kispest

Ecseri út

Pöttyös u.

Határ út

*Danube*

3-0052

train travelers is no. 73, the fastest route between Keleti Station and Nyugati Station. All the information in the "By Bus" section above regarding boarding, ticket validation, and stop-skipping applies to trolleybuses as well.

## BY HÉV

The HÉV is a suburban railway network that connects Budapest to various points along the city's outskirts. There are four HÉV lines; only one, the Szentendre line, is of serious interest to tourists (see chapter 10).

The terminus for the Szentendre HÉV line is Buda's Batthyány tér, also a station of the Red metro line. The train makes 10 stops in northern Buda and Óbuda en route to Szentendre. Most hotels, restaurants, and sights in those areas are best reached by the HÉV (so indicated in the directions given throughout this book). To reach Óbuda's Fő tér (Main Square), get off at the Árpád híd (Árpád Bridge) stop.

The HÉV runs regularly between 4am and 11:30pm. For trips within the city limits, the cost is one transit ticket, self-validated as on a bus or tram. Tickets to Szentendre cost 169 Ft (85¢), minus 60 Ft (30¢) (for the portion of the trip within city limits) if you have a valid day pass. HÉV tickets to destinations beyond the city limits are available at special HÉV ticket windows at the Batthyány tér station or from the conductor on board (no penalty assessed for such purchase).

## BY COGWHEEL RAILWAY & FUNICULAR

Budapest's **cogwheel railway** (*fogaskerekű*) runs from Városmajor, across the street from the Hotel Budapest on Szilágyi Erzsébet fasor in Buda, to Széchenyi-hegy, terminus of the Children's Railway (Gyermek Vasút) and site of Hotel Panoráma. The cogwheel railway runs from 4:30am to 11pm, and normal transportation tickets (self-validated on board) are used. The pleasant route twists high into the Buda Hills; at 60 Ft (30¢), it might be worthwhile to take it just for the ride.

The **funicular** (*sikló*) connects Buda's Clark Ádám tér, at the head of the Széchenyi Chain Bridge, with Dísz tér, just outside the Buda Castle. The funicular is one of only two forms of public transportation serving the Castle District (the Várbusz and bus no. 16 are the other possibilities; see "By Bus," above). An extremely steep and short ride, the funicular runs from 7:30am to 10pm (closed on Monday of even weeks for maintenance). Tickets cost 180 Ft (90¢) for adults and 100 Ft (50¢) for children.

## BY TAXI

Budapest taxis are unregulated, so fares vary tremendously between the different fleets and among the private unaffiliated drivers. Perhaps because there are more taxi drivers than the level of business can support, many drivers are experts at fleecing foreigners. However, if you watch out for yourself, taxis are still a bit cheaper than in the West.

Several **fleet companies** have good reputations in Budapest. These fleets have honest drivers and competitive rates. The most highly recommended company is **Fő Taxi** (☎ 1/222-2222). Fő Taxi fares include a basic rate of 50 Ft (25¢), 120 Ft (60¢) per kilometer (100 Ft [50¢] if you call for the taxi), and 22 Ft (11¢) per minute of waiting time (20 Ft [10¢] if you call for the taxi). A Fő Taxi ride from Castle Hill to central Pest, just to cite one example, should cost about 600 Ft ($3). Other reliable fleets include **Volántaxi** (☎ 1/166-6666), **City Taxi** (☎ 1/211-1111), **Yellow Pages** (☎ 1/155-5000), and **6x6** (☎ 1/266-6666). Call one of these companies from your hotel—or ask the clerk to call for you—even if there are other private taxis waiting around outside. Following our advice, Frommer's reader Karen Harrington took a Fő Taxi from the train station to her hotel for 230 Ft ($1.15). When she left for the station a few days later she asked the clerk to call her a Fő Taxi, but he responded "No need. We have Hotel Taxi." That hotel taxi ended up costing Ms. Harrington 800 Ft ($4) for the same trip.

Many **private drivers** are honest, but of course you can't be sure of this until it comes time to pay the fare. Your best bet is to avoid them altogether, particularly those drivers known to Hungarians as "hyenas," who hang around at the airports, hotels, and tourist sights. Their tricks include fast meters, meters with unusually high base rates, and return-trip surcharges. You should never agree to pay for a driver's return trip. A driver who asks to be paid in anything but forints is likely trying to cheat you. Avoid flat rates, which will no doubt be far higher than one that the meter would register.

**Tipping** is usually 10%. Hungarians usually round the bill up. If you think you have been cheated by the driver, then you certainly should not tip.

Though most people call for a taxi or pick one up at a taxi stand, it is possible to **hail** one on the street, though the rates are slightly higher (see above). At **taxi stands** in Budapest, the customer chooses with whom to do business; go with a cab from one of the recommended fleets, even if it's at the back of the line.

All these warnings notwithstanding, you'll find the majority of the fleet drivers to be polite, honest, and pleasant. Some speak English and enjoy chatting with passengers and pointing out sights.

## BY CAR

There's no reason to use a car for sightseeing in Budapest. You may, however, wish to rent a car for trips out of the city (see chapters 10 through 13). Although Hertz, Avis, and Budget offices can be found in town and at the airports, marginally better deals can be had from some of the smaller companies. You are urged to reserve a rental car as early as possible. If you reserve from abroad, ask for written confirmation by fax. If you don't receive confirmation, it's wise to assume that the reservation has not been properly made.

We have quoted rates for the least expensive car currently listed by each of these recommended agencies.

**Denzel Europcar InterRent,** VIII. Üllői út 60-62, 1082 Budapest. (☎ 1/313-1492 or 1/313-0207, fax 1/313-1492) offers the Suzuki Swift for 4,500 Ft ($22.50) per day (insurance included), plus 27 Ft (14¢) per kilometer. They also have a rental counter at each airport: Ferihegy I (☎ 296-6680) and Ferihegy II (☎ 296-6610).

**Adria Rent-a-Car,** XVIII. Haladás u. 32/a, 1183 Budapest, (☎ 06-20/380-818), also features the Suzuki Swift, at 3,800 Ft ($19) per day (insurance included), plus 28 Ft (14¢) per kilometer.

**LRI Airport Rent-A-Car,** with counters at both airports, (☎ or fax 1/296-7170 or 296-8553), offers the Volkswagen Polo for $23 per day (insurance included) and 23¢ per kilometer.

### DRIVING TIPS

**DRIVING REGULATIONS**    Hungarian police impose on-the-spot fines for driving violations. The speed limit in Hungary is 50kmph (30 m.p.h.) in built-up areas, 80kmph (50 m.p.h.) on main roads, and 120kmph (75 m.p.h.) on motorways. Safety belts must be worn in the front seat and, when available, in the back seat; children under 6 may not sit in the front seat. Horns may not be used in built-up areas, except in an emergency. Headlights must be on at all times on the major intercity roads and highways. Drunk-driving laws are strictly enforced; *any* alcohol content in the driver's blood is illegal.

Cars are required to have in them at all times a first-aid kit and a reflective warning triangle. A decal indicating country of registration is also required. These items should be included in all rental cars. If you're driving a rental car from Bulgaria, France, Greece, Israel, Poland, Italy, Romania, or the former USSR, make sure you have the so-called Green Card (proof of international insurance), not automatically given by all rental agencies. Hungarian police set up random checkpoints, where cars are pulled over and drivers made to present their papers. If all your papers are in order, you'll have no trouble. Still, foreigners residing in Budapest and driving cars with foreign plates report being routinely stopped by police and fined for rather ridiculous infractions. One Frenchman considers the fines a monthly expenditure—something so regular he must budget for them!

There are plenty of gas stations along major routes. Newly built sections of the major highways outside Budapest require payment of a toll.

**BREAKDOWN SERVICES**   The Hungarian Auto Club (**Magyar Autóklub**) operates a 24-hour emergency breakdown service: Call ☎ 088.

The Autóklub also has an **International Aid Service Center,** at II. Rómer Flóris u. 4/a (☎ 1/212-2821), established specifically for foreign motorists. Services provided include emergency aid, towing, and technical advice.

**PARKING IN BUDAPEST**   Parking is very difficult in central Pest and parts of central Buda, but little problem elsewhere in the city. You'll notice that people park virtually anywhere—on the sidewalk, in crosswalks, etc. Cars do occasionally get towed from illegal spots (to Szent István Park). If you find a boot on your car or your car has been towed, call ☎ 1/307-6776, or try 1/118-0800 (Budapest Police Headquarters). On many central streets a *fizető* sign indicates that there's a fee for parking in that area. Purchase a ticket from the machine and leave the ticket on the dashboard (visible from the window). In some cases, the parking fee is collected by an agent who approaches you as you park. Fees are generally 120 Ft (60¢) per hour. Some neighborhoods, notably Buda's Castle District, allow vehicular access only to cars with special resident permits. There are three parking garages, all in the Inner City, at V. Aránykéz u. 4–6, V. Szervita tér 8, and VII. Nyár u. 20.

## BY TRAIN

Train travel within Hungary is generally very efficient; trains almost always depart right on time and usually arrive on time. In the train stations, departures (*érkező vonatok*) are listed on the yellow poster, while arrivals (*induló vonatok*) are listed on the white poster. A train posted as *személy* is an interminable local train, which stops at every single village and town on its route. A *sebes* (speedy) train makes more selective stops, but is, essentially, another type of local train. Always opt for a *gyors* (fast) or Intercity train to get to your destination in a timely manner. All Intercity trains, and gyors trains that are marked *R,* require a seat reservation (*helyjegy*); ask for the reservation when purchasing your ticket. A seat reservation for a gyors train costs 70 Ft (35¢), while one for an Intercity train costs 250 Ft ($1.25). You must sit in your assigned seat; if you want a seat in a nonsmoking car ask for "nem dohányozni." The gyors train is typically an old, gritty rumbling train with the classic eight-seat compartments. The Intercity, a state-of-the-art, clean, modern train, is said to travel faster, but our experience has shown us that there's virtually no difference between the two in terms of speed.

## BY BICYCLE

Budapest is not a bicycle-friendly city by any stretch of the imagination, though an effort to incorporate bicycle lanes into the city streets is now underway. The project is far from complete, but eventually Budapest may be a nice place for a bike ride. As it currently stands, we do not recommend bicycling in the city for safety reasons. This said, the brave and undaunted can rent bikes from Bringóhintó on Margaret Island for 1,000 Ft ($5) per day or 450 Ft ($2.25) per hour. A 5,000 Ft ($25) deposit is required, and you must present your passport for identification. The address is XIII. Hajós A. sétány, ☎ 1/201-1796 or 1/202-6457. Charles Apartment House, at I. Hegyalja út 23, ☎ 1/201-1796 or 1/202-3414, also rents bikes, as do various bicycle shops in the city (ask at Tourinform for a current list). Also look for the map titled "Kerékpárral Budapesten" ("Budapest on Bike"), which shows biking trails and streets with bike lanes. Incidentally, Margaret Island is closed to cars and, thus, is ideal for casual bike riding.

## FAST FACTS: Budapest

**Airport**   See "Getting There," in chapter 2.

**American Express**   Budapest's main American Express office is between Vörösmarty tér and Deák tér in central Pest, at V. Deák Ferenc u. 10, 1052 Budapest (☎ 1/266-8680; fax 1/267-2028). All American Express travel services are provided—client mail, money exchange, ticketing, traveler's check and charge-card replacement. It's open Monday through Friday from 9am to 6:30pm in summer (9am to 5:30pm in winter) and on Saturday from 9am to 2pm. There's an American Express cash ATM on the street in front and also at the airport terminal of Ferihegy II.

For lost traveler's checks, call ☎ 00/800-04411 for the U.K. direct operator. Ask to call collect to ☎ 44-273-571600, or to dial direct (you pay), call ☎ 00/44-273-571600. For lost AMEX cards, call ☎ 1/267-2024 in Budapest from 8am to midnight; after midnight and on Sundays when the office closes early, your call will be automatically transferred to the U.K.

A satellite American Express office was recently opened in the Hilton Hotel on Castle Hill. Hours are Monday through Friday, 9am to 8pm in summer, 9am to 5pm in winter.

**Area Code**   The country code for Hungary is 36; the city code for Budapest is 1.

**Baby-sitters**   Ficuka Baby Hotel, V. Váci u. 11b, I em. 9 (☎ 1/138-2836, ask for Judit Zámbo), will send an English speaking baby-sitter to your hotel for 550 Ft ($2.75) for 1 hour for one child, or 950 Ft ($4.75) per hour for two children. For four or more children, two baby-sitters are issued. Baby-sitters are trained in first aid, developmental psychology, and early childhood learning. Often they are students from ELTE University. Reserve a baby-sitter by phone between 8am and 8pm, Monday through Friday.

For longer stays in Budapest, we recommend Korompay Family Day Care, XI. Menesi út 19 (☎ 1/166-5740), for children 15 months and older. Mrs. Katalin Korompay and her assistant Sylvia are both former kindergarten teachers. The Korompay house, a 5-minute walk from Buda's Móricz Zsigmond kőrtér, is spacious and clean with plenty of toys and kid-size furniture. There is a large garden with a sandbox. Mrs. Korompay cooks vegetarian meals for lunch. Teachers and children sit down to eat together. A warm, wholesome place. A half day (8:30am to 1pm) costs 900 Ft ($4.50), while a full day (8:30am to 5pm) costs 1,700 Ft ($8.50).

**Bookstores**   See "Bookstores," in chapter 8.

**Business Hours**   Most **stores** are open Monday through Friday from 10am to 6pm and on Saturday from 9 or 10am to 1 or 2pm. Many shops close for an hour at lunchtime, and most stores are closed Sunday, except those in the central tourist areas. Many shop owners and restaurateurs also close for 2 weeks in August. On weekdays, food stores open early, at around 6 or 7am, and close at around 6pm. Certain grocery stores, called "nonstops," are open 24 hours; there's a nonstop in Nyugati Station. **Banks** are usually open Monday through Thursday from 8am to 3pm and on Friday from 8am to 1pm. **Museums** in Budapest are usually open Tuesday through Sunday from 10am to 6pm.

**Car Rentals**   See "Getting Around," earlier in this chapter.

**Climate**   See "When to Go," in chapter 2.

**Currency**   See "Money," in chapter 2.

**Currency Exchange**   The hours of private currency-exchange booths vary greatly, but those in hotels and travel agencies are generally open Monday through Friday from 8am to 6pm and on Saturday and Sunday from 8am to 1pm.

**Doctors & Dentists**   IMS, a private outpatient clinic at XIII. Váci út 202 (☎ 1/ 129-8423), has English-speaking doctors and is used by many foreigners living in Budapest; it's reached via the Blue metro line (Gyöngyös utca). Payment can be made with cash or credit/charge cards. IMS also operates an emergency service after hours and on weekends, III. Vihar u. 29 (☎ 1/250-1899). Many luxury hotels have a staff dentist or a private dentist with rented office space. For further dental options, ask at Tourinform. Other relevant emergency medical numbers include AIDS Anonymous (☎ 1/215-7650) and the 24-hour medical needs hot line (☎ 1/118-8212).

**Documents Required**   See "Visitor Information & Entry Requirements," in chapter 2.

**Driving Rules**   See "Getting Around," earlier in this chapter.

**Drugstores**   See "Pharmacies," below.

**Electricity**   Hungarian electricity is 220 volts, AC. If you plan to bring any North American electrical appliances, you'll need a 110–220 volt transformer/converter. Transformers are available at electrical supply stores throughout the city. We recommend **Trakis-Hetra Ltd.,** at VII. István u. 10, (☎ 1/342-5338 or 322-1459). The nearest metro station is Keleti pu. (Red line). If there is a transformer built into the adapter of the appliance, as in many laptop computers, you will need only a small adapter to fit the North American flat plugs into the round holes in the wall. This adapter may be hard to find in Budapest.

**Embassies**   The embassy of **Australia** is at XII. Királyhágó tér 8-9 (☎ 1/ 201-8899); the embassy of **Canada,** at XII. Budakeszi út 32 (☎ 1/275-1200); the embassy of **the Republic of Ireland,** at V. Szabadság tér 7 (☎ 1/302-9600); the embassy of the **United Kingdom,** at V. Harmincad u. 6 (☎ 1/266-2888); and the embassy of the **United States,** at V. Szabadság tér 12 (☎ 1/267-4400). **New Zealand** does not have representation in Hungary.

**Emergencies**   Dial ☎ 104 for an ambulance, ☎ 105 for the fire department, or ☎ 107 for the police. To reach the 24-hour English-speaking emergency service, dial ☎ 1/118-8212.

**Eyeglasses**   *Optika* is the Hungarian name for an optometrist's shop; Pest's Outer Ring Boulevard (Nagykörút) would be a good place to search one out. The word for eyeglasses is *szemüveg*.

**Fax/Telex**   Faxes and telexes can be sent from the main telecommunications office, at Petőfi Sándor u. 17 (near Deák tér). It's open Monday through Friday from 8am to 8pm and on Saturday from 9am to 11pm. A one-page fax to the United States costs 525 Ft ($2.70); two pages cost 775 Ft ($3.90). Internet access is also available. Log on for 300 Ft ($1.50) a half hour, 500 Ft ($2.50) one hour. Downtown luxury hotels also often have fax services.

**Holidays** See "When to Go," in chapter 2.

**Language** Hungarian (*Magyar*), a member of the Finno-Ugric family of languages, is unrelated to any of the languages of Hungary's neighboring countries. By and large, Hungarians know how obscure their language is and welcome and encourage any attempts made by foreigners to communicate. Many Hungarians speak German and/or English. Particularly in Budapest, you shouldn't have much problem making yourself understood. Everyone involved in tourism speaks at least a little English.

*Colloquial Hungarian* (published by Routledge, Chapman, Hall) is a good phrase book and comes with a cassette.

**Laundry & Dry Cleaning** Ask at your hotel or pension. Private room hosts are usually happy to make a little extra money doing laundry. Self-service launderettes (*patyolat*) are scarce in Budapest. As far as we know, the city's only centrally located Laundromat is at VII. Rákóczi út 8. It's open Monday through Friday, 7am to 5pm and Saturday, 7am to 1pm.

**Libraries** The United States Information Service (USIS) has a public reading room in the Central Bank building, at V. Szabadság tér 7-9 (☎ 1/302-6200 or 1/302-0426). A new project is underway at USIS to replace the books and magazines with a high-tech electronic information service consisting of CD-ROMs, databases, and online services with a business emphasis. It's open Tuesday and Thursday from 11am to 5pm.

The British Council library is at VII. Benczúr u. 26 (☎ 1/321-4039). It's open Monday through Thursday from 11am to 6pm and on Friday from 11am to 5pm.

**Lost Property** The BKV (Budapest Transportation Authority) lost-and-found office is at VII. Akácfa u. 18 (☎ 1/322-6613). For items lost on a train or in a train station, call ☎ 1/129-8037. For items lost on an intercity bus (not on a local BKV bus), call ☎ 1/118-2122.

**Repair** Luggage and handbag repair is done at any workshop called *Táska javítás* or *Táska klinika.* It's strikingly cheap. Try the táska javítás in Divat-Kellék, at Kálvin tér 2 (☎ 1/111-2970), near the Kálvin tér metro station (Blue line). The seamstress is Mrs. Balogh. It's open on Monday from 2 to 5:30pm and Tuesday through Friday from 1 to 4pm.

**Luggage Storage** There are left-luggage offices *(ruhatár)* at all three major railroad stations. At Keleti, it's in the main waiting room alongside Track 4. It's open 4am–midnight. At Nyugati, it's in the waiting room behind the international ticket office and it's open 24 hours. The cost is 120 Ft (60¢) per day; for larger bags (35kg/75 lb. and up), 240 Ft ($1.20). There are also self-storage lockers in Keleti and Nyugati stations for 150 Ft (75¢) per day; get exact change (3×50 Ft coins) from the left-luggage office attendant. Déli Station has a new locker system in operation in the main ticket-purchasing area; the lockers are very large, and directions for use are provided by a multilingual computer. The cost is 120 Ft (60¢) per day. The Erzsébet tér bus station, near Deák tér in central Pest, has a left-luggage office, charging 80 Ft (40¢) per bag; it's open Monday through Thursday from 6am to 7pm, on Friday from 6am to 8pm, and on Saturday and Sunday from 6am to 6pm.

**Mail/Post Office** Mail can be received by clients at American Express (see above); a single AMEX traveler's check is sufficient to prove that you're a client. Others can receive mail ℅ Poste Restante, Magyar Posta, Petőfi Sándor u. 17–19, 1052 Budapest, Hungary. This confusing office (open Monday through Friday from 8am to 8pm and on Saturday from 8am to 3pm), not far from Deák tér (all metro lines), is the city's main post office. There are 24-hour post offices near Keleti and Nyugati stations.

At presstime, an airmail postcard costs 84 Ft (42¢); an airmail letter, 112 Ft (56¢) and up. The rate for letters mailed in Budapest to a Budapest address is 20 Ft (10¢), and postcards cost 16 Ft (8¢). For letters mailed to other parts of Hungary, the rate is 27 Ft (14¢); for postcards, 20 Ft (10¢).

**Maps**   See "City Layout" under "Orientation," earlier in this chapter.

**Money**   See "Money," in chapter 2.

**Names**   Hungarians write their names with the family name first, followed by the given name. When mentioning Hungarian names in this book we have employed the more common form of given name followed by family name. The only exception is with street names, where we have used the Hungarian style: hence Ferenc Deák (the man) but Deák Ferenc utca (the street).

**Newspapers & Magazines**   *The International Herald Tribune, USA Today, The Guardian, The Financial Times, The Times of London, The European, Newsweek,* and *Time* are all commonly found in luxury hotels and at kiosks and bookstores in the neighborhood around Váci utca. At larger newsstands you can also find *People, Vogue, Harpers,* and, once in a blue moon, *The New York Times.* Try the news shop next to the Telecommunications office at Petőfi Sándor u. 17 (near Deák tér). Look also for the *Budapest Sun,* an English-language weekly. In addition to articles on current events and politics in Hungary, the paper provides weekly listings of theater, movies, exhibitions, and special events. For longer stays in Budapest, get yourself a copy of *The Phone Book,* an excellent resource, published by CoMo Media (☎ 1/266-4916).

**Pharmacies**   The Hungarian word is *gyógyszertár,* or occasionally, *patika.* Generally, pharmacies carry only prescription drugs. Some hotels advertise "drugstores," but these are just shops with soap, perfume, aspirin, and other nonprescription items. There are a number of 24-hour pharmacies in the city—every pharmacy posts the address of the nearest one in its window. If necessary, ask for a specific address at Tourinform.

**Photographic Needs**   The price of film is about the same as in the West, but the price to develop film is almost twice what it is in the West. Photo booths are located throughout the city in underpasses and department stores.

**Radio**   A short-wave radio can pick up the BBC, Voice of America, Radio Moscow, and other English-language stations.

**Religious Services in English**   Roman Catholic masses are held at 5pm on Saturday in the Jesuit Church of the Sacred Heart, VII. Mária u. 25 (☎ 1/118-3479). Nondenominational services are given on Sunday at 10:30am at the Óbuda Community Center, III. Kiskorona u. 7 (☎ 1/250-0288). Presbyterian and Anglican services are held on Sunday at 11am at VI. Vörösmarty u. 51 (☎ 1/163-7940). The Christian Science Society is located at II. Kútvölgyi út 20-22. Consult "Programme in Hungary" and "Budapest Panorama," available at Tourinform and most hotels, for other English-language religious services.

**Rest Rooms**   The word for toilet in Hungarian is *WC* (pronounced vay-tsay). *Női* means "women's"; *férfi* means "men's."

**Safety** By Western standards, Budapest is a very safe city—muggings and violent attacks are rare. Nevertheless, tourists are always prime targets. Teams of professional pickpockets plague Budapest. They operate on crowded trams, metros, and buses. Be particularly careful on bus no. 26 (Margaret Island) and trams no. 4 and 6 or in any other crowded setting. The pickpocket's basic trick is to create a distraction to take your attention away from yourself and your own safety. Avoid being victimized by wearing a money belt under your clothes instead of wearing a fanny pack or carrying a wallet or purse. No valuables should be kept in the outer pockets of a knapsack.

Sadly, nonwhite people need to be wary of racist gangs, who, though small in number, have made some highly publicized attacks in the past few years. Such crimes are usually committed late at night.

**Shoe Repair** The Hungarian word is *cipész* or *cipő javitás*. Scarcely a neighorhood in the city is without a cipész. Ask your hotel reception for the nearest one.

**Smoking** The antismoking crusade has not yet reached Hungary. Nevertheless, smoking is forbidden in many public places (including all public transport). *Dohányzás tilos* or *Dohányozni tilos* means "No Smoking."

**Taxes** Taxes are included in all restaurant prices, hotel rates, and shop purchases. Foreigners are entitled, upon leaving the country, to a refund of the 25% VAT on some purchases. See chapter 8 for details.

**Taxis** See "Getting Around," earlier in this chapter.

**Telephone** The Hungarian phone system has been recently privatized, though service still does not meet Western standards. For best results, dial slowly and don't be too quick to trust a busy signal; rather, keep trying.

Budapest telephone numbers are constantly changing as Matáv continues to upgrade its system. All numbers starting with "1" may be subject to change by the year 2000. In many, but not all, of these cases, the 1 will simply be replaced with 3. If you find that the number you want has changed (you will hear a recording: "*a hívott szám megváltozott*"), dial 198 for **local directory assistance.** If the operator speaks no English, try calling CoMo Media, publishers of the English language phone book, at 1/266-4916.

You can access the international operator from most public phones, though older phones are less reliable; a 20-Ft coin is required to start the call. You can reach the **AT&T** operator at 00/800-01111, the **MCI** operator at 00/800-01411, and the **Sprint** operator at 00/800-01877.

Other **country direct** access numbers connect you to operators in the country you're calling, with whom you can arrange your preferred billing. **Australia Direct** is 00/800-06111, **Canada Direct** is 00/800-01211, **New Zealand Direct** is 00/800-06411, and **U.K. Direct** is 00/800-04411 (BT) or 00/800-04412 (Mercury).

You can also use **direct dial;** Hungarian telephone books list the numbers of all countries that can be directly dialed. If you don't have access to a telephone book, 09 is the number for the international operator. Direct dial to the **United States** and **Canada** is 00/1; to the **U.K.,** 00/44; to **Australia,** 00/61; and to the **Republic of Ireland,** 00/353. A few Eastern European countries cannot be called by direct dial, and should be accessed from the main telephone office (see below).

Another option, and apparently the cheapest one, is "Phone USA," a prepaid phone card that allows you to call home for 99¢ per minute. The flat rate applies

24 hours a day, 7 days a week. There is no surcharge or connecting fee. Cards cost 4,750 Ft ($23.75) for 60 units (approximately 30 minutes). For more information, visit their website: www.datanet.hu/wwt. In Budapest, cards can be purchased at the American Express office and at certain Ibusz offices.

The **area code** for Budapest is 1, and all phone numbers in Budapest (except mobile phones, see below) have seven digits. Most other towns in Hungary have a two-digit area code and six-digit telephone numbers. To make a call from one Hungary area code to another, first dial 06; when you hear a tone, dial the area code and number. Remember to dial slowly. Numbers that begin with 06-20, followed by a six-digit number, are **mobile phone numbers** in Hungary. These are increasingly popular among business people and some of the listings in this book are mobile phone numbers. Be aware that you pay for a long distance call when you call a mobile phone.

Public **pay phones** charge varying amounts for local calls depending on the time of day that you place your call. You'll get anywhere from 2 to 10 minutes for each 10-Ft coin. It's cheapest to call late in the evenings and on weekends. Public phones operate with old and new 10- and 20-Ft coins or with phonecards (in 50 or 100 units) which can be purchased from post offices, tobacco shops, and some street vendors. It is only worth buying a phonecard if you plan to make a lot of local calls.

The **main telecommunications office,** at Petőfi Sándor u. 17 (near Deák tér), is open Monday through Friday from 8am to 8pm and on Saturday from 9am to 3pm. Telephone calls, as well as faxes and telexes, can be made to anywhere in the world. It costs 200 Ft ($1) per minute to call the United States from this office. Ask at the main desk for a telephone guide information pamphlet in English.

Hotels typically add a surcharge to all calls (although some allow unlimited free local calls), so you're advised to use public telephone booths (often found in hotel lobbies), the telephone office, or the post office.

**Time Zone**    Hungary is on Central European time, 2 hours ahead of Greenwich mean time and 6 hours ahead of eastern standard time from March 26 to September 26; from September 27 to March 25 (during the equivalent of daylight saving time), the difference is 1 hour and 5 hours, respectively.

**Tipping**    Tipping is generally 10%. Among those who welcome tips are waiters, taxi drivers, hotel employees, barbers, cloakroom attendants, toilet attendants, masseuses, and tour guides.

**Water**    Tap water in Budapest is generally considered safe for drinking. Mineral water, which many Hungarians prefer to tap water, is called *ásványvíz*. Purified bottled water (*szénsav mentes*) is sold in delicatessens and groceries in the tourist areas.

# Where to Stay in Budapest    4

Budapest's hotels range from beautiful, historic turn-of-the-century gems to drab, utilitarian establishments typical of the city's socialist period. Although the most notable establishments—among them the stunning art nouveau Hotel Gellért and the city's other "thermal" hotels, Hotel Béke Radisson, and Castle Hill's distinctive Hilton Hotel—are among the city's priciest, accommodation rates in Budapest are among the lowest of any European capital.

Despite the number of new hotels and pensions that have opened in recent years, Budapest retains its reputation as a city without enough guest beds. Indeed, in high season it can be quite difficult to secure a hotel or pension room or hostel bed (although private rooms are always available), so make reservations and get written confirmation well ahead if possible.

When booking, keep in mind that if you want a room with double beds, it should be specifically requested; otherwise you are likely to get a room with two twin beds. Single rooms are generally available, as are extra beds or cots. Hungarian hotels use the word "apartment" to describe the kind of room we call a "suite" (that is, connected rooms, without a kitchen). In these listings, we have referred to such rooms as suites.

**BUDGET LODGINGS**    Although there is an unfortunate dearth of recommendable budget hotels in Budapest, travelers can take advantage of the wealth of good alternative accommodations. Small pensions, rooms in private homes, and a number of good youth hostels make the city inviting to travelers on any budget. Remember that location plays a significant role in cost, with inflated prices for centrally located accommodations the norm. Budapest's efficient public transportation means that reaching downtown from points outside will not be as difficult as you might expect; if you're on a budget, consider staying outside the center in a room removed from the din and smog (and prices) of inner Pest. Pensions in the Buda Hills are far cheaper than downtown hotel rooms; what's more, they are generally located in quiet residential neighborhoods, and most have lovely gardens. We have selected what we consider to be the nicest of the many pensions in the Buda Hills. We also urge you to consider booking a room in Buda's sleepy, but centrally located, Watertown neighborhood, home to a number of recommended hotels.

**ACCOMMODATIONS AGENCIES**    Most accommodations agencies can secure private room rentals, help reserve hotel and pension rooms, and book you into a youth hostel. The most established agencies are the former state-owned travel agents Ibusz, Cooptourist, MÁV Tours, and Budapest Tourist. Although newer, private agencies have proliferated, the older ones tend to have the greatest number of rooms listed. There are agencies in both airports (open 24 hours), all three major train stations, throughout central Pest, and along the main roads into Budapest for travelers arriving by car. The main **Ibusz reservations office** is at Ferenciek tere 10 (☎ 1/ **118-6866;** fax 1/118-4983), reached by the blue metro line. The number to call if you're interested in booking a room in a private home through Ibusz is 1/118-1120. All major credit and charge cards are accepted.

Be aware that tourists have reported that agents may urge them to take a more expensive room than they wanted. Stick to your guns; the agent will eventually help you reserve a room where (and in the general price range) you desire.

**SEASONS**    Most hotels and pensions in Budapest divide the year into three seasons. **High season** is roughly from March or April through September or October. The week between Christmas and New Year's, Easter week, the period of the Budapest Spring Festival, and the weekend of the Grand Prix (second weekend in August) are also considered high season. **Mid season** is usually considered the months of March and October and/or November. **Low season** is roughly November through February, except Christmas week. Some hotels discount as much as 50% in low season, while others offer no winter discount; be sure to inquire.

**PRICE CATEGORIES**    Many hotels and pensions in Budapest list their prices in German marks (DM); a few list them in U.S. dollars. This is done solely as a hedge against forint inflation; all hotels in Budapest accept payment in Hungarian forints as well as foreign currencies. We have converted the DM prices into dollar prices. We based our calculations on an exchange rate of DM 1.75 to $1, the rate at press time. As this exchange rate fluctuates over time, of course, the price of a room in dollars will fluctuate along with it.

All hotels are required to charge a 12% value-added tax (VAT). Some build the tax into their rates whereas others tack it on on top of their rates. When booking a room, ask whether the VAT is included in the quoted price.

In the following sections, hotels are listed according to four price categories: **Very Expensive,** over $170 for a double room; **Expensive,** $100 to $170 for a double room; **Moderate,** $60 to $100 for a double room; and **Inexpensive,** under $60 for a double room. Hotels are also listed within price categories according to neighborhood.

Hotels in Hungary are rated by the international star system. The ratings, however, are in our view somewhat arbitrary and are not included in our entries for that reason.

## 1 Best Bets

- **Best Historic Hotel:** The splendid, sprawling **Hotel Gellért,** XI. Gellért tér 1 (☎ 1/185-2200), first opened in 1918, is still one of the city's most elegant and charming hotels. The art nouveau Gellért Baths (and outdoor pool) are the most popular in Budapest.
- **Best for Business Travelers:** The **Kempinski Hotel Corvinus,** V. Erzsébet tér (☎ 1/266-1000), is the hotel of choice for corporate visitors, with conference facilities, a state-of-the-art business center, and an efficient staff.
- **Best for a Romantic Getaway:** Any of the pensions in the Buda Hills might suffice, but the **Vadvirág Panzió,** II. Nagybányai út 18 (☎ 1/176-4292), is particularly fetching, surrounded as it is by sloping gardens and terraces.

- **Best for Families:** Parents will appreciate the location of the **Hotel Liget,** VI. Dózsa György út 106 (☎ 1/269-5300)—across the street from City Park, home to the zoo, amusement park, and circus.
- **Best Moderately Priced Hotel:** The brand new **Hotel Astra Vendégház,** I. Vám u. 6 (☎ 1/214-1906), opened in 1997, is perfectly situated in Buda's quaint Watertown neighborhood, just a 10-minute walk from the Castle District, and minutes from the Danube embankment.
- **Best Budget Hotel:** The **Charles Apartments,** I. Hegyalja út 23 (☎ 1/201-1796), are comfortable and clean flats with full bathrooms and kitchens. Two people can share an apartment for $40.
- **Best Pension:** The charming **Gizella Panzió,** XII. Arató u. 42/b (☎ 1/249-2281), built into a hill, has a lovely view of the valley in a quiet neighborhood that's relatively easy to reach by bus. The rooms are quaint and sunny.
- **Best Location:** This one is a tie between the only two hotels in Buda's elegant Castle District overlooking the river: The **Hilton Hotel,** I. Hess András tér 1–3 (☎ 1/214-3000), is a luxurious place right next door to the Matthias Church and the Fisherman's Bastion, while **Hotel Kulturinnov,** I. Szentháromság tér 6 (☎ 1/155-0122), is a modest guest house just across the square.
- **Best Service:** At the **San Marco Guest House,** III. San Marco u. 6 (☎ 1/388-9997), the charming proprietors, who speak fluent English, are happy to go out of their way to provide guests with whatever they need: restaurant reservations, theater tickets, train schedules, and more.
- **Best Spa:** The two "thermal hotels"—**Helia,** XIII. Kárpát u. 62–64 (☎ 1/270-3277), and **Aquincum Corinthia,** III. Árpád fejedelem utja 94 (☎ 1/250-3360)—have complete spa facilities that all guests can use free of charge. Relax in the swimming pool, sauna, thermal bath, Jacuzzi, or steam bath.
- **Best View:** You'll see the full Pest skyline or overlook the delightful streets of the Castle District at the **Hilton Hotel,** I. Hess András tér 1–3 (☎ 1/214-3000), widely considered the city's finest hotel (although its design remains controversial).

## 2 The Inner City & Central Pest

### VERY EXPENSIVE

#### Budapest Marriott

V. Apáczai Csere Janos u. 4, 1052 Budapest. ☎ **1/266-7000.** Fax 1/266-5000. 382 rms. A/C MINIBAR TV TEL. DM 359–369 ($205–$210) double. Breakfast DM 28–32 ($16–$18.25) extra. AE, DC, EURO, JCB, MC, V. Metro: Deák tér (all lines).

Rather dowdy and off-putting on the outside, but measuring up to international standards of luxury on the inside, the Marriott is a clean and efficient option that springs few surprises. Accessible to Pest's main shopping and business areas, it hugs the Danube promenade between the Erzsébet and Chain bridges. Rooms, all of which look out to the river (most have balconies), are comfortable, having been renovated after the Marriott chain took over the hotel in 1993 (from the Inter-Continental chain). All 382 accommodations have in-room safes. The lobby has a clubby gentlemen's club feel. Nonsmoking rooms and others equipped for guests with disabilities are available.

At press time, the Marriott was completing a new executive residence designed for long-term stays, the Millenium Court, a few blocks away. The complex, built around the historic *Vasudvar* (Iron Court), will consist of 108 one- and two-bedroom luxury apartments and studios, primarily serving those international businesspeople in the process of relocating to Hungary (30- to 90-day stays). Units will offer the privacy and

# Budapest Accommodations

Alba Hotel Budapest **10**

Aquincum
  Corinthium Hotel **2**

Best Western Hotel Art **19**

Budapest Marriott **15**

Charles Apartments **12**

City Panzió Ring **31**

City Panzió Pilvax **21**

Danubius Grand Hotel
  Margitsziget **3**

Family Hotel **32**

Intercontinental
  Budapest Hotel **14**

Hilton Hotel **6**

Hotel Astra Vendégház **7**

Hotel Béke Radisson **29**

Hotel Centrál **35**

Hotel Citadella **16**

Hotel Délibáb **34**

Hotel Ersébet **20**

Hotel Express **11**

Hotel Gellért **17**

Hotel Kulturinnov **5**

Hotel Liget **33**

Hotel MEDOSZ **28**

Hotel Nemzeti **25**

Hotel Orion **13**

Hotel Papillon **1**

Hotel Victoria **9**

International
  Apartment Hotel **8**

K & K Opera Hotel **27**

Kempinski Hotel Corvinus **22**

King's Hotel **23**

Lotus Youth Hostel **30**

Marco Polo Hostel **24**

Mellow Mood
  Guesthouse **26**

Peregrinus Vendégház **18**

Radio Inn **36**

Thermal Hotel **4**

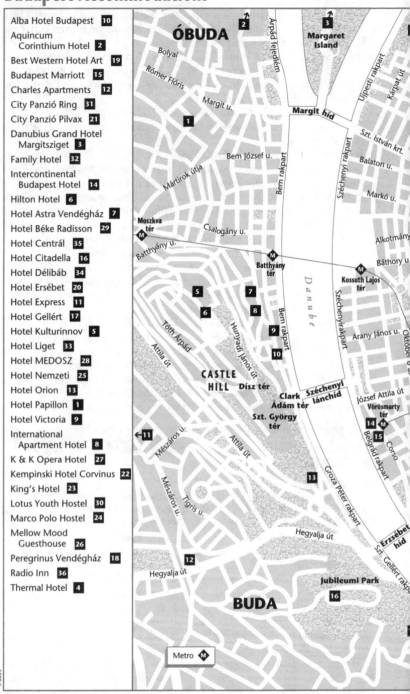

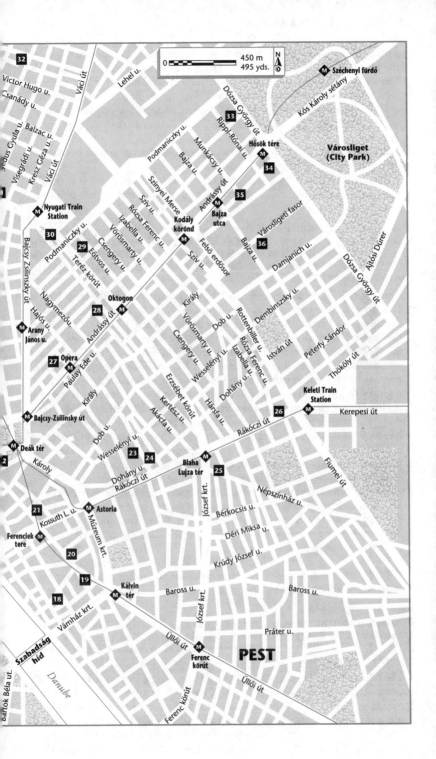

32

Victor Hugo u.

Csanády u.

Jedus Gyula u.

Visegrádi u.

Balzac u.

Kresz Géza u.

Váci út

Váci út

Lehel u.

Dózsa György út

Kós Károly sétány

Széchenyi fürdő

33

Rippl-Rónai u.

Hősök tére

Városliget
(City Park)

Podmaniczky u.

Munkácsy u.

Bajza u.

34

Nyugati Train
Station

Bajcsy Zsilinszky út

Szinyei Merse

Andrássy út

35

Bajza
utca

Városligeti fasor

Bajza u.

Damjanich u.

Dózsa György út

Aitósi Dürer

30

Podmaniczky u.

Szív u.

Rózsa Ferenc u.

Kodály
körönd

Felső erdősor

Szív u.

36

29

Izabella u.

Csengery u.

Eötvös u.

Vörösmarty u.

Teréz körút

28

Oktogon

Andrássy út

Király

Dob u.

Rottenbiller u.

Dembinszky u.

István út

Peterfy Sándor

Thököly út

Nagymező u.

Hajós u.

Arany
János u.

27

Opera

Paulay Ede u.

Király

Vörösmarty u.

Csengery u.

Wesselényi u.

Rózsa Ferenc u.

Izabella u.

Dohány u.

Keleti Train
Station

Bajcsy-Zsilinsky út

Dob u.

Wesselényi u.

Erzsébet körút

Kertész u.

Akácfa u.

Hársfa u.

26

Kerepesi út

Deák tér

2

Károly

23

24

Dohány u.
Rákóczi út

Blaha
Lujza tér

25

Rákóczi út

Fiumei út

József krt.

Népszínház u.

21

Kossuth L. u.

Astoria

Múzeum krt.

Bérkocsis u.

Ferenciek
tere

20

Déri Miksa u.

Krúdy József u.

19

Kálvin
tér

Baross u.

József krt.

Baross u.

18

Vámház krt.

Szabadság
híd

Danube

Bartók Béla út.

Üllői út

Ferenc
körút

Ferenc körút

Üllői út

Práter u.

PEST

0 ▭▬▭▬▭ 450 m
495 yds.

N

61

furnishings of a private residence, with fully equipped kitchens, in addition to grocery, thrice-weekly housekeeping services, and food-and-beverage signing privileges at the Marriott hotel. A health club will also be on the premises. Millenium Court should be open for guests as of early 1998; call the Budapest Marriott for additional information.

**Dining/Entertainment:** The Marriott has three restaurants serving Hungarian and international fare—The Duna Grill, The Csárda Restaurant, and the Beer Garden Terrace.

**Services:** Room service (24-hour), laundry, baby-sitting, safe-deposit boxes, travel desk, and currency exchange.

**Facilities:** Soundproof windows, fitness center, squash court, gift shop, swimming pool, sauna, massage, solarium, sun terrace, meeting facilities (including translation services).

### Inter-Continental Budapest Hotel

V. Apáczai Csere J. u. 12–14, 1052 Budapest. ☎ **1/327-6333.** Fax 1/117-9808. 370 rms, 12 suites. A/C MINIBAR TV TEL. DM 340–380 ($194–$217) double; DM 700 ($399) suite. Breakfast DM 15–25 ($8.55–$14.25) extra. AE, CB, EURO, JCB, MC, V. Parking 2,500 Ft ($12.50) per day. Metro: Deák tér (all lines).

This luxury hotel, located right on the Danube embankment in the Inner City of Pest, was the Fórum Hotel in a previous incarnation. It is not to be confused with the Budapest Marriott, a hotel situated just down the street, which was once called the Inter-Continental. Built in 1981, the uInter-Continental has 370 rooms, including one presidential suite and 10 junior suites. Rooms overlooking the Danube have spectacular views of the Chain Bridge and Castle Hill. The rooms, decorated with contemporary Hungarian artworks, are plush and luxurious, without the depressing, claustrophobic feeling found in some of Budapest's modern hotels. Since becoming part of the Inter-Continental chain, all rooms are being renovated (at press time, all but three floors were entirely renovated, and the rest should be finished by the time this guide hits bookstores). There's a safe in every room, and bathrooms feature a wide selection of toiletries, built-in hair dryers, and complimentary bathrobes. There is also video message retrieval and video check-out, accessed from the TV in your room. Nonsmoking rooms and rooms equipped for travelers with disabilities are available.

**Dining/Entertainment:** International/Hungarian cuisine is available in the elegant Silhouette Restaurant. There's piano music nightly, and outdoor dining is possible on Pest's famous Dunakorzó (Danube promenade). A less expensive restaurant serving all meals, The Grill, is also on the premises. The Viennese-style Wiener Kaffeehaus is said by some to offer the best pastries in Budapest.

**Services:** Room service (24-hour), laundry, baby-sitting, safe-deposit boxes.

**Facilities:** Soundproof windows, business center, barbershop, hairdresser, drugstore, fitness center, swimming pool, sauna, massage, solarium, conference facilities.

### Hotel Béke Radisson

VI. Teréz krt. 43, 1067 Budapest. ☎ **1/301-1611.** Fax 1/301-1615. 239 rms, 8 suites. A/C MINIBAR TV TEL. DM 290–350 ($165–$200) double; DM 600 ($342) suite. Breakfast DM 20 ($11.40) extra. AE, EURO, JCB, MC, V. Parking DM 21 ($12) per day. Metro: Nyugati pu. (Blue line) or Oktogon (Yellow line).

The Béke Radisson, excellently situated not far from Nyugati railway station on Pest's Outer Ring (Nagykörút), carries on a long tradition. In 1913, the Hotel Brittania opened on the same spot. An art nouveau gem, it was one of the most modern Budapest hotels of its time. Unfortunately, the hotel was badly damaged in World War II, and it was not until 1955 that it was reopened under the hopeful name Béke (meaning "peace"). The hotel underwent renovations again in the 1980s, reopening in 1985 after a reconstruction notable for its respect of the hotel's original design. Rooms are smartly furnished in dark wood, each with a safe, and the bathrooms have built-in hair dryers. The soundproof windows don't exactly muffle all the noise from the busy boulevard below. Nonsmoking rooms and rooms equipped for travelers with disabilities are available. Hotel Béke Radisson has its own home-page. Visit it at: www.radisson.com. You can also make contact via e-mail: ib@budzh.sih.dk.

**Dining/Entertainment:** The Shakespeare Restaurant serves breakfast and lunch in a bright, cheerful room with a skylight and Shakespearean frescoes by Jenő Haranghy, preserved from the original Hotel Brittania. The elegant Szondi Restaurant (named after a Hungarian hero who fought the Turks) serves Hungarian/international dinners accompanied by Gypsy music. The restaurant is decorated with Turkish weaponry and frescoes and stained-glass windows (also from the original hotel) depicting battle scenes and other scenes from Szondi's life. László Héjja, the chef, has an excellent reputation. In the Zsolnay Cafe, delicious pastries are served on hand-painted Zsolnay porcelain. The decor here is also carefully chosen, and pays respect to the original hotel: Venetian mirrors, chandeliers, a grand piano. There is also a casino just off the lobby.

**Services:** Room service, dry cleaning, laundry, baby-sitting, car rental, travel desk.

**Facilities:** Swimming pool, sauna, massage, solarium, business center, fitness center, drugstore, gift shop, beauty salon, conference room.

### ✪ Kempinski Hotel Corvinus

V. Erzsébet tér, 1051 Budapest. ☎ **800/426-3135** in North America, 0-800/86-8588 in Britain, or 1/266-1000. Fax 1/266-2000. 367 rms, 28 suites. A/C MINIBAR TV TEL. DM 530 ($302) double; DM 630–3,200 ($359–$1,824) suite. Children 11 and under stay free in parents' room. Breakfast DM 29 ($16.50) extra. AE, EURO, JCB, MC, V. Parking DM 22 ($12.55) per day. Metro: Deák tér (all lines).

Located in the heart of Pest, just off Deák tér, this slick German-run hotel, opened in 1993, is gaining a reputation as the hotel of choice for corporate visitors (and also musicians—the Rolling Stones and Michael Jackson stayed here) to Budapest. The Kempinski is far and away the most expensive place in town. The building itself is, at least from the outside, a monstrous cement edifice, one of a number of ugly new buildings marring this neighborhood. From the inside, however, everything is quietly, and unmistakably, luxurious. The rooms are as well appointed as one might expect from a hotel of this price, and soundproof windows shield guests from the noise of the busy traffic below.

**Dining/Entertainment:** The hotel's Bistro Jardin is a casual eatery. The Corvinus is a gourmet restaurant serving exceptional international cuisine. Pub V offers four kinds of beer on draft. The hotel also has a coffee shop and a lobby bar. The American-style buffet breakfast has received rave reviews.

**Services:** Room service (24-hour), laundry and dry cleaning (weekdays only), car rental. The concierge will help arrange your travel needs, including airplane tickets.

**Facilities:** Swimming pool, sauna, solarium, fitness room, massage, business center, conference facilities, newsstand, beauty parlor, barbershop, gift shop, boutiques.

## EXPENSIVE

### Hotel Erzsébet

V. Károlyi Mihály u. 11–15, 1053 Budapest. ☎ **1/328-5763.** Fax 1/118-9237. 123 rms. A/C MINIBAR TV TEL. DM 250 ($143) double. Rates include breakfast. Rates 20% lower in low season. Discounts for groups of 10 or more. AE, EURO, JCB, MC, V. Free parking available for 12 cars. Metro: Ferenciek tere (Blue line).

Originally built in 1872, the Erzsébet Hotel took as its namesake the queen of Austria-Hungary. The present hotel is the result of a total reconstruction in 1985. Its central Pest location is unbeatable: just a few minutes' walk from the southern, and less busy, end of Váci utca. Rooms are smartly furnished, with many features of a luxury hotel. If you want a modern, centrally located hotel at slightly lower prices, this could be the place for you.

**Dining/Entertainment:** The János Pince is a Hungarian wine-cellar restaurant.

**Services:** Laundry, dry cleaning on request, baby-sitting on request, car rental.

**Facilities:** Two small conference rooms, gift shop, banquet hall, garden.

### Hotel Nemzeti

VIII. József krt. 4, 1088 Budapest. ☎ **1/269-9310** or 1/303-9310. Fax 1/314-0019. 76 rms. A/C MINIBAR TV TEL. DM 190 ($108) double. Rates include breakfast. Rates 30% lower in low season. AE, DC, MC, V. Parking available for DM 10 ($5.70) in neighborhood garage. Metro: Blaha Lujza tér (Red line).

The turn-of-the-century Hotel Nemzeti, just off Blaha Lujza Square, underwent a 1987 restoration that returned much of its original art nouveau splendor. This is perhaps Pest's most handsome and historic hotel. Its biggest drawback is its location; though centrally located, the hotel directly overlooks what has become perhaps the busiest square of the Outer Ring. Half the rooms face the heavily trafficked street, while the other half face into a lovely interior courtyard (you would do well to request one of the latter). The rooms were recently renovated with modern furnishings and new carpeting. Safes and hair dryers have also been installed. Rooms have wonderful high ceilings and spacious bathrooms. The rooms on the top (fifth) floor are most interesting, with slanted ceilings and funky windows (there is an elevator). Mr. Kormany, the manager, really cares for the place, and it shows.

**Dining/Entertainment:** In addition to the lobby pub, the hotel has a restaurant, recently restored to its formal elegance as one of Budapest's most fashionable eateries.

**Services:** Room service, laundry, car rental.

### K & K Hotel Opera

VI. Révay u. 24, 1065 Budapest. ☎ **1/269-0222.** Fax 1/269-0230. 205 rms. AC MINIBAR TV TEL. DM 255–320 ($145–$182) double. Rates 5% lower in low season. Rates include breakfast. AE, DC, EURO, MC, V. Parking DM 13 ($7.40). Metro: Opera (Yellow line).

Operated by the Austrian K & K hotel chain, this tasteful, elegant establishment opened in 1994 and expanded in 1997. Directly across the street from the Opera House in central Pest, the hotel building blends nicely with surrounding architecture. The interior design is equally pleasing. Each room has a safe, and the hotel has a sauna and fitness room. The staff is uniformly friendly and helpful. This hotel is within close proximity not just to the Opera House, but to Budapest's theater district as well. Visit the K & K Hotel chain's website at www.kuk.at, or contact them by e-mail at kk.hotels.headoffice@szg.kuk.at.

## MODERATE

### ✪ King's Hotel

VII. Nagydiófa u. 25–27. ☎ and fax **1/352-7675.** 75 rms, 4 suites. TV TEL. $70–$80 double; $140 suite. AE, DC, MC, V. Free parking available on street. Metro: Astoria (Red line).

The King's Hotel opened for business in 1995 in a beautifully renovated and restored *fin-de-siècle* building in the heart of Pest's Jewish district. Despite the somewhat drab modern furnishings, the rooms retain a 19th-century atmosphere, many with small balconies overlooking the quiet residential street. The reception is uniformly friendly and helpful. The hotel restaurant is strictly Kosher and is open for breakfast, lunch, and dinner; food is prepared under the observation of Rabbi Hoffman. Conference rooms are available. Many of the rooms have air-conditioning.

### Best Western Hotel Art

V. Királyi Pál u. 12, 1053 Budapest. ☎ **1/266-2166.** Fax 1/266-2170. 32 rms. AC MINIBAR TV TEL. DM 170 ($97) double. Rates include breakfast. AE, EURO, V. Parking available for a fee. Metro: Kálvin tér (Blue line).

This hotel, opened in a fully restored turn-of-the-century building in 1994, is brilliantly located on a quiet side street in the southern end of Pest's Inner City. The reception is a bit stuffy and overly formal for a hotel of this size and quality, but the rooms are clean and comfortable. This is a great alternative to the more expensive, larger luxury hotels in the busier part of the Inner City. The hotel has a sauna and fitness room.

### City Panzió Pilvax

V. Pilvax köz 1-3, 1052 Budapest. ☎ **1/266-7660.** Fax 1/117-6396. 32 rms. TV TEL MINIBAR. DM 156 ($89) double. Rates 25% lower in low season. Rates include breakfast. AE, DC, MC, V. Parking DM 26 ($14.80) (garage is at nearby Hotel Taverna). Metro: Ferenciek tere (Blue line).

Opened in 1997, this is one of three new Inner City pensions owned by the Taverna Hotel group, which also owns the large Hotel Taverna on Váci utca. The staff is friendly, and the rooms are clean and efficient, but the place clearly lacks the charm found in many of the pensions in the Buda Hills. It costs a bit more, too, but the location is obviously what you are paying for. The pension is on a narrow, quiet street just a few minutes by foot from the hubbub of central Pest. Not too long ago, your only downtown options were luxury hotels or battered old establishments; now your choices are broader. Visit Taverna's homepage at http://www.hungary.net/taverna, or make contact by e-mail at 100324.235@compuserve.com.

### City Panzió Ring

XIII. Szent István krt. 22, 1137 Budapest. ☎ **1/111-4450.** Fax 1/111-0884. 20 rms. TV TEL MINIBAR. DM 156 ($97) double. Rates 25% lower in low season. Rates include breakfast. AE, DC, EURO, MC, V. No parking available. Metro: Nyugati pu (Blue line).

Opened in 1997, this is another of three new central Pest pensions owned by the Taverna Hotel group, which also owns the large Hotel Taverna on Váci utca. This pension is located on Pest's bustling Outer Ring boulevard (hence the name), on the fringes of the fashionable Újlipótváros neighborhood. It is just a block away from Nyugati railway station, and a 10-minute walk to the Danube embankment and to Margaret Island, the city's loveliest park. The rooms are clean and small, without character. It is a perfectly adequate place, but if you are looking for a pension with old-world charm, you'll have to stray farther from the center of the city. For more information, you can visit Taverna's homepage at http://www.hungary.net/taverna, or make contact by e-mail at 100324.235@compuserve.com.

## INEXPENSIVE

### Hotel MEDOSZ

VI. Jókai tér 9, 1061 Budapest. ☎ **1/153-1700** or 1/374-3000. Fax 1/332-4316. 70 rms. TV TEL. DM 80 ($46) double. Rates include breakfast. Rates 15% lower in low season. No credit cards. Parking difficult in neighborhood. Metro: Oktogon (Yellow line).

The MEDOSZ was formerly a trade-union hotel for agricultural workers. Its location on sleepy Jókai tér, in the heart of Pest's theater district and not far from the Opera House, is as good as it gets off the river in central Pest. Although the hotel has not been renovated since privatization (and the staff has yet to learn to smile), it remains a great value given its location. The rooms are simple but clean. There's a restaurant and bar in the hotel. Laundry service is available. Next door to Hotel MEDOSZ is one of Budapest's special treats for children: a puppet theater (*bábszínház*).

**✪ Peregrinus Vendégház**

V. Szerb u. 3, 1056 Budapest. ☎ **1/266-4911.** Fax 1/266-4913. 26 rms. TV TEL MINIBAR. 11,500 Ft ($57.50) double. Rates include breakfast. No credit cards. No parking. Metro: Kálvin tér (Blue line).

Peregrinus Vendégház is ideally located in the heart of the Inner City of Pest, across the street from a historic Serbian Church on a small side street half a block from Váci utca, popular pedestrian-only street. This is the guest house of Pest's ELTE University. Many guests are affiliated with the university, but the guest house is open to the public. You should reserve at least a week ahead of time. The building dates from the turn of the century and was renovated when it was opened in 1994. The rooms are simple but comfortable. Payment must be in cash in Hungarian forints.

## 3 Central Buda

### VERY EXPENSIVE

**✪ Hotel Gellért**

XI. Gellért tér 1, 1111 Budapest. ☎ **1/185-2200.** Fax 1/166-6631. 233 rms. MINIBAR TV TEL. DM 326–378 ($186–$215) double; DM 466–500 ($266–$285) suite. Rates include breakfast. Spa packages available. AE, DC, MC, V. Free parking. Tram: 47 or 49 from Deák tér.

First opened in 1918, this splendid, sprawling art nouveau hotel was most recently restored in 1970. It's somewhat run-down now, but still one of the most elegant and charming hotels in Budapest. Located at the base of Gellért Hill in Buda, on the bank of the Danube, the Gellért is one of several thermal hotels in Budapest managed or owned by Danubius Hotels. While the majority of guests don't come for the official spa treatment, there are a number of spa-related facilities that all guests can use free of charge: indoor swimming pool and outdoor swimming pool with waves (in summer), steam room, and the art nouveau Gellért Baths, perhaps the most popular of Budapest's thermal baths (most tourists visit them at least once during their stay).

The hotel lobby is circular with marble columns and a mezzanine level. The quality and size of the rooms vary greatly—it seems to be hit or miss. Twenty rooms have air-conditioning. Some rooms with balconies offer great views over the Danube, but these rooms can be noisy since the hotel fronts loud and busy Gellért Square.

**Dining/Entertainment:** The Duna Restaurant serves international/Hungarian cuisine and features gypsy music. On the ground floor are the Brasserie and the Coffeehouse, both with terraces.

**Services:** Room service, baby-sitting, travel desk.

**Facilities:** Spa facilities (see above), laundry, gift shop, beauty salon/barber, newsstand, conference facilities, business center, and simultaneous translators.

### EXPENSIVE

**✪ Alba Hotel Budapest**

I. Apor Péter u. 3, 1011 Budapest. ☎ **1/175-9244.** Fax 1/175-9899. 95 rms. A/C MINIBAR TV TEL. DM 200 ($114) double. Rates include breakfast. Rates 20% lower in low season. AE, DC, EURO, MC, V. Parking DM 22 ($12.55) per day. Many buses run to Clark Ádám tér, including no. 16 from Deák tér.

Opened in 1990, the Alba Hotel Budapest belongs to a Swiss chain, and the Swiss influence is pervasive—from the buffet breakfast that features half a dozen kinds of

Muesli to the antiseptically clean rooms. The hotel is nestled in a tiny cobblestoned alley in Buda's Watertown, directly beneath Buda Castle. It has 7 floors, but only rooms on the top floor have views; the two best are number 706, which has a view of the castle, and number 707, which overlooks Matthias Church. Other 7th-floor rooms offer a pleasing vista of red Buda rooftops. Just 15 of the rooms have air-conditioning.

**Services:** Room service, laundry, small conference room, car rental.

### ✪ Hotel Astra Vendégház

I. Vám u. 6, 1011 Budapest. ☎ **1/214-1906.** Fax 1/214-1907. 12 rms. AC TV TEL MINIBAR. DM 178 ($101) double. Rates include breakfast. Rates 10% lower in low season. AE, DC, MC, V. Parking available on street. Metro: Batthyány tér (Red line).

This little gem of a hotel was opened in 1996 in a renovated 300-year-old building on a quiet side street in Buda's lovely Watertown neighborhood. The rooms are large, with wood floors and classic Hungarian style furniture; the overall effect is a far more homey and pleasant space than that found in most hotel rooms. Indeed, the hotel is tasteful through and through, and the staff friendly. Some rooms overlook the inner courtyard, while others face onto the street. There is a dark cellar bar with a pool table, and a simple unadorned breakfast room.

### Hotel Budapest

II. Szilágyi Erzsébet fasor 47, 1026 Budapest. ☎ **1/202-0044.** Fax 1/212-2729. 280 rms, 9 suites. MINIBAR TV TEL. DM 213 ($121) double; DM 240–290 ($137–$165) suite. Rates include breakfast. Rates 20% lower in low season. AE, DC, MC, V. Parking 1,300 Ft ($6.50) per day. Tram: 56 from Moszkva tér to Fogaskerekű Vasút.

A metallic-looking 1960s Socialist cylinder from the outside, the Hotel Budapest was recently refurbished in response to guests' criticism. It now sports newly upholstered furniture, new carpeting, and bright white (instead of drab gray) paint—the result is a clean modern look. The suites have air-conditioning.

The hotel soars above the neighborhood and offers numerous views; each room boasts a full wall of windows. Your room may overlook the Danube or face up into the hills of Buda. Request a room on a high floor. The vista over the city from the roof garden is simply breathtaking at night. The hotel is within walking distance of Moszkva tér, Buda's central transportation hub, and just across the street from the base of the cogwheel railway, which takes you straight up into the Buda Hills. Locals love to hate the Hotel Budapest, and while it's somewhat of a blight on the landscape, it's also an intriguing place. Room service, laundry, and baby-sitting are available.

**Dining/Entertainment:** The hotel has two restaurants, the smaller of which is air-conditioned, a beer cellar, and a nightclub.

**Facilities:** Roof garden, sauna, conference rooms.

### Hotel Orion

I. Döbrentei u. 13, 1013 Budapest. ☎ **1/156-8933** or 1/156-8583. Fax 1/175-5418. 32 rms. A/C TV TEL. DM 185 ($105) double. Rates include breakfast. Rates lower in low season. AE, DC, EURO, MC, V. Free parking. Tram: 19 from Batthyány tér to Döbrentei tér.

Conveniently located in Buda's Watertown neighborhood, between Castle Hill and the Danube, this small five-story hotel is tucked away on a relatively quiet street near many of the city's best sights. Though the rooms are bright and cheerful enough, and five have balconies, unfortunately they enjoy neither castle nor river views. Döbrentei tér, a messy but convenient transportation hub, is a few minutes away by foot.

**Dining/Entertainment:** The hotel has a small restaurant serving Hungarian/international cuisine.

**Services:** Tourism desk, car rental.

### ✪ Hotel Victoria

I. Bem rakpart 11, 1011 Budapest. ☎ **1/201-8644.** Fax 1/201-5816. 27 rms. A/C MINIBAR TV TEL. DM 195 ($111) double; DM 350 ($200) suite. Rates include breakfast. Rates 25% lower in low season. AE, DC, EURO, MC, V. Parking in garage DM 15 ($8.55). Tram: 19 from Batthyány tér to the first stop.

The Hotel Victoria, located in Buda's lovely Watertown district, is separated from the Danube bank only by the busy road that runs alongside the river. It's situated in a narrow building, with only three rooms on each of its nine floors. This design makes two-thirds of the rooms corner rooms with large double windows providing great views over the river to Pest's skyline beyond. The rooms are quite large, with spacious bathrooms. The middle rooms, though smaller than the corner rooms, also have windows facing the river. Unfortunately, noise from the busy road beneath your window may disturb your rest. The hotel is just minutes by foot from both Batthyány tér and Clark Ádám tér, with dozens of metro, tram, and bus connections. Visit Hotel Victoria's Web site at: www.justweb.com/hotel-victoria. Or send an e-mail to: victoria@mail.datanet.hu.

**Services:** Room service (24-hour), safe, laundry, baby-sitting, car rental.

**Facilities:** Bar, sauna, mini business center, conference rooms, beauty salon.

### ✪ International Apartment Hotel

I. Donáti u. 53, 1015 Budapest. ☎ **1/156-7198.** Fax 1/214-3660. 11 apts. TV TEL. Individual apts. $98, $140, $215, or $280 (reduced rates for long-term stays). Breakfast $5 extra. AE, DC, MC, V. Parking available on street. Metro: Battyhány tér (Red line).

This unique establishment, opened in 1994, is located in a lovely apartment building in Buda's Watertown district. The owner, a German art collector, purchased 11 apartments in the building, renovated them, and installed an elevator for his guests. There is no sign on the street, just a bell with the name "International Apartment Hotel." Reception is on the 4th floor. The place is a 5-minute walk from the metro station, on a quiet street in the upper part of Watertown. The apartments are all quite different from one another, both in terms of size and in terms of facilities and decor (hence the huge disparity in price). Each apartment is generously decorated with original artworks in a distinct motif, and each apartment has a different style of modern furniture. Some apartments have balconies, while some have decks; some have glorious views, others do not. All apartments enjoy fully equipped kitchens with microwave, toaster, coffeemaker, etc. In addition, all the apartments have a CD player (each with an eclectic CD collection), a VCR (free videos available for borrowing), an answering machine, and a fax machine. Two apartments have air-conditioning, and several have built-in Jacuzzis. Meal and shopping service are available for a fee, as is laundry service. This is the perfect choice for business travelers who are spending more than a few days in Budapest—this is a place to come home to.

## INEXPENSIVE

### ✪ Charles Apartment House

I. Hegyalja út 23, 1016 Budapest. ☎ **1/201-1796.** Fax 1/212-2584. 26 apts. TV TEL. $40–$45 apt for 1 or 2, $54 apt for 3. Rates 10%–15% lower in low season. MC V. Parking 1,000 Ft ($5) per day or for free on a nearby side street. Bus: 78 from Keleti pu. to Mészáros utca.

This is one of the better housing deals in Budapest. Owner Károly Szombati has amassed 22 apartments in a single apartment building in a dull but convenient Buda neighborhood (near the large luxury Hotel Novotel), in addition to four apartments in nearby buildings. It is a 30-minute walk to downtown Pest, or a 5-minute bus ride. All accommodations are ordinary Budapest flats in ordinary residential buildings. The furnishings are comfortable and clean, and all apartments have full bathrooms and kitchens. Hegyalja út is a very busy street, but only two apartments face out onto it; the rest are in the interior or on the side of the building. A nearby park has tennis courts and a track. There is a restaurant, a pub, and a grocery store in the neighborhood. The friendly, English-speaking reception is open 24 hours. Laundry service is available, as are bicycle rentals. Inquire by e-mail at: CHARLES@mail.matav.hu.

### Hotel Papillon

II. Rózsahegy u. 3/b, 1024 Budapest. ☎ and fax **1/212-4003** or 1/212-4003. 20 rms. TV TEL. DM 100 ($57) double. Rates include breakfast. Rates 20%–25% lower in low season. AE, EURO, JCB, MC, V. Four free spaces in hotel lot with nighttime security guard. Bus: 91 from Nyugati pu. to Zivatar utca.

The Hotel Papillon, opened in 1992 as a joint Hungarian-German venture, is a pleasing Mediterranean-style white building on a quiet Buda side street. It is located in the area where central Buda begins to give way to the Buda Hills—an easy bus ride to the center of the city. A Mediterranean feeling pervades the interior and spare pink guest rooms as well. Seven rooms have terraces; all have refrigerators. There's a bar and restaurant on the premises, as well as a small swimming pool. In summer the restaurant serves meals on an outdoor terrace. Laundry service is available.

## 4  The Castle District

## VERY EXPENSIVE

### ✪ Hilton Hotel

I. Hess András tér 1–3, 1014 Budapest. ☎ **1/214-3000.** Fax 1/156-0285. 322 rms and suites. A/C MINIBAR TV TEL. DM 365–530 ($208–$302) double; DM 580–720 ($331–$410) suite. Children stay free in parents' room. Breakfast DM 29 ($16.55) extra. AE, CB, DC, EURO, MC, V. Parking for a fee in garage. Bus: "Várbusz" from Moszkva tér or 16 from Deák tér. Funicular: From Clark Ádám tér.

One of only two hotels in Buda's elegant Castle District (the other is Hotel Kulturinnov), the Hilton, built in 1977, is widely considered the city's finest hotel. Its location, on Hess András tér, next door to Matthias Church and the Fisherman's Bastion, is no less than spectacular. The hotel's award-winning design incorporates both the ruins of a 13th-century Dominican church (the church tower rises above the hotel) and the baroque facade of a 17th-century Jesuit college (the hotel's main entrance). The ruins were carefully restored during the hotel's construction, and the results are uniformly magnificent. Although the building is clearly modern, its tasteful exterior blends in fairly well with the surrounding Castle District architecture. More expensive rooms have views over the Danube, with a full Pest skyline; rooms on the other side of the hotel overlook the delightful streets of the Castle District. All rooms are handsomely furnished. The bathrooms have built-in hair dryers.

**Dining/Entertainment:** The luxurious Dominican Restaurant has an international menu; dinner is accompanied by piano music. The colorful Kalocsa Restaurant has a Hungarian menu and nightly Gypsy music. The Margareeta Cafe, with outdoor tables behind the hotel by the Fisherman's Bastion, has coffee and pastries, in addition to afternoon barbecue lunches in the summertime. Drinks are served in the Faust Wine Cellar, the Codex Cocktail Bar, and the Lobby Bar. There's a casino in the hotel, and the lovely Dominican Courtyard is the site of summer concerts.

**Services:** Room service, baby-sitting, travel desk, American Express satellite office.

**Facilities:** Business center, conference facilities, doctor/dentist on call, laundry, newsstand, free airport minibus, beauty salon, antiques shop, florist, photo shop, souvenir shop.

# MODERATE

## ✪ Hotel Kulturinnov

I. Szentháromság tér 6, 1014 Budapest. ☎ **1/155-0122** or 1/175-1651. Fax 1/175-1886. 16 rms. TEL. 13,000 Ft ($65) double. Rates include breakfast. AE, DC, MC, V. Parking 2,000 Ft ($10) per night. Bus: "Várbusz" from Moszkva tér or 16 from Deák tér. Funicular: From Clark Ádám tér.

This is the guest house of the Hungarian Culture Foundation, a foundation dedicated to forging ties with ethnic Hungarians in neighboring countries. Although it is open to the public, few travelers seem to know about it. There are three reasons to stay here: location, location, location. Hotel Kulturinnov is right in the middle of Buda's lovely Castle District; your only other accommodation choice up here is the Hilton, at four or five times the cost. Rooms at the guest house are clean and simple. Each room is equipped with a refrigerator. The hotel is located directly across the street from Matthias Church and the Plague Column, but the entrance is unassuming and practically unmarked. Go through the iron grille gateway and pass through an exhibition hall, continuing up the grandiose red-carpeted staircase to the right.

# 5  Outer Pest

# VERY EXPENSIVE

## ✪ Thermal Hotel Helia

XIII. Kárpát u. 62–64, 1133 Budapest. ☎ **1/270-3277.** Fax 1/270-2262. 254 rms (5 with wheelchair access), 8 suites. A/C MINIBAR TV TEL. DM 320 ($182) double; DM 460 ($262) suite. Rates include breakfast. Spa packages available. AE, DC, EURO, MC, V. Free parking. Trolleybus: 79 from Keleti Station.

Designed by a Finnish architect, this Hungarian-Finnish joint venture (opened in 1990) features tall windows and crisp, sharp angles. Guest rooms are bright and sunny. Some rooms have balconies, and four suites have private saunas. Nonsmoking rooms and rooms equipped for visitors with disabilities are available.

The Thermal Hotel Helia is one of four so-called thermal hotels in Budapest managed or owned by Danubius Hotels. While the majority of guests do not come for the official spa treatment, there are a number of spa-related facilities that all guests can use free of charge: swimming pool, sauna, thermal bath, Jacuzzi, steam bath, and fitness room.

**Dining/Entertainment:** The Restaurant Saturnus, open for dinner only, offers international cuisine with live music. The adjoining Restaurant Jupiter, open for both lunch and dinner, has a fixed-price buffet table with a well-stocked salad bar.

**Services:** Room service (6am to 10:30pm), baby-sitting, safe-deposit boxes. The concierge will assist with travel arrangements.

**Facilities:** Spa facilities (see above), conference facilities, business center, gift shop, drugstore, souvenir shop, beauty salon/barber.

# EXPENSIVE

## ✪ Family Hotel

XIII. Ipoly u. 8/b, 1133 Budapest. ☎ **1/120-1284.** Fax 1/129-1620. 10 rms, 3 suites. A/C MINIBAR TV TEL. DM 180 ($103) double; DM 240 ($137) suite. Rates include breakfast. Rates 10%–15% lower in low season. AE, DC, JCB, MC, V. Parking 600 Ft ($3) per day. Trolleybus: 79 from Keleti pu. to Ipoly utca.

A charming, elegant little place opened in 1991, the Family Hotel stands two blocks from the Danube in a quiet, mostly residential neighborhood in the Újlipótváros (New Leopold Town), just north of the Inner City of Pest. Szent István Park, a pleasant neighborhood park, is only five minutes away by foot. Perhaps the nicest thing about this hotel is the low-key, tasteful atmosphere; it has only one bar (in the Hungarian/international restaurant) and there's very little for sale elsewhere. The suites—all duplexes—are among the nicest rooms in the city, with skylights over the upstairs bedrooms and enormous floor-to-ceiling windows. All rooms in the hotel are spacious, with simple wood furniture and large bathrooms. The wonderfully big suites are suitable for families.

**Services:** Room service.

**Facilities:** Sauna, massage, conference room.

### ○ Hotel Liget

VI. Dózsa György út 106, 1068 Budapest. ☎ **1/269-5300.** Fax 1/269-5329. 139 rms. A/C MINIBAR TEL. DM 204 ($116) double. Rates include breakfast. Rates 25% lower in low season. AE, EURO, JCB, MC, V. Parking DM 15 ($8.55) per day in garage. Metro: Hősök tere (Yellow line).

Although unabashedly modern and somewhat out of sync with the surrounding architecture, the Hotel Liget is well located just off Pest's Heroes' Square and across the street from the Fine Arts Museum and the City Zoo. It is a 30-minute walk to the center of Pest, but the Yellow metro line whisks you into the center in no time at all. The rooms are comfortable and modern, if unimaginatively furnished. The American Embassy is said to put up guests here. Hotel Liget has a homepage on the world wide web. Visit it at: www.hungary.net\taverna.

**Dining/Entertainment:** There's a breakfast room and a coffee/cocktail bar on the premises.

**Services:** Room service, laundry, travel agency.

**Facilities:** Sauna, massage, nonsmoking floor.

## MODERATE

### ○ Hotel Centrál

VI. Munkácsy Mihály u. 5–7, 1063 Budapest. ☎ **1/321-2000.** Fax 322-9445. 36 rms, 6 suites. MINIBAR TV TEL. $86 double; $100–$140 suite. Rates include breakfast. Rates 40% lower in low season. AE, EURO, MC, V. Free parking. Metro: Bajza utca (Yellow line).

It's a bit ugly from the outside, but don't be fooled by its appearance. The Centrál is a little gem of a hotel, located in an exclusive embassy neighborhood just off Pest's Andrássy út, a minute's walk from Heroes' Square and the City Park, and a 25-minute walk to the center of Pest. The lobby is small and tasteful, with marble columns. The enormous suites are marvelous—featuring luxuriously large double beds and spacious bathrooms, as well as vintage Hungarian furniture, carpets, and prints. There's a safe in each suite and at the reception desk. The standard rooms, although quite nice, can't compare to the suites. All rooms have a terrace.

The hotel restaurant serves very good Hungarian fare on world-famous Herend china. Prices are moderate in spite of the regal setting.

## INEXPENSIVE

### Hotel Délibáb

VI. Délibáb u. 35, 1062 Budapest. ☎ **1/342-9301** or 1/322-8763. Fax 1/342-8153. 34 rms. TV TEL. 8,500 Ft ($42.50) double. Rates include breakfast. No credit cards. Parking in neighborhood difficult. Metro: Hősök tere (Yellow line).

The Hotel Délibáb enjoys a wonderful location across the street from Heroes' Square and City Park, in an exclusive Pest neighborhood that's home to most of the city's embassies. It's a 30-minute walk to the center of Pest, or a 5-minute ride on the

Yellow metro line. Rooms here are surprisingly spacious and have nice wood floors; the fixtures are old, but everything works and is clean. There are refrigerators in some of the rooms.

## Detty Panzió

XIV. Gervay u. 23, 1145 Budapest. ☎ **1/252-0820,** 1/383-2756, or 1/383-0390. Fax 1/383-4928. 15 rms. A/C TV TEL. DM 70–120 ($40–$68) double. Rates include breakfast. Rates 10% lower in low season. Discounts for stays of more than 1 week. AE, EURO, JCB, MC, V. Free parking. Bus: 7 Red from Keleti pu. to the last stop; then a 5- to 10-minute walk.

A pleasant and surprising find, the Detty, opened in 1989, is a Buda-like pension in Pest. Tucked away on a quiet, tree-lined street in the remote but attractive Zugló district, it offers extremely clean and tastefully furnished rooms with big windows. The Detty may well be the only budget establishment in town to offer air-conditioning in every room. There's a tiny bar off the cozy reception area, a sauna and solarium, and a small garden with a wading pool. The pension provides laundry service on request. Dogs are welcome.

## ✪ Radio Inn

VI. Benczúr u. 19, 1068 Budapest. ☎ **1/342-8347** or 1/322-8284. Fax 1/322-8284. 32 apts. TV TEL. 5,000–12,000 Ft ($25–$60) apt for 1 to 3. Breakfast 900 Ft ($4.50) extra. V. Parking available on street. Metro: Bajza utca (Yellow line).

As the official guest house of Hungarian National Radio, the Radio Inn houses many visiting dignitaries, and also offers apartments to individual tourists. Reserve well ahead of arrival. The inn is in an exclusive embassy neighborhood (next door to the embassy of the People's Republic of China), a stone's throw from City Park, and a block from Pest's grand Andrássy út. The metro's Yellow line takes you into the center of Pest in 5 minutes; alternatively, it's a 30-minute walk. There's an enormous private courtyard filled with flowers behind the building. The huge apartments (all with fully equipped, spacious kitchens) are comfortably furnished and painstakingly clean. Note that the toilets and bathrooms are separate, European style. The management is somewhat old-system (read: begrudging with information, slightly suspicious of foreigners), yet cordial. Laundry service is available.

## Richter Panzió

XIV. Thököly út 111, 1145 Budapest. ☎ **1/363-3956,** 1/363-5735, or 1/363-5761. Fax 1/363-3956. 29 rms. TV TEL. DM 100 ($57) double. Rates include breakfast. Rates 15%–20% lower in low season. No credit cards. Free parking. Bus: 7 Black from Keleti pu. to Kolumbusz (or Columbus) utca.

Across the street from the towering Honvéd Hotel, the Richter Panzió sits in a busy part of Pest's Zugló neighborhood, just 5 minutes by bus from Keleti Station (on a night-bus route). The pension, opened in 1991 by the famous Hungarian circus family of the same name, is manned by a friendly staff. The guest rooms are delightful, with light-wood floors and huge windows. Most rooms have double beds; the six rear rooms have terraces. There's a small bar in the cozy lobby, and an outdoor deck, plus a whirlpool, sauna, and pool table. Laundry service is available.

# 6 Óbuda

## VERY EXPENSIVE

## ✪ Aquincum Corinthia Hotel

III. Árpád fejedelem utja 94, 1036 Budapest. ☎ **1/250-3360** or 1/250-4177. Fax 1/250-4672. 304 rms, 8 suites. A/C MINIBAR TV TEL. DM 304 ($173) double; DM 429 ($245) suite.

Spa packages available. AE, DC, EURO, MC, V. Parking available for DM 16 ($9) in garage. Train: HÉV suburban railway from Batthyány tér to Árpád híd.

Located on the bank of the Danube, just minutes from Óbuda's lovely Old City center, the Aquincum Corinthia Hotel was opened in 1991. This is a "thermal" hotel, though not all guests come for the spa facilities. Spa-related facilities that all guests can use free of charge include a swimming pool, sauna, thermal baths, Jacuzzi, steam bath, Scottish shower, and fitness room. This delightful, modern hotel is built on the site of a supposed Roman spa; hence its Roman theme. The rooms are cheerful, with soundproof windows, complimentary bathrobes, and built-in hair dryers.

**Dining/Entertainment:** In the elegant Restaurant Ambrosia, open only for dinner, you'll find a Hungarian/international menu with vegetarian and dietetic offerings. There's live piano music nightly. The Restaurant Apicius serves both lunch and dinner, with a salad bar and buffet lunch. The Iris Bar has live music and—here's a new one—a magician!

**Services:** Room service, laundry and dry cleaning, baby-sitting, safe, Ibusz desk, car rental.

**Facilities:** Spa facilities (see above), conference facilities, beauty salon, newsstand, antiques shop, gift shop, business center, drugstore.

# INEXPENSIVE

## ✪ Hotel Római

III. Szent János u. 16, 1039 Budapest. ☎ and fax **1/188-6167** or 1/168-7479. 20 rms; 16 apts. TV TEL. DM 98 ($56) double; DM 112 ($64) apt (for parties of 4 or more). Rates 20% lower in low season. Breakfast DM 7 ($4). AE, EURO, V. Free parking in hotel lot. Train: Suburban HÉV line from Batthyány tér to Római Fúrdő; then bus no. 34 to Szent János utca.

A former resort for minor Communist Party officials, this hotel is a bit off the beaten track, but its location in the Római Fúrdő section of Óbuda, on the banks of the Danube, is refreshingly peaceful. The lobby is spacious and comfortable, with pool tables and a bar. The rooms show their age, but the beds are authentic double beds, and every room has a balcony, a refrigerator, and a fresh coat of paint. An extension was added in 1993, with spiffier rooms. There's a restaurant, an outdoor swimming pool, and large garden. It takes a while to get here from the center of Budapest, but you will feel as if you are staying out in the country.

## ✪ San Marco Guest House

III. San Marco u. 6, 1034 Budapest. ☎ **1/388-9997** or 1/439-7525. Fax 1/388-997. 5 rms (2 with shared shower and toilet). A/C TV. 6,000–7,000 Ft ($30–$35) double. Rates include breakfast. Rates 10%–15% lower in low season. EURO, JCB, MC, V. Parking available on street or for a fee in a nearby garage. Tram: 17 from Margit híd (Buda side) to Nagyszombat utca. Bus: 60 from Batthyány tér to Nagyszombat utca.

Paul and Eva Stenczinger, with assistance from daughter Andrea, run this small pension on the top floor of their house. They speak fluent English and will help guests with restaurant reservations, theater tickets, taxis, train tickets, and other matters, including scams and safety concerns. They will also point out the best neighborhood restaurants for a quiet and delicious dinner. The house is comfortable and homey but unassuming—much like the residential Óbuda neighborhood it's located in. Three rooms face the back, where there's a flower-filled garden (breakfast is served here in summer). All rooms have slanted ceilings and good windows. Most of the Stenczingers' business consists of returning guests. When the editor of this guide stayed here, the owners, although exhausted from hosting the family of an Irishman who had married a Budapest native, nonetheless regaled visitors with tales of life in Communist Hungary.

## 7 The Buda Hills

### EXPENSIVE

#### Petneházy Country Club

II. Feketefej u. 2–4, 1029 Budapest. ☎ **1/176-5992** or 1/176-5982. Fax 1/176-5738. 45 bungalows. MINIBAR TV TEL. DM 195 ($111) small bungalow for 2, DM 245 ($140) large bungalow for 4. Rates include breakfast. Weekly rates available. Rates 10% lower in low season. AE, DC, DISC, EURO, MC, V. Free parking. Drive or take a cab.

The word "bungalow" does not do justice to the handsome Scandinavian-style wooden cabins of the Petneházy Country Club, opened in 1991. Cozily furnished, each bungalow has a private sauna, kitchen, and porch. Each is spacious, bright, and sparkling clean. Four smaller bungalows are tailored for guests with disabilities. Deep in the Cold Valley (Huvösvölgy) region of the Buda Hills, Petneházy is unfortunately beyond the reach of Budapest's public transportation system, so you really need a car to get here. A Fő Taxi would probably cost $15 to $20 to get here from the center. Just down the road is the Petneházy Lovasiskola, for horseback riding in the nearby hills (see "Outdoor Activities & Sports," in chapter 6).

**Dining/Entertainment:** There are a restaurant, with an outdoor barbecue serving specialties from the grill, and a bar. A ragtime band performs every Thursday night in the summer.

**Facilities:** Swimming pool, tennis, solarium, bicycle rental, horseback riding, golf driving range, conference rooms, gift shop.

### MODERATE

#### Budai Hotel

XII. Rácz Aladár u. 45–47, 1121 Budapest. ☎ **1/248-0707** or 1/249-2186. Fax 1/186-8987. 23 rms. MINIBAR TV TEL. DM 125 ($71) double; DM 150 ($86) suite. Rates include breakfast. Rates 20% lower in low season. AE, EURO, MC, V. Free parking in street opposite the hotel, or in secure garage for DM 6 ($3.40). Tram: 59 from Moszkva tér to the last stop.

A 15-minute winding walk from the tram station, the Budai sits high in a quiet section of the Wolf Meadow (Farkasrét) district of the Buda Hills. The rooms are simply furnished; some have terraces. The rooms on the top floor have the best views of the surrounding hills. There's a restaurant and bar on the premises and extensive terrace-dining space.

#### Hotel Panda

II. Pasaréti út 133, 1026 Budapest. ☎ **1/176-1935** or 1/176-1932. Fax 1/176-1002. 28 rms and suites. MINIBAR TV TEL. DM 120 ($68) double; DM 150 ($86) suite. Rates include breakfast. Rates 10% lower in low season. AE, EURO, MC, V. Free parking. Bus: 5 from Marcius 15 tér or Moszkva tér to Pasaréti tér (the last stop).

Opened in 1990, the Hotel Panda is on Pasaréti Square, in a pleasant neighborhood in the Buda Hills. There's a grocery store and several other businesses in the square. The hotel reception is friendly and efficient. However, the desirability of the rooms varies greatly. Rooms facing the front (10 in all) have terraces, with southern exposure and nice views. Rooms elsewhere in the hotel, with smaller windows and without terraces, can get a bit stuffy. Most bathrooms have a window; all have a bidet. While the larger suites are quite large, the smaller ones are identical in size to normal double rooms. A restaurant serves international/Hungarian cuisine, and there's plenty of terrace space for dining. The *Budapest Atlas* mislocates the hotel, placing it much lower down on Pasaréti út, at number 33. You can inquire by e-mail at: panda@magnet.hu

## Hotel Panoráma

XII. Rege u. 21, 1121 Budapest. ☎ **1/395-6121.** Fax 1/395-4265. 36 rms, 53 bungalows.
MINIBAR TV TEL (rms); TV (bungalows). DM 150 ($86) double; DM 155–200 ($88–$114) bungalow. Room rates include breakfast (except in bungalows, which have kitchenettes; breakfast
DM 6/$3.40). Rates 40%–50% lower in low season. AE, DC, EURO, V. Free parking. Cog Railway: Széchenyi-Hegy.

Best reached by the cog railway (a standard part of Budapest's public transit system,
with normal running hours), the Hotel Panoráma is high in the Buda Hills, standing alone in a serene neighborhood of Freedom Hill (Szabadság-Hegy). The hotel was
renovated in 1989; the lobby is small, but the hallways feature comfortable armchairs.
The staff is extremely friendly and helpful. Rooms are bright and clean, with spectacular views. The bungalows are dimmer, decorated in a hunting lodge motif, but
each has a private patio. The whole complex is situated in a shady grove that stays
relatively cool even in the hottest months. The southern terminus of the Children's
Railroad (Gyermek Vasút) is a 5-minute walk. The hotel features a restaurant and a
bar, as well as a swimming pool and sauna.

## Hotel Queen Mary

XII. Béla király út 47, 1121 Budapest. ☎ and fax **1/156-8377.** 20 rms, 2 suites. MINIBAR
TV TEL. DM 120 ($68) double; DM 140–160 ($80–$91) suite. Rates include breakfast. Rates
30% lower in low season. AE, EURO, MC, V. Free parking. Bus: 28 from Moszkva tér to Béla
király út.

Opened in 1992, this hotel is situated high up in the hills in a tranquil, affluent
neighborhood. The rooms are modern and efficient, but lack character. Each room
has a terrace; those on the ground floor share the terrace with adjacent rooms.
Unfortunately, the hotel has less garden space than most Buda pensions. There is,
however, a sauna, solarium, and restaurant (serving only dinner) with outdoor dining in summer. The hotel also has a laundry service.

## ○ Gizella Panzió

XII. Arató u. 42/b, 1121 Budapest. ☎ and fax **1/249-2281.** 8 rms, 6 suites. MINIBAR TV TEL.
DM 120 ($68) double; DM 140 ($80) suite. Rates lower in low season. EURO, MC, V. Free parking. Tram: 59 from Moszkva tér to the last stop.

This fine pension in the Buda Hills is a 10-minute walk from the nearest tram station. Built on the side of a hill, it has a lovely view and a series of terraced gardens
leading down to the swimming pool. The pension also features a sauna, solarium, fitness room, and bar. Guest rooms are all unique but uniformly quaint and sunny.
Owner Gizella Varga clearly has good taste. A sightseeing car and driver can be
arranged for guests upon request.

# INEXPENSIVE

### Beatrix Panzió

II. Széher út 3, 1021 Budapest. ☎ and fax **1/176-3730.** 12 rms, 2 suites. TV TEL. DM 90–120
($51–$68) double; DM 130–150 ($74–$86) suite. Rates include breakfast. Rates 20% lower in
low season. No credit cards. Free parking in secured lot. Tram: 56 from Moszkva tér to the 7th
stop.

The Beatrix Panzió, situated in the Buda Hills and opened in 1991, is an agreeable,
modern place, with smart, comfortable rooms. The suites have private balconies.
There is also a sauna and sundeck for guests' use. In good weather, breakfast is served
in the garden. Management sometimes cooks a traditional Hungarian barbecue
(hearty gulyás over an open fire) for DM 4 ($2.30) per person. Laundry service is
available. The pension also operates its own minibus for sightseeing tours. Széher út

is a small but heavily traveled road. A grocery store is conveniently located down the street.

### G.G. Panoráma Panzió

II. Fullánk u. 7, 1026 Budapest. ☎ and fax **1/176-4718.** 4 rms. TV TEL (shared). $45–$69 double. Breakfast $3 extra. No credit cards. Parking available on street. Bus: 11 from Batthyány tér to Majális utca or 91 from Nyugati pu.

G.G. are the initials of Mrs. Gábor Gubacsi, the friendly English-speaking owner of this small guest house. All guest rooms are on the top floor of the Gubacsi home, located on a steep quiet street in the elegant Rose Hill (Rózsadomb) section of the Buda Hills. Several bus lines from different parts of the center converge on the neighborhood, making it a fairly convenient place to stay. The rooms are small, but tastefully furnished; they share a common balcony, which has a great vista of the hills. There's also a common kitchen and dining area for the guests, with full facilities (including minibar), as well as garden space for picnics, reading, and relaxing. It's a casual but classy place, and the Gubacsis take good care of their guests.

### Siesta Villa

II. Madár u. 8/a, 1025 Budapest. ☎ and fax **1/275-1318.** 3 rms. TV TEL. DM 99 ($56) double. Rates include breakfast. Rates 10% lower in low season. No credit cards. Free parking. Bus: 11 from Batthyány tér to the last stop; then a 15-minute walk.

Deep in the heart of a fashionable section of the Buda Hills, this lovely little pension's only drawback is that it's a good 15-minute walk from the bus stop. There are three guest rooms, each with a spacious bathroom and large windows. In summer, breakfast is served in the garden, and budget travelers will appreciate that the drinks in the common self-service minibar are priced at supermarket prices. The owner, Dr. Ágota Borbás, speaks adequate English and lives on the premises. She is currently in the process of adding a small separate guest house with kitchen, suitable for a family.

### St. Christoph Villa

II. Galóca u. 20, 1028 Budapest. ☎ **1/176-8604.** 5 rms. TV TEL. DM 80 ($46) double. Rates include breakfast. Rates 15% lower in low season. No credit cards. Free parking. Bus: 56 from Moszkva tér to the last stop, then 64 to Kossuth Lajos utca.

Opened in 1991, St. Christoph Villa is a small family-run pension in a pleasant but remote neighborhood of the Buda Hills. The bright rooms have large windows and solid blond-wood furniture. Each room is different—nos. 4 and 5 are the nicest. The common indoor space is unimpressive, but the garden is lovely. Breakfast is served outside in nice weather. If the owners take to you, they're likely to treat you to a traditional gulyás party one evening in the garden.

### ✪ Vadvirág Panzió

II. Nagybányai út 18, 1025 Budapest. ☎ **1/176-4292** or 1/275-0200. Fax 1/176-4292. 10 rms, 5 suites. TV TEL. DM 85–120 ($48–$68) double; DM 140–170 ($80–$97) suite. Rates include breakfast. AE, MC, V. Parking available in private garage for DM 8 ($4.55) per day or for free on street. Bus: 5 from Március 15 tér or Moszkva tér to Pasaréti tér (the last stop).

A 10-minute walk from the bus stop, the Vadvirág (its name means wildflower) is in a gorgeous part of the Buda Hills just a few blocks behind the Béla Bartók Memorial House. Sloping gardens and terraces surround the pension. Inside, the hallways are decorated with prints by the recently deceased Hungarian-born op artist Victor Vasarely. The rooms are all different; most are small but tastefully furnished. Half the rooms have balconies. Some have refrigerators. Room 2 is the best in the house: It's a small suite with a balcony. There's a sauna (DM 15/$8.55 per hour) and a small restaurant with plenty of outdoor seating.

# 8  Margaret Island

## EXPENSIVE

### Danubius Grand Hotel Margitsziget

XIII. Margitsziget, 1138 Budapest. ☎ **1/311-100** or 1/111-1000. Fax 1/153-3029. 152 rms, 10 suites. MINIBAR TV TEL. DM 275–315 ($157–$180) double; DM 375–425 ($214–$242) suite. Rates include breakfast. Rates 10%–20% lower in the low season. Spa packages available. AE, DC, EURO, MC, V. Parking 1,800 Ft ($9) the first night, 1,200 Ft ($6) succeeding nights.

On the northern tip of lovely Margaret Island, in the middle of the Danube, this hotel was originally built in 1873. Destroyed in World War II, it was restored and reopened in 1987. It is connected by an underground tunnel to the adjacent Thermal Hotel Margitsziget. While the majority of guests don't come for the official spa treatment, a number of spa-related facilities of the Thermal Hotel can be used free of charge: swimming pool, sauna, and thermal bath.

This is one of only two hotels on Margaret Island, Budapest's most popular park. Though two bridges connect the island with the rest of the city, vehicular traffic (except one city bus) is forbidden except for access to the hotels.

**Dining/Entertainment:** The Széchenyi Restaurant serves international/ Hungarian cuisine, including special dietetic dishes; there is terrace dining. Other dining options include the Begonia Cafe Terrace, the Gösser Brasserie, the Eskimo Ice Salon, and the Victoria Drink Bar. Guests have access to Thermal Hotel Margitsziget's Thermal Star Night Club, with live shows nightly.

**Services:** Room service, laundry, safe, baby-sitting, Danubius Travel Agency desk.

**Facilities:** Conference facilities, business center, souvenir shop, drugstore, access to Thermal Hotel Margitsziget's barber/beauty salon, free use of spa facilities in neighboring Thermal Hotel Margitsziget.

# 9  Staying in Private Rooms

Private rooms have long been considered the best option for budget travelers in Hungary. When you book a private room you get a room in someone's apartment; usually you share the bathroom either with the hosts or other guests. Breakfast is not officially included, but the host will often offer it for a fee (400 to 600 Ft/$2 to $3). A typical breakfast is continental: bread, butter, jam, coffee or tea. You may have limited kitchen privileges (ask in advance to be sure). Some landlords will greet you when you arrive, give you a key, and seemingly disappear; others will want to befriend you, change money, show you around, and cook for you.

Most rooms are quite adequate, some even memorable, but any number of reasons may cause you to dislike your accommodations: Noisy neighborhoods, tiny bathrooms, and wretched coffee are among the complaints we've heard from the occasional displeased traveler. The great majority of guests, though, are satisfied; certainly, staying in a private room provides a window into everyday Hungarian life that would be missed otherwise (except, perhaps, in some of the family-run pensions).

You can book rooms through accommodation agencies (see the information at the beginning of this chapter). Prices vary slightly between agencies, but, generally speaking, rooms cost 2,500 to 4,500 Ft ($12.50 to $22.50), plus a 3% tax. Most agencies add a 30% surcharge (to the first night only) for stays of less than 4 nights. When booking a room, make sure you know its exact location on a map and how to get there before leaving. There's scarcely an address in Budapest that cannot be reached by some form of public transportation, so regard with skepticism anyone who tells

**Family-Friendly Hotels**

**Hotel Gellért** *(see p. 66)*   Children will appreciate both the indoor pool and the outdoor pool with artificial waves at this sprawling art nouveau hotel.

**Hotel Liget** *(see p. 71)*   The Liget has the most kid-friendly location in town: directly across from City Park, site of the zoo, amusement park, and circus.

**Family Hotel** *(see p. 70)*   The duplex suites, which are wonderfully big, are suitable for families.

you that you must take a taxi. In peak season you may need to shop around a bit for the location you want, but you can always find a room somewhere. Arriving at an agency early in the day will afford the best selection.

In Keleti Station, where most international trains arrive, you are likely to be approached by all sorts of people offering you private rooms. Most are honest folks trying to drum up some business personally. The more aggressive ones can be intimidating if not downright annoying; dismiss them out of hand. But keep in mind that when the middleman (the agency) is eliminated, prices tend to be slightly better, so you might consider taking a room from one of these people, especially if you arrive late at night when the agencies are closed or long lines at the agencies drive you to despair. Trust your judgment and don't let anyone pressure you. Feel free to haggle over prices.

## 10  Youth Hostels

There is intense competition between rival youth hostel companies in Budapest now that the transition from state management to private management is complete. The two leaders are **Travellers' Youth Way Youth Hostels** (☎ 140-8585 or 129-8644; fax 120-8425) and **Universum Youth Hostels** (☎/fax 275-7046). Travellers' Youth Way Youth Hostels (formerly known as **More Than Ways Youth Hostels**) has two year-round hostels and eight summer-only hostels, while Universum Youth Hostels has one year-round hostel and four summer-only hostels.

International trains arriving in Budapest are usually met by representatives of these companies. Your best bet is to book a bed in advance at a recommended hostel; if you haven't, you can make phone calls on your arrival and try to secure a hostel bed or you can try your luck with these hawkers. Since they make a commission on every customer they bring in, they tend to be pushy and say whatever they think you want to hear about their hostel. Shop around and don't let yourself be pressured. Most hostels that solicit at the station also have a van parked outside. The ride to the hostel is free, but you may have to wait a while until the van is full.

There is a youth hostel office at Keleti station (☎ 06-20/657-988 or 06-20/468-334), off to the side of track 6 near the international waiting room. This office, open daily 7am to 10pm, can help you book a bed.

In July and August, a number of university dormitories and other empty student housing are converted into hostels. Their locations change from year to year, as do their management. Because of these factors we haven't reviewed them in this guide. The youth hostels and budget lodgings listed below are all open year-round.

The **Hungarian Youth Hostel Federation (Magyar Ifjúsági Szállások Szövetsége)** can be reached at VI. Bajcsy-Zsilinszki út 31, II/3 (☎/fax **1/131-9705 or 111-3297**). They can provide you with a full listing of youth hostels in Hungary,

## The Check, Please: Tips on Tipping

In restaurants in Budapest, the customer has to initiate the paying ritual. You may find that your waiter has disappeared by the time you're ready to settle up. Call over any restaurant employee and ask to pay. The waiter whose job it is to collect payment will be sent to your table. The bill is usually written out on the spot; occasionally you'll be asked to confirm what you ordered. If you think the bill is mistaken, don't be embarrassed to call it into question; locals will commonly do this. Waiters readily correct the bill when challenged.

In all but the fanciest restaurants, after handing over the bill the waiter will remain, waiting patiently for payment. The tip (generally about 10%) should be included in the amount you give him. State the full amount you are paying (bill plus tip) and the waiter will make change. Hungarians never leave tips on the table. Some restaurants may already add a service charge, in which case a tip is unnecessary.

- **Best Wild Game:** At **Aranyszarvas,** I. Szarvas tér 1 (☎ 1/175-6451)—the restaurant's name means the Golden Stag—enjoy venison stew, pheasant, and wild boar.
- **Best Seafood: Horgásztanya Vendéglő,** I. Fö u. 29 ☎ 1/212-3780), is a family-style fish restaurant, just a short block from the Danube in Buda's Watertown.
- **Best Vegetarian Dishes:** At **Marquis de Salade,** VI. Hajós u. 43 (☎ 1/153-4931), the cooks from around the world prepare an amazing assortment of delicious vegetarian dishes. **Govinda,** V. Belgrád rakpart 18, the riverside Indian restaurant run by the Hare Krishnas, comes in a close second here.
- **Best Coffeehouse: Művész Kávéház,** VI. Andrássy út 29 (☎ 1/112-4606), just across from the Opera House, is a certifiable classic and is open late. It serves our favorite coffee, and you can even order decaffeinated coffee here, a rarity in Budapest.
- **Best Pastries:** Our favorite pastry shop is the century-old **Ruszwurm Cukrászda** (☎ 1/175-5284) in the Castle District, at I. Szentháromság u. 7. It's an utterly charming little place.
- **Best New Restaurant:** It may not have stood the test of time, but **Lou Lou,** Vigyázó F. u. 4, ☎1/312-4505, looks like a winner. Opened in late 1996, it's a fashionable yet understated and intimate restaurant in the financial district.

# 2  Restaurants by Cuisine

### ASIAN
Marquis de Salade (The Inner City & Central Pest, *M* )

### COFFEEHOUSES
Angelika Cukrászda (Central Buda)
Cafe Miró (The Castle District)
Gerbeaud's (The Inner City & Central Pest)
Művész Kávéház (The Inner City & Central Pest)

New York Kávéház (The Inner City & Central Pest)
Ruszwurm Cukrászda (The Castle District)
Wiener Kaffehaus (The Inner City & Central Pest)

### CRÊPERIE
Korona Passage (The Inner City & Central Pest, *I* )

**Key to abbreviations:** *VE*=Very Expensive; *E*=Expensive; *I*=Inexpensive; *M*=Moderate

## CZECH/SLOVAK

Prágai Svejk Vendéglő (The Inner
City & Central Pest, *M*)

## GREEK

Taverna Ressaikos (Central
Buda, *M*)
Taverna Dionysos (The Inner City
& Central Pest, *M*)

## FRENCH

Le Jardin de Paris (Central Buda, *E*)

## HUNGARIAN

Akadémia Önkiszolgáló Étterem
(The Castle District, *I*)
Alabárdos (The Castle District, *VE*)
Aranyszarvas (Central Buda, *M*)
Bagolyvár (Just Beyond Central
Pest, *E*)
Csarnok Vendéglő (The Inner City
& Central Pest, *I*)
Csendes Étterem (The Inner City &
Central Pest, *I*)
Fészek (The Inner City & Central
Pest, *M*)
Gundel (Just Beyond Central
Pest,*VE*)
Horgásztanya Vendéglő (Central
Buda, *M*)
Kacsa Vendéglő (Central Buda,*E*)
Kádár Étkezde (The Inner City
& Central Pest, *I*)
Kéhli Vendéglő (Northern Buda
& Óbuda, *VE*)
Kis Buda Gyöngye (Northern Buda
& Óbuda, *E*)
Kispipa Vendéglő (The Inner City
& Central Pest, *M*)
Légrádi Testvérek (The Inner City
& Central Pest, *VE*)
Lou Lou (The Inner City & Central
Pest, *E*)
Makkhetes Vendéglő (The Buda
Hills, *I*)
Malomtó Étterem (Northern Buda
& Óbuda, *M*)
Mérleg Vendéglő (The Inner City
& Central Pest, *M*)
Náncsi Néni Vendéglője (The Buda
Hills, *M*)

Önkiszolgáló (The Castle District, *I*)
Szeged Vendéglő (Central
Buda, *M*)
Szép Ilona (The Buda Hills, *M*)
Udvarház a Hármashatárhegyen
(The Buda Hills, *VE*)
Uj Sipos Halászkert (Northern Buda
& Óbuda, *M*)

## INDIAN GOVINDA

Gandhi Vegeteriánus Éttmrem
(The Inner City & Central Pest, *I*)
Govinda (The Inner City & Central
Pest, *M*)

## INTERNATIONAL

Gundel (Just Beyond Central
Pest, *VE*)
Lou Lou (The Inner City & Central
Pest, *E*)

## KOREAN

Senara (The Inner City & Central
Pest, *E*)

## MEXICAN

Iguana Bar & Grill (The Inner City
& Central Pest, *M*)

## MIDDLE EASTERN

Marquis de Salade (The Inner City
& Central Pest, *I*)
Semiramis (The Inner City
& Central Pest, *I*)

## PIZZA

Marxim (Central Buda, *I*)
Pizzeria Pink Cadillac (The Inner
City & Central Pest, *I*)

## SALAD BAR

Korona Passage (The Inner City
& Central Pest, *I*)

## SEAFOOD

Horgásztanya Vendéglő (Central
Buda, *M*)
Új Sipos Halászkert (Northern
Buda & Óbuda, *E*)

## SZECHUAN

Hong Kong Pearl Garden (Central
Buda, *E*)

## THAI

Chan Chan (The Inner City
& Central Pest, *E*)

## VEGETARIAN

Gandhi Vegeteriánus Étterem (The
Inner City & Central Pest, *I*)
Govinda (The Inner City & Central
Pest, *I*)

## 3 The Inner City & Central Pest

### VERY EXPENSIVE

**Légrádi Testvérek**

V. Magyar u. 23. ☎ 1/118-6804. Reservations highly recommended. Soup 350–450 Ft
($1.75–$2.25); main courses 1,400–2,600 Ft ($7–$13). AE V. Mon–Sat 6pm–midnight. Metro:
Kálvin tér (Blue line). HUNGARIAN.

A very small (just nine tables) and inconspicuously marked restaurant on a sleepy side
street in the southern part of the Inner City, Légrádi Brothers is one of Budapest's
most elegant and formal eateries. The food is served on Herend china, the cutlery is
sterling, and an excellent string trio livens the atmosphere with its repertoire of Hungarian classics. If you're on a budget, pass on the initial, pre-menu offer of hors
d'oeuvres which cost 1,250 Ft ($6.25). The cream of asparagus soup is a fine inter-
pretation of a Hungarian favorite. The chicken paprika served with cheese dumplings
seasoned with fresh dill will surpass any you've tried elsewhere, and the veal cavellier,
smothered in a cauliflower-cheese sauce, is equally sumptuous.

### EXPENSIVE

**Chan Chan**

V. Váci u. 69. ☎1/118-0452. Reservations recommended. Soup 400–800 Ft ($2–$4); main
courses 1,000–4,000 Ft ($5–$20). DC DISC MC V. Daily 11am–4pm & 6pm–11pm.
METRO: Ferenciek tere (Blue line). THAI.

A welcome addition to Budapest's ever-evolving restaurant scene, Chan Chan features
exotic and original Thai cuisine in a rich and lively setting. The extensive menu can
be overwhelming; either stick to Thai dishes you already know or solicit suggestions
from your waiter. Duck soup with bamboo shoots and wild mushrooms makes a nice
appetizer, as do the spring rolls. For a main course, you might try the Mekong cat-
fish soup (a complete meal in itself) or the grilled shark with wild lemon grass and
chili sauce. The freshest ingredients are used. Each dish appears lovingly prepared.
Service is gracious. Chan Chan enjoys an excellent reputation among the city's burgeoning Asian population.

### ✪ Lou Lou

Vigyázó F. u. 4. ☎ 1/312-4505. Reservations recommended. Appetizers 350–1390 Ft ($1.75–
$6.95); main courses 890–2,490 Ft ($4.45–$12.45). DC DISC MC V. Mon–Fri noon–3pm &
7pm–12am; Sat 7pm–12am. Closed Sun. Metro: Deák tér (all lines) or Kossuth tér (red line).
INTERNATIONAL.

This handsome new addition to the Budapest dining scene has people talking. It's
located on a quiet side street not far from Parliament in the financial district, at least
part of the reason why it attracts a good number of foreigners in Budapest on business. Károly Rudits, who formerly manned the kitchen at the Kempinski hotel,
opened this small (just eight tables), candlelit place in 1996. The decor is rustically
elegant. You step down into an intimate space in which the walls are an attractive
Roman yellow, ceilings are vaulted, and the lighting subdued.

# Budapest Dining

Akadémia Önkiszolgáló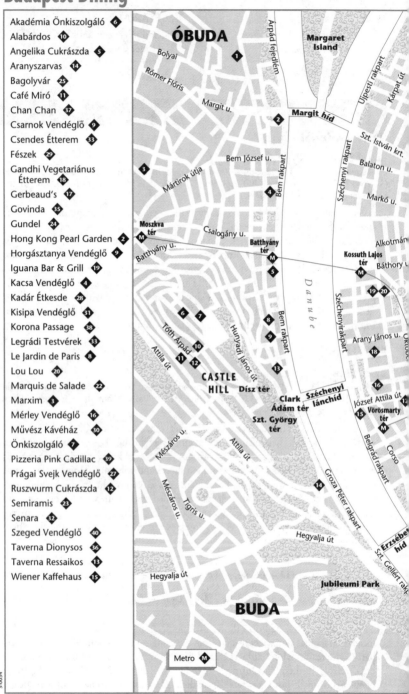

Alabárdos

Angelika Cukrászda

Aranyszarvas

Bagolyvár

Café Miró

Chan Chan

Csarnok Vendéglő

Csendes Étterem

Fészek

Gandhi Vegetariánus
   Étterem

Gerbeaud's

Govinda

Gundel

Hong Kong Pearl Garden

Horgásztanya Vendéglő

Iguana Bar & Grill

Kacsa Vendéglő

Kadár Étkesde

Kisipa Vendéglő

Korona Passage

Legrádi Testvérek

Le Jardin de Paris

Lou Lou

Marquis de Salade

Marxim

Mérley Vendéglő

Művész Kávéház

Önkiszolgáló

Pizzeria Pink Cadillac

Prágai Svejk Vendéglő

Ruszwurm Cukrászda

Semiramis

Senara

Szeged Vendéglő

Taverna Dionysos

Taverna Ressaikos

Wiener Kaffehaus

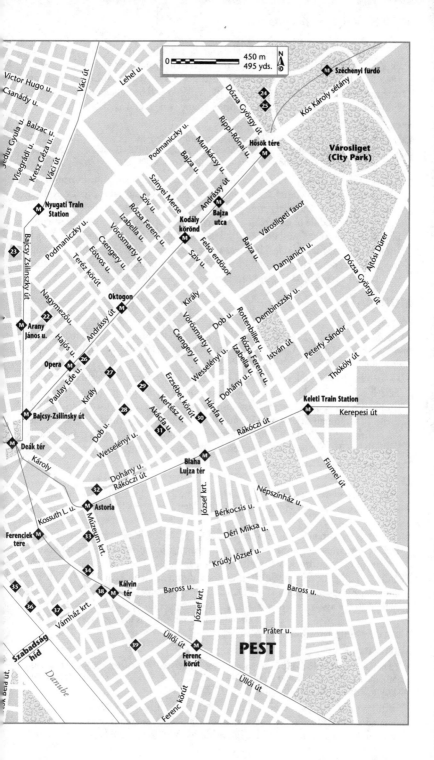

Victor Hugo u.
Csanády u.
Jedus Gyula u.
Balzac u.
Visegrádi u.
Kresz Géza u.
Váci út
Váci út
Lehel u.
Dózsa György út
Kós Károly sétány
 Széchenyi fürdő

Podmaniczky u.
Munkácsy u.
Rippl-Rónai u.
Bajza u.
Hősök tére
Városliget
(City Park)

Nyugati Train
Station
Podmaniczky u.
Szinyei Merse
Rózsa Ferenc u.
Szív u.
Andrássy út
Kodály körönd
Bajza utca
Felsö erdösor
Bajza u.
Városligeti fasor
Damjanich u.
Dózsa György út
Ajtósi Dürer

Bajcsy Zsilinszky út
Nagymezöu.
Izabella u.
Vörösmarty u.
Csengery u.
Eötvos u.
Teréz körút
Szív u.
Király
Oktogon
Andrássy út
Vörösmarty u.
Csengery u.
Dob u.
Rottenbiller u.
Dembinszky u.
Rózsa Ferenc u.
Izabella u.
István út
Peterfy Sándor
Thököly út

Arany
János u.
Hajós u.
Opera
Paulay Ede u.
Király
Wesselényi u.
Dohány u.
Hársfa u.
Keleti Train Station
Kerepesi út

Bajcsy-Zsilinsky út
Erzsébet körút
Kertész u.
Akácfa u.
Rákóczi út

Dob u.
Wesselényi u.

Deák tér
Károly
Dohány u.
Rákóczi út
Blaha Lujza tér
Fiumei út

Kossuth L. u.
Astoria
József krt.
Népszínház u.
Bérkocsis u.

Ferenciek
tere
Múzeum krt.
Déri Miksa u.
Krúdy József u.

Kálvin tér
Baross u.
József krt.
Baross u.

Vámház krt.
Üllői út
Práter u.

Szabadság híd
Üllői út
Ferenc körút
Üllői út

Danube
Ferenc körút

Béla út.

PEST

0    450 m
     495 yds.

N

87

The lengthy menu is in English. For starters, you might try the cold peach soup, excellent and refreshing, followed by the vegetarian strudel, a good deal at 890 Ft ($4.45). Or splurge, opting for the grilled prawns or veal. Lou Lou features an extensive wine list (which is framed on the wall and will be pulled down for you to study), ranging to 4,400 Ft ($22) a bottle. House wine is also available.

### Senara

VII. Dohány u. 5. ☎ **1/269-6549.** Reservations recommended. Main courses 1,200–2,400 Ft ($6–$12); menu meals 1,500–3,780 Ft ($7.50–$18.90). AE, DC, DISC, EURO, MC, V. Mon–Sat 11:30am–2:30pm and 6–11:30pm. Metro: Astoria (Red line). KOREAN.

Senara offers top-flight Korean fare in air-conditioned comfort in the heart of Pest. The tables, divided by tasteful wood-lattice work, have considerable privacy. Korean music plays softly in the background. Many of the meat meals are cooked on a grill sunk into the middle of each table. The menu, though available in English, is complicated and arcane. Your best bet is to select one of the special menu meals, which come with soup, salad, rice, kimchee, and a main course. The delightful Pulkogi menu is a beef-and-chicken combination: You cook the thin strips of meat at your table, dip them in soy sauce, and eat them with rice—a delicious meal!

## MODERATE

### Fészek

VII. Kertész u. 36. ☎ **1/322-6043.** Reservations recommended. Soup 120–240 Ft (60¢–$1.20); main courses 500–1,380 Ft ($2.50–$6.90); menu meals 1,020 Ft ($5.10). AE MC V. Daily noon–1am. Tram: 4 or 6 to Király utca. HUNGARIAN.

Owned by the same folks who own the better-known Kispipa Vendéglő (see below), Fészek is located in the quiet, interior courtyard of a building at the corner of Dob utca and Kertész utca. A small, easy-to-miss sign on the street is the only advertisement. Pass through a dim lobby to enter the restaurant. Savory wild game and freshwater fish dishes are the house specialties. The outdoor dining experience here is without equal in the busy center of Pest. Be sure to reserve ahead of time since Fészek is invariably crowded.

### ✪ Govinda

V. Belgrád rakpart 18. No telephone. Small menu meal 500 Ft ($2.50); large menu meal 800 Ft ($4). Tues–Sun 9am–9pm. Closed Monday. Metro: Ferenciek tere (Blue line). INDIAN VEGETARIAN.

This tiny restaurant, owned and operated by Hare Krishnas, features exceptional Indian vegetarian cuisine. There is no proselytizing; just a bit of incense, traditional Indian music, and friendly (English-speaking) waiters. The chef, trained in India, prepares authentic and exotic offerings for a different menu each day. You choose either a large or small menu meal. The meal includes soup, fresh-baked Indian bread, main dish (an assortment of interesting, savory smaller dishes), a drink (such as spicy ginger ale or lemon rosewater), and a dessert. Everything is lovingly prepared. On a hot day, sit upstairs, where it is air-conditioned.

### Iguana Bar & Grill

V. Zoltán u. 16. ☎ **1/131-4352.** Reservations recommended. Appetizers 300–700 Ft ($1.50–$3.50); main courses 900–1,800 Ft. ($4.50–$9). AE DC MC V. Sun–Thurs noon–midnight, Fri–Sat noon–2am. Metro: Kossuth tér (Red line). MEXICAN.

Run by three thirtysomething American ex-pats, this classy Mexican restaurant opened to immediate success in summer, 1997. The restaurant boasts a spacious, beautifully designed interior with a bilevel dining area. Still, it can be difficult to find a table—especially on the weekend. When you do manage to get seated, crispy home-made tortilla chips and salsa are waiting for you. One of the Czech Republic's best beers, *Budvar*, makes the perfect accompaniment. You might also try the *Iguana Beer*, made especially for the restaurant by a small Csepel Island brewery. Though the chef is Hungarian, he trained in the American Southwest, so the flavors are indeed authentic. Fiery souls should start off with the *Jalapeño Poppers*, breaded jalapeño peppers stuffed with cheese and rolled in a "secret ingredient," which co-owner Cory will proudly reveal if asked. Incidentally, at least one of the owners can be found at the restaurant at all hours, directing operations and chatting with regulars. For an entree, consider one of the daily specials (posted on a blackboard). Beef burritos or *Chicken a la Mo* (named after co-owner Mo) also make excellent choices.

### Kispipa Vendéglő

VII. Akácfa u. 38. ☎ **1/342-2587.** Reservations recommended. Main courses 500–1,380 Ft ($2.50–$6.90); menu meal 1,020 Ft ($5.10). AE MC V. Mon–Sat noon–1am. Closed July and Aug. Metro: Oktogon (Yellow line). HUNGARIAN.

Unobtrusively located on a residential street in Erzsébetváros, behind the old Jewish district, Kispipa (Little Pipe) is a well-lit, medium-size establishment. Unfortunately, it is closed in July and August, but if you are here any other time of year it is worth a visit. The cream-colored walls are lined with vintage Hungarian poster advertisements, and piano music contributes to the relaxed atmosphere. The menu is extensive; wild-game dishes are the house specialty. Five "complete menu" deals offer soup, main course, and dessert for a very reasonable price. Kispipa, formerly one of Budapest's only private restaurants, has played a small part in modern Hungarian history: The political party FIDESZ (Young Democrats) was founded (illegally) here in 1988.

### ❂ Marquis de Salade

VI. Hajós u. 43. ☎ **1/302-4086.** Self-serve salad bar 555 Ft ($2.80) (plates are on the small side); 500–1,500 Ft ($2.50—$7.50); menu meal 520–675 Ft ($2.70—$3.40). V. Daily noon–midnight. Metro: Arany János u. (Blue line). ASIAN/MIDDLE EASTERN/AFRICAN.

Vegetarians will jump for joy here. This cozy little self-service restaurant turns out an amazing assortment of exceptional salads. Located on the edge of Pest's theater district, it is a favorite luncheon spot of Hungarian actors. The connection between the exceptional Eastern cuisine and theater is rooted in the marriage of the owner, a woman from the Central Asian country of Azerbaijan, to Péter Halász, an outstanding member of the ELTE University Theater (whose radical initiatives forced him to leave Hungary in the 1960s, only to return again in 1989 and become a central figure in Budapest's alternative-theater scene). Additionally, the restaurant employs an eclectic mix of eight cooks from six different countries (Russia, Bangladesh, East Africa, Hungary, China, Italy, and the Caucasus Mountains). Offerings reflect this diversity. There's additional seating in the upstairs loft, and plans are afoot to expand to the cellar as well.

### Mérleg Vendéglő

V. Mérleg u. 6. ☎ **1/117-6911.** Soup 130–220 Ft (65¢–$1.10); main courses 420–1,180 Ft ($2.10–$5.90). MC V. Mon–Sat 8am–11pm. Metro: Deák tér (all lines). HUNGARIAN.

This is a moderately priced little restaurant serving unpretentious Hungarian cuisine just a few minutes walk from the central tourist area of the Inner City. In the immediate vicinity of the Atrium Hyatt and Inter-Continental hotels, the restaurant is on Mérleg utca, a quiet side street between Nador utca and the Danube embankment. A perfect alternative to the expensive tourist traps of Váci utca. The place is simple, with tasteful decor and shared tables. Stick with the basic Hungarian dishes; try stuffed cabbage (töltött kaposzta) or paprika chicken (paprikás csirke).

### Prágai Svejk Vendéglő

VII. Király u. 59/b. ☎ 1/322-3278. Soup 250 Ft ($1.25); main courses 700–1,100 Ft ($3.50–$5.50). AE, V. Daily noon–11pm. Tram: 4 or 6 from Nyugati pu. CZECH/SLOVAK.

Hankering for a taste of the neighboring regions? Svejk restaurant offers plump, delicious potato gnocchi served with sheep cheese and bacon. Heartier appetites might order the ragout with steamed knedli. Eight different types of unsurpassable Czech beer are available here. Service is uniformly friendly and quick. The walls feature quotes and illustrations from Jaroslav Hasek's famous novel about the clumsy, fat, ever-failing Svejk, a soldier in the Austro-Hungarian army. Live piano music is featured.

### Taverna Dionysos

V. Belgrád rakpart 16. ☎ 1/118-1222. Appetizers 200–300 Ft ($1–$1.50); main courses 700–900 Ft ($3.50–$4.50). Reservations recommended. MC V. Daily noon–midnight. Metro: Ferenciek tere (Blue line). GREEK.

This faithful rendition of a Greek tavern recently opened on Pest's Danube embankment on the pleasant southern end of the Inner City, not far from the central market hall. The delicious food is authentic Greek fare at reasonable prices in the center of the city. Weather permitting, sidewalk dining is available.

## INEXPENSIVE

### ✪ Csarnok Vendéglő

V. Hold u. 11. ☎ 1/269-4906. Soup 180 Ft (90¢); main courses 460–800 Ft ($2.30–$4); menu meals 460–480 ($2.30–$2.40). MC. Mon–Sat 9am–midnight, Sun noon–10pm. Metro: Arany János utca (Blue line). HUNGARIAN.

On the Inner City's quiet Hold utca (Moon Street), the Csarnok Vendéglő is located between Szabadság tér and Bajcsy-Zsilinszky út, not far from the United States Embassy. Its name comes from the wonderful turn-of-the-century market hall (csarnok) next door. One of the few restaurants in this part of the Inner City, it's even more notable for its uniformly low prices. The menu (in English translation) features typical Hungarian vendéglő fare, heavy as usual on meat dishes. Outdoor seating is available on the sidewalk, but sit inside for the full effect.

### Csendes Étterem

V. Múzeum krt. 13 (enter from side street, Ferenczy István utca). ☎ 1/267-0218. Soup 140–280 Ft (70¢–$1.40); main courses 370–900 Ft ($1.85–$4.50). No credit cards. Mon–Sat noon–10pm. Metro: Astoria (Red line) or Kálvin tér (Blue line). HUNGARIAN/SLOVAK/TRANSYLVANIAN.

Located on the Múzeum körút section of Pest's Inner Ring boulevard, just a few minutes walk from the main tourist area around Váci utca, the Csendes Étterem ("Quiet Restaurant") features inexpensive Hungarian, Slovak, and Transylvanian dishes. The restaurant has a decidedly rustic look, with exposed wooden rafters, wooden booths, and tasteful horse posters decorating the walls. The English-language menu is full of amusing errors (somewhat like the sign we once saw at a Romanian border crossing: "Welcome to Romania. Have a nice tripe.") Csendes is a student hangout; ELTE University is just down the street.

### Gandhi Vegetariánus Étterem

V. Vigyázó Ferenc u. 4. ☎1/269-4944. Soup 200 Ft ($1); small menu meal 480 Ft ($2.40); large menu meal 680 Ft ($3.40). No credit cards. Daily noon–10:30pm. Metro: Deák tér (all lines). VEGETARIAN.

A friendly, new-age restaurant serving interesting vegetarian food in a peaceful atmosphere. Choose from two daily menu options written (in Hungarian and English) on a blackboard. For instance, stuffed squash with Indian ragout and brown rice or potato pumpkin casserole with garlic Roquefort sauce, steamed cabbage and spinach soufflé. Or you can simply order soup (cream of cauliflower perhaps, or lentil) and salad bar, though the salads lack variety. Seating is plentiful. There is a browsing bookshelf stocked with New Age and Eastern literature. Photographs of Gandhi hang on the walls.

### ✪ Kádár Étkezde

VII. Klauzál tér 9. ☎ **1/321-3622.** Soup 120 Ft (60¢); main courses 200–500 Ft ($1–$2.50). No credit cards. Tues–Sat 11:30am–3:30pm. Metro: Astoria (Red line) or Deák tér (all lines). HUNGARIAN.

By 11:45am, Uncle Kádár's, in the heart of the historic Jewish district, is filled with a steady stream of lunchtime regulars—from paint-spattered workers to elderly Jewish couples. Uncle Kádár, a neighborhood legend, personally greets them as they file in. From the outside the only sign of the place is a small red sign saying "Étkezde." And, to be sure, the place is no more than a lunchroom, but it has a wonderful atmosphere. Photographs (many autographed) of actors and athletes decorate the walls. There is an old-fashioned seltzer bottle on every table. The food is simple but hearty. The service is fast and friendly. The menu is only in Hungarian, but if you see something you like on someone else's table you can always point. Try the soup, regardless. Served in a deep bowl, with bread, it's practically a meal in itself. Table sharing is the norm here. Customers pay at the front, then return to hand the waitress a tip.

### ✪ Korona Passage

In the Mercure Korona Hotel, V. Kecskeméti u. 14. ☎ **1/117-4111.** Crêpes 300–500 Ft ($1.50–$2.50); salad bar 190–300 Ft (95¢–$1.50). No credit cards. Daily 10am–10pm. Metro: Kálvin tér (Blue line). CRÊPERIE/SALAD BAR.

This is a great place for lunch in central Pest. The prices here are incredibly low, especially considering that it's in the Mercure Korona luxury hotel. Giant crêpes are made to order—fillings range from cheese to sweet walnut puré—and are delicious. Skip the self-service salad bar, which is never well-stocked. The long, arcade-style restaurant, with a skylight and thriving plants, is bright and clean, air-conditioned, and smoke free. High chairs are available for the little ones. The Hotel Mercure Korona was built at the spot where the original medieval Pest city wall once stood, and a piece of it remains in the restaurant.

### Pizzeria Pink Cadillac

IX. Ráday u. 22. ☎ **1/216-1412** or 218-9382. Pizzas 380–700 Ft ($1.90–$3.50); pasta 320–630 Ft ($1.60–$3.15). Mon–Thurs 11am–11pm, Fri 11am–1am, Sat 1pm–1am, Sun 1pm–11pm. Metro: Kálvin tér (Blue line). PIZZA.

Run by an enterprising young woman from Arad, Romania, this glitzy little pizzeria offers some of the city's best pizza. Lasagna and other pasta dishes are also served. Ingredients are fresh. Everything is tasty. Free delivery is available. Pink Cadillac is located on Ráday utca, one of Central Pest's up-and-coming streets. In fact, plans are afoot to convert the entire length of the street into a pedestrian-only zone, like Váci utca.

### ✪ Semiramis

V. Alkotmány u. 20. ☎ **1/111-7627.** Main courses 370–700 Ft ($1.85–$3.50). No credit cards. Mon–Sat noon–9pm. Metro: Kossuth tér (Red line). MIDDLE EASTERN.

Located just a block from Parliament and a few blocks from Nyugati Station, this little eatery is best suited for lunch since it tends to run out of the more popular dishes by evening. Seating is primarily upstairs in a small and cozy loft decorated with Middle Eastern tapestries and colorful straw trivets. The waiters are uniformly friendly, and all speak English. Everything is delicious, including the house specialty, chicken breast with spinach (spenótos csirkemell), which consists of far more spinach than chicken. Vegetarians can easily build a meal out of several appetizers; try the yogurt-cucumber salad (yogurtos saláta) and the fül (a zesty garlic and fava bean dish).

# 4  Just Beyond Central Pest

## VERY EXPENSIVE

### ✪ Gundel

XIV. Állatkerti út 2. ☎ 1/322-1002 or 321-3550. Reservations highly recommended. Soup 700 Ft ($3.50); main courses 2,350–4,980 Ft ($11.75–$24.90). AE, DC, EURO, MC, V. Daily noon–4pm and 7pm–midnight. Metro: Hősök tere (Yellow line). HUNGARIAN/INTERNATIONAL.

Budapest's fanciest and most famous restaurant, Gundel was reopened in 1992 by the well-known restaurateur George Lang, owner of New York's Café des Artistes. The Hungarian-born Lang, author of *The Cuisine of Hungary*, along with his partner Ronald Lauder, son of Estée Lauder and a one-time New York gubernatorial candidate, has spared no effort in attempting to re-create the original splendor for which Gundel, founded in 1894, achieved its international reputation. Located in City Park, Gundel has an opulent dining room and a large, carefully groomed garden. The kitchen prides itself on preparing traditional dishes in an innovative fashion. Lamb and wild-game entrees are house specialties. The menu also tends to highlight fruits and vegetables in season. In late spring, for instance, don't miss out on the asparagus served in hollandaise with grilled salmon. Gundel has perhaps the most extensive wine list in town, and the waiters are well versed in its offerings. The homemade fruit ice cream served in the shape of the fruit makes for a delectable dessert, as does the famous Gundel torta, a decadently rich chocolate layer cake. Budget-minded travelers should consider eating at Bagolyvár, the less fancy "home-style" restaurant next door, also owned by George Lang (see "Expensive," below).

## EXPENSIVE

### ✪ Bagolyvár

XIV. Állatkerti út 2. ☎ 1/321-3550. Reservations recommended. Soup 220–320 Ft ($1.10–$1.60); main courses 1,190–3,000 Ft ($5.95–$15). AE, MC, V. Daily 11am–11pm. Metro: Hősök tere (Yellow line). HUNGARIAN.

Bagolyvár (Owl Palace) offers something unique to the budget traveler—a taste of Gundel, Budapest's most famous (and most expensive) restaurant, at less than wallet-flattening prices. George Lang, the well-known owner of Gundel, wanted to offer Hungarian "home-style" cooking to the general public at a reasonable price, and thus was born his second Budapest eatery, located just next door to Gundel in City Park. The Bagolyvár menu is limited to half a dozen main courses (supplemented by daily specials), which include roast veal with green beans as well as layered Savoy cabbage. Delicious desserts include chocolate poppy-seed cake and fresh fruit salad. The food is carefully prepared and presented. The decor and ambience are pleasant and unpretentious. Outdoor dining is available in the restaurant's garden.

## 5   Central Buda

### EXPENSIVE

#### Hong Kong Pearl Garden

II. Margit krt. 2. ☎ **1/212-3948** or 1/212-3131. Reservations recommended. Soup 480–760 Ft ($2.40–$3.80); main courses 960–1,680 Ft ($4.80–$8.40); menu meals 1,350–9,800 ($6.75–$49). AE, DC, MC, V. Mon–Sat noon–11:30pm, Sun noon–11pm. Tram: 4 or 6 to the Buda side of the Margaret Bridge. SZECHUAN.

In a prime location just over the Margaret Bridge on Buda's Margit körút, the Hong Kong Pearl Garden opened in 1993. Though Budapest is now saturated with Chinese restaurants, this one remains among the most popular. The atmosphere is luxurious but not suffocating. The tables are nicely spaced and the lighting is restrained; many windows provide ample natural light. There's live piano music in the evenings. Service is on the slow side, but the staff are uniformly friendly and all speak some English. There's a variety of duck dishes—including Peking duck (order in advance)—but the house specialties are the seafood dishes.

#### ✪ Kacsa Vendéglő

I. Fő u. 75. ☎ **1/201-9992.** Reservations recommended. Soup 350–500 Ft ($1.75–$2.50); main courses 1,300–2,300 Ft ($6.50–$11.50). AE, DC, EURO, MC, V. Daily 6pm–1am. Metro: Batthyány tér (Red line). HUNGARIAN.

Kacsa (meaning "duck") is located on the main street of Watertown, the Buda neighborhood that lies between Castle Hill and the Danube. Here you'll find an intimate, elegant, and understated dining atmosphere. A string trio is appealing, but the service seems overly attentive and ceremonious. Enticing main courses include roast duck with morello cherries, haunch of venison with grapes, and pike-perch Russian style. The vegetarian plate is the best we had anywhere. For dessert, sample the assorted strudels, prepared with fruits in season.

#### Le Jardin de Paris

I. Fő u. 20. ☎ **201-0047.** Reservations recommended. Soup 250–350 Ft ($1.25–$2.25); appetizers 350–1,200 Ft ($1.75–$6); main courses 1,200–1,800 Ft ($6–$9). AE, DC, MC, V. Daily noon–12am. Metro: Batthyány tér (Red line). FRENCH.

In the heart of Buda's Watertown, just across the street from the hideous Institut Français, is this wonderful little French bistro. A cozy cellar space, it is decorated with an eclectic collection of graphic arts. A jazz trio entertains diners. The menu contains a variety of nouvelle French specialties, and the wine list features French as well as Hungarian vintages. Presentation is impeccable; the waiters are not overbearing.

### MODERATE

#### ✪ Aranyszarvas

I. Szarvas tér 1. ☎ **1/175-6451.** Reservations recommended. Soup 290–320 Ft ($1.45—$1.60); main courses 890–1,200 Ft ($4.45–$6). AE, CB, DC, EURO, MC, V. June–Aug, daily noon–11pm; Sept–May, daily 4pm–11pm. Bus: A number of buses serve Döbrentei tér, including number 8 from Március 15 tér. HUNGARIAN.

The Golden Stag is located in a historic building in central Buda's Tabán district, just below and to the south of Castle Hill. There's indoor seating in a dining room with a restrained wild-game motif, but on pleasant nights customers dine on the outdoor terrace. A string trio is available to serenade, but must be requested in advance. As the name and decor suggest, this restaurant serves wild game, and the menu lists a variety of reasonably priced dishes, such as hunter's saddle of hare, Serbian wild boar, and venison stew. The desserts are worth sampling as well, particularly the mixed strudel, prepared with seasonal fruit.

### ✪ Horgásztanya Vendéglő

I. Fő u. 27. ☎ **1/212-3780.** Soup 250–290 Ft ($1.25–$1.45); main courses 690–1,290 Ft ($3.45–$6.45). No credit cards. Daily noon–11pm. Metro: Battyhány tér (Red line). HUNGARIAN.

Just a short block from the Danube, in Buda's Watertown (Víziváros), the Horgásztanya Vendéglő is a family-style fish restaurant. Although the restaurant specializes in fish dishes, non-fish eaters can enjoy dining here too; the extensive menu (in English) lists a variety of Hungarian specialties. The decor is traditional Hungarian and unpretentious.

### Szeged Vendéglő

XI. Bartók Béla út 1. ☎ **1/166-6503.** Soup 200–300 Ft ($1–$1.50); main courses 700–1,500 Ft ($3.50–$7.50). No credit cards. Daily noon–11pm. Tram: 47 or 49 from Deák tér to Hotel Gellért. HUNGARIAN.

Come to this classic vendéglő for a taste of Szeged, the southern Hungarian city admired for its cuisine (see chapter 13 for information on trips to Szeged). The house specialties are spicy fish dishes, including the famous fish soup, *Szeged halászlé*. The restaurant is a touch old-school, but the food is good and hearty. Gypsy music is performed nightly. The restaurant is just down the street from the Hotel Gellért, not far from Buda's Móricz Zsigmond körtér.

### ✪ Taverna Ressaikos

I. Apor Péter u. 1. ☎ **1/212-1612.** Reservations recommended. Soup and appetizers 250–700 Ft ($1.25–$3.50); main courses 650–1,090 Ft ($3.25–$5.40). AE, EURO, MC. Daily noon–midnight. Bus or tram: Any to Clark Ádám tér, including bus no. 16 from Deák tér. GREEK.

Located in the heart of Buda's Watertown (Víziváros), just next door to the Hotel Alba Budapest, the Taverna Ressaikos features carefully prepared food at reasonable prices. Portions are generous. Try the calamari or the sumptuous lamb in wine. The menu also features a number of interesting goat dishes. Vegetarians can easily make a meal out of appetizers such as stuffed tomatoes, spanikopita, and tsatsiki. The live guitar music in the evenings can get a bit too loud, and the service, while attentive, is definitely on the slow side.

## INEXPENSIVE

### ✪ Marxim

II. Kisrókus u. 23. ☎ **1/316-0231.** Pizza 240–550 Ft ($1.20–$2.75); pasta 290–420 Ft ($1.45–$2.10). No credit cards. Mon–Thur noon–1am, Fri–Sat noon–2am, Sun 6pm–1am. Metro: Moszkva tér (Red line). PIZZA.

On a gritty industrial street near Moszkva tér, Marxim's chief appeal lies not in its cuisine but in its decor. The motif is Marxist nostalgia; the entrance is marked by a small neon red flag. The cellar space is decorated with barbed wire, more red flags, banners, posters, and cartoons recalling Hungary's dark past. Amazingly, this is one of just a few places in Budapest where you can still see this kind of stuff, so thoroughly have symbols of the Communist period been whisked away. (Another place, of course, is *Szoborpark* [Statue Park]; see chapter 6 for details.) Several years ago, Marxim was unsuccessfully prosecuted under a controversial new law banning the display of the symbols of "hateful" political organizations. The loud, smoky cellar space has a barlike atmosphere. A number of beers are available on draft.

## 6   The Castle District

### VERY EXPENSIVE

**Alabárdos**

I. Országház u. 2. ☎ **1/214-3814** or 214-3139. Reservations required. Soup 400–750 Ft ($2–$3.75); main courses 1,500–4,500 Ft ($7.50–$22.50); fixed-price lunch (with drinks) 1,900–3,450 Ft ($9.50–$17.25). AE, DC, MC, V. Mon–Sat noon–4pm and 7pm–midnight. Bus: Várbusz from Moszkva tér or 16 from Deák tér to Castle Hill. Funicular: From Clark Ádám tér to Castle Hill. HUNGARIAN.

In the heart of the Castle District, Alabárdos offers nouvelle cuisine Hungarian style in a small, posh setting. The historic building it's housed in has several medieval details; 15th-century arches can be seen in the courtyard. The atmosphere inside is hushed and elegant, although slightly pretentious. The walls are judiciously decorated in a medieval motif. A keyboardist performs unobtrusively. Meals are served on Zsolnay porcelain, from Pécs. Weather permitting, outdoor dining is available in the courtyard.

### INEXPENSIVE

**Akadémia Önkiszolgáló Étterem**

I. Orszagház u. 3. Soup 60–100 Ft (30¢–50¢); main courses 160–340 Ft (80¢–$1.70). Mon–Fri 11:30am–2pm. Bus: Várbusz from Moszkva tér or 16 from Deák tér to Castle Hill. Funicular: From Clark Ádám tér to Castle Hill. HUNGARIAN.

Located on the third floor of an unmarked building, this is one of two humble self-service cafeterias—both of which are open only for lunch and only on weekdays—offering incredibly cheap and hearty meals in the Castle District. Basic Hungarian fare, good for fortifying your tired legs, is available: soups, meat entrees, dumplings, and pickled or boiled vegetables. Few tourists are in evidence here. Take the elevator or stairs to the third floor.

**✪ Önkiszolgáló**

I. Hess András tér 4 (in the Fortuna Courtyard). Soup 60–100 Ft (30¢–50¢); main courses 120–300 Ft (60¢–$1.50). Mon–Fri 11:30am–2:30pm. Bus: Várbusz from Moszkva tér or 16 from Deák tér to Castle Hill. Funicular: From Clark Ádám tér to Castle Hill. HUNGARIAN.

Located directly across the street from the Hilton Hotel, in the Fortuna Courtyard (where the bookstore Litea is located, see chapter 8), this is the second of the two self-service cafeterias in the Castle District. The entrance is marked only by a small sign posting the open hours; it is the second door on the left inside the archway, up one flight of stairs. Just follow the stream of locals at lunchtime. This is a no-frills eatery. Point out your selections, share a table, and bus your own tray when you are done. The atmosphere is more appealing here than at the cafeteria down the street.

## 7   The Buda Hills

### VERY EXPENSIVE

**✪ Udvarház a Hármashatárhegyen**

I. Hármashatárhegyi út 2. ☎ **1/188-8780** or 188-6921. Reservations recommended. Soup 300–450 Ft ($1.50–$2.25); main courses 1,300–2,900 Ft ($6.50–$14.50). AE, CB, DC, DISC, MC, V. May–Oct, Tues–Sun 11am–11pm; Nov–Apr, Tues–Fri 6–11pm, Sat–Sun 11am–11pm. Bus: 65 from Kolosy tér in Óbuda to the last stop. HUNGARIAN.

This lovely restaurant high in the Buda Hills boasts several elegant dining rooms, in addition to tables on the terrace with a great panoramic view of the surrounding hills.

Dinner here makes for a full evening; in the courtyard there's a folklore show, with music and dance. The menu features a large variety of Hungarian specialties, particularly fish and game specialties. Other than by taxi, the only way to get here is by taking bus no. 65 to the last stop (note that the last bus heads back at 10pm).

## MODERATE

### ✪ Náncsi Néni Vendéglője

II. Órdögárok út 80. ☎ **1/397-2742.** Reservations recommended for dinner. Main courses 400–850 Ft ($2–$4.25). AE, CB, DC, DISC, EURO, JCB, MC, V. Daily noon–11pm. Tram: 56 from Moszkva tér to the last stop, then change to bus 63 to Széchenyi utca. HUNGARIAN.

Decorated with photographs of turn-of-the-century Budapest (including a copy of the coffee-shop picture that appears on the cover of John Lukacs's sentimental *Budapest, 1900*), this popular but remote restaurant is located high in the Buda Hills. There's outdoor garden dining in the summer, with live accordion music at night. The menu features typical Hungarian dishes, prepared with great care. The restaurant is near St. Christoph Villa and the Petneházy Country Club.

### Szép Ilona

II. Budakeszi út 1–3. ☎ **1/275-1392.** Soup 290–610 Ft ($1.45–$3.05); main courses 780–1,550 Ft ($3.90–$7.75). No credit cards. Daily 11:30am–10pm. Bus: 158 from Moszkva tér (departs from Csaba utca, at the top of the stairs, near the stop from which the Várbusz departs for the Castle District). HUNGARIAN.

This cheerful, unassuming restaurant serves a mostly local clientele. There's a good selection of Hungarian specialties; try the borjúpaprikás galuskával (veal paprika) served with galuska (a typical Central European style of dumpling). There's a small sidewalk-side garden for summer dining. The Szép Ilona is located in a pleasant Buda neighborhood; after your meal, have a stroll through the tree-lined streets.

## INEXPENSIVE

### ✪ Makkhetes Vendéglő

XII. Németvölgyi út 56. ☎ **1/155-7330.** Soup 145–320 Ft (75¢–$1.60); main courses 480–890 Ft ($2.40–$4.45). No credit cards. Daily 11am–10pm. Bus: 105 from Deák tér. HUNGARIAN.

In the lower part of the Buda Hills, Makkhetes (the name means "7 of Acorns," a Hungarian playing card) is a rustic little neighborhood eatery. The crude wood paneling and absence of ornamentation gives it a distinctly country atmosphere. The regulars (the waiters seem to know everyone who enters) start filing in at 11:30 for lunch. The food is good and the portions large. You won't go wrong with the paprika csirke galuskával (chicken paprika with dumplings). Outdoor dining is available.

## 8 Northern Buda & Óbuda

## VERY EXPENSIVE

### Kéhli Vendéglő

III. Mókus u. 22. ☎ **1/250-4241.** Reservations recommended. Soup 450–900 Ft ($2.25–$4.50); main courses 1,280–2,920 Ft ($6.40–$14.60). AE. Mon–Fri 5pm–midnight, Sat–Sun noon–midnight. Train: HÉV suburban railway from Batthyány tér to Árpád híd. HUNGARIAN.

Housed in a historic Óbuda building, Kéhli is an upscale traditional Hungarian restaurant with a cozy dining room and an enclosed garden. Located behind the Aquincum Corinthia Hotel in Óbuda's old city, the restaurant can be a bit difficult to find. One of the house specialties is Szinbád's Favorite, named for the famous pirate introduced

> ## 🏠 Family-Friendly Restaurants
>
> **Bagolyvár** *(see p. 92)*   This is the place to go if your visit to the child-oriented sights in City Park takes you to the lunch or dinner hour. Under the same management and right next door to the famous (and pricey) Gundel, Bagolyvár offers excellent home-style cooking at very moderate prices. High chairs are available. There was a litter of kittens running about the patio while we lunched.
>
> **Gerbeaud's** *(see p. 98)*   Be sure to make a stop at Budapest's most famous coffeehouse for a special dessert. It's an elegant place, but in good weather you can get a table outside on bustling Vörösmarty tér and watch the kids play around (and on) the square's fountain.
>
> **Marxim** *(see p. 94)*   Come to this cellar restaurant for good ole pizza and pasta; teenagers will appreciate what may be Budapest's most bizarre restaurant decor, an evocation of Communist ghosts past.
>
> **Korona Passage** *(see p. 91)*   Crêpes are kid-friendly food, and here you can watch them being made right at the counter. High chairs are available.

to Hungary by 20th-century novelist Gyula Krúdy; the dish consists of pork stuffed with chicken liver rolled in bacon and served in a paprika-and-mushroom sauce. Another dish worth sampling is the roast goose liver with garlic. Dinner is accompanied by live music.

## EXPENSIVE

### ✪ Kis Buda Gyöngye

III. Kenyeres u. 34. ☎ **1/368-6402** or 368-9246. Reservations highly recommended. Soup 350–500 Ft ($1.75–$2.50); main courses 880–3,200 Ft ($4.40–$16). AE DC MC V. Mon–Sat noon–midnight. Closed Sun. Tram: 17 from Margit híd (Buda side). HUNGARIAN.

On a quiet side street in a residential Óbuda neighborhood, Kis Buda Gyöngye (Little Pearl of Buda) is a favorite of Hungarians and tourists alike. This lively, cheerful establishment features an interior garden, which sits in the shade of a wonderful old gnarly tree. Inside, an eccentric violin player entertains diners. The standard Hungarian fare is prepared with great care. Consider the goose plate, a rich combination platter including roast goose leg, goose cracklings, and goose liver. Service can be slow.

## MODERATE

### ✪ Malomtó Étterem

II. Frankel Leó u. 48. ☎ **1/326-2847**. Reservations recommended for dinner. Soup 110–220 Ft (55¢–$1.10); main courses 690–1,600 Ft ($3.45–$8). AE, DC, EURO, MC, V. Daily noon–midnight. Tram: 4 or 6 to Margit híd (Buda side), then walk along Frankel Leó utca to the Lukács Baths (Lukács Fürdó). HUNGARIAN.

Right across the street from the Lukács thermal baths, the Malomtó (named for the nearby Mill Pond) sits at the base of a hill. There are two outdoor terraces, well shaded from the road, and live guitar music nightly. The menu features a good variety of Hungarian wild game specialties and seafood dishes, in addition to the standard Hungarian specialties. You might notice that the menu posted outside differs from the one distributed at the tables, though this seems to be related more to mismanagement than to any attempt at deception. Since the main-course portions are themselves huge, you may want to bypass soup and salad. The *Bélszín kedvesi módra* (beef and goose liver in a creamy mushroom sauce) is sumptuous. On a recent visit, we tried the *sztrapacska oldalassal* (pork ribs with ewe cheese dumplings) and found it delightful. Service can be on the slow side.

**Uj Sipos Halászkert**

III. Fő tér 6. ☎ **1/250-1064** (public phone in lobby). Reservations recommended. Soup 250–400 Ft ($1.25–$2); main courses 750–1,600 Ft ($3.75–$8). 10% service charge added to the bill. AE, CB, DC, DISC, MC, V. Daily noon–midnight. Train: Suburban HÉV line to Árpád híd. HUNGARIAN/SEAFOOD.

In its own handsome building on Óbuda's dignified main square, this restaurant consists of several rooms with a comfortable air of worn elegance. Though the exterior of the restaurant has received a fresh paint job and the addition of the word "Uj" (new) to the name of the place, the inside is, to our eyes, unchanged. The menu specializes in Hungarian seafood dishes. A string trio enhances the atmosphere, and there is a small interior garden area.

## 9 Coffeehouses

Like Vienna, imperial Budapest was famous for its coffeehouse culture. Literary movements and political circles alike were identified in large part by which coffeehouse they met in. Sándor Petőfi, the revolutionary poet of 1848 fame, is said to have instructed his friend János Arany, another leading Hungarian poet of the day, to write to him in care of the Pilvax Coffee House, as he spent more time there than at home. Although Communism managed to dull this cherished institution, a few classic coffeehouses have miraculously survived the tangled tragedies of the 20th century.

All the classic coffeehouses offer delicious pastries and coffee in an atmosphere of luxurious (if occasionally faded) splendor. Many offer small sandwiches, some serve ice cream, and some feature bar drinks. Pastries are displayed in a glass case and generally cost between 100 and 300 Ft (50¢ and $1.50); coffee costs 100 to 300 Ft (50¢ to $1.50). Table sharing is common, and lingering for hours over a single cup of coffee or pastry is perfectly acceptable. See chapter 1, "Coffee & Tea," for Hungarian coffee terms and additional information.

### THE INNER CITY & CENTRAL PEST

**Gerbeaud's**

V. Vörösmarty tér 7. ☎ **1/118-1311.** Daily 9am–9pm. Metro: Vörösmarty tér (Yellow line).

Gerbeaud's is probably Budapest's most famous coffeehouse. Founded in 1858, it has stood on its current spot since 1870. Whether you sit inside amid the splendor of turn-of-the-century furnishings or outside on one of Pest's liveliest squares, you will be sure to enjoy the fine pastries that have made the name Gerbeaud famous. Its reputation and location ensure that it's filled to capacity throughout the year; good luck getting a table in the late afternoon.

**✪ Művész Kávéház**

VI. Andrássy út 29. ☎ **1/352-1337** or 351-3942. Daily 9am–midnight. Metro: Opera (Yellow line).

### Impressions

*The cafes are never empty here . . . Everyone loiters on the Corso, for no one is in a hurry in Budapest. If a cool breeze comes up, the waiters bring small steamer rugs for their patrons.*

—Grace Humphrey, American memoirist, 1936

Just across Andrássy út from the Opera House, Művész (Artist) is one of Budapest's finest traditional coffeehouses. The lush interior includes marble table tops, crystal chandeliers, and mirrored walls. Despite its old-world grandeur, Művész retains a casual atmosphere. There are tables on the street, but sit inside for the full coffeehouse effect. Decaffeinated cappuccino is available, still a rarity in Budapest. Elaborate ice-cream sundaes seem to be a favorite with locals and tourists alike.

### New York Kávéház

VII. Erzsébet krt. 9–11. ☎ **1/322-3849** or 322-1648. Daily 9am–midnight. Metro: Blaha Lujza tér (Red line).

On the ground floor of a spectacular art nouveau palace built at the end of the 19th century, the New York Coffeehouse has a history as rich as the ornate decoration of its interior. In the early 20th century, it was perhaps the city's best-known meeting place for artists, poets, writers, and actors; and portraits of famous regulars line the walls upstairs. From 1954 to 1989, it was known as the Hungaria. In spite of the seemingly precarious condition of the building (the scaffolding outside appears to be permanent—it's been up at least 10 years), the interior has been carefully restored. Rather expensive but mediocre meals (main courses from 1,800 to 3,000 Ft/$9 to $15), are served in a sunken room in the center, but this establishment is best suited for coffee and pastries. A ticket collector is stationed at the door, charging what appears to be a cover; however, the 300 Ft ($1.50) you pay will be subtracted from your order.

### Wiener Kaffehaus

In the Intercontinental Budapest Hotel, V. Apáczai Csere János u. 12–14. ☎ **1/327-6333** or 117-8088. Daily 9am–10pm. Metro: Deák tér (all lines).

A faithful reproduction of a Viennese coffeehouse, located inside one of Budapest's finer luxury hotels, the Wiener Kaffehaus serves up delicious pastry. The bonbons are particularly popular, and are available in variously sized gift packages.

## CENTRAL BUDA

### ✪ Angelika Cukrászda

I. Batthyány tér 7. ☎ **1/201-4847** or 212-3784. Daily 10am–10pm. Metro: Batthyány tér (Red line).

The Angelika Cukrászda is housed in a historic building next to St. Anne's Church on Buda's Batthyány tér. The sunken rooms of this cavernous cafe provide the perfect retreat on a hot summer day. Stained-glass windows, marble floors, and emerald-green upholstery contribute to the quiet old-world atmosphere. You can choose from among a selection of excellent pastries and teas (a rarity in Budapest, a city of serious coffee addicts). There is also a small gallery inside the coffeehouse, where artworks are displayed.

## THE CASTLE DISTRICT

### Cafe Miró

I. Úri u. 30. ☎ **1/175-5458**. Daily 9am–midnight. Bus: Várbusz from Moszkva tér or 16 from Deák tér to Castle Hill. Funicular: From Clark Ádám tér to Castle Hill.

A recent addition to the Castle District, the trendy Cafe Miró features salads as well as the standard pastries, coffees, and teas. Open until midnight (unusual in this neighborhood), the cafe is particularly striking for its whimsical interior design, which, in turquoise, rusty orange, and lemon yellow, aims to evoke the work of Catalan artist Joan Miró. The crowd consists of young and hip Hungarians mixed with camera-wielding tourists.

⊗ **Ruszwurm Cukrászda**

I. Szentháromság u. 7. ☎ **1/175-5284.** Daily 10am–7pm. Bus: Várbusz from Moszkva tér or 16 from Deák tér to Castle Hill. Funicular: From Clark Ádám tér to Castle Hill.

More than a century old, the Ruszwurm is an utterly charming little place, with two rooms outfitted with small tables and chairs and wall shelves lined with antiques. It can be very difficult to find a free table, and the two out front on the sidewalk seem forever occupied. A particularly tasty pastry is the *Dobos torta,* a multilayered cake with a thin caramel crust on top.

## 10 Snacks on the Run

Budapest is a great place for snacking. There are kiosks and *bufes* turning out impromptu meals near every major transportation hub. Below are our favorites— good alternatives to the international fast-food joints proliferating in Budapest. Generally, you can pick up a meal on the run for 300 Ft ($1.50) or less.

**Déli railway station**    Try the **Gyros Bufe** in the upper level of the station (enter from Alkotás út). Delicious gyros sandwiches, made from turkey, are sold here.

**Moszkva tér**    Hungarian-style fast-food sandwiches are available 24 hours a day from the **Györsbufe** (Fast Buffet) kiosk. As you emerge from the metro (Red line), it's to the left of the clock; look for the line of people. The menu changes daily, but usually two or three types of hot sandwiches are available: Húsos meleg szendvics is meat sauce and melted cheese on half a baguette; gomba meleg szendvics is the same, but with a mushroom rather than meat sauce; and hamburger is, well, a Hungarian variant on the tradition (*sajtos* is with cheese). Hamburger hús nélkül has no burger; it is a bun stuffed with fixings, the best choice for vegetarians. All sandwiches cost 100 to 120 Ft (50¢ to 60¢).

**Nyugati railway station**    In the underpass beneath Nyugati railway station (beneath the *Skala Metro* department store), you will find an unnamed **stand** selling fried chicken sandwiches. Ranging from 170 to 225 Ft (85¢ to $1.15) apiece, they make a great snack. Not far away, at IV. Visegrádi u. 1, is **Ramen House Miyako,** considered by many to be Budapest's best Japanese noodle house. It's open daily until 1am. The excellent **Turkish bakery,** just down the street toward the Danube, at IV. Szent István krt. 13, sells freshly baked pita bread and a broad selection of baklava and other lovely pastries.

**Bajcsy-Zsilinszky út**    Bagels were born in Eastern Europe, and though they haven't been seen much here for half a century or more, they have recently been reintroduced in Budapest. The place is **New York Bagel,** across the street from the Bazilika at VI. Bajcsy-Zsilinszky út 21 (Metro: Arany Janos utca, on the Blue line). While these are not quite New York bagels, they're tasty enough. Bagels cost 54 Ft (27¢), with added charges for various spreads and toppings, including cream cheese and lox, both hard to find elsewhere in Budapest. Bagel sandwiches run from 240 to 550 Ft ($1.20 to $2.75). Try the mixed bagel (vegyes), baked with Hungarian paprika. There's free delivery on Monday through Friday (10am to 8pm) to most districts on orders of 500 Ft ($2.50) or more.

**Oktogon**    Next door to Burger King, on Andrassy út, you'll find an outlet of **Prima Pék,** a bakery chain with a distinctive orange sign that offers great pastries. If you like what you try, keep your eyes open; Prima Pék shops are found throughout the city.

**Deák tér**    In the Inner City's Deák tér neighborhood, we recommend two snacking options. Hungarian fast-food meals are available from **Paprika,** at V. Városház

u. 10, at the corner of Pilvax köz. Meals are just 260 Ft ($1.30), and a picture of every dish is posted on the wall for easy ordering. Try the *töltött kaposzta* (stuffed cabbage) or *töltött paprika* (stuffed pepper). Prefer something sweet? Try the **Kürtőskalács** window on the corner of Károly körút and Bárczy István utca (V. Károly krt. 30). Kürtőskalács is an exquisite, light honey bread shaped like a cylinder; traditionally the dough is wrapped around a bottle and baked in an extremely hot oven. Here it is baked on a metal pipe. A decidedly superior kürtőskalács is sold from a kiosk in Móricz Zsigmond körtér (see below).

**Keleti railway station**   Time to kill before catching your train? Savory Balkan specialties are sold at **Ari Balkan Étterem,** VIII. Kerepesi út 1 (near the Hotel Park). This is a small cellar establishment with pictures on the wall of all the dishes available. The food is also displayed under a glass counter. The old "point and order" method works well here. It's open daily until 11pm. Another option is **El Fayoumi Étterem,** at VIII. Nefelejcs u. 5. Delicious gyros and falafels are dispensed here. In the mood for something sweet? The unnamed **pastry trailer** permanently parked at the head of Nefelejcs utca, in front of the Kentucky Fried Chicken outlet, offers a soft, flaky kakaos csiga (chocolate snail) and equally fresh brioche.

**Blaha Lujza tér**   Next door to the Hotel Nemzeti, at VIII. József krt. 2, you'll find **Hot Pot Forró Krumpli,** a little place with all sorts of baked potatoes for sale. It's a perfect treat on a chilly day.

**Astoria**   Directly in front of Pizza Hut, you'll find a tiny sidewalk kiosk called **Pizza Kucko.** This place was here long before Pizza Hut arrived on the scene, and guess what? Their pizza is better! If you don't believe it, take a look at the long lines every day at lunchtime.

**Móricz Zsigmond körtér**   This busy Buda transportation hub is the site of the single most delicious sweet snack available in this entire city full of sweets. We refer, of course, to the **kürtőskalács** sold in the little kiosk in the triangle in front of McDonald's. This is a delicious honey bread quite unlike anything else you've ever tasted. The one sold here is delightfully fresh. The kiosk is open every day, but closes at 7:30 pm.

# 6

# Exploring Budapest

**H** istoric Budapest is surprisingly small, and many sights listed in the following pages can be reached by foot from the city center. Take the time to stroll from one attraction to the next; you'll find yourself passing magnificent, if now somewhat faded, examples of the city's distinctive architecture.

## SUGGESTED ITINERARIES

### If You Have 1 Day

Spend a few hours in the morning exploring the Inner City and central Pest. Walk the length of Váci utca, the city's trendiest shopping street, to Vórósmarty tér. Stop for cappuccino and a slice of apple strudel (*almás rétes*) at the sumptuous Gerbeaud coffeehouse. Stroll along the Danube as far as the neo-Gothic Parliament building, noting along the way the Chain Bridge and the Gresham Palace. Lunch with the locals at Mérleg Étterem on Mérleg utca. Save the whole afternoon for visiting the major sites of Castle Hill and exploring the cobblestoned streets of the Castle District.

### If You Have 2 Days

On your first day, see Pest, as above, saving the Castle District for tomorrow. Walk the Outer Ring boulevard, noting Nyugati Railway Station and the New York Palace, grand examples of turn-of-the-century architecture. Stop for coffee and a slice of *dobos torta* (layer cake) at the exquisite New York Kavehaz, inside the Palace. Later, head to Buda's Gellért Hotel and unwind in its medicinal spa waters. Refreshed, hike up the stairs of Gellért Hill to see the Liberation Monument and an unparalleled panorama of the city.

Devote most of your second day to the Castle District, as above. Visit some smaller museums as well, like the Music History Museum (check for a recital) or the Military History Museum. Head back to Pest later to see Heroes' Square and City Park. Splurge on dinner at Gundel, where visiting royalty dined in turn-of-the-century Budapest. Afterward, stroll the length of grand Andrássy út back toward the center of Pest.

### If You Have 3 Days

Spend Days 1 and 2 as suggested above. Spend one evening attending a concert at the Ferenc Liszt Music Academy, Budapest's finest hall.

On the third day, take a boat up the Danube to Szentendre, a charming riverside town, home to a flourishing artist's colony. Don't miss the Margit Kovács Museum, where the work of Hungary's most innovative ceramic artist can be seen. Return in time for a final dinner at elegant Kacsa Vendéglő in Budapest's Watertown.

### If You Have 5 Days or More

In the morning of Day 4, visit central Pest sights you may have missed, like the Opera House or St. Stephen's Basilica. After lunch, cross the Chain Bridge to Watertown, Buda's historic riverside neighborhood. See St. Anne's Church, the Capuchin Church, and the Király Baths, one of the only remaining examples of Turkish architecture in Budapest. Later, take a ride through the scenic Buda Hills on the Children's Railroad.

On the fifth day, first thing in the morning, visit one of Pest's authentic indoor market halls and sample Hungary's scrumptious fruit in season. Head to the Ethnographical Museum or the Applied Arts Museum, treasure troves of the rich Hungarian culture. After lunch, get away from the hustle and bustle of the city on Margaret Island. Stroll through the rose gardens, rent a bike, or just sunbathe in this peaceful setting. Later, as the sun is setting, return to the Castle District for a final look.

# 1  The Top Attractions in Pest, Buda & Óbuda

## PEST
### MUSEUMS

Museums are closed on Mondays, except where noted. Most museums offer substantial student and senior discounts. Many also offer a family rate. Inquire at the ticket window.

### Néprajzi Múzeum (Ethnographical Museum)

V. Kossuth tér 12. ☎ **1/332-6340.** Admission 200 Ft ($1). Tues–Sun 10am–6pm. Metro: Kossuth tér (Red line).

Directly across Kossuth tér from the House of Parliament, the vast Ethnographical Museum is located in the stately neo-Renaissance/eclectic former Hungarian Supreme Court building. The ornate interior rivals that of the Opera House. A ceiling fresco of Justitia, the goddess of justice, by the well-known artist Károly Lotz, dominates the lobby. Although a third of the museum's holdings are from outside Hungary, concentrate on the items from Hungarian ethnography. The fascinating permanent exhibition, "From Ancient Times to Civilization," features everything from drinking jugs to razor cases to chairs to clothing.

### Szépművészeti Múzeum (Museum of Fine Arts)

XIV. Hősök tere. ☎ **1/343-9759.** Admission 200 Ft ($1), free for students. Tues–Sun 10am– 5:30pm. Metro: Hősök tere (Yellow line).

Planned at the time of the 1896 millennial celebration of the Magyar Conquest, the Museum of Fine Arts opened 10 years later in this neoclassical behemoth on Heroes' Square, at the edge of City Park. The museum is the main repository in Hungary of foreign art; as such, it ranks among Central Europe's major collections. A significant part of the collection was acquired in 1871 from the Esterházys, an enormously wealthy family who had spent centuries amassing great art. There are eight departments: Egyptian Art, Antiquities, Baroque Sculpture, Old Masters, Drawings and Prints, 19th- and 20th-century Masters, and Modern Sculpture. Most great names associated with the old masters—Tiepolo, Tintoretto, Veronese, Titian, Raphael, Van Dyck, Brueghel, Rembrandt, Rubens, Hals, Hogarth, Dürer, Cranach, Holbein,

# Budapest Attractions

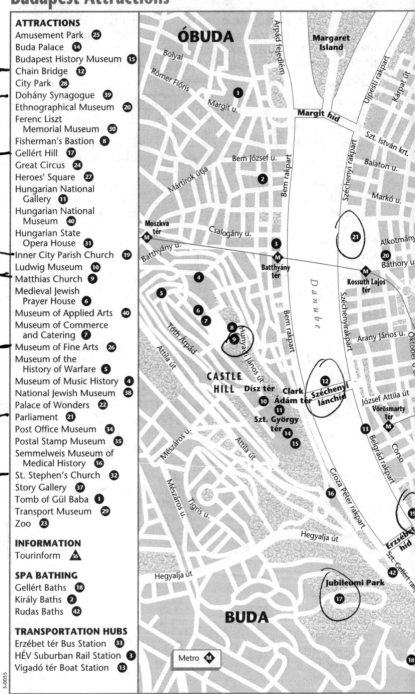

**ATTRACTIONS**
Amusement Park 25
Buda Palace 14
Budapest History Museum 15
Chain Bridge 12
City Park 28
Dohány Synagogue 39
Ethnographical Museum 20
Ferenc Liszt
  Memorial Museum 30
Fisherman's Bastion 8
Gellért Hill 17
Great Circus 24
Heroes' Square 27
Hungarian National
  Gallery 11
Hungarian National
  Museum 40
Hungarian State
  Opera House 31
Inner City Parish Church 19
Ludwig Museum 10
Matthias Church 9
Medieval Jewish
  Prayer House 6
Museum of Applied Arts 40
Museum of Commerce
  and Catering 7
Museum of Fine Arts 26
Museum of the
  History of Warfare 5
Museum of Music History 4
National Jewish Museum 38
Palace of Wonders 22
Parliament 21
Post Office Museum 34
Postal Stamp Museum 35
Semmelweis Museum of
  Medical History 16
St. Stephen's Church 32
Story Gallery 37
Tomb of Gül Baba 1
Transport Museum 29
Zoo 23

**INFORMATION**
Tourinform 36

**SPA BATHING**
Gellért Baths 18
Király Baths 2
Rudas Baths 42

**TRANSPORTATION HUBS**
Erzsébet tér Bus Station 33
HÉV Suburban Rail Station 3
Vigadó tér Boat Station 13

3-0055

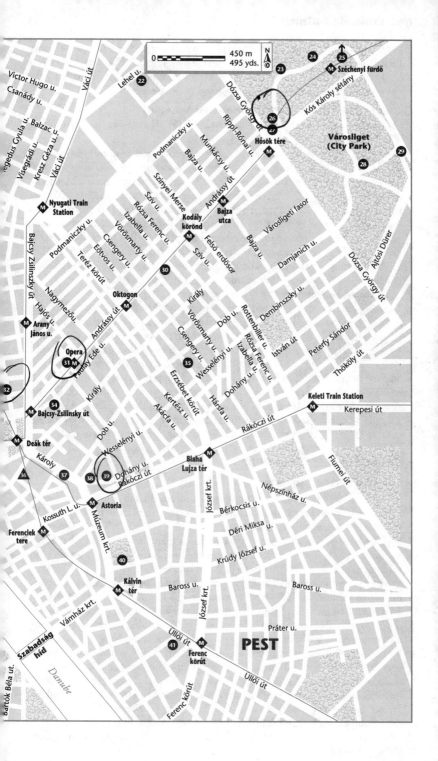

0 ⟞⟞⟞⟞⟞ 450 m
495 yds.

N

Victor Hugo u.
Csanády u.
...gedus Gyula u.
Balzac u.
Visegrádi u.
Kresz Géza u.
Váci út
Váci út
Lehel u. ㉒
Dózsa György út
Rippl-Rónai u.
Hősök tére ㉖ ㉔ ㉓
㉕ Széchenyi fürdő
Kós Károly sétány
Podmaniczky u.
Munkácsy u.
Bajza u.
Andrássy út
Szinyei Merse
Városliget (City Park) ㉘ ㉙
Nyugati Train Station
Podmaniczky u.
Rózsa Ferenc u.
Izabella u.
Vörösmarty u.
Csengery u.
Eötvos u.
Teréz körút
Kodály körönd
Balzac utca
Felső erdősor
Bajza u.
Városligeti fasor
Damjanich u.
Dózsa György út
Aitósi Dürer
Szív u.
Szív u.
㉚
Nagymező u.
Oktogon
Andrássy út
Király
Vörösmarty u.
Csengery u.
Dob u.
Rottenbiller u.
Dembinszky u.
István út
Peterfy Sándor
Thököly út
Arany János u.
Hajós u.
Opera ㉛
Paulay Ede u.
Wesselényi u.
Izabella u.
Rózsa Ferenc u.
㉟
Keleti Train Station
Bajcsy-Zsilinszky út
㉜
Király
Erzsébet körút
Kertész u.
Akácfa u.
Dohány u.
Hársfa u.
Rákóczi út
Kerepesi út
㉞
Bajcsy-Zsilinsky út
Deák tér
Károly
㊱ ㊲ ㊳ ㊴
Dob u.
Wesselényi u.
Dohány u.
Rákóczi út
Blaha Lujza tér
József krt.
Népszínház u.
Fiumei út
Kossuth L. u.
Múzeum krt.
Astoria
Bérkocsis u.
Ferenciek tere
Déri Miksa u.
Krúdy József u.
㊵
Kálvin tér
Baross u.
József krt.
Baross u.
Vámház krt.
Üllői út
Práter u.
Szabadság hid
bartók Béla ut.
Danube
㊶
Ferenc körút
Üllői út
Ferenc körút
PEST

Goya, Velázquez, El Greco, and others—are represented here. Of 19th-century French artists, the museum is best represented by Delacroix, Corot, and Manet. It has been said, though, that while the museum suffers no shortage of works by the old masters, it can boast precious few outright masterpieces.

## ❂ Nemzeti Múzeum (Hungarian National Museum)

VIII. Múzeum krt. 14. ☎ 1/138-2122. Admission 250 Ft ($1.25). Tues–Sun 10am–6pm. Metro: Kálvin tér (Blue line).

The Hungarian National Museum, an enormous neoclassical structure built in 1837–47, was one of the great projects of the early 19th-century Age of Reform, a period that also saw the construction of the Chain Bridge and the National Theater (no longer standing), as well as the development of the modern Hungarian national identity. The museum played a major role in the beginning of the Hungarian Revolution of 1848–49; on its wide steps on March 15, 1848, the poet Sándor Petőfi and other young radicals are said to have exhorted the people of Pest to revolt against the Habsburgs. The very presence of such an imposing structure in the capital, and its exhibits proudly detailing the accomplishments of the Magyars, played a significant role in the development of 19th-century Hungarian nationalism.

The museum's main attraction is the crown of St. Stephen (King Stephen ruled 1000–38), ceremoniously returned by U.S. Secretary of State Cyrus Vance to Hungary in 1978 from the United States, where it had been stored since the end of World War II. Few Hungarians would assert, however, that the two-tiered crown on display ever actually rested on Stephen's head: Its lower part was evidently a gift to King Géza I (1074–77), and its upper part was built for Stephen V, almost 250 years after the first Stephen's death. Out of respect, visitors must put slippers on over their shoes when entering the room where the crown is displayed. The two main museum exhibits on view are "The History of the Peoples of Hungary from the Paleolithic Age to the Magyar Conquest" and "The History of the Hungarian People from the Magyar Conquest to 1989." "The Hungarian Royal Insignia" is another permanent exhibit.

## HISTORIC SQUARES & BUILDINGS

### Hősök tere (Heroes' Square)

Situated at the end of Pest's great boulevard, Andrássy út, and at the entrance to its most famous park, City Park (Városliget), the wide open plaza of Hősök tere (Heroes' Square) is one of the symbols of the city. During the country's Communist era, Socialist holidays were invariably celebrated with huge military reviews in the square. In 1989, a rally here on the day of the reburial of Imre Nagy (executed after the 1956 revolution) attracted 300,000 people to the square.

The square, like the park beyond it, was laid out for the 1896 Magyar Conquest millennial celebration. In its center stands the 118-foot-high Millennial Column; arrayed around the base of the column are equestrian statues of Árpád and the six other Magyar tribal leaders who led the conquest. Behind the column, arrayed along a colonnade, are 14 heroes of Hungarian history, including King Stephen I, the country's first Christian king (first on left); King Matthias Corvinus, who presided over Buda's Golden Age in the 15th century (sixth from right); and Lajos Kossuth, leader of the 1848–49 War of Independence (first on right). The statues were restored in 1996, in honor of the 1,100th anniversary of the Magyar Conquest. Flanking Heroes' Square are two of Budapest's major museums: the Museum of Fine Arts and the Exhibition Hall. Take the metro to Hősök tere (Yellow line). (*Note:* Despite its convenience, avoid eating at Városligeti Étterem, a restaurant across the street from the square—the waiters are rude and dishonest.)

## ✪ Magyar Állami Operaház (Hungarian State Opera House)

VI. Andrássy út 22. ☎ **1/153-0170.** Admission (only on guided tours) 600 Ft ($3). Tours given daily at 3 and 4pm. Metro: Opera (Yellow line).

Completed in 1884, the Opera House, on Pest's elegant Andrássy út, is the crowning achievement of the famous Hungarian architect Miklós Ybl's career. Budapest's most celebrated performance hall, it boasts a fantastically ornate interior featuring frescoes by two of the best-known Hungarian artists of the day, Bertalan Székely and Károly Lotz. Both inside and outside are dozens of statues of such greats as Beethoven, Mozart, Verdi, Wagner, Smetana, Tchaikovsky, and Monteverdi.

Home to both the State Opera and the State Ballet, the Opera House has a rich and evocative history. A political scandal marked the opening performance in 1884. Ferenc Liszt had written a piece to be performed especially for the event, but when it was discovered that he had incorporated elements of the *Rákóczi March*, a patriotic (and anti-Habsburg) Hungarian melody, he was prevented from playing it. Well-known directors of the Opera House have included Gustav Mahler and Ferenc Erkel. See "The Performing Arts," in chapter 9, for information on performances.

### Parliament

V. Kossuth tér. ☎ **1/268-4437.** Admission (by guided tour only): 30-minute tour in English, 700 Ft ($3.50), Mon–Fri, 10am and 2pm and Sat, 10am. Ibusz offers a 2-hour tour in English for 2,400 Ft ($12) on Wed, Fri, and Sat. Starting times vary day to day, depending on Parliament permission. Contact Ibusz ☎ 1/118-1139 to reserve. Closed when Parliament is in session. Metro: Kossuth tér (Red line).

Budapest's great Parliament building, completed in 1902, was built to the eclectic design of Imre Steindl. It mixes a predominant neo-Gothic style with a neo-Renaissance dome. Standing proudly on the Danube bank, visible from almost any riverside vantage point, it has from the outset been one of Budapest's symbols, though until 1989 a democratically elected government had convened here exactly once ( just after World War II, before the Communist takeover). Built at a time of extreme optimism and national purpose, the building was self-consciously intended to be one of the world's great houses of Parliament. It is one of the largest state buildings in Europe. The main copula is decorated with statutes of Hungarian kings. On either side of the copula are waiting rooms leading into the respective houses of Parliament. Here the members of Parliament are said to gather during breaks in the session to smoke and chat. Note the cigar holders on the side of the doors. The waiting room on the Senate side (blue carpet) is adorned with lovely statues of farmers, peasants, tradesmen, and workers. The statues that decorate the waiting room on the representatives' side (red carpet) are of sailors, soldiers, postal officials, etc. The interior decor is predominantly neo-Gothic. The ceiling frescoes are by Károly Lotz, Hungary's best-known artist of that genre. Look for the largest hand-made carpet in Europe, from the small Hungarian village of Békésszentandrás.

## CHURCHES & SYNAGOGUES

### ✪ Dohány Synagogue

VII. Dohány u. 2–8. ☎ **1/342-8949.** Admission by donation. Officially open Tue–Fri 10am–3pm, Sun 10am–1pm. Metro: Astoria (Red line) or Deák tér (all lines).

Built in 1859, this is the world's second-largest synagogue (and the largest in Europe). Budapest's Jewish community still uses it. The architecture has striking Moorish elements; the interior is vast and ornate, with two balconies, and the unusual presence of an organ.

The synagogue has a rich but tragic history. Adolf Eichmann arrived with the occupying Nazi forces in March 1944 to supervise the establishment of the Jewish

*When I got tired of the noisy streets of Pest and the artificial gay life there, I loved to wander about quaint silent Buda, where everything and everybody seemed to have stood still a couple of centuries ago.*
—Elizabeth Keith Morris, English memoirist, 1931

ghetto and the subsequent deportations. He set up his headquarters inside the synagogue itself. Up to 20,000 Jews took refuge inside the synagogue complex, of whom 7,000 did not survive the bleak winter of 1944–45. They're buried in the courtyard, where you can also see a transported piece of the original brick ghetto wall. An ambitious restoration was recently completed, funded in large part by a foundation set up by the American actor Tony Curtis, who is of Hungarian-Jewish descent. The building's original splendor is now apparent. The National Jewish Museum is inside the Synagogue complex (see "More Museums & Sights," below).

### ✪ Belvárosi Plébániatemplom (Inner City Parish Church)
V. Március 15 tér. ☎ 1/118-3108. Free admission. Mon–Sat 6am–7pm, Sun 8am–7pm. Metro: Ferenciek tere (Blue line).

The Inner City Parish Church, standing flush against the Erzsébet Bridge in Pest, is one of the city's great architectural monuments. The 12th-century Romanesque church first built on this spot was constructed inside the remains of the walls of the Roman fortress of Contra-Aquincum. In the early 14th century, a Gothic church was built, and this medieval church, with numerous additions and reconstructions reflecting the architectural trends of the time, stands today. Both Gothic and baroque elements can be observed on the exterior. Inside are niches built in both styles, as well as a *mihrab* (prayer niche) dating from the Turkish occupation, evidence of its conversion in those years to a mosque. The painting on the altar is the work of the 20th-century artist Pál Molnár (his work can also be seen in St. Anne's Church). The church was almost torn down when the Erzsébet Bridge was built in the late 19th century. Fortunately, an alternative plan won out, calling for the new bridge to wind around the church in a serpentine fashion (this interesting construction is best viewed from Gellért Hill). Daily mass is held at 6:30am and 6pm; Sunday mass at 9am, 10am, noon, and 6pm.

### Bazilika (St. Stephen's Church)
V. Szent István tér 33. ☎ 1/117-2859. Church, free; treasury, 80 Ft (40¢); tower, 200 Ft ($1). Church, daily 7am–7pm, except during services; treasury and Szent Jobb Chapel, Mon–Sat 9am–5pm, Sun 1–5pm; tower, daily 10am–4:30pm. Metro: Arany János utca (Blue line) or Bajcsy-Zsilinszky út (Yellow line).

Although not a basilica in the technical sense of the word, Hungarians like to call St. Stephen's "The Basilica" in honor of its sheer size: It's the largest church in the country. The Basilica took over 50 years to build (the collapse of the dome in 1868 caused significant delay); three leading architects, two of whom (József Hild and Miklós Ybl) died before work was finished, presided over its construction. It was finally completed in 1906, but during its long construction Pest had undergone radical growth; strangely, while the front of the church dominates sleepy Szent István tér, the rear faces out onto the far busier Inner Ring boulevard. The bust above the main entrance is of King Stephen, Hungary's first Christian king. Inside the church, in the Chapel of the Holy Right (Szent Jobb Kápolna), you can see Hungarian Catholicism's most cherished—and bizarre—holy relic: Stephen's preserved right hand. The church was considered so sturdy that it was used to store important documents and artworks during World War II bombing. There are great views from the tower, but the climb is not recommended for the weak of knees or lungs. If a church ever needed a good spring cleaning, this is it. Organ concerts are held here at 7pm on Monday evening in summer. Daily mass is held at 8am, 5:30pm, and 6pm; Sunday mass at 8am, 9am, 10am, noon, 6pm, and 7:30pm.

# BUDA
## MUSEUMS

### Budapesti Történeti Múzeum (Budapest History Museum)
I. In Buda Palace, Wing E, on Castle Hill. ☎ 1/175-7533. Admission 200 Ft ($1). Guided tours in English for serious history buffs, 5,000 Ft ($25) available upon advance request. May 15–Sept 15, daily 10am–6pm; Sept 16–May 14, daily 10am–5pm. Closed Tues. Bus: Várbusz from Moszkva tér or 106 from Deák tér to Castle Hill. Funicular: From Clark Ádám tér to Castle Hill.

This museum, also known as the Castle Museum, is the best place to get a sense of the once-great medieval Buda. It might be worth it to you to splurge for a guided tour; even though the museum's descriptions are written in English, the history of the palace's repeated construction and destruction is so confusing and arcane that it's difficult to understand what you're really seeing.

"The Medieval Royal Palace and its Gothic Statues" exhibit consists almost entirely of rooms and artifacts uncovered during the post–World War II excavation and rebuilding of the palace. A visit here is more notable perhaps for the rooms and halls themselves than for the fragments and occasional undamaged pieces of statues, stone carvings, earthenware, and the like. The recently opened "History of Budapest Since 1686" exhibit is most notable for its photographs.

### ✪ Nemzeti Galéria (Hungarian National Gallery)
I. In Buda Palace, Wings B, C, and D, on Castle Hill. ☎ 1/175-7533. Admission 150 Ft (75¢). Guided tours in English for 1,000 Ft ($5). Mar 16–Nov 14, Tues–Sun 10am–6pm; Nov 15–Mar 15, Tues–Sun 10am–4pm. Bus: Várbusz from Moszkva tér or 106 from Deák tér to Castle Hill. Funicular: From Clark Ádám tér to Castle Hill.

A repository of Hungarian art from medieval times to the 20th century, the Hungarian National Gallery is an enormous museum whose entire collection you couldn't possibly view during a single visit. The museum dates its founding to the great reform period of the mid-19th century, and moved to its present location in Buda Palace in 1975. Few people outside Hungary are familiar with even the country's best-known artists. Nevertheless, Hungary has produced some fine artists, particularly in the late 19th century, and this is the place to view their work. The giants of the time are the brilliant Mihály Munkácsy, whose masterpieces include *The Lintmakers, Condemned Cell,* and *Woman Carrying Wood;* László Paál, a painter of village scenes, among whose best pictures are *Village Road in Berzova, Path in the Forest at Fontainbleau,* and *Depth of the Forest;* Károly Ferenczy, whose mastery of light is seen in *Morning Sunshine* and *Evening in March;* and Pál Szinyei Merse, the plein-air artist, whose own development paralleled that of the early French impressionists (see *Picnic in May*). Some other artists to look for are Gyula Benczúr, who painted grand historical scenes; Károly Lotz, best known as a fresco painter (Opera House, Matthias Church), here represented by a number of nudes and several fine thunderstorm paintings; and Bertalan Székely, a painter of historical scenes and landscapes. József Rippl-Rónai's canvases are premier examples of Hungarian post-impressionism and art nouveau (see *Father and Uncle Piacsek Drinking Red Wine* and *Grandmother*), while Tivadar Csontváry Kosztka, the "Rousseau of the Danube," is considered by some critics to be a genius of early modern art. See "The Art of Hungary," in chapter 1, for more information on Hungary's artists.

## A FAMOUS CHURCH

### ✪ Mátyás Templom (Matthias Church)

I. Szentháromság tér 2. ☎ **1/115-5657.** Church, free; exhibition rooms beneath the altar, 100 Ft (50¢). Daily 9am–5pm. Bus: Várbusz from Moszkva tér or 106 from Deák tér Castle Hill. Funicular: From Clark Ádám tér to Castle Hill.

Officially named the Church of Our Lady, the symbol of Buda's Castle District and the protector Saint of all of Hungary, is popularly known as Matthias Church after the much-loved 15th-century king who was twice married here. Although the structure dates to the mid-13th century, like other old churches in Budapest it has an interesting history of destruction and reconstruction, always being refashioned in the architectural style of the time. The last two Hungarian kings (Habsburgs) were crowned in the church: Franz Joseph in 1867 (Liszt wrote and performed his *Coronation Mass*) and Charles IV in 1916. The church interior is decorated with works of two outstanding 19th-century Hungarian painters, Károly Lotz and Bertalan Székely. Organ concerts are held here on most Friday evenings from June to September at 8pm. Daily mass is held at 7am and 6pm; Sunday mass at 7am, 8:30am, 10am, noon, and 6pm.

## SPECTACULAR VIEWS

### Halászbástya (Fisherman's Bastion)

The neo-Romanesque Fisherman's Bastion, perched on the edge of Buda's Castle District near Matthias Church and the Hilton Hotel, affords a marvelous panorama of Pest. Built at the turn of the last century, it was intended mainly for decorative purposes, despite its military appearance. Looking out over the Danube to Pest, you can see (from left to right): Margaret Island and the Margaret Bridge, Parliament, St. Stephen's Basilica, the Chain Bridge with the Hungarian Academy of Sciences and the Gresham Palace behind it, the Vigadó Concert Hall, the Inner City Parish Church, the Erzsébet Bridge, and the Szabadság Bridge. There is an annoying charge of 100 Ft (50¢) just to take in the view from the upper balcony. To get to the Halászbástya, take the Várbusz from Moszkva tér or bus no. 106 from Deák tér, or funicular from Clark Ádám tér to Castle Hill.

### Gellért Hegy (Gellért Hill)

Gellért Hill, towering 230m (750 ft.) above the Danube, offers the single best panorama of the city. The hill is named after the Italian Bishop Gellért, who assisted Hungary's first Christian king, Stephen I, in converting the Magyars. Gellért became a martyr when he was rolled in a barrel to his death from the side of the hill on which this enormous statue now stands. The bishop defiantly holds a cross in his outstretched hand. On top of Gellért Hill you'll find the **Liberation Monument,** built in 1947 supposedly to commemorate the Red Army's liberation of Budapest from Nazi occupation, though many believe that Admiral Horty, Hungary's wartime leader, had planned the statue prior to the liberation to honor his fighter-pilot son who was killed in the war. A mammoth statue, it's one of the last socialist realist memorials you'll find in Hungary. The statue's centerpiece, a giant female figure holding a leaf aloft, is affectionately known as *Kiflis Zsuzsa* (*kifli* is a crescent-shaped roll eaten daily by many Hungarians, while Zsuzsa, or Susie, is a common girl's name). Hungarian children like to call the smaller flame-holding figure on her side *Fagylaltos fiú* (the boy with the ice-cream cone). Also atop Gellért Hill is the **Citadella,** a symbol of power built by the Austrians in 1851, shortly after they crushed the Hungarian War of Independence of 1848–49. It costs 90 Ft (45¢) to enter the Citadella, open daily from 8am to 6pm. To get here, take bus no. 27 from Móricz Zsigmond körtér.

## Impressions

*How much beauty there is in the Chain Bridge, what elegant silence, haughty humility, charming lightness, and archaic melancholy!*
—Antal Szerb, 20th-century Hungarian writer

## ÓBUDA
### ROMAN RUINS

The ruins of Aquincum, the once-bustling capital of the Roman province of Pannonia, are spread throughout the southern part of Óbuda. The various sites are far enough away from each other, and the layout of modern Óbuda sufficiently anti-pedestrian, that it's difficult to see everything. Fortunately, two major sites are right across the street from each other, near the Aquincum station of the suburban HÉV railroad. The ruined **Amphitheater of the Civilian Town** is directly beside the HÉV station. It's open all the time and you're free to wander through (you should know, though, that homeless people now live inside its walls). The main Budapest-Szentendre highway cuts through Óbuda, causing no small amount of pedestrian frustration. Across it stand the ruins of the **Civilian Town.** Everything is visible from the roadside, except for the collection of the **Aquincum Museum,** at III. Szentendrei u. 139 ( ☎ 1/250-1650). This neoclassical structure was built at the end of the 19th century in harmony with its surroundings. The museum exhibits coins, utensils, jewelry, and pottery from Roman times. Entry is 200 Ft ($1). It's open April to October only, Tuesday through Sunday from 10am to 6pm. Take the HÉV suburban railroad from Batthyány tér to Aquincum.

## BRIDGING PEST & BUDA
### SZÉCHENYI LÁNCHÍD (THE CHAIN BRIDGE)

The Chain Bridge is, along with Parliament, the dominant symbol of Budapest. As the first permanent bridge across the Danube (1849), it paved the way for the union of Buda, Óbuda, and Pest into a single city. Prior to 1849, people relied on a pontoon bridge that had to be dismantled when ships passed and could be swept away in stormy weather. The initiative for the Chain Bridge came from the indefatigable Count István Széchenyi, the leading figure of Hungarian society during the mid-19th-century Age of Reform. The Scotsman Adam Clark, for whom the square on the Buda side of the bridge is named, came to Budapest to supervise the massive project; he remained in the city until his death many years later. The bridge was blown up by the retreating Nazis in World War II, but was rebuilt immediately after the war. Located in the heart of the city, it's best admired at night (until midnight), when it's lit up like a chandelier. It's an easy walk across if you're heading to Castle Hill—or merely want a mid-river view of Pest.

## 2  More Museums & Sights in Pest, Buda & Óbuda

## PEST

### ✪ Iparművészeti Múzeum (Museum of Applied Arts)
IX. Üllői út 33–37. ☎ 1/217-5222. Admission 120 Ft (60¢); free Tues. Tues–Sun 10am–6pm. Metro: Ferenc körút (Blue line).

It's worth a trip to the Museum of Applied Arts just to see the marvelous building it's housed in, designed by Ödön Lechner in the 1890s. Lechner, whose most famous

# Where Have All the Statues Gone?

Ever wonder where all the vanished Communist statues went after the fall? Only a few short years ago Budapest, and the rest of Hungary for that matter, was filled with memorials to Lenin, to Marx and Engels, to the Red Army, and to the many lesser-known figures of Hungarian and international Communist history. Boldly torn from their pedestals in the aftermath of 1989, they sat for a few years in warehouses gathering dust, until a controversial plan for a **Socialist Statue Park**—Szoborpark Múzeum—was born. It sounded like a great idea, a must-see for Western tourists. However, the park's inconvenient location and the relatively small number of statues on display (reflecting nothing of their former ubiquitousness) make it much less than it could be. Another drawback is that the best examples of the genre, dating from the Stalinist period of the late 1940s and 1950s, were removed from public view long before 1989 and have presumably been destroyed.

Located in the XXII district (extreme southern Buda) on Balatoni út (☎ **1/227-7446**), the museum park is a memorial to an era and to despotism, but more than anything else perhaps, to bad taste. The museum gift shop sells all sorts of Communist-era memorabilia, such as T-shirts, medals, and Red Army marching songs on cassette. Admission is 200 Ft ($1). The park is open March to October 10am to 5pm, June to August, 8am to 8pm. To get here, take the black-lettered bus no. 7 from Ferenciek tere to Kosztolányi Dezsó tér. Board a yellow bus (to Érd) at Platform 6 for a 20-minute ride to the park.

creation is the Town Hall in the Great Plain city of Kecskemét (see chapter 13), is the architect who was most adventurous in combining traditional Hungarian folk elements with the art nouveau style of his time. The building's ceramic decoration comes from the famous Zsolnay factory in Pécs. If you're impressed by this structure, pay a visit to the former Post Office Savings Bank on Hold utca, another fine example of Lechner's work (see "Walking Tour 3—Leopold Town & Theresa Town," in chapter 7). The museum's permanent exhibits are divided into five sections: furniture; textiles; metalwork; ceramics, porcelain, and glass; and an eclectic display of books, leather, and ivory. Much of the museum's space is given to temporary exhibitions.

## Nemzeti Zsidó Múzeum (National Jewish Museum)

VII. Dohány u. 2–8. ☎ **1/342-8949**. Admission by donation. Mon–Sat 10am–3pm, Sun 10am–1pm. Metro: Astoria (Red line) or Deák tér (all lines).

The museum is located in the Dohány Synagogue complex; a tablet outside informs visitors that Theodor Herzl, the founder of Zionism, was born on this spot. The four-room museum is devoted to the long history of Jews in Hungary. Displays include Sabbath and holiday items (including some gorgeous examples of Herend Passover plates) and ritual and everyday artifacts. The last room contains a small but moving exhibit on the Holocaust in Hungary.

## ✪ Postamúzeum (Post Office Museum)

VI. Andrássy út 3. ☎ **1/269-6838**. Admission 50 Ft (25¢). Tues–Sun 10am–6pm. Metro: Bajcsy-Zsilinszky út (Yellow line) or Deák tér (all lines).

The exhibits here are of limited interest, but the building itself and the apartment in which the museum is situated—the opulently furnished former Sexlehner family flat—are simply dazzling. Chandeliers dangle from the frescoed ceilings and intricately carved wood moldings trim the walls.

# Óbuda & Margaret Island Area

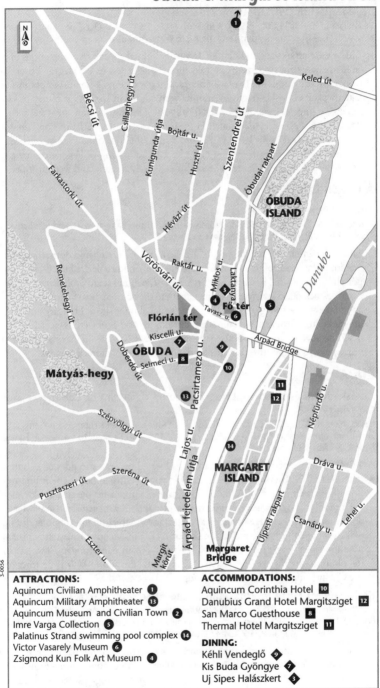

**ATTRACTIONS:**

Aquincum Civilian Amphitheater ❶
Aquincum Military Amphitheater ⓭
Aquincum Museum  and Civilian Town ❷
Imre Varga Collection ❺
Palatinus Strand swimming pool complex ⓮
Victor Vasarely Museum ❻
Zsigmond Kun Folk Art Museum ❹

**ACCOMMODATIONS:**

Aquincum Corinthia Hotel 🔟
Danubius Grand Hotel Margitsziget 🔢
San Marco Guesthouse 🔢
Thermal Hotel Margitsziget 🔢

**DINING:**

Kéhli Vendeglő ❾
Kis Buda Gyöngye ❼
Uj Sipes Halászkert ❸

113

## Béyegmúzeum (Postal Stamp Museum)

VII. Hársfa u. 47. ☎ **1/341-5526.** Admission 50 Ft (25¢). May–Oct, Tues–Sun 10am–6pm; Nov–Apr, Tues–Sun 10am–4pm. Tram: 4 or 6 to Wesselényi utca.

This may seem like an attraction of decidedly limited appeal, but generations of philatelists the world over have admired the artistic creations of Magyar Posta. This wonderful little museum has rack after rack of the country's finest stamps. The mistakenly printed upside-down "Madonna with Child" in Rack 49 is Hungary's most valuable stamp. The stamps of Rack 65 abjectly demonstrate how the worst inflation the world has ever seen devastated Hungary in the 1940s. Variations on Lenin and Stalin can be seen in Racks 68 to 77, and Racks 70 to 80 contain numerous brilliant examples of socialist realism. You don't have to be a stamp collector to enjoy a visit to the Postal Stamp Museum. The staff is extremely friendly and well informed.

## A JEWISH CEMETERY

### Kozma Cemetery

X. Kozma u. 6. ☎ **1/342-1335.** Free admission. Mon–Thurs 8am–4pm, Fri and Sun 8am–2pm. Tram: 37 from Blaha Lujza tér to the next to last stop.

The city's main Jewish cemetery is in the eastern end of the Kőbánya district, a long train ride from the center of town. An estimated half-million people are buried here. A vast, peaceful place, it's still in use today. Ornate art deco tombs stand proudly near the main entrance, their faded grandeur a testament both to the status of those buried beneath them and to the steady passage of time. The cemetery is also the site of Hungary's most moving Holocaust memorial, a set of nine walls with the names of victims etched in. About 6,500 names appear, of the 600,000 Hungarian Jews estimated to have perished in the war. Survivors and relatives have penciled in hundreds of additional names.

# BUDA

## Kereskedelmi és Vendéglátóipari Múzeum (Museum of Commerce and Catering)

I. Fortuna u. 4. ☎ **1/175-6249.** Admission 80 Ft (40¢). Wed and Thurs 10am–5pm; Sat and Sun 10am–6pm. Bus: Várbusz from Moszkva tér or 106 from Deák tér to Castle Hill. Funicular: From Clark Ádám tér to Castle Hill.

These are two separate but related exhibits located on opposite sides of a courtyard in the Castle District; a single ticket entitles you to entry to both. The prime attraction of the catering exhibit is the antique baking equipment: pie tins, cookie molds, and utensils. The commerce exhibit has a wider appeal, with assorted (somewhat randomly assembled) vintage items: cigar boxes, advertisements, liquor bottles, fountain pens, sewing equipment, and ration books. A "Gyula Meinl" display shows that the ubiquitous Austrian grocery chain had an early presence in Hungary. Two fascinating photos (why they're here is inexplicable) show the World War II destruction of the Chain Bridge and the Erzsébet Bridge.

## Hadtörténeti Múzeum (Museum of the History of Warfare)

I. Tóth Árpád sétány 40. ☎ **1/156-9522.** Admission 250 Ft ($1.25). Apr–Sept Tues–Sun 10am–6pm, Oct–Mar, Tues–Sun 10am–4pm. Bus: Várbusz from Moszkva tér or 106 from Deák tér to Castle Hill. Funicular: From Clark Ádám tér to Castle Hill.

Housed in a former barracks in the northwestern corner of the Castle District, this museum has exhibits from the time of the Turkish occupation to the 20th century. Uniforms, decorations, models, weapons, maps, and photographs are unfortunately accompanied only by Hungarian text. The Turkish weaponry display is particularly interesting, but the highlight is undoubtedly the room devoted to the 1956 Hungarian

Uprising. Here, consecutive panels of large, mounted photographs detail the 13 chaotic days. Artifacts round out the display, in particular a Soviet flag with the center cut out (where the hammer and sickle were), and the legendary hand of Stalin, the only known surviving piece of the giant statue of the Soviet dictator whose public destruction was one of the failed uprising's dramatic moments. Toy soldiers are available in the gift shop.

### Ludwig Museum

I. In Buda Palace, Wing A, on Castle Hill. ☎ 1/175-9575. Admission 100 Ft (50¢); free Tues. Tues–Sun 10am–6pm. Bus: Várbusz from Moszkva tér or 106 from Deák tér to Castle Hill. Funicular: From Clark Ádám tér to Castle Hill.

In the northern end of the Buda Palace, this was formerly the Museum of the Hungarian Worker's Movement. Now converted to a more politically correct purpose, it houses a less-than-inspiring permanent exhibition of contemporary Hungarian and international art.

### Középkori Zsidó Imaház (Medieval Jewish Prayer House)

I. Táncsics Mihály u. 26. ☎ 1/342-1335. Free admission. May–Oct Tues–Fri 10am–2pm, Sat–Sun 10am–6pm. Bus: Várbusz from Moszkva tér or 106 from Deák tér to Castle Hill. Funicular: From Clark Ádám tér to Castle Hill.

This tiny, medieval Sephardic synagogue was unexpectedly discovered in the 1960s during general excavation work in the Castle District. It dates to approximately 1364, when Jews were allowed to return to the Castle District, from which they had been expelled four years earlier by King Lajos. But after the massacre of Jews that occurred in Buda in the late 17th century (following the defeat of the occupying Turks by a Habsburg-led Christian army), the synagogue was turned into an apartment and, over the ensuing centuries, forgotten. A nearby excavation unearthed the ruins of another, much larger, synagogue dating from 1461; all that remains of it are a keystone, on display now inside this synagogue, and three stone columns standing in the courtyard here. Some Hebrew gravestones are also on display behind a grate in the entryway; the small one in the center of the front row dates from the 3rd century A.D. The English-speaking caretaker will give you a free informal tour if you express an interest.

### Semmelweis Orvostörténeti Múzeum (Semmelweis Museum of Medical History)

I. Apród u. 1–3. ☎ 1/175-3533. Admission 80 Ft (40¢). Tues–Sun 10:30am–5:30pm. Take any bus or tram to Döbrentei tér (for example, bus no. 8 from Március 15 tér).

This museum, which traces the history of medicine from ancient times to the modern era, is located in the former home of Ignác Semmelweis, Hungary's leading 19th-century physician. Semmelweis is hailed as the "savior of mothers" for his role in identifying the cause of puerperal (childbed) fever and preventing it by advocating that physicians wash their hands between patients. The museum, spread over four rooms, displays everything from early medical instruments to anatomical models to old medical textbooks. There's also a faithfully reconstructed 19th-century pharmacy. Descriptions are only in Hungarian, but many exhibits are self-explanatory. In the Semmelweis Memorial Room, two bookcases display the eminent scholar's collection of medical texts. Keen eyes might notice the seven volumes of Osler's *Modern*

### Impressions

*There is no other town of the land of the faithful, and perhaps in all the world which gushes forth in such wonderful abundance its springs to cure all ills, as Buda.*
—Evlia Chelebi, Turkish traveler, 16th century

> **❷ Did You Know?**
>
> • A network consisting of 10 kilometers (6 miles) of tunnels, built in the Middle Ages for military purposes, lies underneath Buda's Castle District. Visitors can join up with nighttime lantern tours through Buda's bowels, as it were.
>
> • Budapest was the site of the European continent's very first underground metro line, which you can still ride today (the Yellow line).
>
> • Budapest did not become a unified city until 1873, when Pest, Buda, and Óbuda merged.
>
> • All of Budapest's bridges were blown up by the retreating Nazis in the final days of World War II.
>
> • The Red Army liberated Pest from Nazi occupation on January 18, 1945, but did not manage to liberate Buda until February 13.
>
> • The Swedish diplomat Raoul Wallenberg, stationed in Budapest, saved thousands of Jews from Nazi deportation by issuing fake passports and setting up "safe houses," only to disappear himself into the Soviet gulag after the city's liberation.
>
> • Budapest's Jewish population (about 80,000) is the largest of any European city outside Russia.
>
> • Budapest is home to the northernmost Turkish shrine in Europe, the tomb of Gúl Baba.
>
> • The elusive chess champion Bobby Fischer, who recently came out of hiding, is rumored to be living in Budapest.

*Medicine,* written long after Semmelweis's death; they were a gift from U.S. President George Bush to the late József Antall, who became the prime minister of Hungary after the first democratic elections in 1990. Antall had previously been director of the Semmelweis Museum.

## A MUSLIM SHRINE

### ✪ Gúl Baba Türbéje (Tomb of Gúl Baba)
II. Mecset u. 14. Admission 100 Ft (50¢). Tues–Sun 10am–6pm. Tram: 4 or 6 to the Buda side of Margaret Bridge; the most direct route to Gúl Baba tér is via Mecset utca, off Margaret utca.

The unfortunate Turkish dervish Gúl Baba died at dinner. It was no ordinary meal either, but a 1541 gala in Matthias Church celebrating the conquest of Buda. Gúl Baba was a member of a Turkish order involved in horticulture, specifically in the development of new species of roses; today his tomb, located in a wonderfully steep, twisting neighborhood at the beginning of the Hill of Roses (Rózsadomb) district, is maintained as a Muslim shrine by the Turkish government. The descriptions are in Hungarian and Turkish, but an English-language pamphlet is available on request. The tomb is set in a park, surrounded by lovely rose gardens. The ancient tomb is the northernmost Muslim shrine in Europe. The museum was recently restored, and was reopened in 1997 in an official ceremony attended by Turkey's President Demirel.

## ÓBUDA

### ✪ Lakásmúzeum (Zsigmond Kun Folk Art Museum)
III. Fő tér 4. ☎ **1/250-1020.** Admission 100 Ft (50¢); English-language guidebook 50 Ft (25¢). Tues–Sun 2–6pm. Train: HÉV suburban railroad from Batthyány tér to Árpád híd.

Here in Zsigmond Kun's former apartment you can admire his wonderful collection of Hungarian folk art. For almost a century he traveled around Hungary collecting and documenting folk art. On display are ceramics and brandy flasks, tapestries and chairs, sheep bells, shepherds' hats, and hundreds of other examples of Hungarian folk art. The 104-year-old Kun is said to enjoy excellent health and to be writing his memoirs. The museum staff speaks fondly of "Zsigmond Bácsi" (Uncle Zsigmond).

## ✪ Varga Imre Gyűjtemény (Imre Varga Collection)

III. Laktanya u. 7. ☎ **1/250-0274.** Admission 100 Ft (50¢). Tues–Sun 10am–6pm. Train: HÉV suburban railroad from Batthyány tér to Árpád híd.

Imre Varga is Hungary's best-known contemporary sculptor. This small museum, just off Óbuda's Fő tér, shows a good cross section of his sensitive, piercing work. Historical subjects on display inside the museum range from the pudgy, balding figure of Imre Nagy, reluctant hero of the 1956 Hungarian Uprising, to the dapper, capped Béla Bartók. The museum also has a garden where Varga's sad, broken figures stand forlornly or sit on benches resting their weary feet; cats also live in the garden, enhancing the atmosphere. For an example of the sculptor's work in a public context, see the recently installed statue of Imre Nagy near Parliament.

## Victor Vasarely Museum

III. Szentlelek tér 1. ☎ **1/250-1540.** Admission 60 Ft (30¢); free Wed. Tues–Sun 10am–6pm. Train: HÉV suburban railroad from Batthyány tér to Árpád híd.

This museum, devoted to the works of the Hungarian-born founder of op art, was opened in 1987 after the artist donated some 400 works to the Hungarian state. A huge, airy place, it extends over two floors. On display is a full range of Vasarely's colorful, geometric art. Vasarely died just recently, in the spring of 1997.

## AN ARCHITECTURAL WONDER

### Leo Frankel Synagogue

III. Frankel Léo u. 49. Not officially open to the public. Tram: 17 from the Buda side of Margaret Bridge.

Still in use today, the Frankel Leo Synagogue is about as bizarre an architectural creation as Budapest has to offer. This seemingly normal apartment building looks no different from its neighbors—until you notice the Star of David and the menorah carved into its facade. But that's just the beginning: The synagogue is lodged inside and completely fills the interior courtyard. The two structures were built contemporaneously in the late 19th century. Apparently, there were enough Jews living there who didn't feel like having to walk to prayer.

The whole scene is best viewed from above. Climb the stairs, or take the antique elevator, to gain perspective. The synagogue itself is not open regularly, but entry is not necessary to appreciate it. (You can enter the apartment building if not the synagogue.) An official tour of the synagogue is possible with Chosen Tours (see "Specialty Tours," below).

# 3  Parks, Gardens & Playgrounds

Hungarians love a stroll in the park, and on weekends and summer afternoons, it seems as if the whole of Budapest is out enjoying what Hungarians lovingly refer to as "the nature."

Popular **Margaret Island (Margit-sziget)** has been a public park since 1908. The long, narrow island, connected to both Buda and Pest via the Margaret and Árpád bridges, is barred to most vehicular traffic. In addition to three important ruins—the Dominican Convent, a 13th- to 14th-century Franciscan church, and a 12th-century Premonstratensian chapel—facilities on the island include the Palatinus Strand open-air baths (see "Spa Bathing & Swimming," below), which draw upon the famous thermal waters under Margaret Island; the Alfréd Hajós Sport Pool; and the Open Air Theater. Sunbathers line the steep embankments along the river, and bicycles are available for rent. (See "Getting Around by Bike" in chapter 3.) There are also several snack bars and open-air restaurants. Despite all this, Margaret Island is a quiet, tranquil place. In any direction off the main road you can find well-tended gardens or a patch of grass under the shade of a willow tree for a private picnic. Margaret Island is best reached by bus no. 26 from Nyugati tér, which runs the length of the island, or tram no. 4 or 6, which stops at the entrance to the island midway across the Margaret Bridge. (*Warning:* These are popular lines for pickpockets. See "Fast Facts: Safety" in chapter 3.)

**City Park (Városliget)** is an equally popular place to spend a summer day, and families are everywhere in evidence. Heroes' Square, at the end of Andrássy út, is the most logical starting point for a walk in City Park. Built in 1896 as part of the Hungarian millennial celebrations, it has been the site of some important moments of Hungarian history. The lake behind the square is used for boating in summer and for ice skating in winter. The Vajdahunyad Castle was built as a temporary structure in 1896 for the millennial celebration to demonstrate the different architectural styles in Hungary; it was so popular that a permanent structure was eventually designed to replace it. The park's Animal Garden Boulevard (Állatkerti körút), the favorite street of generations of Hungarian children, is where the zoo, the circus, and the amusement park are all found (see "Especially for Kids," below). Gundel, Budapest's most famous restaurant, is also here, as are the Széchenyi Baths, with a splendid outdoor pool. The southern end of City Park is considerably less crowded, with fewer buildings. The Transport Museum is among the few sights here, while the nearby Petőfi Csarnok is the venue for a variety of cultural events.

The Yellow metro line makes stops at Hősök tere (Heroes' Square), at the edge of the park, and Széchenyi Fürdő, in the middle of it.

There are numerous parks and nature reserves in the **Buda Hills.** You can ride the Children's Railroad through the hills or the János Hill chair lift to its highest point (see "Especially for Kids," below). The Buda Hills are a great place to explore on your own; you'll hardly ever stray too far from a bus or tram line, and yet you'll feel as if you're in the countryside, far from a bustling capital city. Moszkva tér is the best place to start an excursion into the hills. Pick up tram no. 56 or bus no. 21, 22, or 28; get off when you see an area you like.

Our 20-month-old son, Aryeh, spent several months in Budapest and served as our official consultant on **playgrounds.** You can depend on his recommendations; this kid knows a good playground when he sees one. The Hungarian word for playground is *játszótér* (or *játszó kert*).

His favorite is in **Károly kert,** a wonderful little enclosed park in the southern half of the Inner City, bordered by Ferenczy István utca, Magyar utca, and Henszlmann Imre utca. To enter the park, you must pass through a gigantic wrought-iron gate. Once inside, you'll find an enclosed area with swings and seesaws; an enclosed miniature soccer pitch; a sandbox with a slide emptying into it (common in Hungarian playgrounds); and a fairly shaggy field. In the middle is a fountain surrounded by flowers. The equipment here is not as modern or as varied as at some of the city's other playgrounds, but the place has a distinct old-world charm and its location in the Inner City makes it a convenient destination.

Another fine playground is located not far from Buda's busy transportation hub, Móricz Zsigmond körtér. At the intersection of Villányi út and Tas Vezér utca (directly across the street from the Hotel Flamenco), this playground is entirely self-enclosed (no dogs allowed), it is very large, and it has lots of modern equipment. Everything is clean and well-maintained.

Pest's **City Park** (see above) has a nice playground called *Iskolás játszókert*. It is in the southwest corner of the park, near the intersection of Dózsa György út and Ajtósi Dürer sor. This narrow, rectangularly shaped playground has a great wooden climbing structure and innovative swings— a tire swing and a hammock swing.

Margaret Island, for all its charm, lacks a decent playground. The best it has to offer is just off the main road to the left after you pass the stadium at the head of the island.

If you find yourself in Buda's Watertown district (perhaps on our Watertown walking tour, see chapter 7), and you need to make a little play stop, there is a small, neighborhood playground on Franklin utca, between Donáti utca and Iskola utca. It is a quiet, residential area.

Another neighborhood playground is found in **Pillangó Park,** just across the street from the Pillangó utca station of the metro (Red line). This playground is situated in the midst of a huge Socialist-era housing development in outer Pest. The architecture is not pretty, but this is how most people live in Budapest; it's worth a look. The playground features a manually operated merry-go-round for the little ones, and another nearby playground has a cable swing for bigger kids.

Rainy day desperation? Take the kids to the Moszkva tér McDonald's, which has a rather nice indoor playground. No one seems to care whether you are a customer or not.

# 4  Especially for Kids

The following attractions are for kids of all ages, since just about everyone loves a train ride in the hills, a Ferris wheel, or a good puppet show. Three attractions here—the zoo, the amusement park, and the circus—are located in City Park (Városliget), along the famed Animal Garden Boulevard (Állatkerti körút). You could easily spend a whole children-oriented day here.

See also later in this chapter for information on the Palatinus Strand outdoor swimming pool complex and horse and pony riding in the Buda Hills.

## MUSEUMS

### Természettudományi Múzeum (Museum of Natural History)

VIII. Ludovika tér 6. ☎ **1/313-5015.** Admission 200 Ft ($1) adults, 90 Ft (45¢) children over 3, free for children under 3; free admission on Fridays from 1pm–6pm. Open Wed–Mon, 10am–6pm. Closed Tuesdays. Metro: Nagyvárad tér (Blue line).

Opened in 1996, the museum features a large "discovery room" on the first floor, in which all the exhibits are interactive. Participation in them is both educational and fun. The museum is nicely situated next to Orczy Kert (Orczy Garden), a large park featuring over 100 different species of trees and a small lake. Until after World War II, the park belonged to the Ludoviceum, the Hungarian Military School, which now houses the museum.

### Csodák Palotája (Palace of Wonders)

XIII. Váci út 19. ☎ **1/270-6131.** Admission 300 Ft ($1.50) adults, 250 Ft ($1.25) children over 3, free for children under 3. Tue–Fri, 9am–5pm; Sat–Sun, 10am–6pm. Metro: Lehel tér (Blue line). From the metro station, walk north on Váci út (in direction of Bulcsu utca and Déval utca).

## Impressions

*The last time we were here we happened to see the breaking of the winter's ice, and it was a wondrous sight to behold the great blocks borne down by the swift current, heave and struggle and beat against each other, and then clash headlong against the massive stonework of the Chain Bridge, with a crash like that of a volley of musketry.*
> —Nina Elizabeth Mazuchalli, English traveler, 1881

Opened in 1997, and sponsored in part by the Soros Foundation, Csodák Palotája is an interactive science center featuring dozens of fun, educational exhibits in one large room—for instance, lasers, optical puzzles, and mazes. Best for kids over 3 years old.

### Mesegaléria
V. Károly krt. 22, ☎ 1/117-7843). Free admission. Tue–Sat, 10am–6pm. Metro: Astoria (Red line).

This art gallery for kids features enchanting original illustrations from Hungarian children's literature. Works by Károly Reich and Piroska Szántó are particularly lovely. The work is hung at the appropriate eye-level; all works are for sale.

# FAMILY FUN IN CITY PARK

### ✪ Vidám Park (Amusement Park)
XIV. Állatkerti krt. 14–16. ☎ 1/343-0996. Free admission; rides 100–200 Ft (50¢–$1). Apr–Sept, daily 10am–8pm; Oct–Mar, 10am–6pm. Metro: Széchenyi fürdő (Yellow line).

Much frequented by Hungarian families, Vidám Park (literally "Happy Park"), unlike Disneyland or Copenhagen's Tivoli, is eminently affordable. Two rides in particular are not to be missed. The 100-year-old **Merry-Go-Round (*Körhinta*)**, constructed almost entirely of wood, was recently restored to its original, delightful grandeur. The riders must actively pump to keep the horses rocking. Authentic wurlitzer music plays. As the carousel spins round and round, it creaks mightily. The **Ferris wheel (*Óriáskerék*)** is also wonderful, although it has little in common with the rambunctious Ferris wheels of the modern age. A gangly, bright yellow structure, it rotates at a liltingly slow pace, gently lifting you high into the sky for a remarkable view. The Vidám Park also features Europe's longest wooden **roller coaster.**

Parents must pay for a ticket when accompanying young children, even if the child is too young to go on a ride by him or herself.

Next door is a toddlers' amusement park **(Kis Vidám Park),** although several rides in the Vidám Park are also suitable for toddlers.

### Közlekedési Múzeum (Transport Museum)
XIV. Városligeti krt. 11. ☎ 1/343-0565. Admission 100 Ft (50¢); free Wed. Tues–Fri 10am–5pm, Sat–Sun 10am–6pm. Trolleybus: 74 from Károly körút (pick it up on Dohány utca, across the street from Dohány Synagogue).

Located near the Petőfi Csarnok in the little touristed southeastern corner of City Park, this wonderful museum features large-scale working models of various kinds of historic transportation mechanisms, especially trains. On weekends, a film on aviation history is shown at 11am. The aviation exhibit is housed in the Petőfi Csarnok, an all-purpose community center nearby.

### Állatkert (Zoo)
XIV. Állatkerti krt. 6–12. ☎ 1/343-6075. Admission Mon–Fri, 150 Ft (75¢) adults, 100Ft (50¢) students, 80 Ft (40¢) children 14 and under; Sat–Sun, 200 Ft ($1) adults, 150 Ft (75¢) students,

100 Ft (50¢) children 14 and under. Daily 9am–6pm (to 3pm in winter). Metro: Hősök tere or Széchenyi fürdő (Yellow line).

Opened in 1866, the zoo is located near the circus and the amusement park on City Park's famous Animal Garden Boulevard, a favorite spot for Hungarian youngsters for 130 years. Although the zoo has been modernized several times, it still retains the sad flavor of an old-style, fairly inhumane zoo. Nice attractions here are the pony rides and two important examples of art nouveau architecture: the main entrance gate and the elephant house. Two recently renovated greenhouses contain spectacular tropical plants.

## A RAILROAD & CHAIR LIFT

### Gyermekvasút (Children's Railroad)

Hungarian children, specially trained and under adult supervision, run this scenic narrow-gauge railway, making it especially exciting for youngsters. The youthful engineers are dressed in miniature versions of the official MÁV (Hungarian State Railways) uniforms, with all the appropriate paraphernalia. The railway was built in the late 1940s and was formerly run by the Young Pioneers, the youth movement of the Communist Party, although these days it has no political affiliation. The train winds its way slowly through the Buda Hills, providing numerous panoramas along the way. One-way travel time is 45 minutes; call the Széchenyi Hegy terminus ( ☎ 1/395-5420) for more information.

A round-trip costs 140 Ft (70¢), half price for children 13 and under. It's open Monday through Friday from 10am to 5pm and on Saturday and Sunday from 10am to 6pm; closed on Mondays from September through March. To the Széchen yi-hegy terminus, take the cogwheel railway (fogaskerekú vasút) from Városmajor (across the street from the Hotel Budapest, on Szilágyi Erzsébet fasor in Buda) to the last stop. To the Hűvösvölgy terminus, take tram no. 56 from Moszkva tér to the last stop.

### ✪ János-Hegy Libegő (János Hill Chair Lift)

This somewhat primitive chair lift, at XII. Zugligeti út 93, takes you up János Hill to within a steep 10-minute walk of Budapest's highest point. At the top is the neo-Romanesque **Erzsébet Kilátó (Lookout Tower),** built in 1910. Presently it costs 50 Ft (25¢) to climb the tower (well worth it for the glorious view); you'll find a nondescript snack bar there. We expect this to change, however, since a private company just purchased the rights to develop the lookout tower; a "cultural and entertainment center" is planned. You can ride the chair back down, hike back down to the no. 158 bus, or, if you have a map of the Buda Hills, hike out to any number of other bus connections. Call Tourinform ( ☎ 1/117-9800) for more information.

A one-way trip costs 150 Ft (75¢) for adults, 80 Ft (40¢) for children; a round-trip is 200 Ft ($1) for adults, 160 Ft (80¢) for children. The chair lift operates April 1 through September 15, 9am to 5pm; September 16 through March 31, 9am to 4pm. Closed on Mondays of odd weeks. Take bus no. 158 from Moszkva tér to the last stop.

## ENTERTAINMENT: THE CIRCUS, PUPPET THEATERS & FOLK DANCING

### Nagy Cirkusz (Great Circus)

XIV. Állatkerti krt. 7. ☎ **1/343-9630.** Tickets 250–520 Ft ($1.75–$2.60); children under 4 free. Metro: Hősök tere or Széchenyi fürdő (Yellow line).

It's not the Big Apple Circus or Cirque de Soleil, but kids love it just the same. Actually, Budapest has a long circus tradition, though most Hungarian circus stars opt for the more glamorous and financially rewarding circus life abroad. When buying tickets it's helpful to know that *porond* means ring level and *erkély* means balcony. The box office is open from 10am to 7pm. Performances are held Wednesday through Sunday, except in September and October.

○ **Bábszínházak (Puppet Theaters)**

Kids from all countries love Hungarian puppet theater. The shows are all in Hungarian, but with such standard fare as *Cinderella, Peter and the Wolf,* and *Snow White,* no one has trouble following the plot. The audience is an important part of the show: Hungarian children shriek "*Rossz farkas!*" ("Bad wolf!"), for instance, at every appearance of the villainous wolf in *Peter and the Wolf.* Budapest has two puppet theaters, with the season running from September to mid-June. Tickets are extremely cheap, usually in the 150- to 350-Ft (75¢ to $1.75) range. The **Budapest Puppet Theater (Budapesti Bábszínház)** is at VI. Andrássy út 69 (☎ 1/321-5200); the nearest metro station is Oktogon (Yellow line). The **Kolibri Puppet Theater (Kolibri Bábszínház)** is at VI. Jókai tér 10 (☎ 1/153-4633); Jókai tér is halfway between the Oktogon and Opera stations of the Yellow metro line. Shows start at various times throughout the day, and tickets are available all day at the box offices.

**Táncház (Folk Dancing)**

This participatory evening of folk music and folk dancing ranks as one of the best cultural experiences your kids can have while visiting Hungary. The music is always live, with some of the leading Hungarian folk bands playing. The **FMH Cultural House (Szakszervezetek Fővárosi Művelődési Háza),** XI. Fehérvári út 47 (☎ 1/203-3868) hosts a táncház just for kids every Tuesday, from 5:30pm–6:30pm, for 100 Ft (50¢). Tram no. 47 from Deák tér gets you there. The **First District Cultural Center,** at I. Bem rakpart 6 (☎ 1/201-0324), also hosts a táncház hour for kids every Friday evening, September through May, at 5pm, preceding its regular táncház. The First District Cultural Center is near Clark Ádám tér, which is served by a large number of buses and trams, including bus no. 16 from Deák tér.

## IN-LINE SKATING & ICE SKATING

**Görzenál Roller Blading**

III. Árpád fejedelem út 2000. ☎ **1/250-4800.** Admission 300 Ft ($1.50); students 200 Ft ($1). Daily 10am–10pm. Bus: 6 from Nyugati pu. Train: HÉV suburban railway from Battyhány tér to Árpád fejedelem.

If your kids enjoy in-line skating, skateboarding, and trampolining, this is the place for them. Rental skates are available, and for a small fee you can spend the day.

**JégPálya (Ice Rink)**

XIII. Váci út 178. ☎ **1/465-1209.** Admission 250 Ft ($1.25) for 2 hours. Daily 9am–9pm. Metro: Gyöngyösi utca (Blue line).

This ice skating rink is located in the first Western-style shopping mall in Budapest, the Duna Plaza. Skates can be rented (rental is actually included in the admission price). This small rink, suitable only for kids, will at least keep them busy while you shop.

**Pólus Center**

XV. Szentmihályi u. 131. ☎ **1/419-4070.** Admission 200 Ft ($1) for 1 hour. 100 Ft (50¢) to rent skates. Trolley bus: 6 from Keleti station.

Pólus Center rink is twice the size of the rink in the Duna Plaza shopping mall.

## 5  Sightseeing for the Music Enthusiast

Three museums in Budapest celebrate the contributions that great Hungarian artists have made to the realm of music.

The greatest Hungarian composer of the 19th century, and one of the country's most famous sons, was undoubtedly Ferenc (Franz) Liszt (1811–96). Although Liszt spent most of his life abroad, he maintained a deep interest in Hungarian culture and musical traditions, as evidenced by his well-known "Hungarian Rhapsodies." He also was one of the great virtuoso pianists of his century. Liszt created the symphonic poem, its first manifestation being *Les Preludes* (1848). He served as the first president of Budapest's Academy of Music, which is named after him.

If Liszt was the towering figure of 19th-century Hungarian music, Béla Bartók (1881–1945) and Zoltán Kodály (1882–1967) were the giants of the 20th century. The founders of Hungarian ethnomusicology, Bartók and Kodály traveled the back roads of the country in the early 1900s, systematically recording Hungarian and Gypsy folk music. Peasant folk music had for hundreds of years been an important part of rural Hungarian culture, but by the turn of the century it was in danger of being lost. In addition to saving an enormous wealth of music from oblivion, Bartók and Kodály made some important discoveries in their research, noting both the differences and the interrelationships between Hungarian and Gypsy folk music, which had over time fused considerably. Both men were composers, and the influence of the folk music they so cherished can be heard in their work. Kodály established the internationally acclaimed Kodály method of musical education and lived to become the grand old man of Hungarian music, while Bartók died relatively young in the United States, an impoverished, embittered refugee from fascism.

Regularly scheduled concerts are given at the museums below; see the listings for details. For complete schedule information, check Budapest's free bimonthly *Koncert Kalendárium,* available at the Central Philharmonic Ticket Office on Vörösmarty tér.

### Bartók Béla Emlékház (Béla Bartók Memorial House)

II. Csalán u. 29. ☎ **1/176-2100.** Museum, 100 Ft (50¢); concerts, 300–500 Ft ($1.50–$2.50). Open Tues–Sun, 10am–6pm. Bus: 5 from Március 15 tér or Moszkva tér to Pasaréti tér (the last stop).

High in the Buda Hills, this little museum is housed in Béla Bartók's final Hungarian home. Every year on September 26th, the date of Bartók's death, the Bartók String Quartet performs in the museum. Concerts are also performed on Friday evenings in spring and autumn.

### Liszt Ferenc Emlékmúzeum (Ferenc Liszt Memorial Museum)

VI. Vörösmarty u. 35. ☎ **1/322-9804.** Admission 80 Ft (40¢). Mon–Fri 10am–6pm, Sat 9am–5pm. Closed Aug. Metro: Vörösmarty utca (Yellow line).

Located in the apartment in which Liszt spent his last years, this modest museum features several of the composer's pianos, including a child's Bachmann and two Chickering & Sons grand pianos. Also interesting are the many portraits of Liszt done by the leading Austrian and Hungarian artists of his time, including two busts by the Hungarian sculptor Alajos Stróbl. Concerts are performed here on Saturdays at 11am. The museum was closed for renovations at press time, but is due to reopen by summer 1998.

### Zenetörténeti Múzeum (Museum of Music History)

I. Táncsics M. u. 7. ☎ **1/214-6770** (ext. 250). Admission 80 Ft (40¢). Tues–Sun 10am–6pm. Bus: Várbusz from Moszkva tér or 106 from Deák tér to Castle Hill. Funicular: From Clark Ádám tér to Castle Hill.

Various instruments and manuscripts are displayed in this museum, housed in a historic building in Buda's Castle District. You'll find a reproduction of Béla Bartók's workshop as well as the Bartók Archives. Concerts are performed here twice a month; tickets are 400 Ft ($2).

## 6 Organized Tours

### BOAT & BUS TOURS

**Ibusz** (☎ 1/118-1139 or 1/118-1043), with decades of experience, sets the standards with organized tours in terms of both quality and quantity. Ibusz offers 11 different boat and bus tours, ranging from basic city tours to special folklore-oriented tours. Ibusz tours operate all year, with an abbreviated schedule in the off-season. All buses are air-conditioned, and all guides speak English. Some sample offerings are: a 3-hour **Budapest City Tour** for 3,600 Ft ($18), a 2-hour **Parliament Tour** (Parliament can only be visited on an organized tour, although it can be visited for free; see earlier in this chapter) for 2,400 Ft ($12), and a 2-hour **Folklore Evening** on the Danube for 7,900 Ft ($38). Bus tours leave from the Erzsébet tér bus station, near Deák tér (all metro lines); boat tours leave from the Vigadó tér landing. There's also a free hotel pickup service 30 minutes before departure time. For a full list of tours, pick up the Ibusz "Budapest Sightseeing" catalog, available at all Ibusz offices and most hotels. Tours can be booked at any Ibusz office and at most major hotels, or by calling Ibusz directly.

The Hungarian company **MAHART** operates daily sightseeing cruises on the Danube. The Budapest office of MAHART is at V. Belgrád rakpart (☎ 1/118-1704, 1/118-953, and 1/118-1586). Boats depart from Vigadó tér (on the Pest waterfront, between the Erzsébet Bridge and the Chain Bridge and near the Budapest Marriott hotel) on weekends and holidays in the spring and every day in summer. Additionally, MAHART organizes group boat tours up and down the Tisza River from April 1 to October 15. These tours are booked through separate agencies in the towns of departure (Tokaj, Kisköre, Tiszacsege, Szolnok, Szeged, and many others along the river). Ask at MAHART for further information and the telephone numbers necessary for booking.

**Legenda,** Fraknó utca 4 (☎ 1/117-2203), a private company founded in 1990, offers three boat tours on the Danube. A boat tour is a great way to get your measure of the scope and scale of the Hungarian capital, and a majority of the city's grand sights can be seen from the river. The daytime tour, called "Duna Bella," operates twice daily and includes a stop at Margaret Island. Tickets cost 2,100 Ft ($10.50). The nighttime tour is called "Danube Legend" and is a bit hokey, but worth it for the view of the city all lit up. "Danube Legend" tickets cost 2,500 Ft ($12.50), which includes refreshments. Tours run from mid-April to mid-October; all boats leave from the Vigadó tér port, Pier 6 or 7. Tickets are available through most major hotels, at the dock, or through the Legenda office.

### SPECIALTY TOURS

**Chosen Tours** (☎ 1/319-6800; fax 1/166-5165) specializes in tours related to Jewish life and heritage in Budapest. The 1¹/₂- to 2-hour guided walking tour of Pest's historic Jewish Quarter is a good introduction to that fascinating neighborhood. Tours run Sunday through Friday, beginning at 10:30am in front of the Dohány Synagogue, on Dohány utca. The walking tour costs $11. Reserve a place or just show up. Chosen Tours also offers a 2- to 3-hour, air-conditioned bus tour of Jewish sights throughout the city. Called "Budapest Through Jewish Eyes," it costs $11 and runs

Sunday through Friday, beginning at 2pm. Reserve a place beforehand. The meeting point is also the Dohány Synagogue. You can do both tours for a combined ticket price of $17. Other tours, available on the basis of private booking, include a tour of Jewish art, a tour to Szentendre, as well as tours catering to individual needs and interests.

## 7   Spa Bathing & Swimming: Budapest's Most Popular Thermal Baths

Hungarians are great believers in the medicinal powers of thermal bathing, and few can deny that time spent in thermal baths is enjoyable and relaxing. The baths of Budapest have a long and proud history, stretching back to Roman times. Under Turkish occupation, the bath culture flourished, and several still-functioning bathhouses—Király, Rudas, and Rácz—are among the architectural relics of the Turkish period. In the late 19th and early 20th centuries, Budapest's "golden age," several fabulous bathhouses were built: the extravagant eclectic Széchenyi Baths in City Park, the splendid art nouveau Gellért Baths, and the solid neoclassical Lukács Baths. All are still in use and are worth a look even for nonbathers.

Thermal bathing is an activity steeped in ritual. For this reason, and because bathhouse employees tend to be unfriendly relics of the old system, many foreigners find a trip to the baths stressful or confusing at first. As with any ritualistic activity, it helps to spend some time observing before joining in. Even then, you are likely not to know what to do or where to go. The most confusing step may well be the ticket window with its endless list of prices for different facilities and services, often without English translations. Chances are you're coming to use one of these facilities or services: *uszoda,* pool; *termál,* thermal pool; *fürdő,* bath; *gőzfürdő,* steam bath; massage; and sauna. Towel rental is *törülköző* or *lepedő.* An entry ticket generally entitles you to a free locker in the locker room (*öltöző*); you can usually opt to pay an additional fee for a private cabin (*kabin*).

Remember to pack a bathing suit—and a bathing cap, if you wish to swim in the pools—so you won't have to rent vintage 1970 models when you visit Budapest's famous thermal baths. Towels are provided. If you wear eyeglasses and are essentially left groping without them, you might want to consider wearing contacts when you go to the baths. That way you won't have to deal with your glasses fogging up or feel your way around the facilities. You should tip attendants from 20 to 50 Ft. (10¢ to 25¢) and masseurs 100 Ft. (50¢). Most bathhouses have snack bars in the lobbies where you can score a cold juice or sandwich after your bath.

## THE MOST POPULAR THERMAL BATHS IN BUDAPEST

You may wish to visit the bathhouses mentioned above for their architecture and ambience, but we suggest using the facilities at the baths listed below. These are the best in terms of service and sanitary conditions. Also remember that spa facilities are available at the two Thermal Hotels: Helia and Acquincum Corintnia (see chapter 4).

### Gellért Baths

Budapest's most spectacular bathhouse, the Gellért Baths are located in Buda's Hotel Gellért, the oldest Hungarian spa hotel and an art nouveau jewel, at XI. Kelenhegyi út 4 (☎ 1/166-6166). Enter the baths through the side entrance.

The exterior is in need of restoration, but once inside the lobby you'll be delighted by the details. The unisex indoor pool is without question one of Europe's finest, with marble columns, majolica tiles, and stone lion heads spouting water. The

# Fear & Bathing in Budapest

Budapest, a city constructed above more than 100 thermal springs, has earned a reputation as a bather's paradise. The local bath culture dates nearly to the city's founding: Once a Celtic settlement called Ak-Ink (meaning "abundant waters"), it was conquered and renamed Aquincum by the Romans, who built the first thermal baths. Today visitors to Budapest can visit any of at least 10 bath houses.

Despite the opportunity to immerse oneself in such history, some may find that the mere words "bath culture" conjure all sorts of nervous imagery. My daily visits to the thermal baths were one of the highlights of my recent trip to Budapest—but not because of any lurid experiences. For little more than $5 (except at the slightly more expensive Hotel Gellért), you can spend an entire morning or afternoon indulging in the full spa treatment: hot and cold bathing pools, swimming, sauna, and medicinal or therapeutic massage. While some of the baths are less luxurious than more expensive Western-style spas, soaking is immensely relaxing after a day of touring and a great way to participate alongside Hungarians in a dearly held national ritual.

Although some bath houses, particularly the male-only Király and Rudas Baths, are rumored to be popular with gay men on the prowl, this did not hamper my experience at any of the thermal baths I visited. Most people, straight or gay, needn't be intimidated. The baths are clean and people generally mind their own business. (If you are concerned about getting hit on, however, you're better off going to one of the more touristed baths, such as Gellért or Széchenyi.)

Each of the bath houses is different, in terms of architecture, services, and the way things are run. My favorites were the Gellért Hotel, a spectacular palace of relaxation with a Gaudiesque indoor pool and carved columns; Széchenyi Baths in City Park, where men play interminable chess matches while wading waist-deep in

segregated Turkish-style thermal baths, one off to each side of the pool through badly marked doors, are also glorious though in need of restoration. The outdoor roof pool attracts great attention for 10 minutes every hour on the hour when the artificial wave machine is turned on. There are separate nude sunbathing decks for men and women, but you'll have to figure out where they are. In general, you need patience here.

Admission to the thermal bath costs 400 Ft ($2); 15-minute massage is 450 Ft ($2.25) plus tip. Lockers are free; a cabin can be rented for 200 Ft ($1). Admission to all services costs 1,200 Ft ($6) for adults and 600 Ft ($3) for children. Prices are posted in English. The thermal baths are open all year, daily from 6am to 7pm, with the last entrance 1 hour before closing. Take tram no. 47 or 49 from Deák tér to Szent Gellért tér.

## Király Baths

The Király Baths, at I. Fő u. 84 (☎ 1/202-3688), are one of Budapest's most important architectural monuments to Turkish rule, and a place where Hungarian culture meets the Eastern culture that influenced it.

The bath itself, built in the late 16th century, is housed under an octagonal domed roof. Sunlight filters through stained-glass windows. In addition to the thermal bath, there are sauna and steam bath facilities. After your treatment, wrap yourself in a cotton sheet and lounge with a cup of tea in the relaxation room. If you don't care to the thermal pool; and Rudas, a 16th-century octagonal Turkish bath where subdued rays of light filter through small holes in the domed ceiling. The Rudas is a bit dark, and to some minds dingy, but a bath here is a singular experience. Bathing rituals practiced during the Ottoman Empire have remained undaunted by the passing of centuries and political regimes.

Procedure can be confusing at any of the baths, however; only a couple have multilingual attendants or signs posted in a language other than Hungarian. Start by renting an individual dressing room cubicle. Once inside the locker room, present your ticket to an attendant, who may or may not grunt instructions to you, but will definitely lead you to a stall. After you change out of your street clothes, the attendant will lock the door behind you, keeping one key and giving another to you. After you finish with your bath, you'll have to find him to unlock the door.

At the male-only baths, you'll be given a gossamer cotton apron to wear. Try your best to make the skimpy, backless patch of cloth cover your groin, then make your way to the steaming thermal pool. This may involve some wrong turns down mysterious corridors. While some baths have *termál* rooms clearly indicated, others, more obscure, may seem like funhouses. Your best bet is to trace the route of the satiated bodies filing out.

Not knowing the ritual, exactly, I went from hot bath to shower to massage to shower to hot bath to cold tub. After lounging in the thermal baths, I found the brutally cold waters terrifically restorative. The hygienic massage, lasting either 15 or 30 minutes, was a brusque rubdown performed with some sort of milky lotion, in long, powerful strokes from one's shoulders to ankles. Although the gruff nature of the masseurs is initially disconcerting, relax. The Romans and Turks did it, and so can you.

—Neil E. Schlecht

bathe, you're still welcome to take a peek at the interior. The Király baths are open on different days for men and women. Reportedly, the men's bath is frequented by a largely gay crowd.

Men can use the baths on Monday, Wednesday, and Friday from 6:30am to 6pm. Women are welcome on Tuesday and Thursday from 6:30am to 6pm and on Saturday from 6:30am to noon. It costs 300 Ft ($1.50) to bathe. Take the Red line metro to the Batthyány tér stop.

**Rudas Baths**

Near the Erzsébet Bridge on the Buda side, I. Döbrentei tér 9 (☎ 1/156-1322), is another of Budapest's classic Turkish baths. The baths are for men only (and are a known pick-up spot), while both sexes are admitted to the swimming pool.

The first baths were built on this site in the 14th century, although the Rudas Bathhouse dates to the late 16th century. It boasts an octagonal pool and domed roof; some of the small window holes in the cupola have stained glass, while others are open to the sky. Diffuse light streams in. You'll find most of the same services and facilities as at the Király: thermal bath, sauna, and steam bath.

The baths are open from 6am to 6pm on weekdays, 6am to 12pm on weekends. The thermal baths cost 350 Ft ($1.75). Take bus 7 and get off at the Buda side of the Erzsébet Bridge, turn left and venture down to the riverside. Or walk: It's just across the river. The baths are the first prominent building you encounter.

## Széchenyi Baths

The Széchenyi Baths are perhaps second only to the Gellért Baths in terms of facilities and popular appeal. Part of an immense health spa, they are located in the City Park, at XIV. Állatkerti út 11-14 (☎ 1/121-0310).

Ivy climbs the walls of the sprawling pool complex here. On a nice day, crowds of bathers, including many families and tourists, visit the palatial unisex outdoor swimming pool. Look for the older gentlemen concentrating intently on their chess moves, even while half-immersed in the thermal pool. Turkish-style thermal baths are segregated and located off to the side of the pool.

Admission to the thermal baths costs 220 Ft ($1.10); massage and dressing cabins are extra. Individual prices are posted in English. The thermal baths are open daily from 6am to 6pm, while the pool is open from 8am to 6pm daily. Metro: Széchenyi fürdő (Yellow line).

# AN OUTDOOR POOL COMPLEX

### Palatinus Strand

In the middle of Margaret Island is without question Budapest's best located *strand* (literally "beach," but better translated as "outdoor pool complex"), at XIII. Margit-sziget (☎ 1/112-3069). It's a fantastic place, fed by the Margaret Island thermal springs. There are three thermal pools, a vast swimming pool, a smaller artificial wave pool, a water slide, segregated nude sunbathing decks, and large, grassy grounds. The waters of the thermal pools are as relaxing as at any of the bathhouses, but the experience here is not as memorable as it is at the older bathhouses. Facilities include Ping-Pong tables, pool tables, trampoline, and dozens of snack bars: in other words, a typical Hungarian *strand*.

The single admission price for all pools is 300 Ft ($1.50) for adults and 200 Ft ($1) for children and teenagers; 200 Ft ($1) after 5pm Monday through Friday. Open May through September, daily from 8am to 7pm, with the last entry at 6pm. Take bus no. 26 from Nyugati pu.; beware of pickpockets on the bus!

## 8 Outdoor Activities & Sports

**GOLF**   For information, contact the **Budapest Golf Club,** V. Bécsi út 5 (☎ 1/117-6025). The nearest golf course is located on Szentendre Island, 25 minutes north of Budapest by car. Call or fax the course directly at 26/392-463. You can also access information about golf courses in Hungary via the Internet: www.datanet.hu/concorde/golf/golf.htm.

**HORSEBACK RIDING**   Riding is a popular activity in Hungary, and a good place to mount up is the **Petneházy Lovasiskola** (Riding School), at II. Feketefej u. 2 (☎ 1/176-5937). As far out in the Buda Hills as you can go without leaving the city limits, the school is located in open country, with trails in the hills. The hourly prices are great: Free riding on the track with a trainer is 900 Ft ($4.50) for adults, 800 Ft ($4) for children; open riding with a guide is 1,100 Ft ($5.50) for adults, 900 Ft ($4.50) for children. There are also ponies for children. The Petneházy Country Club is down the road. At the stable is a great little *csárda,* recently renovated; you might want to have lunch here. The stable is open year-round, Tuesday through Sunday, 9am to noon and 2pm to 4pm. Take bus no. 56 (56E is fastest) from Moszkva tér to the last stop, then bus no. 63 to Feketefej utca, followed by a 10-minute walk.

**HUNTING**   Foreigners must have a hunting license in order to hunt in Hungary. For information on hunting seasons and other regulations, contact **MAVAD RT,**

I. Úri u. 39 (☎ **1/175-9611;** fax 1/155-6705). Also, see "Package Tours" under "Getting There," in chapter 2, for information on **Wingshooting Adventures,** an American company that organizes hunting tours in Hungary.

**IN-LINE SKATING & ICE SKATING**   There are several options for both in Budapest. While at least one of the ice rinks is more appropriate for children, adults can rent in-line and ice skates elsewhere in the city. See "Especially for Kids," above.

**SQUASH   City Squash Courts,** at II. Marczibányi tér 13 (☎ 1/325-0082), has four courts. An easy walk from Moszkva tér (Red metro line), their hourly rates— *per court*—are 2,400 Ft ($12) for 1 hour of play during peak hours (Monday through Friday from 5pm to 10pm) and 1,800 Ft ($9) for 1 hour of play at other times (daily from 7am to 5pm and 10pm to midnight). Racquets can be rented for 400 Ft ($2); balls can be purchased. Open daily from 7am to midnight. The **Hotel Marriott Squash Court,** at V. Apáczai Csere J. u. 4 (☎ 1/266-4290), also rents out court time ($15 per hour) and racquets (300 Ft/$1.50).

**TENNIS**   If you plan to play tennis in Budapest, bring your own racquet along since most courts don't rent equipment; when it is available, it's usually primitive.

Many of Budapest's luxury hotels, particularly those removed from the city center, have tennis courts that nonguests can rent. The **MTK Sport Complex,** in Buda at XI. Bartók Béla út 63, (☎ **1/209-1595**), boasts 15 outdoor clay courts. The fee is 700 Ft ($3.50) per hour during the day or 1,400 Ft ($7) per hour at night, under floodlights. Three outdoor courts are covered by a tent year-round; from October through April all courts are covered and the price of play throughout the day is 1,400 Ft ($7) per hour (again to cover the cost of lighting). Equipment is not available for rental. Open daily 6am to 10pm. Móricz Zsigmond körtér, a transportation hub served by countless buses and trams, is only 5 minutes away by foot.

# 7

# Strolling Around Budapest

**B**udapest is best seen on foot. The following walking tours are intended to introduce you to the texture and color of the city. Many of the city's top attractions—the Buda Palace and Parliament, the National Gallery, and the National Museum among them—are visited on these tours, but dozens of minor sites—vintage pharmacies and quiet courtyards, market halls and medieval walls—are visited as well. On these walking tours special attention is paid to the hidden Budapest, the glorious details that taken together make this the memorable city that it is.

## WALKING TOUR 1
## The Inner City

**Start:** Deák tér.
**Finish:** Danube Promenade.
**Time:** 3 to 4 hours (excluding museum stops.
**Best Times:** Tuesday through Saturday.
**Worst Times:** Monday, when museums are closed, and Sunday, when stores are closed.

The medieval city of Pest, like most medieval cities, was surrounded by a protective wall. The wall is long gone, though some remnants remain, which we'll see on this tour. The historic part of the city, inside the walled area, is still known as the Belváros, or Inner City. The Erzsébet Bridge divides the Inner City into two parts: The busier northern half features luxury hotels along the Danube Promenade (Dunakorzó) and the boutiques and shops of the pedestrian-only Váci utca; the quieter southern half, meanwhile, is largely residential, but is also home to the main buildings of Eötvös Loránd University and a number of lovely churches. This sleepy southern half is undergoing a revitalization since the 1996 extension of the pedestrian-only status of Váci utca. Pest's Inner Ring boulevard (Kiskörút) wraps around both halves, tracing the line of the former medieval city wall. This walking tour spends equal time in each half of the Inner City, visiting museums, churches, stores, courtyards, and a great market hall en route. We'll end with a leisurely stroll down the Danube Promenade.

Begin at Deák tér, where all three metro lines converge. If you have any questions about theater tickets, activities, or excursions, now would be a good time to pop into:

1 Tourinform
2 Underground Railway Museum
3 Szervita tér
4 City Hall
5 Pest County Hall
6 Franciscan Church
7 Eötvös Loránd University
    (ELTE) Library
8 University Square
9 Monument to 1838 Danube Flood
10 Károly kert
11 Medieval City Wall
12 Hungarian National Museum
13 Központi Antikvárium
🕳 Múzeum Kávéház/Korona Passage
14 Calvinist Church

15 Central Market Hall
16 Main Customs House
17 Váci utca
18 Serbian Orthodox Church
19 Inner City Parish Church
20 Váci utca
21 Atlantisz Book Island
22 Pharmacy
23 Zsolnay Shop
24 Vali Folklor
25 Margit Kovács ceramic relief
26 Philantria Flower Shop
27 National Philharmonic Ticket Office
🕳 Gerbeaud's
28 Roosevelt tér
29 Danube Promenade (corso)

1. Tourinform, at V. Sütő u. 4. Budapest's main tourist information bureau has helpful information on lodging, cultural programs, and excursions. Alternatively, you could start with a visit to the:

2. Underground Railway Museum, located in the underground passage beneath Deák tér. Here you can see a beautifully preserved original train from the European continent's first underground system, built in Budapest in 1896.

   From nearby Szomory Dezső tér, head down Fehérhajó utca toward Szervita tér, formerly Martinelli tér. Ahead of you, you'll notice Váci utca, the crowded pedestrian street. The tour will return there later; for now, turn left into:

3. Szervita tér. This is the site of the early 18th-century baroque Servite Church, the column of the Virgin Mary, and the former Török Banking House with its colorful Secessionist mosaic.

   Continue now on Városház utca (City Hall Street), which begins to the left of the church. Dominating this street is the 18th-century:

4. City Hall, the largest baroque edifice in Budapest. The lime-green neoclassical building at Városház u. 7 is the 19th-century:

5. Pest County Hall. After a visit to the inner courtyards, you will see, as you emerge onto busy Kossuth Lajos utca, the Erzsébet Bridge to your right, with the northern slope of Gellért Hill behind it. Directly across the street (reached via the underpass) is the:

6. Franciscan Church. A church stood here as early as the 13th century, but the present church dates from the 18th century. The relief on the building's side depicts Miklós Wesselényi's heroic rescue effort during the awful Danube flood of 1838. Next door, a shop sells religious artifacts, including hand-painted icons from Bulgaria, Ukraine, and Russia.

   Continuing south on Ferenciek tere, the striking neoclassical building with the colorful dome is the:

7. Eötvös Loránd University (ELTE) Library. Continuing straight on Károlyi Mihály utca, the next big square is:

8. University Square (Egyetem tér), site of the ELTE Law School; the baroque University Church, with a copy of the *Black Madonna* of Czestochowa above the altar; and the Sándor Petőfi Literary Museum, a veritable shrine to Hungarian literary heroes (almost all are largely unknown outside Hungary).

9. A small (waist-level) monument to the 1838 Danube flood sits at the corner of Szerb utca and Király Pál utca; a map shows the extent of the flooding. Notice that the entire Inner City was underwater! Now turn left onto Henszlmann Imre utca. After half a block you will see:

10. Károly kert, on your left. This beautifully maintained neighborhood park has benches in the shade, swings, a miniature soccer pitch, and a lovely fountain with begonias growing around it. The park is filled with children all day long. Exit the park onto Magyar utca, and pass through the courtyard of Magyar u. 28, on the corner of Magyar utca and Henszlmann Imre utca. In the middle of the courtyard is a well-preserved section of:

11. Pest's medieval city wall, dating to the 15th century. Emerge onto busy Múzeum körút. Across the street is the massive neoclassical:

12. Hungarian National Museum. Legend has it that the fiery poet Sándor Petőfi recited his incendiary "National Song" on the museum steps on the first day of the 1848 anti-Habsburg Hungarian Revolution. The museum's most famous exhibit is the legendary Hungarian crown jewels of King Stephen; in reality, Stephen never saw these jewels since they postdate him by several centuries. The jewels have an astonishing history nonetheless: complex tales of theft, subterfuge, and rescue.

Spirited out of Hungary before the Soviet liberation of 1945, they ended up in U.S. government hands. President Carter ceremoniously returned them to the Hungarian government in 1978. The National Museum is one of those museums where, depending on your interest, you can spend 10 minutes or 10 hours.

This part of Múzeum körút has long been known for its *antikvária*, stores selling rare books and maps. At Múzeum krt. 13–15, you'll find the:

13. **Központi Antikvárium.** Another antikvárium, called Honterus, is ahead at Múzeum krt. 35.

**☕ TAKE A BREAK**  Choose between the **Múzeum Kávéház,** Múzeum krt. 12 (☎ 1/267-0375), suitable either for a Hungarian lunch or just for coffee and pastries, or **Korona Passage,** an airy crêperie/salad bar in the Korona Hotel on nearby Kálvin tér (☎ 1/117-4111).

Nearby Kálvin tér is named for the 19th-century:

14. **Calvinist Church,** which graces it. Medieval Pest's Kecskeméti Gate stood on Kálvin tér, on the site of the bridge passage between the two buildings of the Hotel Korona.

You're now on the Vámház (Customs House) körút section of the Inner Ring. Rounding the bend, you'll see just ahead the green span of the Szabadság (Freedom) Bridge, with the Gellért Hotel towering beyond in Buda. Head down Vámház körút, and turn right onto Veres Pálné utca, making a short detour off the körút. At the first corner, Bástya utca, at the rear of a playground, is another fine piece of the medieval town wall.

Back on Vámház körút, proceed to the:

15. **Central Market Hall (Központi Vásárcsarnok).** This is the largest and most spectacular of Budapest's late–19th-century market halls. Recently renovated and reconstructed, the bright, airy hall houses a wide assortment of fresh-produce vendors, dispensing dairy products, meat and poultry, vegetables, and fruit. Escalators lead to a mezzanine level where traditional folk items are sold. Fast-food and drink booths are also upstairs. While the new market hall is clean and extremely pleasant, it clearly lacks the homey grit and verve of a traditional market, such as the outdoor market in Szeged (See chapter 13).

Next door to the market is the eclectic-style former:

16. **Main Customs House.** Now a university building, it sits sprawled on the Danube—from which you can admire the graceful span of the Szabadság Bridge, our personal favorite of Budapest's six bridges.

17. Now take the **Váci utca** all the way back down to the southern end of the Inner City. Take a short detour at **Szerb utca** (turn left), named for the lovely 18th-century:

18. **Serbian Orthodox Church.** Set off from the street by a small garden, this lovely church dates to the mid–18th century. Interestingly, the paintings on the iconostasis reflect the Italian Renaissance instead of the more typical Byzantine style. Return to Váci utca, and continue walking north. This is the section of Váci utca that was recently transformed into a pedestrian-only street.

At Kossuth Lajos utca, turn left toward the Danube. Passing under the Erzsébet Bridge, you're now back in the northern, more crowded half of the Inner City. Towering above you is the:

19. **Inner City Parish Church.** Built and rebuilt numerous times since the 12th century, the church displays Gothic and baroque elements on the outside, while inside are niches built in both those styles, as well as a *mihrab* (prayer niche) dating from the Turkish occupation.

Pass under the archways of the ELTE Arts Faculty building (walking away from the river), and the next street is:

**20.** Váci utca again. This is its more crowded half. At Váci u. 31–33, is the:

**21.** Atlantisz Book Island. Here you'll find the best selection of English-language books about Hungary, both colorful coffee-table books and more serious literary and historical titles.

At Váci u. 34, on the corner of Kígyó utca (Snake Street), is a wonderful old:

**22.** pharmacy, furnished with antique wooden cabinets and drawers. Nearby, at Kígyó u. 4, you'll find the:

**23.** Zsolnay Shop. Here you'll find Budapest's widest selection of delightfully gaudy Zsolnay porcelain, from the southern city of Pécs. Even if you don't intend to buy, come just to see some fabulous examples of this internationally known china.

Proceed down Váci utca now. You'll probably make various stops along your way, but one of them should definitely be at:

**24.** Vali Folklor, in the courtyard of Váci u. 23. This tiny shop offers a fine assortment of authentic secondhand Hungarian folk costumes, as well as tapestries, ceramics, and figurines.

Just down Régiposta utca, across the street from McDonald's, above the door of Régiposta u. 13, is a lovely, but faded:

**25.** Margit Kovács ceramic relief of a horse and coach. Kovács was Hungary's greatest ceramic artist. A superb museum dedicated to her work can be visited in the small town of Szentendre, on the Danube Bend (see "Szentendre," in chapter 10). Look for the art nouveau interior of the:

**26.** Philantria Flower Shop, at Váci u. 9. Note the whimsical carved moldings, as well as wall murals recalling the style of Toulouse-Lautrec.

Váci utca ends in Vörösmarty tér, one of Pest's loveliest squares, which has a number of attractions in addition to the monumental statue of the great Romantic poet Mihály Vörösmarty, author of "The Appeal," Hungary's "second national anthem." Nearby is the:

**27.** National Philharmonic Ticket Office (Nemzeti Filharmónia Jegypénztár), at Vörösmarty tér 1. Here you can buy advance tickets for most Budapest performances; no commission is charged. In the same building is the Hungaroton Record Store, with an excellent selection of both classical and folk music.

Across the square, half a block away, at Deák Ferenc u. 10, is the American Express office. But certainly the best-known feature of Vörösmarty tér is Gerbeaud's, the legendary coffeehouse.

☕ **TAKE A BREAK**   Gerbeaud's, at Vörösmarty tér 7, founded in 1858, has been on this site since 1870. The decor and the furnishings are classic turn of the century, while the pastries are among the city's best. In summertime, try any of the fresh fruit strudels (*gyümölcs rétes*).

Your next stop is:

**28.** Roosevelt tér (described in "Walking Tour 3: Leopold Town and Theresa Town," below). The Buda Palace looms on Castle Hill directly across the river, which is spanned here by the Széchenyi Chain Bridge. Here, where the statue of the great 19th-century educator József Eötvös stands, is the beginning of the fabled:

**29.** Danube Promenade (Dunakorzó). Gone are the traditional coffeehouses that once lined its turn-of-the-century length between the Chain Bridge and the Erzsébet Bridge. In their place rise luxury hotels, the most monstrous of which is the concrete behemoth called the Budapest Marriott. Nevertheless, Budapest still comes to stroll here: Join the throngs, equal parts native and tourist. The glorious unobstructed view of Buda across the river remains as it ever was. Castle Hill towers above the Watertown, whose many steeples pierce the sky. Along the promenade you'll find artists, musicians, vendors, and craftspeople, not to mention various hustlers and lowlifes.

## WALKING TOUR 2
## The Castle District

**Start:** Roosevelt tér, Pest side of Chain Bridge.
**Finish:** Tóth Árpád sétány, Castle District.
**Time:** 3 to 4 hours (excluding museum stops).
**Best Times:** Tuesday through Sunday.
**Worst Time:** Monday, when museums are closed.

A limestone-capped plateau rising impressively above the Danube, Castle Hill was first settled in the 13th century; it remains the spiritual capital of Hungary. The district has been leveled periodically, most recently by the 1945 Soviet shelling of Nazi forces. It was always painstakingly rebuilt in the prevailing style of the day, thus shifting from Gothic to baroque to renaissance. After World War II, an attempt was made to incorporate various elements of the district's historic appearance into the general restoration. Castle Hill, recently added to UNESCO's list of World Cultural Heritage sites, consists of two parts: the Royal Palace itself and the so-called Castle District, a mostly reconstructed medieval city. The Royal Palace now houses a number of museums, including the Hungarian National Gallery. The adjoining Castle District is a compact, narrow neighborhood of cobblestoned lanes and twisting alleys; restrictions on vehicular traffic enhance the old-world feel and tranquillity. Prime examples of every type of Hungarian architecture, from early Gothic to neo-Romanesque, can be seen. A leisurely walk in the Castle District will be a warmly remembered experience.

To get an accurate picture of the dimensions and grandeur of Castle Hill, start the walking tour in Pest's Roosevelt tér, on the:

1. **Széchenyi Chain Bridge.** One of the outstanding symbols of Budapest, the first permanent bridge across the Danube was originally built in 1849 and then destroyed by Nazi dynamite during World War II. The 1949 opening ceremony of the reconstructed bridge was held 100 years to the day after its original inauguration.

Arriving in Buda, you're now in:

2. **Clark Ádám tér.** This square was named for the Scottish engineer who supervised the building of the bridge and afterward made Budapest his home. From Clark Ádám tér, take the:

3. **Funicular (*sikló*).** It will transport you up to the Royal Palace in just a minute or two. Dating from 1870, it too was destroyed in World War II and was not rebuilt until 1986. You can also walk up the steep stairs to Castle Hill. Whichever method of ascent you choose, when you arrive at the top, turn and look left at the statue of the:

4. **Turul.** The mythical eagle is perched on the wall looking out over the Danube to Pest. The eagle is said to have guided the ancient Magyars in their westward migration. The main courtyard of the palace, from which the museums are entered, is on the building's far side, but first go down the nearby stairs to see the:

5. **Equestrian Statue of Prince Eugene of Savoy.** Prince Eugene was one of the leaders of the united Christian armies that ousted the Turks from Hungary in the late 17th century. Inside the palace are a number of museums. You might want to visit them now or return after the walking tour. The first is the:

6. **Hungarian National Gallery.** The museum houses much of the greatest art ever produced by Hungarians. Don't miss the works of the 19th-century artists Mihály Munkácsy, László Paál, Károly Ferenczy, Pál Szinyei Merse, Gyula Benczúr, and Károly Lotz. Nor should you overlook József Rippl-Rónai, the great art nouveau painter of the turn-of-the-century period. Proceed to the:

7. **Budapest History Museum.** The highlights here are the Gothic rooms and statues uncovered during the post–World War II excavation and rebuilding of the Royal Palace. The rooms and all their contents, dating back as far as the 14th century, were buried for hundreds of years. Next we have the:

8. **Széchenyi National Library.** The library is named for Ferenc Széchenyi (not his more famous son István, after whom the Chain Bridge is named), who founded it in 1802. It now houses the world's greatest collection of "Hungarica," with some four million holdings. In Wing A of the Buda Palace is the:

9. **Ludwig Museum.** This repository of contemporary and international art was formerly the Museum of the Hungarian Worker's Movement.

   Exiting the palace, pass the new excavations and go through Dísz tér (where bus no. 16 can be caught later). Bearing right at the small grassy triangle with the statue of the swordsman, emerge onto Tárnok utca. On the left side of the street, you'll find the:

10. **Golden Eagle Pharmacy Museum (Arany Sas Patikamúzeum),** at Tárnok u. 18. Renaissance and baroque pharmacy relics are displayed in this odd and cavernous little museum. Just ahead on Tárnok utca is:

11. **Holy Trinity Square (Szentháromság tér).** The central square of the Castle District is where you'll find the Holy Trinity Column, or Plague Column, dating from the early–18th century, and the:

12. **Matthias Church (Mátyás templom).** Officially called the Church of Our Lady, this symbol of the Castle District is universally known as Matthias Church because Matthias Corvinus, one of Hungary's most revered kings, was married twice inside it. There's an ecclesiastical art collection inside, and organ concerts are held Friday evenings in the summer. Next door to the church is the:

13. **Hilton Hotel.** The Castle District's only hotel, the Hilton tastefully incorporates two ruins into its award-winning design: a 13th-century Dominican church, with a tower rising above the hotel, and the baroque facade of a 17th-century Jesuit college, the hotel's main entrance. Summer concerts are held in the Dominican Courtyard. Behind the Hilton is the:

14. **Fisherman's Bastion (Halászbástya).** This sprawling neo-Romanesque structure affords a marvelous panorama of Pest. Looking out over the Danube to Pest, you can see (from left to right): Margaret Island and the Margaret Bridge, Parliament, St. Stephen's Basilica, the Chain Bridge, the Vigadó Concert Hall, the Inner City Parish Church, the Erzsébet Bridge, and the Szabadság Bridge. Avoid the overpriced restaurant housed inside the Fisherman's Bastion.

   ☕ **TAKE A BREAK** You may want to stop at Litea, a bookstore and tearoom located in the Fortuna Passage, opposite the Hilton. You can browse, then sit and enjoy a cup of tea while looking over your selections. If it is lunch you desire, head to the Önkiszolgáló in the same Fortuna Passage. In this self-service cafeteria you can get an incredibly cheap and good Hungarian lunch. It is open only on weekdays and

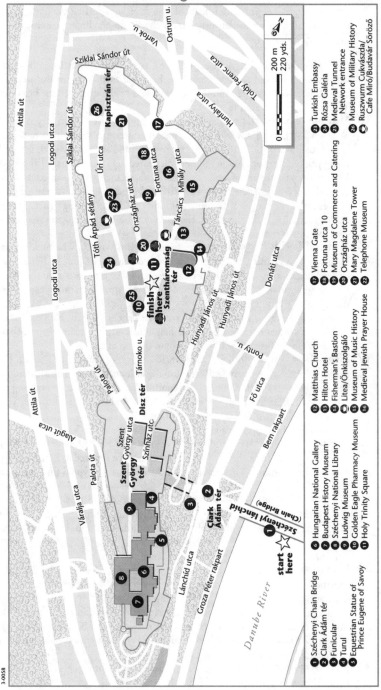

**N**

0    200 m
     220 yds.

26 Kapisztrán tér
21
17
18
22 23
Úri utca
19
Fortuna utca
16
15
Táncsics Mihály utca
20
13
11
24
14
Szentháromság tér
12
25
10
**finish here**

Dísz tér
Tárnoko u.
Palota út

Szent György tér
Színház utca

Clark Ádám tér

Szécheny lánchíd
(Chain Bridge)

2
3
4
9
5
6
8
7

**start here**

Danube River

3-0058

1 Széchenyi Chain Bridge
2 Clark Ádám tér
3 Funicular
4 Turul
5 Equestrian Statue of Prince Eugene of Savoy
6 Hungarian National Gallery
7 Budapest History Museum
8 Széchenyi National Library
9 Ludwig Museum
10 Golden Eagle Pharmacy Museum
11 Holy Trinity Square
12 Matthias Church
13 Hilton Hotel
14 Fisherman's Bastion
15 Litea/Önkiszolgáló
16 Museum of Music History
17 Medieval Jewish Prayer House
17 Vienna Gate
18 Fortuna utca 10
19 Museum of Commerce and Catering
20 Országház utca
21 Mary Magdalene Tower
22 Telephone Museum
23 Turkish Embassy
24 Rózsa Galéria
25 Medieval Tunnel Network entrance
26 Museum of Military History
27 Ruszwurm Cukrászda / Cafe Miró/Budavár Söröző

137

only for lunch. The entrance is marked by a small sign posting the open hours; it is the second door on the left inside the archway, up one flight of stairs. Just follow the stream of Hungarians.

Because the entire length of each of the Castle District's north-south streets is worth seeing, the tour will now take you back and forth between the immediate area of Szentháromság tér and the northern end of the district. First head down Táncsics Mihály utca, to the:

**15. Museum of Music History,** at Táncsics Mihály u. 7. Beethoven stayed here for a spell in 1800, when it was a private home. It now houses the archives of the great composer Bartók. The building next door, at Táncsics Mihály u. 9, served for many years as a prison. Among those incarcerated here were Mihály Táncsics, the 19th-century champion of land reform after whom the street is named, and Lajos Kossuth, the leader of the 1848–49 anti-Habsburg revolution. Táncsics utca was the center of the medieval Jewish community of Buda. During general postwar reconstruction work in the 1960s, the remains of several synagogues were uncovered. Nearby is the:

**16. Medieval Jewish Prayer House,** at Táncsics Mihály u. 26. The building dates from the 14th century. In the 15th and 16th centuries the Jews of Buda thrived under Turkish rule. The 1686 Christian reconquest of Buda was soon followed by a massacre of Jews. Many survivors fled Buda; this tiny Sephardic synagogue was turned into an apartment.

After exiting the synagogue, retrace your steps about 10 yards back on Táncsics Mihály utca, turn left onto Babits Mihály köz, and then turn left onto Babits Mihály sétány. This path will take you onto the top of the:

**17. Vienna Gate (Bécsi kapu),** one of the main entrances to the Castle District. From the top of the gate, you can look out onto the fashionable Rose Hill (Rózsadomb) neighborhood in the Buda Hills. The enormous neo-Romanesque building towering above Bécsi kapu tér houses the National Archives. Bécsi kapu tér is also home to a lovely row of houses (nos. 5 to 8).

From here, head up Fortuna utca to the house at:

**18. Fortuna u. 10.** This is certainly one of the district's most photographed houses. It dates originally from the 13th century, but has been restored to Louis XVI style. The facade incorporates medieval details. At Fortuna u. 4 you'll find the charming, unassuming:

**19. Museum of Commerce and Catering.** Mostly food-related artifacts from the turn of the century are lovingly displayed at this unique museum. The museum is open Wednesday to Friday from 10am to 5pm, Saturday and Sunday from 10am to 6pm only.

Return to Szentháromság tér and start down:

**20. Országház utca.** This is one of two streets in the Castle District best suited for viewing a mysterious Hungarian contribution to Gothic architecture. Niches of unknown function were built into the entryways of medieval buildings. When uncovered during reconstruction, the niches were either preserved or incorporated into the designs of new, modern structures. Niches can be seen in Országház u. 9 and 20, while number 28 has wooden doors of enormous proportions.

Országház utca ends in Kapisztrán tér, site of the:

**21. Mary Magdalene Tower.** Once part of a large 13th-century church, the tower is the only part that survived World War II.

Now take Úri utca back in the direction of the Royal Palace. In a corner of the courtyard of Úri u. 49, a vast former cloister, stands the small:

**22. Telephone Museum.** The museum's prime attraction is the actual telephone exchange (7A1-type rotary system), in use from 1928 to 1985, which is housed in it. In the courtyard is a lovely grassy area where you can sit. Úri u. 45 houses the:

**23. Turkish Embassy.** Ironically, this is the only embassy in the Castle District, which from 1541 to 1686 was the seat of Turkish rule in Hungary. Also on Úri utca are Gothic niches galore, seen in the entryways of nos. 40, 38, 36, 34, 32, and 31. Beautiful gardens fill the courtyards of many buildings on Úri utca. If the entranceways are open, take a peek inside.

No doubt you've noticed the presence in the Castle District of a large number of art galleries. Hungarian naïve and primitive art is on display in:

**24. Rózsa Galéria,** at Szentháromság u. 13. Prices start at about $150.

Úri u. 9 is the entrance to the:

**25. Medieval Tunnel Network,** which weaves its way through the almost 15km (9 miles) of rock beneath the Castle District. The only part of this network you can actually see is home to the Buda Wax Works (guided tour required), an unimpressive, tacky exhibit on the "legends" of early Hungarian history.

Úri utca ends back in Dísz tér. Take tiny Móra Ferenc utca (to the right) to Tóth Árpád sétány, the promenade that runs the length of the western rampart of the Castle District. This is a shady road with numerous benches. At its northern end, appropriately housed in the former barracks at Tóth Árpád sétány 40, is the:

**26. Museum of Military History.** To our minds, the highlight of this expansive museum is the room devoted to the 1956 Hungarian Uprising, one of the few violent episodes of Budapest's history in which the Castle District was not a primary venue. The 13 chaotic days of the Uprising are detailed by consecutive panels of large mounted photographs. The legendary hand of Stalin is here, too—the only piece known to remain from the giant statue whose public destruction was a dramatic moment of the failed Uprising.

The walking tour ends back near Szentháromság tér, where you can catch the Várbusz down to Moszkva tér, or from Dísz tér you can get bus no. 16 to Deák tér.

**☕ WINDING DOWN**   The Ruszwurm Cukrászda, Szentháromság u. 7, has been here since 1827. This little coffeehouse and pastry shop is the only classic of its kind in the Castle District. Its pastries are among the city's best. The recently opened Cafe Miró, Úri u. 30, is a world apart, with an intriguing interior design paying homage to the Spanish artist Joan Miró. The cafe mainly features desserts and coffees (iced coffee, too) and stays open until midnight, unusual in the Castle District. Just down the street, at Úri u. 13, is Budavár Söröző, a good spot for a snack, espresso, or beer. It has just two tiny tables inside and three or four outside on the sidewalk.

## WALKING TOUR 3
### Leopold Town & Theresa Town

**Start:** Kossuth tér, site of Parliament.

**Finish:** Művész Coffeehouse, near the Opera House.

**Time:** About 3 hours (excluding museum visits and the Opera House tour).

**Best Times:** Tuesday through Sunday. Note that if you want to visit the Parliament building, you should secure your ticket in advance.

**Worst Time:** Monday, when museums are closed.

In 1790, the new region developing just to the north of the medieval town walls of Pest was dubbed Leopold Town (Lipótváros) in honor of the emperor, Leopold II. Over the next 100 years or so, the neighborhood developed into an integral part of Pest, housing numerous governmental and commercial buildings; Parliament, government ministries, courthouses, the Stock Exchange, and the National Bank were all built here. This tour will take you through the main squares of Leopold Town. You'll also walk briefly along the Danube and visit a historic market hall. Along the way, you can stop to admire some of Pest's most fabulous examples of art nouveau architecture, as well as the city's largest church. Then you'll cross Pest's Inner Ring boulevard, leaving the Inner City, and head up elegant Andrássy út, on the edge of Theresa Town (Terézváros). There you'll see some wonderful inner courtyards and finish the tour after visiting the dazzling State Opera House (try to arrive here by 3 or 4pm if you'd like to tour the Opera House).

Exiting the Kossuth tér metro (Red line), you'll find yourself on the southern end of:

**1. Kossuth tér.** Walk toward Parliament, passing the equestrian statue of the Transylvanian prince Ferenc Rákóczi II, hero of an early–18th-century anti-Habsburg revolt. Exiled after the failure of his revolt, Rákóczi wandered from Poland to France and then to Turkey, where he remained until his death. You can't miss, on your left, one of the symbols of Budapest, the neo-Gothic:

**2. House of Parliament.** Unless you've only just arrived in Budapest, you certainly will have seen this massive structure hugging the Danube. The Parliament building, designed by Imre Steindl and completed in 1902, had been used only once by a democratically elected government prior to 1989. Unfortunately, you can only enter by guided tour (the half-hour tour is worthwhile for the chance to go inside). The eclectic-style building across the street from Parliament, the former Supreme Court, now houses the:

**3. Ethnographical Museum.** The museum boasts more than 150,000 objects in its collection. The *From Ancient Times to Civilization* exhibition contains many fascinating relics of Hungarian life. Walk past the statue of 1848 revolutionary hero Lajos Kossuth; after 45 years in exile, the stubborn Kossuth died in Torino, Italy, but received a hero's burial in Budapest.

Now enter the small park by the Danube at the northern end of Kossuth tér. There's a sensitive Imre Varga statue of Mihály Károlyi, first president of the post–World War I Hungarian Republic. Károlyi, too, died in exile. In 1962, 7 years after his death, his ashes were brought back to his homeland. Across the Danube, to your left, you can see Castle Hill and the church steeples of Watertown (Víziváros) beneath it. The bridge visible to your right is the Margaret Bridge.

Here, you have two options. The more intrepid, and those traveling without children, can turn left, go down the stairs, and scurry across the busy two-lane road to the river embankment. Walk south along the blustery embankment; after completing this circumnavigation of Parliament, cross back and come up the set of stairs. Others can simply circle back to the southern end of Parliament. You'll find a small statue of Attila József, the much-loved interwar working-class poet, whose tragic suicide (by jumping under a train at Lake Balaton) is imitated from time to time in Hungary.

Cross the tram tracks and, walking away from the river, pass through Vértanúk tere. Here stands:

**4. Imre Varga's statue of Imra Nagy.** Nagy was the reformist communist who led the failed 1956 Hungarian Uprising. He was executed after the Soviet-led invasion. The

# Walking Tour—Leopold Town & Theresa Town

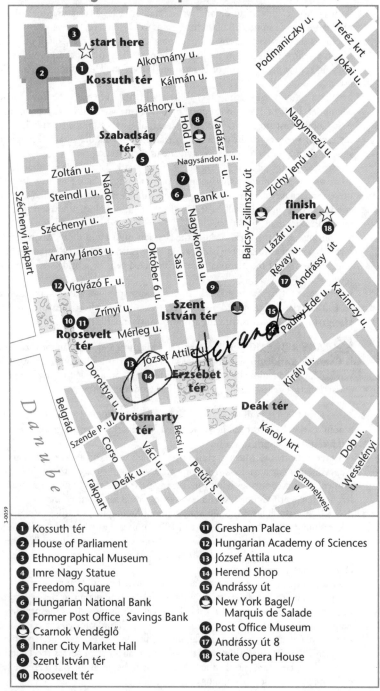

1. Kossuth tér
2. House of Parliament
3. Ethnographical Museum
4. Imre Nagy Statue
5. Freedom Square
6. Hungarian National Bank
7. Former Post Office  Savings Bank
   Csarnok Vendéglő
8. Inner City Market Hall
9. Szent István tér
10. Roosevelt tér
11. Gresham Palace
12. Hungarian Academy of Sciences
13. József Attila utca
14. Herend Shop
15. Andrássy út
   New York Bagel/
   Marquis de Salade
16. Post Office Museum
17. Andrássy út 8
18. State Opera House

3-0059

statue, called "Witnesses to Blood," was erected in 1996, 7 years after the re-burial of Nagy attracted some 300,000 Hungarians to Hősők tere.

Now walk a few blocks down Nador utca and turn left onto Zoltán utca. The massive yellow building on the right side of Zoltán utca is the Former Stock Exchange, now headquarters of Hungarian Television. The front of the building is on:

5. **Freedom Square (Szabadság tér).** Directly in front of you is the Soviet Army Memorial, built in 1945 and topped by one of the few Red Stars remaining in post-Communist Budapest. The American Embassy is at Szabadság tér 12. Paying careful attention to the often unruly traffic here, walk diagonally through the square, aiming for its southeast corner, site of the eclectic:

6. **Hungarian National Bank (Magyar Nemzeti Bank).** Leaving Szabadság tér via Bank utca, you can enter the National Bank through a side entrance. Its well-preserved, ornate lobby reminds one more of an opera house than a bank; its air-conditioned skylit main hall has rows of soft, comfortable chairs where you can take a breather.

Continue on Bank utca, making the first left onto Hold utca (Moon Street), formerly known as Rosenberg házaspár utca, for Ethel and Julius Rosenberg. Next door to the rear of the National Bank, connected to it by a bridge, is the newly restored:

7. **former Post Office Savings Bank (Posta Takarékpénztár).** The bank was built in 1901 to the design of Ödön Lechner, the architect who endeavored to fuse Hungarian folk elements with the art nouveau style of his time.

☕ **TAKE A BREAK** On the corner of Hold utca and Nagysándor József utca is **Csarnok Vendéglő,** Hold u. 11 (☎ 1/112-2016). This unassuming little vendéglő, visited mainly by neighborhood residents, is suitable for a typical Hungarian lunch. The restaurant's name is taken from the nearby:

8. **Inner City Market Hall (Belvárosi Vásárcsarnok),** built in 1897. This vast, cavernous market hall has been newly restored. The market is one of the city's liveliest; pick up some fruit in season.

Emerge from the Market Hall onto Vadász utca and turn right. Passing Nagysándor József utca, look right for a great view of the colorful tiled roof of the former Post Office Savings Bank you recently passed. Turn right on Bank utca and left on Hercegprímás utca. After a few blocks, you'll find yourself in:

9. **Szent István tér.** This is the site of the famous St. Stephen's Basilica, Budapest's largest church. Built between 1851 and 1905, it is well worth a stop. In the Szent Jobb Kápolna, behind the main altar, you can see an extraordinary holy relic: Stephen's preserved right hand. Monday-night organ concerts are held in the church in summer.

Head down Zrínyi utca, straight across the square from the church entrance. As you pass Október 6 utca, you might want to make a slight detour to **Bestsellers,** the English-language bookstore at no. 11. Bestsellers stocks travel books, especially on Eastern Europe. Returning now to the Danube, you'll find yourself emerging into:

10. **Roosevelt tér,** at the head of the famous Chain Bridge. Built in the revolutionary year 1848–49, the bridge was the first permanent span across the Danube. Roosevelt Square itself is really too full of traffic to be beautiful, but there are several important and lovely buildings here, including:

11. **The Gresham Palace.** Built in 1907, it is one of Budapest's best-known art nouveau buildings. Unfortunately, it has now fallen into a woeful state of disrepair. You can

pass through its main courtyard through any of three gates, including one on Zrínyi utca. To your right, as you face the river, is the neo-renaissance facade of the:

12. **Hungarian Academy of Sciences.** Like the Chain Bridge, it was the brainchild of the 19th-century Count István Széchenyi (called "the Greatest Hungarian"), who completed it in 1864. A statue of Széchenyi adorns the square. Guards prevent access beyond the Academy lobby, but it's worth a peek inside. A statue of Ferenc Deák, architect of the 1867 Compromise with Austria, is in a shady grove in the square's southern end by the Atrium Hyatt Hotel.

Turn left away from the river onto bustling:

13. **József Attila utca.** This street was named for the poet whose statue embellishes Kossuth tér. You're now walking along a portion of the Inner Ring (Kiskörüt), which separates the Inner City (Belváros) to your right from Leopold Town (Lipótváros) to your left. At József nádor tér you may want to stop in at the:

14. **Herend Shop.** Herend china is perhaps Hungary's most famous product, and this museumlike shop is definitely worth a look.

Continuing up József Attila utca, you'll pass Erzsébet tér, site of Budapest's main bus station, just before reaching Bajcsy-Zsilinszky út. Endre Bajcsy-Zsilinszky, a heroic leader of Hungary's wartime anti-fascist resistance, was executed by the Arrow Cross (Hungary's Nazis) on Christmas Eve 1944. Crossing Bajcsy-Zsilinszky út, you'll find yourself at the head of stately:

15. **Andrássy út.** Lined with trees and a wealth of beautiful apartment buildings, this is *fin-de-siècle* Pest's greatest boulevard.

☕ **TAKE A BREAK**    Walk one short block to your left on Bajcsy-Zsilinszky út to **New York Bagel,** at VI. Bajcsy-Zsilinszky út 21 (metro to Arany János utca on the Blue line). Try the tuna melt or the turkey salad on a mixed bagel (vegyes), baked with Hungarian paprika. Or, if you crave a proper meal, drop into **Marquis de Salade,** a bit farther down Bajcsy-Zsilinskky út at VI. Hajós u. 43, for delightful vegetarian cuisine.

Returning now to Andrássy út, look for no. 3, a building with a stunning entryway, which is the:

16. **Post Office Museum.** Its main attraction is clearly the opulently appointed apartment in which it's located. Imagine: This is how the wealthy of Andrássy út used to live! The frescoes in the entryway are by Károly Lotz, whose frescoes also decorate the Opera House and Matthias Church, in the Castle District.

Cross over to the even-numbered side of Andrássy. Stop to peek into other entryways and courtyards. Take a look in the vestibule of:

17. **Andrássy út 8.** Here you'll find more ceiling frescoes and painted glass courtyard doors; the courtyard is typical of this kind of Pest apartment building. Andrássy út 12, a building belonging to the once-feared Interior Ministry, has a gorgeous entryway and an inner courtyard with frescoes covering the walls. A policeman sometimes guards the entrance, but tourists are welcome.

Continue on Andrássy út until reaching the neo-renaissance:

18. **State Opera House.** Designed by Miklós Ybl and built in 1884, the Opera House survived the siege of Budapest at the end of World War II nearly unscathed. In fact, its huge cellars provided shelter for thousands during the bombing. Turning left on Hajós utca, walk around the Opera House. There are a number of music stores on Hajós utca. The street directly behind the Opera House, Lázár utca, affords an unusual view of the Bazilika. And if you are lucky, you can hear performers practicing through open windows on Dalszinház utca. Opera House

English-language tours (the only way, short of attending a performance, that you can get a look inside) are daily at 3 and 4pm year-round and start at the front entrance; the cost is 600 Ft ($3) per person.

You'll find the Opera station of the Yellow metro line just in front of the Opera House.

## WALKING TOUR 4
## The Jewish District

**Start:** Dohány Synagogue.
**Finish:** Wesselényi utca.
**Time:** About 2 hours (excluding museum visit).
**Best Times:** Sunday through Friday.
**Worst Time:** Saturday, when the museum and most shops are closed.

The Jewish district of Pest has a long and ultimately tragic history. It first sprang up in medieval times just beyond the Pest city wall (which stood where today's Inner Ring boulevard stands), as Jews were forbidden to live inside the town. Later, Pest expanded beyond the medieval walls, and the Jewish district actually became one of the city's more centrally located neighborhoods. The huge synagogues that you'll see on this tour give some idea of its former vitality. Under the German occupation in World War II the district became a walled ghetto, with 220,000 Jews crowded inside; almost half didn't survive the war. Sadly, the neighborhood is now more or less in a state of decay; buildings are crumbling, garbage is strewn about, graffiti cover the walls. Still, though, this compact little neighborhood is filled with evocative sights.

Halfway between Astoria (Red metro line) and Deák tér (all metro lines) is the:

1. **Dohány Synagogue.** This striking Byzantine building, Europe's largest and the world's second-largest synagogue, was built in 1859 and is still used by Budapest's *Neolog* (Conservative) Jewish community. The synagogue is newly cleaned and restored. The small freestanding brick wall inside the courtyard, to the left of the synagogue's entrance, is a piece of the original:

2. **Ghetto Wall,** which isolated Budapest's Jews inside this district during World War II. This is not actually where the wall stood, however: It was situated on Károly körút, the nearby stretch of the Inner Ring boulevard. To the left of the wall, on the spot marked as the birthplace of Theodor Herzl, the founder of modern Zionism, is the:

3. **National Jewish Museum.** On display are ornaments and art from the long history of Hungarian Jewry. The last of the four rooms is given over to a moving exhibit on the Holocaust in Hungary. (Note the open hours: May through October only, Monday through Friday from 10am to 3pm and Sunday from 10am to 1pm.) The synagogue courtyard can be entered through the rear of the complex on Wesselényi utca. Inside the courtyard is a newly unveiled:

4. **Holocaust Memorial.** Designed by Imre Varga, the well-known contemporary Hungarian sculptor, the memorial is in the form of a weeping willow tree. Thin metal leaves, purchased by survivors and descendants to honor martyred relatives, are slowly filling the many branches.

Now head down Rumbach utca. On the right, near the corner of Rumbach utca and Dob utca, is the rather bizarre-looking:

5. **Memorial to Charles Lutz.** Lutz was the Swiss consul who aided Swedish diplomat Raoul Wallenberg's heroic attempts to save Budapest's Jews from the Nazi death camps. The inscription from the Talmud reads: "Saving one soul is the same

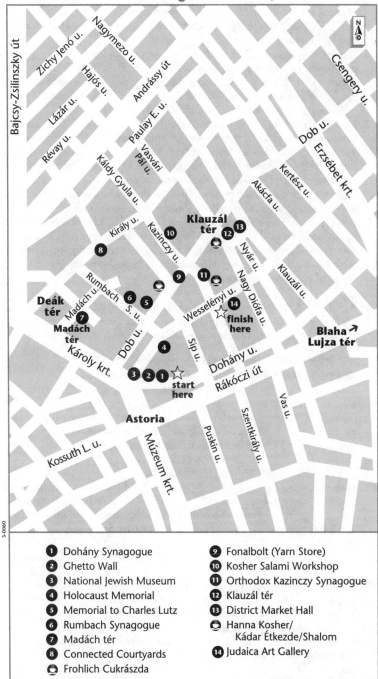

1. Dohány Synagogue
2. Ghetto Wall
3. National Jewish Museum
4. Holocaust Memorial
5. Memorial to Charles Lutz
6. Rumbach Synagogue
7. Madách tér
8. Connected Courtyards
9. Frohlich Cukrászda
9. Fonalbolt (Yarn Store)
10. Kosher Salami Workshop
11. Orthodox Kazinczy Synagogue
12. Klauzál tér
13. District Market Hall
🍴 Hanna Kosher/
     Kádar Étkezde/Shalom
14. Judaica Art Gallery

as saving the whole world." A lonely memorial to the far better known Wallenberg stands irrelevantly on Szilágyi Erzsébet fasor, far away in Buda. Half a block farther on Rumbach utca is the:

6. **Rumbach Synagogue.** This handsome yellow-and-rust–colored building is in its own way as impressive as the Dohány Synagogue. Built in 1872 by the Vienna architect Otto Wagner, the Orthodox synagogue is no longer in use. You can't go inside as it's under reconstruction, but the facade itself is worth seeing.

　　At the corner of Madách út, take a look at the giant archway of:

7. **Madách tér.** In the 1930s, a plan was drawn up for the creation of a great boulevard similar in form and style to Andrássy út. World War II put an end to the ambitious project, and the grand Madách tér leads only to itself now. Looking through the arch (presently under restoration) on a clear day, you get an unusual view of Gellért Hill, crowned by the Liberation Monument.

　　Take a right onto Király utca, which forms the northern border of the historic Jewish district. At Király u. 13, head through the long series of:

8. **connected courtyards.** These emerge onto Dob utca, back in the heart of the Jewish district. This kind of complex—residential buildings connected by a series of courtyards—is typical of the Jewish district. As you can readily see, these courtyards are in extremely poor condition, dirty and run-down with graffiti-covered walls and abandoned apartments.

　　☕ **TAKE A BREAK**　**Frohlich Cukrászda,** Dob u. 22, is the only functioning Kosher cukrászda (sweet shop) left in the district. Here you can purchase pastries, rolls, or ice cream. (The shop closes for two weeks at the end of August.)

　　Knitters should be sure to stop at the nearby:

9. **Fonalbolt (Yarn Store),** at Dob u. 27. The prices are unbeatable.

　　Half a block to the left off Dob utca on Kazinczy utca, at no. 41, is the:

10. **Kosher Salami Workshop (Szalámi és Kolbászáru Üzem).** Salami, famous throughout Hungary, is handmade here with ancient machinery. If you make a purchase, be sure to admire the equally ancient cash register in the corner. The sign outside directing you to the entrance is deceptive; simply enter via the doorway in front of you.

　　Back at Kazinczy u. 29 is the:

11. **Orthodox Kazinczy Synagogue.** Built in 1913 and still active, today much of it is in great decay, although the synagogue has a well-maintained courtyard in its center. There are a number of apartments in which members of the community live. While hundreds of tourists a day visit the Dohány Synagogue, far fewer make the trip here.

　　Go all the way through the courtyard, emerge onto Dob utca, turn right, and head into:

12. **Klauzál tér.** This is the district's largest square and its historic center. A dusty park and playground fill the interior of the square. There are a number of sights on Klauzál tér, including two lunch options (see below). At Klauzál tér 11, you'll find the:

13. **District Market Hall (Vásárcsarnok).** One of the half dozen or so great steel-girdered market halls built in Budapest in the 1890s, this one now houses a Skála grocery store. The entrance area is filled with smaller vendors selling fruit or vegetables.

　　☕ **TAKE A BREAK**　You have three lunch options in Klauzál tér and its immediate vicinity, each with a markedly different character. **Hanna Kosher Restaurant,** back at the Kazinczy Synagogue (☎ 1/142-1072), the city's only

Orthodox Kosher restaurant, is the domain of the elderly Jews who live inside the synagogue complex. **Kádár Étkezde,** at Klauzál tér 9 (☎ 1/121-3622), is a simple local lunchroom (open only Tuesday through Saturday from 11:30am to 3:30pm) serving a regular clientele, ranging from young paint-spattered workers to elderly Jews. The **Shalom Restaurant,** at Klauzál tér 2 (☎ 1/322-1464), a somewhat fancier establishment, does a brisk business with tourists.

If you like, head back on Nagydiófa utca to Wesselényi utca, where you can end the walking tour at the:

14. **Judaica Art Gallery,** at Wesselényi u. 13. Here you'll find Jewish-oriented books, both new and secondhand (some are in English). Clothing, ceramics, art, and religious articles are also for sale. Other quick-stop shopping possibilities a few blocks off Klauzál tér are an excellent and inexpensive map store and a Kosher grocery (Kóser Élelmiszerek Boltja), both located in the building at Nyár u. 1.

# WALKING TOUR 5
## Tabán & Watertown (Víziváros)

**Start:** The Pest side of the Erzsébet Bridge.
**Finish:** The Buda side of the Margaret (Margít) Bridge.
**Time:** About 2 to 3 hours (excluding museum visits).
**Best Time:** Any time.

This tour will take you through the narrow, twisting neighborhood along the Buda side of the Danube. Tabán, the area between Gellért Hill and Castle Hill, was once a vibrant but very poor workers' neighborhood. The neighborhood was razed in the early 20th century for "sanitary reasons"; now only a handful of Tabán buildings stand below the green expanse of parks where the rest of Tabán once was. The neighborhood directly beneath Castle Hill, opposite the Inner City of Pest, has been called Víziváros (Watertown) since the Middle Ages. Historically home to fisherman who made a living on the Danube, Víziváros was surrounded by walls in Turkish times. The neighborhood still retains a quiet integrity; above busy Fő utca (Main Street), which runs one street up from and parallel to the river the length of Watertown, you'll wander along aged, peaceful lanes.

Begin the walking tour on the Pest side of the:

1. **Erzsébet Bridge.** The nearest metro stations are Ferenciek tere (Blue line) and Vörösmarty tér (Yellow line). The original Erzsébet Bridge was completed in 1903, but like all the city's bridges was destroyed by the Germans in World War II; the present bridge was constructed in 1964. Note how the bridge skirts around the Inner City Parish Church, which dates to the 12th century. Cross the bridge on the right side with the flow of traffic. In order to do this, you'll need to be in front of the church; there's a staircase opposite, leading up to the bridge.

In front of you is Gellért Hill; the statue of Bishop Gellért bears his cross defiantly on the mountainside. From here, vengeful pagans, recalling the cruelties of the conversion to Christianity, forced the Italian bishop who had aided King Steven's crusade into a barrel and rolled him to his death in the river far below.

Upon reaching Buda, descend the steps, and, passing the statue of Queen Erzsébet, note the tablet commemorating the anti-fascists who, on this spot in 1944, blew up a statue of Gyula Gömbös, a leading Hungarian fascist of the interwar period. You're now at the bottom of the historic Tabán district. Walk away from the bridge, toward the yellow church whose steeple is visible above the trees. Your first stop here in Buda is the:

2. **Tabán Parish Church.** You can enter this church, built in 1736. Inside you'll find a copy of a 12th-century carving called the "Tabán Christ." The original is in the Budapest History Museum (inside the Buda Palace). Passing the church, you now see in front of and above you the southern end of the Buda Palace. Watertown is the long, narrow strip of Buda that lies on a slope between Castle Hill and the Danube. Before proceeding to it, note the tile-roofed Stag House on Szarvas tér diagonally across the street. One of Tabán's few remaining buildings, it now houses the Aranyszarvas Restaurant.

If you cross to that side of the street, you can see across busy Attila út (the street that runs behind Castle Hill) two graffiti-covered pillarlike chunks of the:

3. **Berlin Wall.** Its presence here recalls the pivotal role Hungary played in the fall of East German communism. Thousands of East German vacationers crossed the border from Hungary into Austria after the "Iron Curtain" was dismantled there in late summer 1989. This exodus was a major spark in the popular movement that led ultimately to the collapse of the East German regime and the breaching of the Berlin Wall.

Continue now down Apród út. The rust-and-white building at Apród út 1–3 is the:

4. **Semmelweis Medical History Museum.** Named after one of Hungary's greatest physicians, the museum has furnishings of the 19th-century Szentlélek Pharmacy. Proceed to:

5. **Ybl Miklós tér.** This narrow square on the Danube is named for Hungary's most celebrated architect. The lovely building at the square's southern end is the former Várkert (Castle Garden) Kiosk; it's now a casino. The patio ceiling is covered with sgraffito. Directly across the street from Miklós Ybl's statue is the Várkert Bazar. It's now in a frightful state of disrepair, but you can still admire the ornate archways and stairs.

Walk the length of the old Bazar to Lánchíd utca, so named because it leads into Clark Ádám tér, the Buda head of the Chain Bridge. Walking away from the river, take the steep set of stairs on your left up to quiet canyonlike:

6. **Öntőház utca.** In summer, the terrace gardens of the residential buildings here thrive. Flowers, small trees and shrubs, ivy, and grape vines are cultivated with care.

Turn right, winding back down to Lánchíd utca just before it spills into:

7. **Clark Ádám tér.** This is a busy traffic circle named for the Scottish engineer who supervised building the Chain Bridge in 1848–49. After completing his assignment, Clark grew so fond of Budapest that he remained here until his death. In addition to the bridge, many attractions are sited here. Immediately to your left is the:

8. **Funicular** (*sikló*), which goes up to the Buda Palace. In front of the funicular is the "Zero Kilometer Stone," the marker from which all highway distances to and from Budapest are measured.

Straight across the square from the Chain Bridge is:

9. **The Tunnel.** Built between 1853 and 1857, it connects Watertown with Christina Town (Krisztinaváros) on the other side of Castle Hill. The joke of the day was that the tunnel was built so that the precious Chain Bridge could be placed inside when it rained. Just across the street from the tunnel, a set of stairs marks the beginning of the long climb up to Castle Hill.

Passing straight through the square, you'll find yourself at the head of Watertown's:

# Walking Tour—Taban & Watertown (Víziváros)

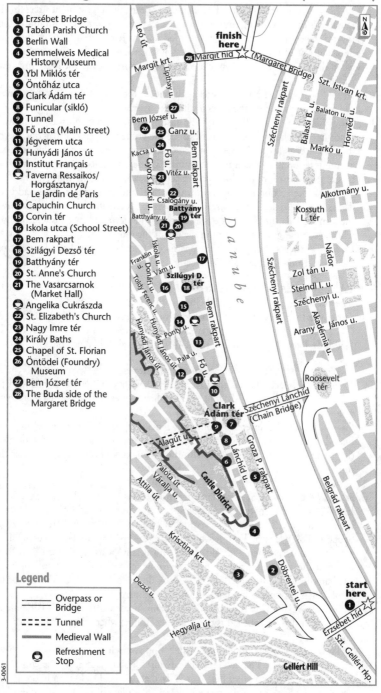

1. Erzsébet Bridge
2. Tabán Parish Church
3. Berlin Wall
4. Semmelweis Medical History Museum
5. Ybl Miklós tér
6. Öntőház utca
7. Clark Ádám tér
8. Funicular (sikló)
9. Tunnel
10. Fő utca (Main Street)
11. Jégverem utca
12. Hunyádi János út
13. Institut Français
   Taverna Ressaikos/ Horgásztanya/ Le Jardin de Paris
14. Capuchin Church
15. Corvin tér
16. Iskola utca (School Street)
17. Bem rakpart
18. Szilágyi Dezső tér
19. Batthyány tér
20. St. Anne's Church
21. The Vasarcsarnok (Market Hall)
   Angelika Cukrászda
22. St. Elizabeth's Church
23. Nagy Imre tér
24. Király Baths
25. Chapel of St. Florian
26. Öntödei (Foundry) Museum
27. Bem József tér
28. The Buda side of the Margaret Bridge

## Legend

— Overpass or Bridge
- - - - Tunnel
▨▨▨ Medieval Wall
⬤ Refreshment Stop

3-0061

10. **Fő utca (Main Street).** You'll be either on or near this long, straight street for the remainder of this walking tour. As you pass Jégverem utca, make a minute detour toward the river to examine the solid wood door at Jégverem u. 2. Note the small door cut out of the larger one, presumably a gatekeeper's door in days gone by when the main doors were kept closed except for carriages and the like. Now head left on:

11. **Jégverem utca.** At Kapucinus utca, you can see the steep old tile rooftops down the street. Continue up the stairs to the next street:

12. **Hunyádi János út.** Walk through the absurdly tall, narrow doorway of Hunyádi János út 9. Peek into the courtyard to see the crude wooden construction of the inner terrace landings. Hunyádi János út 4, across the street, has a dazzling enclosed atrium interior above the inner courtyard; its timeless beauty is sharply contrasted by the sheer horror of the dungeonlike cellar, clearly visible beneath you.

At the intersection of Magas utca, turn right and cross the street. Head back down toward Fő utca, via Szőnyeg utca. Crossing Kapucinus utca, continue down the steps at Pala utca. Here are the rooftops you viewed from a distance a short while ago. Emerge onto Fő utca at the site of the monstrous:

13. **Institut Français.** Note also the reconstructed remains of a medieval house across the street from this French cultural center.

☕ **TAKE A BREAK** **Taverna Ressaikos,** I. Apor Péter u. 1 (☎ 1/135-0361), serves delicious, carefully prepared Greek cuisine (see "Central Buda," in chapter 5). Other meal options include **Horgásztanya** (The Fisherman's Den), I. Fő u. 29 (☎ 1/212-3780), where Hungarian seafood is served in a rustic setting, and **Le Jardin de Paris,** I. Fő u. 20 (☎ 1/201-0047), a delightful French bistro.

Across the street from Horgásztanya is the former:

14. **Capuchin Church.** This is the first of several Watertown churches included on this tour. Note the Turkish door and window frames on the church's southern wall. Just past this church is:

15. **Corvin tér.** Several interesting buildings, including the home of the Hungarian State Folk Ensemble, are located here. There is presently a major archaeological dig going on at this square. Note also the row of very old baroque houses at the top of the square.

Head above Corvin tér to:

16. **Iskola utca (School Street).** Turn right on Iskola utca and left up the Donáti lépcső (stairs) to Donáti utca; a clay frieze of two horsemen adorns the residential building to the left, opposite the stair landing. Turn right and walk to the next set of stairs, Toldy lépcső. Turn left up the stairs and right onto Toldy Ferenc utca, a residential street lined with old-fashioned gas lampposts. This street is so tranquil that the only other tourists are likely to be following this very walking tour. At Franklin utca, turn right and head back down to Iskola utca. Turn right on Iskola, then left onto Vám. Cross Fő utca, heading to the:

17. **Bem rakpart,** the Danube embankment. Directly across the river is Parliament. The next bridge on your left is the Margaret Bridge, where this walking tour will end.

Turn right now and you'll immediately find yourself in:

18. **Szilágyi Dezső tér.** The neo-Gothic Calvinist Church dates from the end of the 19th century. The composer Béla Bartók lived at Szilágyi Dezső tér 4 in the 1920s. The Danube bank near this square is the site of a piece of Hungary's darkest history. Here the Arrow Cross (*Nyilas*), the Hungarian Nazis, massacred thousands

of Jews in 1944 and 1945, during the last bitter winter of World War II. Many were tied together into small groups and thrown alive into the freezing river.

Returning now to Fő utca, turn right and continue on toward Watertown's main square. You may want to stop in at the Herend Village Pottery shop at Bem rakpart 37, on the ground floor of the housing block. You'll find several attractions along:

**19. Batthyány tér.** One of its principal sights is the 18th-century:

**20. St. Anne's Church.** One of Hungary's finest baroque churches, it was almost destroyed in the early 1950s when the Hungarian dictator Mátyás Rákosi (known as "Stalin's most loyal disciple") had the idea that when his mentor visited him at his office in Parliament, he would be loathe to look across the Danube at a Buda skyline dominated by churches. Fortunately, Rákosi's demented plan was never realized.

**21. The Vasarcsarnok (Market Hall),** in Batthyány tér. One of several built in Budapest in 1897 but no longer a public market, today it houses a large, well-stocked grocery store (open on Sunday). The interior might be worth a look. Two doors down is the former White Cross Inn, a rococo building, which, like St. Anne's, dates from the 18th century. The legendary philanderer Casanova is said to have spent a night here, hence the name of the ground-floor nightclub. Next door, at Batthyány tér 3, above the first-floor windows of the building, are several enchanting but shamefully dirty clay friezes.

☕ **TAKE A BREAK**   Next door to St. Anne's Church in the former presbytery is **Angelika Cukrászda,** I. Batthyány tér 7. This lovely, traditional Budapest coffee house is the perfect place for a little rest. Delicious pastries are served in low-ceilinged, cavernous rooms, clearly designed for ecclesiastical purposes.

Continuing along Fő utca, the next church on your right is:

**22. St. Elizabeth's Church.** Be sure to have a look at the baroque interior: The carved pulpit is the handiwork of friars. The frescoes date from the 19th century.

You're now approaching the northern border of Watertown; larger streets—like Batthyány utca and Csalogány utca—now bisect Fő utca. You can no longer see Castle Hill. The next square is:

**23. Nagy Imre tér.** A small park hidden behind a Total gas station, the square is named for the reform Communist leader who played a leading, if slightly reluctant, role in the 1956 Hungarian Revolution. The prisonlike building on the corner is the Military Court of Justice, where Nagy was secretly tried and condemned to death in 1958, thus providing Hungary with yet another martyr. Nagy's rehabilitation and reburial in June 1989 was a moment of great unity in Hungary, and a statue of him was recently erected near Parliament (see "Walking Tour 3," above). The main entrance to the Military Court of Justice is on Fő utca.

Two blocks farther, at Fő u. 82–86, is the:

**24. Király Baths.** This 16th-century bathhouse is now one of the city's major monuments to the period of Turkish rule. Even if you're not going in to bathe, you should take a peek at the gorgeous interior. The baths are open on different days for men and women (see "Spa Bathing & Swimming," in chapter 6).

Next door, at the corner of Fő utca and Ganz utca, is the baroque:

**25. Chapel of St. Florian.** Today this is a Greek Orthodox church; have a look inside the vestibule.

Turn left on Ganz utca, passing through the small park between the baths and the church. You're suddenly in a strange postindustrial landscape, at the end of which is, appropriately, the:

**26.** Öntödei (Foundry) Museum. The museum is housed inside the original structure of the famed Abraham Ganz Foundry. From the outside, it's hard to imagine the vast barnlike interior. The collection of antique cast-iron stoves is the
highlight.

Turn right onto Bem József utca, a street with many fishing and army-navy-type
supply stores, heading back down toward the Danube, where you'll find yourself
in:

**27.** Bem József tér, named after the Polish general who played a heroic role in the
1848–49 Hungarian Revolution. On October 23, 1956, the square hosted a rally
in support of the reform efforts in Poland. The rally, and the subsequent march
across the Margaret Bridge to Parliament, marked the beginning of the famous
1956 Hungarian Uprising.

Turn left onto Lipthay utca, which is parallel to the river. Admire the buildings
on your left along this street before ending the tour at:

**28.** The Buda side of the Margaret Bridge. Here you can pick up the no. 4 or
no. 6 tram and head either to Buda's Moszkva tér (Red metro line) or across
the river to Pest's Outer Ring boulevard.

## 1 The Shopping Scene

**MAIN SHOPPING STREETS**   All year long, tourists and locals alike throng the pedestrian-only **Váci utca,** from the stately Vörösmarty tér, the center of Pest, across the roaring Kossuth Lajos utca, all the way to Vámház krt. Váci utca, and most of the pedestrian streets bisecting it, are lined with shops. Boutiques, not visible from the street, also fill the courtyards. The increasing prevalence of Euro-fashion items is a fairly recent development on Váci utca. Increased "Western-style" prices are also relatively new. Váci utca, was formerly (as recently as the 1980s), known throughout the country as *the* street for good bookshops. Sadly, only three bookstores remain. The street is otherwise largely occupied by the aforementioned clothing boutiques and an overwhelming number of folklore/souvenir shops. An exception to this is the southern section of the street, from Kossuth Lajos utca to Vámház körút, which was recently made into a pedestrian-only way. For the moment at least, it retains a leisurely and less commercial quality.

Another favorite shopping haunt is the **Castle District** in Buda; with its abundance of folk-art boutiques and art galleries, it's a popular area for souvenir hunters.

While locals might window-shop in these two neighborhoods, they tend to do their serious shopping elsewhere. One favorite street is Pest's **Outer Ring** (Nagykörút); another bustling shopping street is Pest's **Kossuth Lajos utca,** off the Erzsébet Bridge, and its continuation **Rákóczi út,** which extends all the way out to Keleti Station. In Buda, Hungarian crowds visit the shops of **Margit körút** and the neighborhood of **Móricz Zsigmond körtér,** where the Buda Skála department store is located.

**HOURS**   Most stores are open Monday through Friday from 10am to 6pm and on Saturday from about 9am to about 1pm. Some stores stay open an hour or two later on Thursday, while some close for an hour at lunchtime. Most shops are closed Sunday, except for those in downtown Pest. Payment by credit or charge card in tourist shopping areas is usually possible.

**TAXES & REFUNDS**   Prices in Hungary carry a built-in 25% value-added tax (VAT). Individuals making noncommercial purchases exceeding 25,000 Ft ($125) are entitled to a VAT refund on the amount over 25,000 Ft; this entitlement does not apply to works of art or antiques, however. The refund process is rather elaborate. In most shops, the salesperson can provide the necessary VAT reclaim form and will fill it out for you. In addition, make sure that you receive a separate receipt indicating the VAT amount. Your name, home address, and passport number should be entered on this receipt. No more than 90 days may elapse from the time of purchase and time of export; no more than 183 days can elapse from the time of export and submission of the claim for a refund. Save not only sales receipts, but also currency-exchange receipts (or credit/charge-card receipts); attach the original invoice and the Customs certification to the refund claim form. Use one claim form per sales receipt. Receive certification from Customs by presenting the object of purchase upon export (for instance, at the airport), or else submit the claims by mail to: **Foreigners' Refund Office** of the APEH Budapest Directorate, XI. Bartók Béla út 156, Budapest (☎ **1/203/0888** or 1/156-9800). For further information (and to obtain a claim form in advance of departure if the store did not provide one), visit the office directly or call. Information and forms are also available through **Intertrade,** I. Csalogány u. 6–10 (☎ **1/ 156-9800;** fax 1/175-0616). You can also obtain information over the web: www.taxfree.se.

**SHIPPING & CUSTOMS**    Very few shops will organize shipping for you. You can ship a box to yourself from any post office, but the rules on packing boxes are as strict as they are arcane. The Hungarian postal authorities prefer that you use one of their official shipping boxes, for sale at all post offices. They're quite flimsy, however, and have been known to break open in transit.

Hungarian Customs regulations do not limit the export of noncommercial quantities of most goods. However, the export of some food staples like coffee and chocolate is strictly regulated (but rarely enforced). There is no limit on wine, but only 1 liter of spirits and 400 cigarettes may be exported.

## 2  Best Buys

### HUNGARIAN FOLK ITEMS

Folkloric objects are the most popular souvenirs among foreigners visiting Budapest. The state-owned Folkart shops (Népművészeti Háziipar) have a great selection of handmade goods at unbeatable prices. Popular items include pillow cases, pottery, porcelain, dolls, dresses, skirts, and sheepskin vests.

Another source of authentic folk items is the ethnic Hungarian women who come to Budapest with bags full of handmade craftwork from Transylvania, a region of Romania heavily populated with ethnic Hungarians. The police have driven them from the main tourist shopping streets, and they now congregate where they can. Keep your eyes open for these vendors, unmistakable in their characteristic black boots, dark-red skirts, and red or white kerchiefs tied around their heads. Their prices are generally quite reasonable, and bargaining is customary. In summer 1996, they tended to congregate along the Szabadság bridge and at Moszkva tér. Now, instead, Moszkva tér is the site of a daily soup kitchen, serving the homeless; a startling new reality in Hungary, the price of free-market capitalism in the eyes of many.

### PORCELAIN, FOODSTUFFS & MARKETS

Another popular Hungarian item is **porcelain,** particularly from the country's two best-known producers, Herend and Zsolnay. Although both brands are available in the West, here you'll find a better selection and prices about 50% lower.

Typical **Hungarian foods** also make great gifts. Hungarian salami is world famous. Connoisseurs generally agree that Pick Salami, produced in the southeastern city of Szeged, is the best brand. Herz Salami, produced locally in Budapest, is a slightly lesser product. Another typical Hungarian food product is chestnut paste (*gesztenye püré*), available in a tin or block wrapped in foil; it's used primarily as a pastry filling, but can also top desserts and ice cream. Paprika paste (*pirosarany*) is something else you'll scarcely find outside Hungary. It comes most commonly in a bright-red tube. Three types are available: hot (*csípős*), deli style (*csemege*), and sweet (*édes*). All these items can be purchased in grocery stores (*élelmiszer*) and delicatessens (*csemege*).

If you love **open markets,** Budapest is the place for you. There are numerous markets here: flea markets (*használtáru piac*), filled not only with every conceivable kind of junk and the occasional relic of Communism, but also with great quantities of mostly low-quality new items like clothing, cassettes, and shoes; and food markets (*vásárcsarnok, csarnok,* or *piac*), with row after row of succulent fruits and vegetables, much of it freshly picked and driven in from the surrounding countryside. You can also find saffron and several varieties of dried mushrooms for a pittance. By definition, a journey into a market is a journey off the tourist track.

# 3  Shopping A to Z

## ANTIQUES

When shopping for antiques in Budapest, you should know that Hungary forbids the export of many items designated as "cultural treasures." Some purchases come with a certificate allowing export; with other purchases the responsibility is the buyer's alone to go to the correct office (in the Museum of Applied Arts) and apply for the certificate. Our advice is to buy only from those shops that supply the certificate for you. A journey through the Hungarian bureaucracy can be a withering experience.

Although it no longer has a monopoly on the sale of antiques, the still state-owned **BÁV (Bizományi Kereskedoház és Záloghitel Rt.)** continues to control the lion's share of the antiques market in Hungary. Here's a partial list of BÁV shops:

- I. Hess András tér 1 (☎ 1/175-0392), in the Castle District, specializing in porcelain and folk art.
- V. Bécsi u. 1–3 (☎ 1/117-2548), near Deák tér, is the largest of the shops, specializing in antique furniture, chandeliers, carpets, and painting.
- V. Ferenciek tere 5 (☎ 1/118-3773), specializing in carpets.
- V. Kossuth Lajos u. 1–3 (☎ 1/118-4403), just across the street from the Ferenciek tere shop, specializing in antique furniture, chandeliers, and paintings.
- VI. Andrássy út 27 (☎ 1/342-5525), near the Opera House, specializing in antique art, porcelain, and silver.
- VII. Dohány u. 16–18 (☎ 1/342-7935), in the historic Jewish neighborhood, specializing in paintings, furniture, and carpets.
- IX. Tűzoltó u. 14 (☎ 1/212-9824), specializing in furniture.

**Qualitas Antiquitas** is a private company with four locations: The store at I. Krisztina krt. 73 (☎ 1/175-0658), behind the Castle District, specializes in paintings and furniture; the one at V. Falk Miksa u. 32 (☎ 1/111-8471), near Parliament, and the one at Kígyó u. 5 (☎ 1/118-3246) specialize in coins, jewelry, and Herend and Zsolnay porcelain; and the one at VII. Dohány u. 1 (☎ 1/341-5585), near the Dohány Synagogue, specializes in paintings, carpets, and ecclesiastical and glass objects. Qualitas Antquitas also operates an **Auction Hall,** at V. Váci u. 36 (☎ 1/267-3539); auctions are on Mondays at 5pm.

**Ecclesia Szövetkezet,** at V. Ferenciek tere 7 (☎ 1/117-3754), next door to the Franciscan church, has hand-painted icons from Russia, Bulgaria, and Ukraine, starting at around 30,000 Ft ($150); contemporary hand-painted copies start as low as 5,000 Ft ($25).

The **Ecseri Flea Market** (see "Markets," below) also deserves mention here, as numerous private antique dealers operate booths at this one-of-a-kind open-air flea market.

# ART GALLERIES

Budapest is home to a burgeoning—but still fairly unsettled—art gallery scene. The same export rules outlined above regarding antiques apply to all works of art considered to be Hungarian cultural treasures. Before completing a purchase, confirm that you'll be allowed to take the work out of the country; gallery proprietors should have the requisite documentation on hand.

Galleries tend to keep normal store hours (Monday through Friday from 10am to 6pm and on Saturday from 10am to 1 or 2pm, sometimes as late as 6pm). They're concentrated in two areas: the Inner City of Pest and Buda's Castle District. An art dealer by the name of Károly Szalóky has an ambitious plan to transform Várfok utca in the Castle District into a street of contemporary Hungarian artists' galleries. He has already opened two new galleries on the street, **Spiritusz** and **XO Gallery,** in addition to his long-standing **Várfok 14 Gallery,** at Várfok u. 14 (☎ 1/115-2165). Other galleries specializing in contemporary Hungarian art include: **Vár Gallery,** I. Táncsics Mihály u. 17 (☎ 1/155-9802); **Eve Art Gallery,** VI. Király u. 98/b (☎ 1/322-8466); **Luttár Gallery,** XIII. Hegedus Gyula u. 24 (☎ 1/149-5045). **Közép-Európai Gallery,** VI. Andrássy út 1 (☎ 1/268-0026), specializes in contemporary paintings from Central and Eastern Europe (former socialist countries). **Fortuna 11 Gallery,** I. Fortuna u. 11 (☎ 1/201-8984), features both contemporary painting and Herend majolica, as well as folk items and furniture. **Rózsa Gallery,** with two locations at I. Szentháromság u. 13 (☎ 1/155-6866) and V. Petőfi Sándor 9 (☎ 1/268-9174), exhibits Hungarian naïve art. They are closed on weekends. **Studio 1900 Gallery,** XIII. Hegedus Gyula u. 24/b (☎ 129-5553) and **Műgyűjtők Gallery,** V. Kossuth Lajos u. 12 (☎ 1/117-3132), both specialize in 19th- and 20th-century painting. Art students exhibit their work in the **Studio Gallery,** at V. Képíró u. 6 (☎ 1/267-2033). The **Hologram Gallery,** in the Párizsi Udvar (Paris Passage), off V. Ferenciek tere (☎ 1/118-3761), is always filled with people; you can even get hologram business cards here.

# ART SUPPLIES

## Leonart
VI. Bajcsy köz. 3. ☎ **1/153-3750.** Metro: Arany János u. (Blue line).

For the amateur and the professional artist, Leonart offers a wide selection of watercolor, oil, and acrylic paints, as well as brushes, drawing materials, canvas, and paper. Open Monday through Friday, 9am to 5pm.

# BOOKSTORES—NEW & SECONDHAND

## Atlantisz Book Island
V. Piarista köz 1. ☎ **1/267-0966.** Metro: Ferenciek tere (Blue line).

Located in ELTE University's Department of Humanities building, Atlantisz is frequented by local academics and foreign visitors alike. The selection is broad: law, philosophy, sociology, literary criticism, and fiction. Lots of English-language books are on hand. Open Monday through Friday from 10am to 6pm.

## Bestsellers

V. Október 6 u. 11. ☎ **1/112-1295.** Metro: Arany János utca (Blue line).

Budapest's first English-language bookstore, Bestsellers is a popular meeting spot for English speakers. It's located in the middle of the Inner City, not far from Szabadság tér, site of the American Embassy. The store is notable for its assortment of travel books on Eastern Europe. Newspapers and magazines are also available, including some, like *Rolling Stone,* that can be hard to find elsewhere in Budapest. Bestsellers operates a book and CD-ROM ordering service at no extra charge. Open Monday through Saturday from 9am to 6:30pm.

## Biblioteka Antikvárium

VI. Andrássy út 2. ☎ **1/131-5132.** Metro: Arany János utca (Blue line) or Deák tér (all lines).

At the head of Andrássy út, near Bajcsy-Zsilinszky út, this is one of central Pest's better *antikvária* (used- and rare-bookshops). They have five bookcases full of English-language books, and a variety of maps and prints. Open Monday through Friday from 10am to 6pm and on Saturday from 9am to 1pm.

## Honterus Antikvárium

V. Múzeum krt. 35. ☎ **1/117-3270.** Metro: Astoria (Red line) or Kálvin tér (Blue line).

Located near the Központi Antikvárium, across the street from the Hungarian National Museum (Nemzeti Múzeum), this old- and rare-bookstore has more prints and maps on display than any other antikvárium in town. There's a shelf of mostly arcane, out-of-date English-language academic books as well as a stack of *National Geographic* magazines. Open Monday through Friday from 10am to 6pm and on Saturday from 10am to 2pm.

## Központi Antikvárium

V. Múzeum krt. 13–15. ☎ **1/117-3514.** Metro: Astoria (Red line) or Kálvin tér (Blue line).

"Central Antikvárium" is the city's oldest and largest old- and rare-bookstore. Indeed, it is reported to be the largest rare bookstore in all of Central Europe. Opened in 1881 across the street from the Hungarian National Museum on "Antikvárium Row" (Múzeum krt. was *the* antikvárium street during the pre-World War I era, home to 37 different shops at that time), this shop has books, prints, maps, and a shelf of assorted knickknacks. Open Monday through Friday from 10am to noon and 1 to 6pm and on Saturday from 9am to 12:30pm. The "Central Antikvárium" owners have two additional stores nearby: Mediprint, V. Múzeum krt. 17. ☎ 1/117-4948, featuring a unique collection of old medical books; and Kodály Antikvárium, V. Múzeum krt. 21 ☎ 1/117-3347, which sells secondhand sheet music, LPs, and CDs.

## Libri Idegen Nyelvú Könyvesbolt (Libri Foreign-Language Bookshop)

V. Váci u. 32. ☎ **1/118-2718.** Metro: Vörösmarty tér (Yellow line) or Deák tér (all lines).

The foreign-language bookstore of the ubiquitous Libri chain, this shop is located on Váci utca, in downtown Pest. It has a fair selection of Corvina English-language books about Hungary, a section of English-language fiction, English-language magazines and newspapers, and a music section. Open Monday through Friday from 10am to 6pm and on Saturday from 9am to 1pm.

## ✪ Litea: Literature & Tea Bookshop

I. Hess András tér 4. ☎ **1/175-6987.** Mon–Sat 10am–6pm, Sun 1pm–6pm. Bus: Várbusz from Moszkva tér, bus 16 from Deák tér, or funicular from Clark Ádám tér, to Castle Hill.

Situated in the Fortuna courtyard opposite the Hilton Hotel, this bookshop/teahouse stocks a wide range of books on Hungary, CDs and cassettes of the works of Hungarian composers, as well as cards, maps, and other quality souvenirs for serious enthusiasts of Hungarian culture. This is one of the few bookshops that sells what we consider to be the two best architectural guides to Budapest: *Budapest 20th Century Architecture Guide* and *Századeleji Házak Budapesten* (see "Recommended Books," in chapter 1). Take your time browsing; order a cup of tea, sit, and have a closer look at the books that interest you. This calm, no-obligation-to-buy atmosphere is a rare find.

**Studium Könyvesbolt**
V. Váci u. 22. ☎ **1/118-5881.** Metro: Vörösmarty tér (Yellow line) or Deák tér (all lines).

This is the best Váci utca bookshop for those in search of English-language books (mostly Corvina books) about Budapest or Hungary. Coffee-table books, guidebooks, fiction and poetry in translation, and scholarly works are available. There's also a good selection of maps, including the hard-to-find Cartographia trail map of the Buda Hills (A *Budai Hegység*). Open Monday through Friday from 9:30am to 7pm and on Saturday from 10am to 3pm.

## BUTTONS

### ✪ Gomb (Button Store)
V. Váci u. 75. Metro: Ferenciek tere (Blue line).

For the button lover in your life. This tiny shop, on the quieter end of the Váci utca, sells nothing but buttons. There are dozens of drawers full of buttons, most of which have a strikingly retro (outdated) appeal. Dénes Vándorffy, *gombkészitő* (button-maker), is a shopkeeper from the old days, when it was possible to make a living from something as mundane (but necessary) as a button. We can only hope that his little business continues to survive, now that this section of the Váci utca has been made part of the pedestrian tourist-way. Open Monday through Friday, 10am to 2pm.

## CLOTHING & SHOES

We list just a few options, assuming you'll discover the rest on your own.

### Bagatell
V. Váci u. 6. ☎ **1/117-7207.** Metro: Vörösmarty tér (Yellow line) or Deák tér (all lines).

Bagatell is a closet-sized boutique featuring cutting-edge Italian and Austrian women's fashions and accessories—silk, rayon, and cotton. Open Monday through Friday from 10am to 6pm and on Saturday from 10am to 1pm.

### Joker Applied Arts
VII. Akácfa u. 5/a. ☎ **1/341-4281.** Metro: Blaha Lujza tér (Red line).

Located just off Blaha Lujza tér, next door to the Hotel Emke. In business since the late 1970s (a very long time in ever-changing Budapest), Joker features original handmade goods by local artisans, as well as Asian import items. Clothing, shoes, and accessories are for sale. Proprietor Judit Maior died recently and is fondly remembered by her regular customers. Her daughter Andrea now keeps shop. Open Monday through Friday from 10am to 6pm and on Saturday from 10am to 2pm.

### Kaláka Design Studio
V. Haris köz 2. ☎ **1/118-3313.** Metro: Vörösmarty tér (Yellow line) or Deák tér (all lines).

Here you'll find unique women's shoes and clothing by Hungarian fashion designers Vörös Zsuzsa and Bodor Ágnes. Clothing is exquisitely tailored from the finest materials. Kaláka has a second shop in the Castle District, at I. Szentháromság u. 5. Open Monday through Friday from 10am to 6pm and on Saturday from 10am to 2pm.

## Manu-Art

V. Múzeum krt. 7 (in the courtyard). ☎ **1/137-4677.** Metro: Astoria (Red line).

Handcrafted originals by local applied-arts students are the stock in trade here: women's clothing (hand-dyed cottons), funky oversize coffee mugs, and T-shirts. Open Monday through Friday from 10am to 6pm and on Saturday from 10am to 1pm. Manu-Art has two other (smaller) shops, the latter selling just hand-printed T-shirts: VI. Bajcsy-Zsilinszky köz 3 (☎ 1/332-0298) and V. Károly krt. 10, near Astoria (☎ 1/266-8136).

## ✪ V50 Design Art Studio

V. Váci u. 50 ☎ **1/137-5320.** Metro: Ferenciek tere (Blue line).

Valeria Fazekas, fashion designer, has a unique sense for clothes that are both subtle and elegant. Great care goes into every single piece. Her choice of materials is distinctive, her tailoring exquisite. Her hats are nearly works of art. Prices are more than reasonable, but she does not accept credit cards. She has a second shop at V. Belgrád rakpart 16, where she can often be found working late into the night in the upstairs studio. The first shop is open Monday through Saturday, 1pm to 6pm; the second shop is open Monday through Friday, 10am to 6pm and Saturday 10am to 1pm.

# COINS

## Globe Numizmatikai Galéria

V. Nádor u. 5. ☎ **1/137-7940.** Metro: Deák tér (all lines).

This small shop, not far from Deák tér in a quiet part of the Inner City, has a variety of coins and antique paper money for sale. Of particular note are the Roman coins. Open Monday through Thursday from 9am to 3pm, Friday from 10am to 2pm.

Coin enthusiasts might also visit the several coin shops across the street from the Dohány utca Synagogue, near Astoria (Red line metro). Sometimes you can observe a huddle of old men, diehard collectors no doubt, trading old coins with each other on the street in front of these shops.

# DEPARTMENT STORES & MALLS

Sprawling Örs Vezér tere, the eastern terminus of the Red metro line, is home both to Budapest's branch of the internationally known Swedish **Ikea** chain and to the city's first quasi-American-style mall, **Sugár.** The mall's open Monday through Friday from 9am to 6pm and weekends from 9am to 2pm. Individual shops set their own hours within the mall.

Closer to the center, try the ever-crowded **Skála Metro,** at Nyugati tér across from Nyugati Station, or the equally popular **Buda Skála,** on Október 23 utca, near Móricz Zsigmond körtér. Both are open Monday through Friday from 10am to 6pm and on Saturday from 9am to 1pm.

On Váci utca, the **Fortuna Department Store** houses the latest in men's and women's international designer fashions. There's also an elegant perfumery and a cafe on the top floor. Fortuna is air-conditioned. Open Monday through Friday from 10am to 6pm and on Saturday until 3pm.

Three new malls sprouted in Budapest between January and April 1997, like mushrooms after rain. **Duna Plaza,** XII. Váci út 178 (☎ 1/465-1220), is a shopping center/entertainment complex, comprised of 120 different shops (including a Virgin Records Megastore), a nine-screen "Hollywood Cineplex," snackbars and pubs, the best bowling alley in the city, and even a small ice rink. Duna Plaza is also unique in featuring an Internet Club (☎ 1/465-1126; online at www.plazaclub.com), providing 15 PCs and a Mac for use at 600 Ft ($3) per hour, 12 Ft ($.06) per minute for sending e-mail. Duna Plaza is open daily 9am to 9pm; the entertainment complex closes later.

**Polus Center,** at XV Szentmihályi út 131 (☎ 1/419-4028), is now the largest shopping mall in the region. It is home to TESCO, the British supermarket chain, as well as to countless other shops. Wings in the mall have flashy American street names: Rodeo Drive, Sunset Boulevard, Wall Street, etc. A cheesy touch, but evocative of a certain American-style capitalist mania. Open weekdays 10am to 8pm, weekends 10am to 6pm. A mall shuttle bus or else bus 73 (red-lettered) departs for Polus Center from Keleti station.

**Euro Park,** the third and smallest of the new malls, is located at XIX. Üllői út 201 (☎ 1/282-9266). Metro: Határ út (Blue line).

## FOLK CRAFTS

Except for a few specialty shops like the ones listed below, the stores of the state-owned **Folkart Háziipar** should be your main source of Hungary's justly famous folk items. Almost everything is handmade—from tablecloths to miniature dolls, from ceramic dishes to sheepskin vests. You can shop with the knowledge that all items have been passed by a critical jury. This is represented by the distinctive label (or sticker) you'll find on all Folkart products: a circle with a bird in the center, surrounded by the words FOLKART/NÉPMÚVÉSZETI HUNGARY. The private folk-art shops lining Váci utca and the streets of the Castle District tend to be much more expensive, and their products, unlike Folkart's, often tend toward the kitschy (though with some notable exceptions). The main store, **Folkart Centrum,** is at V. Váci u. 14 (☎ 1/118-5840) and is open daily from 9:30am to 7pm.

You'll find a second Folkart store at VIII. Rákóci út 32 (☎ 1/342-0753), with similar offerings at similar prices; unlike Folkart Centrum, this one is closed Sunday.

One outstanding private shop on Váci utca is ✪ **Vali Folklór,** in the courtyard of Váci u. 23 (☎ 1/137-6301). This cluttered shop is run by a soft-spoken man named Bálint Ács who travels the villages of Hungary and neighboring countries buying up authentic folk items. He's extremely knowledgeable about the products he sells, and enjoys speaking with customers (in German or English). When he is not around, his mother keeps shop; she speaks no English. The most appealing items here are the traditional women's clothing. Prices are fair, and Bálint Ács's mother tailors them to size for you in 3 to 4 days time. Open Monday through Friday from 10am to 6pm and on Saturday and Sunday from 10am to 7pm.

Lovers of **dolls** might visit Mrs. Berényi, the gregarious older woman who runs the tiny doll repair shop and store, **Baba Klinika,** at V. Múzeum krt. 5 (☎ 1/267-2445), near Astoria. Open Monday through Friday from 9:30am to 5:30pm and on Saturday from 9:30am to 12:30pm.

✪ **Holló Folkart Gallery,** at V. Vitkovics Mihály u. 12 (☎ 1/117-8103), is an unusual gallery selling handcrafted reproductions of original folk-art pieces from various regions of the country. Beautiful carved and painted furniture is for sale, as well as smaller mirrors, decorative boxes, traditional decorative pottery, and wooden candlesticks. Open Monday through Friday from 10am to 6pm and on Saturday from 10am to 1pm.

## MARKETS

Markets are very crowded, bustling places. Be wary of pickpockets. Carry your valuables under your clothing in a money belt rather than in a wallet (See "Safety" in chapter 3).

## OPEN MARKETS (PIAC)

**Józsefvárosi Piac**
VIII. Kőbányai út. ☎ **1/314-0833.**

The market closest to the city center, the Józsefvárosi piac has been renamed "Four Tigers" as a result of the influx of Chinese vendors. The piac, situated on the side of a railroad yard, near the Józsefváros Station, is not really a flea market in the technical sense of the word since most of the goods are not secondhand. But you'll find bargains aplenty: Chinese silk, Turkish dresses, Russian caviar, vodka, the occasional piece of Stalinist memorabilia, toy tanks, Romanian socks, slippers, and chalky-tasting chocolate. Also for sale are dishes, clocks, pens, combs, clothes, tea, and East European condoms. All prices are negotiable. Foreign currency is welcomed, though you'll attract far less attention by paying in forints. Dozens of languages are spoken in the tightly packed, crowded lanes of this outdoor market, which operates daily from 7am to 6pm. To get here, take tram no. 28 from Blaha Lujza tér or no. 36 from Baross tér (Keleti Station), and get off at Orczy tér.

**Ecseri Flea Market**
XIX. Nagykőrösi út, ☎ **1/280-8840.**

Rows of wooden tables chock-full of old dishes, toys, linens, and bric-a-brac greet you as you enter this market at Nagykőrösi út 156. From the tiny cubicles in the narrow corridors, serious dealers market their wares: Herend and Zsolnay porcelain, Bulgarian and Russian icons, silverware, paintings, furniture, clocks, rugs, prewar dolls and stuffed animals, antique clothing, and jewelry. The Ecseri is clearly something more than your average flea market. Antiques buyers beware, though; you'll need permission from the Museum of Applied Arts to take your purchases out of the country. Haggling is standard. Purchases are in cash only. The market runs Monday through Friday from 8am to 4pm and on Saturday from 8am to 3pm. Take bus no. 54 from Boráros tér.

## FRUIT & VEGETABLE MARKETS (CSARNOK OR PIAC)

There are five vintage market halls (*vásárcsarnok*) in Budapest. These vast cavernous spaces, all wonders of steel and glass, were built in the 1890s in the ambitious grandiose style of the time. Three are still in use as markets and provide a measure of local color you certainly won't find in the grocery store. A visit to any of the markets is well worth the time. Hungarian produce is sensational, and you'll seldom go wrong with a kilo of strawberries, a cup of raspberries, or a couple of peaches.

The **Központi Vásárcsarnok** (Central Market Hall), on IX. Vámház körút (☎ 1/217-7700), is the largest and most spectacular market hall. Located on the Inner Ring (Kiskörút), on the Pest side of the Szabadság Bridge, it has been impeccably reconstructed and was reopened for business in 1995. This bright, trilevel market hall is a pleasure to visit. Fresh produce, meat, and cheese vendors dominate the space. Keep your eyes open for inexpensive saffron and dried mushrooms, as well. The mezzanine level features folk-art booths, coffee and drink bars, and fast-food booths. The basement level houses seafood, pickled goods, a complete selection of spices, and Asian import foods, along with a large grocery store. Open Monday, 6am to 5pm, Tuesday through Friday, 6am to 6pm, and on Saturday from 6am to 2pm. Take the metro to Kálvin tér (Blue line).

The **Belvárosi Vásárcsarnok** (Inner City Market Hall), on V. Hold utca (☎ 1/313-8442), is located in central Pest in the heart of the Lipótváros (Leopold Town), behind Szabadság tér. It houses a large supermarket, in addition to fruit and vegetable vendors. Open on Monday from 6am to 5pm, Tuesday through Friday from 6am to 6pm, and on Saturday from 6am to 2pm. Take the metro either to Kossuth tér (Red line) or Arany János utca (Blue line).

The **Józsefvárosi Vásárcsarnok,** on VIII. Rákóczi tér (☎ 1/313-8442), badly damaged by fire in 1988, was restored to its original splendor and reopened in 1991. There's only a small area of private vendors; the rest of the hall is filled with retail booths. Open on Monday from 6am to 4pm, Tuesday through Friday from 6am to 6pm, and on Saturday from 6am to 1pm. Take the metro to Blaha Lujza tér (Red line) or tram no. 4 or 6 directly to Rákóczi tér.

In addition to these three classic market halls, Budapest has dozens of neighborhood produce markets. Here are two centrally located ones: The **Fehérvári úti Vásárcsarnok,** on XI. Fehérvári út (☎ 1/181-0355), in front of the Buda Skála department store, is just a block from the Móricz Zsigmond körtér transportation hub. Open Monday through Friday from 6am to 6pm. Take tram no. 47 from Deák tér to Fehérvári út, or any tram or bus to Móricz Zsigmond körtér. The **Fény utca Piac,** on II. Fény utca, just off Moszkva tér in Buda, is currently closed for an ambitious reconstruction project; it should reopen at the end of 1998. Open Monday from 6am to 5pm, Tuesday through Friday from 6am to 6pm, and on Saturday from 6am to 1pm. Take the metro to Moszkva tér (Red line). Unfortunately, the renovation will mean higher rental fees, which will drive out many of the elderly and smaller vendors. The renovation of the Központi Vásárcsarnok in 1995 came at the same sad price.

**Lehel tér Piac,** at VI. Lehel tér, is another neighborhood market, and our personal favorite. It is a bustling but not overwhelming place. It has an authentic, workaday ambience you won't find in a newly renovated, gentrified *vásárcsarnok*. Along the sidewalk there are vendors selling household goods (teakettles, potholders, seat cushions, cooking utensils) and clothing (socks, underwear, kids' clothes). Farther in are rows of succulent produce, legumes, nuts, dried fruits, spices, meat, and cheese (including very tasty goat cheese [*kecske sájt*] from Slovakia). Most of the vendors here let you select your own produce, something that you usually aren't permitted to do in the larger vásárcsarnoks. Take the Blue line metro to Lehel tér

## MODELS

### Sas Militaria

V. Sas u. 1. ☎ **1/266-4393.** Metro: Kossuth tér (Red line) or Arany János utca (Blue line).

Perhaps the largest complete model shop in Budapest, Sas Militaria specializes, as its name suggests, in military models, but also sells all sorts of accessories for model building as well. The staff is very knowledgeable. If you're a model enthusiast, don't miss this remarkable shop. Open Monday through Friday from 10am to 6pm and on Saturday from 9:30am to 1:30pm.

## MUSIC

### Violin Universitas

V. Károlyi Mihály u. 19. ☎ **1/117-4103.** Metro: Ferenciek tere (Blue line).

One of the best selections in the city of Hungarian folk music can be found here. Other musical tastes will be satisfied, too. Open daily 9am to midnight.

### Liszt Ferenc Zeneműboltja (Ferenc Liszt Music Shop)

VI. Andrássy út 45. ☎ **1/322-4091.** Metro: Oktogon (Yellow line).

Budapest's musical crowd frequents this shop, located near both the State Opera House and the Ferenc Liszt Academy of Music. Sheet music, scores, records, tapes,

CDs, and books are availab[...]
on Saturday from 10am t[...]

## Wave

VI. Bajcsy-Zsilinszky út 15/d. [...]

On Révay köz, a small [...]
from the rear of St. Ste[...]
garians looking for acid [...]
Age music by Deep F[...]
music shop, called **T**[...]
alternative and punk [...]
concert information [...]
(until 8pm in summ[...]

Virgin, the mam[...]
Mall. See the secti[...]

164    Shopping

# SOUVENIRS & GIFTS

## Interieur Studio

V. Vitkovics Mihály u. 6. ☎ 1/137-7005

A fragrant potpourri scent greets [...]
find wonderful gift possibiliti[...]
hand-dipped candles, teas, an[...]
tion of dried flowers, and [...]
sells handmade Christ[...]
Friday from 10am t[...]

## Vár-Bazár

I. Ostrom u. 10. N[...]
In this clos[...]
hood be[...]
inexp[...]

# PORCELAIN & [...]

## Herend Shop

V. József nádor tér 11. ☎ **1/117-2622.** Metro: Vorosm[...]
lines).

Hand-painted Herend porcelain, first produced in 1826 in the town of Herend near Veszprém in western Hungary, is world renowned. This shop has the widest Herend selection in the capital. Unfortunately, they can't arrange shipping. Even if you don't intend to buy, come just to see some gorgeous examples of Hungary's most famous product. The store is located in Pest's Inner City, on quiet József nádor tér, just a few minutes' walk from Vörösmarty tér. Open Monday through Friday from 10am to 6pm and on Saturday from 9am to 1pm. If you plan a trip to Veszprém or Lake Balaton, you should visit the Herend Museum in Herend (see chapter 11).

## Herend Village Pottery

II. Bem rakpart 37. ☎ **1/156-7899.** Metro: Batthyány tér (Red line).

If Herend porcelain isn't your style (or in your price range), this delightfully casual pottery might be just the thing. Various patterns and solid colors are available; all are dishwasher and oven safe. Because everything is handcrafted, it's possible to order and reorder particular pieces at a later time. Prices are reasonable at this particular shop. They also sell quality crystal from Hungary, known as Ajka crystal. The owners are very knowledgeable, eager to assist but not pushy. Open Monday through Friday from 9am to 5pm and on Saturday from 9am to noon.

A second Herend Village Pottery shop recently opened at V. Váci u. 23 (☎ 1/118-3240; fax 1/118-2094). They sell Herend porcelain as well as village pottery. What is more, they are the only shop to date that offers shipping on large orders. Though the service is costly ($45), you are likely to be saving far more on the price of Herend china purchased here in Hungary.

## Zsolnay Márkabolt

V. Kígyó u. 4. ☎ **1/118-3712.** Metro: Vörösmarty tér (Yellow line) or Deák tér (all lines).

Delightfully gaudy Zsolnay porcelain from the southern city of Pécs is Hungary's second-most-celebrated brand of porcelain, and this shop has Budapest's widest selection. Like the Herend shop, they cannot arrange shipping. Even if you don't intend to buy, come just to see some fabulous examples of Hungary's other internationally known porcelain. The Zsolnay Museum is in Pécs (see chapter 13). Open Monday through Friday from 10am to 6pm and on Saturday from 10am to 1pm.

. Metro: Ferenciek tere (Blue line).

you as you enter this lovely little shop. Here you'll
s: original pottery, unusual baskets, natural cosmetics,
unique handmade boxes and blank books, a huge selec-
beautiful silk-screened papers for gift wrapping. Interieur
nas and Easter decorations in season. Open Monday through
6pm and on Saturday from 10am to 2pm.

phone. Metro: Moszkva tér (Red line).

t-sized subterranean thrift shop, located in the steep, twisting neighbor-
ween Buda's Moszkva tér and the Castle District, you can find all sorts of
nsive knickknacks, including old postcards, some nice plates, and even the
asional piece of Herend china. Márta, the woman who runs the shop, speaks no
nglish, but somehow seems able to converse with English-speakers anyway. Open
Monday through Friday from noon to 6pm.

## TEA & COFFEE

**1000 Tea**
V. Váci u. 65. ☎ **1/137-8217.** Metro: Ferenciek tere (Blue line).

Set back in the courtyard of Váci u. 65 (a teapot-shaped sign points the way), this
cozy little shop is a haven for serious tea drinkers, with 24 different bulk teas available. A wall map, stuck with labels from the various teas, indicates their places of origin. Information as to the harvest of individual teas is also posted—in five languages.
The shop owner and sales clerk are happy to advise and inform you in your selections. Prices range from 500 Ft to 1,700 Ft ($2.50 to $8.50) per 100 grams. Open
Monday through Friday, 11am to 7pm; Saturday, 10am to 2pm.

**Coquan's Kávé**
V. Nádor u. 5. ☎ **1/266-9936.** Metro: Deák tér (all lines).

Opened in 1996, Coquan's serves and sells high quality, freshly ground coffees. It is
currently the only shop of its kind in Budapest, started by an American who no doubt
saw the need. About 20 different types of coffee are available. You can buy in bulk
(500–600 Ft/$2.50–$3 per 120 grams) or by the cup (120 Ft/60¢ for a cup of Italian roast espresso). Try a slice of banana bread or cardamom coffee cake while you're
at it. Coquan's has a second shop at IX. Ráday u. 15 (☎ 1/215-2444). Both shops
are open Monday through Friday, 8am to 7pm; Saturday, 9am to 5pm. The shop
on Ráday utca is also open on Sunday, 9am to 5pm.

## TOYS & KID STUFF

**Burattino Jaték (Burattino Toys)**
IX. Ráday u. 47. ☎ **1/215-5621.** Metro: Kálvin tér (Blue line) (ascend from underpass to Ráday
utca).

This is a closet-sized store specializing in handmade wooden toys: trucks, trains, doll
houses, and fancy building blocks. There are also wonderful hand and finger puppets made from felt (the wolf, the fox, and the turtle are particularly special), as well
as other original and educational toys. Open Monday through Friday, 10am to 6pm;
Saturday 10am to 1pm.

### Toys Anno
VI. Teréz krt. 54. ☎ **1/302-6234.** Metro: Nyugati pu. (Blue line).

Part museum, part specialty shop, Toys Anno might be of more interest to collectors than to kids. The shop sells exact replicas of antique toys from around the world. The tin toys are exceptional, especially the monkeys on bicycles, the lilting Ferris wheel, and the Soviet rocket that prepares for launch by itself. There are also old-fashioned dolls and puzzles. Items are behind glass and tagged with a serial number. You have to ask for prices and display of toys that interest you. The clerk is more than happy to oblige. Open Monday through Friday, 10am to 6pm; Saturday, 9am to 1pm.

### Gyermek Cipő (Children's Shoes)
V. Múzeum krt. 7 (inside the courtyard). ☎ **1/117-8182.** Metro: Astoria (Red line).

This bright, modern shop sells a wide variety of Hungarian and imported toddler and kids' shoes. Prices are more or less comparable to American prices, but the colorful selection and the hand-stitched leather make these shoes something special. A casual, kid-friendly atmosphere pervades; Barney or Sesame Street videos play on a TV. Open Monday through Friday, 10am to 6pm; Saturday, 10am to 2pm.

### Rokiland
VII. Erzsébet krt. 4. ☎ **1/322-2495.** Metro: Blaha Lujza tér (Red line).

This tiny upstairs shop, just off Blaha Lujza tér, has all sorts of handcrafted pipe-cleaner animals. Prices start at around 80 Ft (40¢). Several display windows on the street give you an idea of what's available. The best animals here are clearly the monkeys, which one enthusiastic, thirtysomething American collector we know, has been buying in great quantities since he first came to Hungary almost 7 years ago. They have recently introduced a light brown monkey, in addition to the old dark brown model. The snakes are also great; watch the cashier give each snake an expert twist before putting it into your bag. Incidentally, we have just discovered that these pipe-cleaner animals make great cat toys, too. Open Monday through Friday from 10am to 6pm.

There is also another newly opened Rokiland store just off Váci utca in central Pest; it is at V. Petőfi Sándor u. 3 (☎ 1/117-3131).

## WINE & CHEESE

### La Boutique des Vins
V. József Attila u. 12 (behind the Jaguar dealership). ☎ **1/117-5919.** Metro: Deák tér (any line)

Sophisticated, classy, and friendly, this wine shop is a cut above the others. It is truly *the* place for learning about and/or purchasing Hungarian wines. The owners speak excellent English and are well versed in their merchandise. Try the excellent Villány reds or the whites from the Balaton region. A wide range of Tokaj dessert wines, dating back to 1912, is also available. Prices are reasonable. Open Monday through Friday from 10am to 6pm and on Saturday from 10am to 3pm.

### Nagy Tamás Sajtkereskedése (Thomas Nagy's Cheese Shop)
V. Gerlóczy u. 3. ☎ **1/327-1000.** Metro: Deák tér (all lines).

Opened in 1994, this is the only shop to date dealing exclusively in cheese. The shop sells more than 300 types of hard and soft cheeses, including Hungarian, as well as imported French, Italian, Dutch, and English varieties. Open Monday through Friday from 9am to 6pm and on Saturday from 9am to 1pm.

# 9

# Budapest After Dark

**B**udapest is blessed with a rich and varied cultural life. The Tour-inform office recently boasted that in the average month the city was the site of no fewer than 840 noteworthy performances! In Budapest you can still go to the Opera House, one of Europe's finest, for less than $3 (the most expensive tickets in the house, in the fabulously ornate royal box once used by the Habsburgs, go for less than $25). Almost all of the city's theaters and halls, with the exception of those hosting internationally touring rock groups, offer tickets for as little as $2 to $4. Of course, you can also get $18 to $20 tickets at the same venues. It makes sense in Budapest to select a performance based as much on the venue as on the program. If, for example, the Great Hall of the Academy of Music is the venue, it would be worth your while to consider a program you might not ordinarily be interested in.

The opera, ballet, and theater seasons run from September through May or June, but most theaters and halls also host performances during the summer festivals. A number of lovely churches and stunning halls offer concerts exclusively in the summer. While classical culture has a long and proud tradition in Budapest, jazz, blues, rock, and disco have exploded in the post-Communist era. New clubs and bars have opened up everywhere; the parties start late and last until morning. So put on your dancing shoes or slip your opera glasses into your pocket; whatever your entertainment preference, Budapest nights offer plenty to choose from.

**PROGRAM LISTINGS**  The most complete schedule of mainstream performing arts is found in the free bimonthly *Koncert Kalendárium,* available at the Central Philharmonic Ticket Office in Vörösmarty tér. The *Budapest Sun,* one of two English-language weeklies, has a comprehensive events calendar; it also lists less-publicized events like modern dance and folk music performances. **"Programme in Hungary"** and **"Budapest Panorama,"** the two free monthly tourist booklets, have only partial entertainment listings, featuring what their editors consider the monthly highlights.

**TICKET OFFICES**  For opera, ballet, theater, and concert tickets, you're better off going to one of the commission-free state-run ticket offices than to the individual box offices. There are always schedules posted, and you'll have a variety of choices. If none of the cashiers speaks English, find a helpful customer who can translate for you. On the day of the performance, though, you might have better luck at the box office. The Central Theater Ticket Office (Színházak Központi Jegyiroda), VI. Andrássy út 18 (☎ 1/312-0000), sells tickets to just about everything, from theater and operetta to sports events and rock concerts. The office is open Monday through Thursday from 9am to 1pm and 1:45 to 6pm, on Friday to 5pm; a second branch is at II. Moszkva tér 3 (☎ 1/135-9136), with the same hours from 10am. For **classical performances,** go to the National Philharmonic Ticket Office (Filharmonía Nemzeti Jegyiroda), V. Vörösmarty tér 1 (☎ 1/118-0281), open Monday through Friday from 10am to 1:30pm and 2 to 6pm, and on Saturday from 10am to 2pm. For **opera and ballet,** go to the Hungarian State Opera Ticket Office (Magyar Állami Opera Jegyiroda), VI. Andrássy út 20 (entrance inside the courtyard) (☎ 1/332-7914), open Monday through Friday from 11am to 5pm. For events in the **Spring Festival,** go to the Festival Ticket Service, V. 1081 Rákóczi út 65 (☎ 1/210-2795 or 133-2337), open daily from 10am to 6pm before and during the festival. For **rock and jazz concert** tickets, try Ticket Express, VI. Jókai u. 40. (☎ 1/153-0692).

# 1   The Performing Arts

The major symphony orchestras in Budapest are the Budapest Festival Orchestra, the Philharmonic Society Orchestra, the Hungarian State Symphony Orchestra, the Budapest Symphony Orchestra, and the Hungarian Railway Workers' (MÁV) Symphony Orchestra. The major chamber orchestras include the Hungarian Chamber Orchestra, the Ferenc Liszt Chamber Orchestra, the Budapest String Players, and the newly established Hungarian Virtuosi. Major choirs include the Budapest Chorus, the Hungarian State Choir, the Hungarian Radio and Television Choir, the Budapest Madrigal Choir, and the University Choir.

Budapest is now on the touring route of dozens of major European ensembles and virtuosos. Keep your eyes open for the performances of well-known visitors.

## OPERA, OPERETTA & BALLET

### Erkel Színház (Erkel Theater)
VIII. Köztársaság tér 30. ☎ 1/333-0540. Metro: Keleti pu. (Red line).

The Erkel Theater is the second home of the State Opera and Ballet. The largest theater in Hungary, it seats as many as 2,400 people. Though it was built in art nouveau style in 1911, little of its original character shows through the various renovations it has undergone. If you have a choice, go to the Opera House instead (their seasons—mid-September to mid-June—are the same). Chamber orchestra concerts are also performed here. Ticket prices range from 200 to 1,500 Ft ($1 to $7.50). It's open the same hours as the State Opera House, below.

### Fővárosi Operettszínház (Municipal Operetta Theater)
VI. Nagymező u. 17. ☎ 1/269-3870. Metro: Opera or Oktogon (Yellow line).

In the heart of Budapest's theater district, the Municipal Operetta Theater is the site not just of operetta, but also of rock opera and musicals. Recent hits have included *The Sound of Music, Sugar,* and *Crazy for You.* The off-season is mid-July to mid-August. Ticket prices vary by show, generally ranging from 300 to 2,000 Ft ($1.50 to $10). The box office is open Monday through Friday from 9:30am to 6pm and on Saturday from 1 to 6pm.

### Magyar Állami Operaház (Hungarian State Opera House)
VI. Andrássy út 22. ☎ 1/131-2550. Metro: Opera (Yellow line).

Completed in 1884, the Opera House is the crowning achievement of the famous Hungarian architect Miklós Ybl's career. It's easily Budapest's most famous performance hall, and a tourist attraction in its own right. The lobby is adorned with Bertalan Székely's frescoes; the ceiling frescoes in the hall itself are by Károly Lotz. Guided tours of the Opera House leave daily at 3 and 4pm; the cost is 600 Ft ($3).

The splendid Opera House, home to both the State Opera and the State Ballet, possesses a rich history. A political scandal marked the first opening performance in 1884: Ferenc Liszt had written a piece to be performed especially for the event, but when it was discovered that he had incorporated elements of the *Rákóczi March,* a patriotic Hungarian (and anti-Habsburg) melody, he was prevented from playing it. Gustav Mahler and Ferenc Erkel rank as the Opera House's most famous directors.

Hungarians adore opera, and a large percentage of seats are sold on a subscription basis; buy your tickets a few days ahead of time if you can. The season runs from mid-September to mid-June. Summer visitors, however, can take in the approximately 10 performances (both opera and ballet) of the Summer Festival, in July or August. Seating capacity is 1,260. Ticket prices range from 300 to 4,500 Ft ($1.50 to $22.50). The cheaper tickets may be hard to come by, however. The box office is open Monday through Friday from 11am to 6pm. Performances usually start at 7pm, but some longer shows start as early as 5pm. There are occasional weekend matinees.

## CLASSICAL MUSIC

### Bartók Béla Emlékház (Béla Bartók Memorial House)
II. Csalán út 29. ☎ **1/176-2100.** Tickets 200–300 Ft ($1–$3). Bus: 5 from Március 15 tér or Moszkva tér to Pasaréti tér (the last stop).

This charming little hall is in Béla Bartók's last Budapest residence, which is also the site of a Bartók museum. A regular Friday concert series is given by the Bartók String Quartet, a prolific group founded in 1957 (they play a lot more than just Bartók). Concerts are performed from the end of September through December. For schedule information, check Budapest's free bimonthly *Koncert Kalendárium.* Performances are on Friday at 6pm, and occasionally other days.

### Budapesti Kongresszusi Központ (Budapest Convention Center)
XII. Jagelló út 1–3. ☎ **1/161-2869.** Tickets 500–800 Ft ($2.50–$4). Tram: 61 from Moszkva tér or Móricz Zsigmond körtér.

A large modern hall that's a convention as well as concert site, the Convention Center has established itself in recent years as one of the more important halls in the city. The hall is spacious and comfortable, but lacks the character of the older venues. It's part of the Novotel complex in central Buda. The performance schedule varies.

### Pesti Vigadó (Pest Concert Hall)
V. Vigadó tér 1. ☎ **1/138-4721.** Tickets 400–3,000 Ft ($2–$15). Metro: Vörösmarty tér (Yellow line) or Deák tér (all lines).

Right in the middle of the famed Danube Promenade (Dunakorzó), the Vigadó is one of the city's oldest music halls, dating to 1864. All sorts of classical performances are held here. Although it's one of the city's best-known halls, Hungarian music lovers rate its acoustics and atmosphere second place to the Academy of Music. The concert schedule varies; the box office is always open during the day before a performance.

### Zeneakadémia (Ferenc Liszt Academy of Music)
VI. Liszt Ferenc tér 8. ☎ **1/341-4788** or 1/342-0179. Tickets 500–1,500 Ft ($2.50–$7.50). Metro: Oktogon or Opera (Yellow line).

## Music on a Summer's Eve

During the summer, you'll find several special venues for enjoying classical music. Tickets for all summer-program venues are available at the **National Philharmonic Ticket Office,** V. Vörösmarty tér 1 (☎ 1/118-0281), open Monday through Friday from 10am to 1:30pm and 2 to 6pm, and on Saturday from 10am to 2pm.

The historic outdoor **Dominican Courtyard,** incorporated into the award-winning design of the Castle District's Hilton Hotel, I. Hess András tér 1–3 (☎ 1/214-3000), is the site for a series of classical recitals during the Budapest Summer Program. The schedule varies each year; recitals are usually in July. Ticket prices run 500 to 1,000 Ft ($1.50 to $5). Take the Várbusz from Moszkva tér or bus no. 16 from Deák tér to Castle Hill.

The Castle District's beautiful **Matthias Church** (Mátyás Templom), I. Szentháromság tér 2, holds a regular Friday-night series of organ concerts (7:30pm) from June through September. Concerts start at 7:30pm. Ticket prices are 500 to 2,500 Ft (75¢ to $12.45). You can buy tickets at the National Philharmonic Ticket Office, during the day in the church (9am to 7pm), or just before the performance. Take the Várbusz from Moszkva tér or bus no. 16 from Deák tér to Castle Hill.

Organ concerts are also held Monday evenings at 7pm during July and August at **St. Stephen's Church (Basilica),** Hungary's largest church, V. Szent István tér 33 (☎ 1/117-2859). Every week features a different program. Tickets cost 500 Ft to 1,500 Ft ($2.50 to $7.50) and can be purchased before the performance at the church entry or else at the Central Theater Ticket Office (Színházak Központi Jegyiroda), VI. Andrássy út 18 (☎ 1/312-0000).

The **Dohány Synagogue** is the venue for occasional concerts from May through September. Concerts begin at 7pm, but days are not regular. Tickets cost 500 Ft to 2,000 Ft ($2.50 to $10). For information and tickets, call the Central Theater Ticket Office.

Chamber music concerts are performed in summer in the exquisite Dome Hall of the **Parliament** building, V. Kossuth tér. The concerts feature the Hungarian Virtuosi, led by Miklós Szenthelyi, one of the premiere violinists in the city and a professor at the Music Academy. The atmosphere is absolutely grand. Concerts are held at 6pm on the second Friday of the month, from June to September. Tickets cost 3,000 Ft ($15) and include a tour of the building at 5:15pm, right before the concert. For information and tickets, call the Musica Viva Arts Foundation, V. Vörösmarty tér 1, VI/624 (☎ 1/117-7031), or the Central Theater Ticket Office.

The Great Hall (Nagyterem) of the Academy of Music, with a seating capacity of 1,200, is Budapest's premier music hall. Hungary's leading center of musical education, the Academy was built in the early years of the 20th century; the building's interior is decorated in an art nouveau style. The acoustics in the Great Hall are said to be the best of any hall in the city. If you go to only one performance in Budapest, it should be either at the Opera House or here. Unfortunately, the Great Hall is not used in the summer months; the smaller Kisterem, also a fine hall, is used then. In addition to major Hungarian and international performances, you can also attend student recitals (sometimes for free). A weekly schedule is posted outside the Király utca entrance to the Academy. The box office is open Monday through Friday from 2pm to showtime. Performances are frequent.

# FOLK PERFORMANCES

## Budai Vigadó (Buda Concert Hall)

I. Corvin tér 8. ☎ **1/117-2754.** Tickets 2,800 Ft ($14). Metro: Batthyány tér (Red line).

The Budai Vigadó is the home stage of the Hungarian State Folk Ensemble (Állami Népi Együttes Székháza). The ensemble is the oldest in the country and includes 40 dancers, a 20-member Gypsy orchestra, and a folk orchestra. Under the direction of award-winning choreographer Sándor Timár, the ensemble performs folk dances from all regions of historic Hungary. *The New York Times* called it "a mix of high art and popular tradition. . . . Every dance crackled with high speed." Tickets can be reserved by telephone. The box office is open 10am to 6pm daily. Performances usually start at 7pm on Tuesday, Thursday, and Saturday.

## Szakszervezetek Fővárosi Művelődési Háza (FMH Cultural House)

XI. Fehérvári út 47. ☎ **1/203-3868.** Tickets 2,000 Ft ($10). Tram: 47 from Deák tér.

Another popular folk program venue, the "Folklór Centrum," as some advertisements refer to this theater, features the Budapest Dance Ensemble, the Honvéd Dance Ensemble (the Army's dance troupe), the Bihari Dance Ensemble, and the Rajko Band. The Rajko Band, originally established in the 1950s, is a leading group of young Gypsy musicians (none is older than 25). A 10-minute film on Budapest precedes the performance. Tickets can be reserved by telephone. Performance days are Monday, Wednesday, Friday, and Saturday, May through October. Altogether there are about 100 performances over the course of the season.

# THEATERS

Budapest has an extremely lively theater season from September through June. For productions in English, try the **Merlin Theater,** V. Gerlóczy u. 4 (☎ 1/117-1337), located on a quiet street in the heart of the Inner City. In 1998 it marked its eighth season of English- and German-language dramatic productions. It's the only primarily foreign-language theater in Budapest, and Hungarian and foreign actors are featured. Tickets cost 1,000 to 2,000 Ft ($5 to $10); box office hours vary. Take the metro to Astoria (Red line) or Deák tér (all lines).

For musical productions, try the **Madách Theater,** VII. Erzsébet krt. 29–33 (☎ 1/233-2015), built in 1961 on the site of the famous Royal Orpheum Theater. Ticket prices are 600 to 1,2000 Ft ($3 to $6). The box office is open daily from 1 to 7pm; performances are usually at 7pm. Take tram no. 4 or no. 6 to Wesselényi utca. Also staging musical performances is the **Vigszínház (Merry Theater),** XIII. Szent István krt. 14 (☎ 1/269-3920), which was recently restored to its original delightfully gaudy neo-baroque splendor. Ticket prices are 350 to 1,500 Ft ($1.75 to $7.50). Take the metro to Nyugati pu. (Blue line). Incidentally, in the 1950s the Vigszínház served as the venue for the Hungarian Communist Party's New Year's Eve balls. Stalinist-era dictator Mátyás Rákosi hosted the events, artists and celebrities of the day were on the guest list, and everyone danced and drank the night away.

# 2  The Club Scene

The club scene in Budapest has found fertile ground since the political changes of 1989, so much so, in fact, that clubs come in and go out of fashion overnight. A few, however, like Made Inn Mine and Fregatt, have exhibited solid staying power since the late 1980s. There are few specifically jazz or blues clubs in town; most clubs prefer to be recognized for their decidedly eclectic offerings. Performances usually start late, after 10pm. All establishments serve beer and wine, and many offer mixed drinks as well.

The clubs listed below are the undisputed hot spots at press time, but you'd be wise to check the *Budapest Sun* (available at newsstands) for the latest club information.

### Franklin Trocadero Club

V. Szent István krt. 15. ☎ **1/111-4691.** Cover: 300 Ft ($1.50). Metro: Nyugati pu. (Blue line).

This hip salsa and merengue club on two levels features a large dance floor, several bars, and pool tables. Live Latin music is performed on Wednesday, Friday, and Saturday night. An international crowd mixes with local blondes. Open daily from 9pm to 5am (sometimes open later).

### Hully Gally

XII. Apor Vilmos tér 9. ☎ **1/175-9742.** Cover 1,000 Ft ($5). Tram: 59 from Moszkva tér or Déli pu. to Apor Vilmos tér.

A huge entertainment complex featuring a huge bilevel disco with cheesy live music, two topless bars, a restaurant, and a beer hall. If you like sleaze, especially of the post-Communist, nascent-capitalist variety, this is the place for you. Open daily from 8pm to 5am.

### Made Inn Mine

VI. Andrássy út 112. ☎ **1/111-3437.** Cover 300 Ft ($1.50); Thursdays 500 Ft ($2.50). Metro: Bajza utca (Yellow line).

This very popular club shares the building of the Young Artists' Club (FMK), another rock-music club, but the two establishments are completely different. The air-conditioned Made Inn Mine has a subterranean cavelike atmosphere. Wednesday night features a funk dance party and all drinks are half price. Thursday night is *the* night to be here; you may have to wait in line to enter. Open daily from 8pm to 5am. Kitchen open until 3am.

### Piaf

VI. Nagymező u. 25. ☎ **1/312-3823.** Cover 350 Ft ($1.75), from which 250 Ft ($1.25) goes toward your first drink. Metro: Oktogon (Yellow line).

In the heart of Budapest's theater district, Piaf is a sophisticated French-style night-club, with red velvet chairs and a candlelit atmosphere. Upstairs features live piano music, while downstairs is a bar. Drinks are pricy. Open daily from 10pm to 6am.

### ✪ Fél 10 Jazz Klub

VIII. Baross u. 30. ☎ **06-60/318-467** (mobile phone). Metro: Kálvin tér.

A classy, multilevel club, one of the few whose dance floor isn't crammed with teenagers. The place features live jazz performances nightly, while techno-free dance parties get going in the wee hours of the morning, Wednesday to Sunday. Open Monday through Friday, noon to dawn; Saturday and Sunday, 7pm to dawn.

## 3 The Bar Scene

### ✪ Fregatt

V. Molnár u. 26. ☎ **1/118-9997.** Metro: Ferenciek tere (Blue line).

The first English-style pub in Hungary, though now too crowded and noisy to really feel like one. Hungarians make up the better half of the clientele, but American and other English-speaking expatriates frequent Fregatt too. Guinness stout is on draft. Order at the counter, unlike in most places where waiters attend to you. Live music includes folk, country, and jazz. Open daily from 3pm to midnight.

### Cafe Incognito

VI. Liszt Ferenc tér 3. ☎ **1/342-1471.** Tram: 4 or 6 to Oktogon.

Incognito calls itself a cafe for zoning purposes, but the cozy and dim atmosphere of a bar is unmistakable. A sophisticated but casual place, Incognito opens out onto the street in the summer. There's a full bar. Open Monday through Friday from 10am to midnight and on Saturday and Sunday from noon to midnight.

### Chicago Sörgyár
VII. Erzsébet krt. 2. ☎ **1/269-6753.** Metro: Blaha Lujza tér (Red line).

An American-style microbrewery on one of Pest's busiest squares, the Chicago Sörgyár (sörgyár means "brewery") has Bulls, Cubs, and White Sox paraphernalia on the walls and a diehard expatriate clientele. They come not just for the fairly good home-brewed beer, but for the hamburgers, nachos, and French fries as well. Happy hour with half-price drinks, is Monday through Friday from 4 to 6pm. Open Monday through Thursday from noon to midnight, on Friday and Saturday from noon to 1am, and on Sunday from noon to 11pm.

### Irish Cat Pub
V. Múzeum krt. 41. ☎ **1/266-4085.** Metro: Kálvin tér (Blue line).

This is the first Irish-style pub in Budapest; there's Guinness on tap and a whiskey bar. It's a popular meeting place for ex-pats and travelers. The pub features a full menu. Open Monday through Thursday and Sunday 11am to 3am; Friday and Saturday, 11am to 5am.

### ✪ John Bull Pub
V. Podmaniczky tér 4 ☎ **1/269-3116.** Metro: Arany János utca (Blue line).

One in a chain of popular English pubs, the John Bull has comfortable chairs and plush carpeting. The rooms are well ventilated and the service is impeccable. There's occasional live music (Irish, folk, country), but no cover charge. Open daily from noon to midnight.

Look for other John Bull Pubs in Budapest, one of which is located at XII. Maros u. 28 (☎ **1/156-3565**). All are uniformly pleasant places to socialize, usually with a good number of tourists and ex-pats in attendance.

### Morrison's Music Pub
VI. Révay u. 25. ☎ **1/269-4060.** Metro: Opera (Yellow line).

An almost-twentysomething crowd packs this casual pub every night of the week. There's a small dance floor, an eclectic variety of loud live music, and a number of beers on tap. Open Monday through Saturday, 8pm to 4am.

### Tokaji Borbár (Tokaj Wine Bar)
V. Andrássy út 20. ☎ **1/269-3116.** Metro: Opera (Yellow line).

Here's a casual, unpretentious place to sample the delicious, fruity whites of the famous Tokaj region. Patrons either sit at the bar or stand. Gift boxes of the wines are available; as a special service, they'll print your (or the recipient's) name on the label of the bottle you purchase for 200 Ft ($1) extra; it takes 2 days to have this special label prepared. Open Monday through Saturday from 1pm to 9pm.

## 4  Gay Bars

As with the fickle club scene, "in" bars become "out," or even close down, at a moment's notice. The gay bar scene in Budapest is exclusively male-oriented at this point, though this, too, is liable to change. Search out a copy of the English language phone book (see "Fast Facts" in chapter 3) for a more complete listing of gay bars.

**Angel,** VII. Szövetség u. 33., is a basement establishment, with a bar, restaurant, and huge dance floor. Angel has been around for a while now, and is presumably here to stay. The clientele is not exclusively gay, especially on Friday and Sunday nights, when Angel hosts a now-famous transvestite show, starting at 11pm. Cover charge is 300 Ft ($1.50). No shows and no cover on Thursdays. Open Thursday through Sunday from 10pm to dawn. Take the metro to Blaha Lujza tér (Red line).

**Mystery Bar,** V. Nagysándor József u. 3, is a smaller place, with a larger foreign clientele. There are occasional drag shows and live lounge music. Hours vary. Take the metro to Arany János utca (Blue line).

## 5  Hungarian Dance Houses

Although Hungarian folk music no longer survives as a thriving part of rural life (except, perhaps, in Transylvania, now part of Romania), recent years have seen the growth of an urban-centered folk revival movement known as the *táncház* (dance house). An interactive evening of folk music and folk dancing, held in community centers around town, ranks as one of the best cultural experiences you can have in Hungary. We've listed a few of the best-known places to go below. The format usually consists of about an hour of dance-step instruction followed by several hours of dancing accompanied by a live band, which might include some of Hungary's best folk musicians, in an authentic, casual atmosphere. You can come just to watch and listen if you're nervous about not being able to learn the steps.

The leading Hungarian folk band Muzsikás, whose lead singer is the incomparable Márta Sebestyén (they recently toured the U.S., playing to great acclaim), hosts a táncház every Wednesday (September through June only) at 8pm (250 Ft/$1.25) at the **Marczibányi Square Cultural House (Marczibányi tér Művelődésiház),** II. Marczibányi tér 5/a (☎ 1/212-0803). Take the Red line metro to Moszkva tér. If you're in town and have an evening to catch a Muzsikás performance, don't miss it. The **FMH Cultural House (Szakszervezetek Fővárosi Művelődési Háza),** XI. Fehérvári út 47 (☎ 1/203-3868), hosts a táncház for kids every Tuesday, from 5:30pm to 6:30pm, for 100 Ft (50¢). It also holds a csángó táncház, the oldest and most authentic type of traditional Hungarian folk dance, on Saturday, from 6pm to 11pm, for 200 Ft/$1). Tram no. 47 from Deák tér gets you there.

The **First District Cultural Center,** at I. Bem rakpart 6 (☎ 1/201-0324), hosts the Téka (another well-known folk band, performing on traditional instruments) táncház every Friday evening, September through May (200 Ft/$1). The evening kicks off with a táncház hour for kids, at 5pm. The First District Cultural Center is near Clark Ádám tér, which is served by a large number of buses and trams, including bus no. 16 from Deák tér.

## 6  More Entertainment

**CASINOS**   Budapest has about a dozen casinos, mostly in the luxury hotels. At this point, only hard currency is accepted, but this may change soon. Formal dress is generally required. Following are some of the more popular casinos: **Casino Budapest Hilton,** I. Hess András tér 1–3 (☎ 1/175-1333); **Las Vegas Casino,** in the Atrium Hyatt Hotel, V. Roosevelt tér 2 (☎ 1/266-1234 or 1/117-6022); and **Orfeum Casino,** in the Hotel Béke Radisson, VI. Teréz krt. 43 (☎ 1/301-1600).

**MOVIES**   A healthy number of English-language movies are always playing in Budapest. The best source of listings and addresses is in either the *Budapest Sun* or the free weekly, *Pesti Est,* which has an English-language section for movies. Movies labeled *szinkronizált, mb.,* or *magyarul beszél* mean that the movie has been dubbed and are best to be avoided; *feliratos* means subtitled.

# 10 | The Danube Bend

The Danube Bend (Duna Kanyar), a string of small riverside towns just north of Budapest, is a popular excursion spot for foreigners and Hungarians alike. Inasmuch as the name "Danube Bend" suggests a single change in the river's direction, however, it's a misnomer. The Danube, which enters Hungary from the northwest, flows in a southeasterly direction for a time, forming the border with Hungary's northern neighbor, Slovakia. Just after Esztergom, about 25 miles north of Budapest, the river swings abruptly south. This is the start of the Danube Bend region. The river then swings sharply north again just before Visegrád, and yet again south before Vác. From Vác, it flows more or less directly south, through Budapest and down toward the country's Serbian and Croatian borders.

The delightful towns along the Bend—in particular, Szentendre, Visegrád, Esztergom, and Vác—can easily be seen on day trips from Budapest; they're all within a couple of hours away. The great natural beauty of the area, where forested hills loom over the river, makes it a welcome departure for those weary of the city. Travelers with more time can even make a long weekend out of the Bend.

## 1 Exploring the Danube Bend

### GETTING THERE

**BY BOAT & HYDROFOIL**    From April to September **boats** run between Budapest and the towns of the Danube Bend. In fact, the leisurely boat ride through the beautiful countryside of the region is one of the highlights of an excursion. All boats leave Budapest's Vigadó tér boat landing, stopping to pick up passengers 5 minutes later at Buda's Batthyány tér landing, before continuing up the river.

Schedules and towns served are complicated, so contact **MAHART,** the state shipping company, at the Vigadó tér landing (☎ 1/118-1223) for information. You can also get MAHART information from Tourinform or any Ibusz office.

Round-trip prices are 630 Ft ($3.15) to Szentendre, 690 Ft ($3.45) to Visegrád or Vác, and 750 Ft ($3.75) to Esztergom. Ask about discounts for children.

The approximate travel time from Budapest is 1¹/₂ hours to Szentendre, 2¹/₂ hours to Vác, 3¹/₂ hours to Visegrád, and 5 hours to Esztergom. If time is crucial, you might want to consider taking the train or bus (both of which are also considerably cheaper).

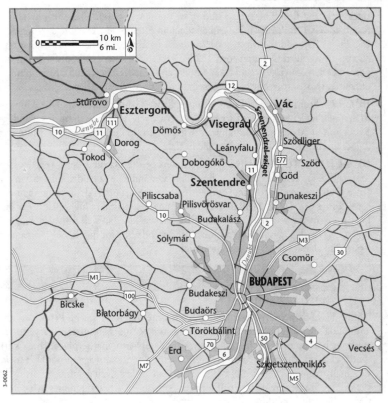

MAHART also runs a much faster (and more expensive) **hydrofoil** nonstop between Budapest's Vigadó tér and Visegrád and Esztergom. The hydrofoil runs late May to early September on Saturday, Sunday, and holidays only. It departs Budapest for Visegrád at 10:50am and returns from Visegrád at 4pm. The trip is 50 minutes. The hydrofoil departs Budapest for Esztergom twice daily, at 8am and 5pm, but makes the return trip only once at 6:15pm. The trip is an hour and 10 minutes.

**BY TRAIN** **To Szentendre:** The HÉV suburban railroad connects Budapest's Batthyány tér with Szentendre. Trains leave daily, year-round, every 20 minutes or so from 4am to 11:30pm. The one-way fare is 109 Ft (55¢); subtract 60 Ft (30¢) if you have a valid Budapest public transportation pass. The trip takes 45 minutes.

**To Visegrád:** There's no direct train service to Visegrád.

Trains depart Nyugati Station to Visegrád-Nagymaros. From there you take a ferry across the river to Visegrád. The ferry service (RÉV) is just across the street from the train station. A ferry leaves every hour throughout the day. The train ticket to Visegrád-Nagymaros costs 133 Ft (65¢); the ferry boat ticket costs 70 Ft (35¢).

**To Esztergom:** Ten trains daily make the run between Budapest's Nyugati Station and Esztergom. The trip takes about 1 1/4 hours. Train tickets cost 266 Ft ($1.35).

**To Vác:** More than 20 trains a day depart Budapest's Nyugati Station for Vác. The trip takes 45 minutes. Tickets cost 168 Ft (85¢).

**BY BUS** Approximately 30 daily buses travel the same interminable route to Szentendre, Visegrád, and Esztergom, departing from Budapest's Árpád híd bus station (at the Blue line metro station of the same name). The one-way fare to Szentendre is 126 Ft (65¢); the trip takes about 30 minutes. The fare to Visegrád is 252 Ft ($1.25), and the trip takes 1¼ hours. To Esztergom, take the bus that travels via a town called Dorog; it costs 252 Ft ($1.25) and takes 1½ hours. The bus that goes to Esztergom via Visegrád takes 4 hours and costs 410 Ft ($2.05). Keep in mind, of course, that all travel by bus is subject to occasional traffic delays.

**BY CAR**    From Budapest, Route 11 hugs the west bank of the Danube, taking you to Szentendre, Visegrád, and Esztergom. Alternatively, you could head "overland" to Esztergom by Motorway 10 highway, switching to Route 111 at Dorog. Motorway 2 goes up the east bank of the Danube to Vác.

**BY GUIDED TOUR**    Although the towns of the Danube Bend (particularly Szentendre) are easily accessible by bus, train, car, and boat, a guided tour may make sense if you're pressed for time and wish to see the major sights of more than one town. **Ibusz** (☎ 1/118-1139 or 1/118-1043) has a selection of high-quality bus and boat tours to the region. For a full list of their offerings, pick up their *Budapest Sightseeing* catalog, available at all Ibusz offices and at major hotels. See "Organized Tours," in chapter 6, for more information.

# 2  Szentendre

21km (13 miles) N of Budapest

The center of Szentendre (pronounced *Sen*-ten-dreh) must rank with Pest's Váci utca and Buda's Castle District as the most touristed spots in all Hungary. In the summer it becomes one huge handcraft and souvenir marketplace, thick with tourists. Despite the excess commercialism, Szentendre remains a gorgeous little town. Originally peopled in medieval times by Serbian settlers fleeing Turkish northward expansion, Szentendre counts half a dozen Serbian churches among its rich collection of historical buildings. The town retains a distinctively Mediterranean flavor, seldom experienced this far north in Europe.

Since the turn of the century, Szentendre has been home to an artist's colony. About one hundred artists currently live and work here. As a result, it has a wealth of museums and galleries, the best of which are listed below. Surprisingly few people visit the museums, distracted perhaps by the shopping opportunities. You'll appreciate the peace and quiet of the many exhibition halls. In Szentendre, you should explore more than the suffocating tourist scene surrounding the main drag Fő tér. Hike up the winding cobblestone streets to the Roman Catholic churchyard at the top of the hill for a lovely view of the red-tile rooftops. Wander down side streets. Szentendre is too small for you to get lost in and too beautiful for a less than thorough look around.

## ESSENTIALS

The information office **Tourinform** is at Dumtsa Jenő u. 22 (☎ 26/317-965 or 26/317-966), with maps of Szentendre (and the Danube Bend region), as well as concert and exhibition schedules. The office can also provide accommodations information and is open Monday through Friday from 10am to 4pm. If you arrive by train or bus, you'll come upon this office as you follow the flow of pedestrian traffic into town on Kossuth Lajos utca. If you arrive by boat, you may find the **Ibusz** office sooner, located on the corner of Bogdányi út and Gőzhajó utca, ☎ 26/313-597. It's open April to October, Monday through Friday from 9am to 6pm and weekends 10am to 2pm. From November to March, it's open weekdays only, 9am to 4pm.

The best source of information, particularly if you are planning to stay in the region more than a day, is **Globe Center,** at Kucsera F. u. 15 (☎ and fax **26/310-030**).

# Szentendre

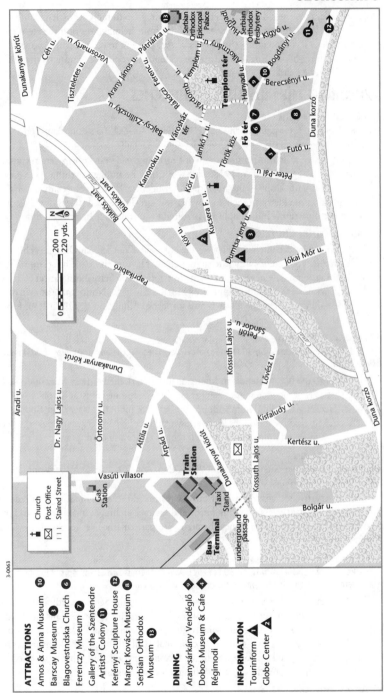

**ATTRACTIONS**

Amos & Anna Museum ⑩
Barscay Museum ③
Blagovestndska Church ⑥
Ferenczy Museum ⑦
Gallery of the Szentendre
Artists' Colony ⑪
Kerényi Sculpture House ⑫
Margit Kovács Museum ⑧
Serbian Orthodox
Museum ⑬

**DINING**

Aranysárkány Vendéglő ⑨
Dobos Museum & Cafe ④
Régimodi ⑤

**INFORMATION**

Tourinform ▲
Globe Center ②

3-0063

Gizella Faragó, the Globe Center travel agent, is extremely knowledgeable and dedicated. From hunting to horseback riding, from helping you find the right pension room to recommending the best *palacsinta* place in town, she truly knows it all. What is more, her wealth of information extends beyond Szentendre to the whole of the Danube bend.

## EXPLORING THE MUSEUMS & CHURCHES

### ✪ Margit Kovács Museum

Vastagh György u. 1. No phone. Admission 250 Ft (90¢). Apr–Oct, Tues–Sun 10am–6pm; Nov–Mar, Tues–Sun 10am–4pm. Walk east from Fő tér on Görög utca.

This expansive museum features the work of Hungary's best-known ceramic artist, Margit Kovács, who died in 1977. Her work may be unlike anything you've ever seen; this museum displays the breadth of her talents. We were especially moved by her sculptures of elderly women and by her folk-art–influenced friezes of village life. When the museum is full, people are required to wait outside before entering.

### Blagovestenska Church

The Blagovestenska church at Fő tér 4 is the only one of the Serbian Orthodox churches in Szentendre you can be fairly sure to find open. The tiny church, dating from 1752, was built on the site of an earlier wooden church from the Serbian migration of 1690. A rococo iconostasis features paintings of Mihailo Zivkovic. Notice that the eyes of all the icons are upon you; the effect is awe-inspiring. Admission is 50 Ft (25¢). Open Tuesday through Sunday, 10am to 5pm.

### ✪ Ferenczy Museum

Fő tér 6. No phone. Admission 90 Ft (45¢). Apr–Oct, Tues–Sun 10am–4pm; Nov–Mar, Fri–Sun 10am–4pm.

Next door to the Blagovestenska in Main Square (Fő tér), the Ferenczy Museum is dedicated to the art of the prodigious Ferenczy family. The featured artist is Károly Ferenczy, one of Hungary's leading impressionists; you can see more of his work in Budapest's National Museum. Works of his lesser-known children, Noémi (tapestry maker), Valer (painter), and Beni (sculptor and medallion maker), are also on display.

### Barcsay Museum

Dumtsa Jenő u. 10. No phone. Admission 90 Ft (45¢). Apr–Oct, Tues–Sun 10am–4pm; Nov–Mar, Fri–Sun 10am–4pm.

The conservative socialist dictates of the day restricted the work of artist Jenő Barcsay (1900–88). Nevertheless, in his anatomical drawings, etchings, and charcoal and ink drawings, Barcsay's genius shines through. We particularly like his pastel drawings of Szentendre streets.

### Serbian Orthodox Museum

Patriarka u. 5. No phone. Admission 60 Ft (25¢). Apr–Oct, Tues–Sun 10am–4pm; Nov–Mar, Fri–Sun 10am–4pm. Walk north from Fő tér on Alkotmány utca.

The Serbian Orthodox Museum is housed next door to the Serbian Orthodox church (services at 10am on Sunday) in one of the buildings of the former episcopate just north of Fő tér. This collection—one of the most extensive of its kind in predominantly Catholic Hungary—features exceptional 16th- through 19th-century icons, liturgical vessels, scrolls in Arabic from the Ottoman period, and other types of ecclesiastical art. Informative labels are in Hungarian and English.

### ✪ Ámos and Anna Muzeum

Bogdányi u. 10. No telephone. Tues–Sun 10am–6pm. 90 Ft (45¢).

This exceptional museum was the former home of artist couple Imre Ámos and Margit Anna, whose work represents the beginning of Expressionist painting in Hungary. Opened after Anna's death in 1991, the collection is Szentendre's best kept secret. Particularly engaging are the drawings Ámos did between periods of forced labor on the Russian front, where he eventually died of typhus. On a lighter note are Anna's wonderful puppets. Amos's art seems influenced by Chagall, whereas Anna's work invokes Miró and Klee.

Outside the museum in the courtyard is Anna's gravesite, around which visitors have left wishing stones from the garden as a token of respect.

### Művésztelepi Galéria (Gallery of the Szentendre Artists' Colony)
Bogdányi u. 51. ☎ **26/311-463.** Admission 60 Ft (45¢). Apr–Oct, Wed–Sun 11am–5pm. Walk north from Fő tér on Bogdányi utca.

Temporary exhibitions of contemporary colony artists are held in this unmarked, nondescript building 10 minutes from the town center. Strikingly different from the tourist-oriented art galleries, the atmosphere is distinctly old system; the work, however, is thoroughly contemporary. Most works on display are for sale.

Fifty or so yards further down Bogdányi utca is the Kerényi Sculpture House and Park at Ady E. u. 5. No phone. Admission 60 Ft (30¢). April through October, Wednesday through Sunday noon to 6pm.

## SIGHTS OUTSIDE TOWN

### Skanzen (Open-Air Ethnographical Museum)
Szabadság-forrás út. ☎ **26/312-304.** Admission 150 Ft (75¢). Apr–Oct, Tues–Sun 9am–5pm. Closed Oct–Mar.

About 3 kilometers (2 miles) northwest of Szentendre is one of Hungary's better *skanzens,* or reproduction peasant villages. This ambitious skanzen represents rural life from all regions of the country. There are several reconstructed 18th- and 19th-century villages, with thatch-roofed houses, blacksmith and weaving shops, working mills, and churches. A guidebook in English is available at the gate.

It's easily reached from Platform 8 of Szentendre's bus station, adjacent to the HÉV station (get off at the Szabadság-forrás stop). Buses depart about once an hour. If you're driving, follow Rte. 10 N. Turn left on Szabadság-forrás út.

### Pap-sziget (Priest's Island)
This island at the northern end of town provides a place to rest and relax, with thermal waters in the outdoor bathing pools. Bring a suit and towel or rent them there. Facilities include basic locker rooms. Buses for Leányfalu and Visegrád pass the bridge to Pap-sziget.

### Golf & Tennis Country Club
Szentendre Island. ☎ **26/392-463.** Fax 26/392-465.

Located in the northern corner of Szentendre Island, just outside the village of Kisoroszi, this country club features an 18-hole golf course with tree-lined fairways. The course is open March 1 to November 15. Clubs are available for rent. Call or fax to reserve a tee time. The country club also has a driving range and tennis courts.

## WHERE TO DINE

### Aranysárkány Vendéglő (Golden Dragon Inn)
Alkotmány u. 1/a. ☎ **26/311-670.** Reservations recommended. Soup 200–250 Ft ($1–$1.25); main courses 500–1,200 Ft ($2.50–$6). No credit cards. Daily noon–10pm. HUNGARIAN.

Located just east of Fő tér on Hunyadi utca, which leads into Alkotmány utca, "The Golden Dragon" is always filled to capacity. The crowd includes a good percentage of Hungarians, definitely a good sign in a tourist town like Szentendre. Indeed, a former chef brought wide fame to this little restaurant with the publication of a cookbook entitled *Four Seasons at the Golden Dragon Inn.* He's gone now, but the food remains excellent.

Long wooden tables set with sterling cutlery provide a relaxed but tasteful atmosphere in this air-conditioned restaurant. You can choose from among such enticing offerings as alpine lamb, roast leg of goose, quail, and venison ragoût. Vegetarians can order the vegetable plate, a respectable show of grilled and steamed vegetables in season. The cheese dumplings would round out the meal. Various beers are on draft.

### Dobos Museum & Cafe

Dumtsa Jenő u. 7. No phone. Free admission. Tues–Sun 10am–6pm.

Be sure to stop in for a slice of authentic *dobos torta,* a sumptuously rich layer cake named after pastry chef József Dobos, who experimented with butter frostings in the 19th century. The success of his recipe was immediate, and he was quickly appointed as the official baker for the Habsburg emperor. Photographs of József Dobos and his formerly secret recipe book are on display in the cafe.

### ✪ Régimodi

Futó u. 3. ☎ **26/311-105.** Reservations recommended. Soup 200–400 Ft ($1–$2); main courses 550–1,600 Ft ($2.75–$8). DC, EURO, JCB, MC, V. Daily noon–midnight. HUNGARIAN.

If you walk directly south from Fő tér, you'll find another excellent choice for dining. An elegant restaurant in a former private home, Régimodi is furnished with vintage Hungarian carpets and chandeliers. Original artworks decorate the walls. Limited terrace dining is available, though you might not want to miss out on eating amid the rich interior decor.

The menu offers a wide range of Hungarian specialties, with an emphasis on game dishes. The wild-deer stew in red wine is particularly sumptuous, while less adventurous diners might opt for the turkey baked with apples. The menu also features numerous salad options. There's an extensive wine list.

## 3  Visegrád

45km (28 miles) NW of Budapest

Halfway between Szentendre and Esztergom, Visegrád (pronounced *Vee*-sheh-grod) is a sparsely populated, sleepy riverside village, which makes its history all the more fascinating and hard to believe. The Romans built a fort here, which was still extant when Slovak settlers gave the town its present name (meaning "High Castle") in the 9th or 10th century. After the Mongol invasion (1241–42), construction began on both the present ruined hilltop citadel and the former riverside palace. Eventually, Visegrád could boast one of the finest royal palaces ever built in Hungary. Only one king, Charles Robert (1307–42), actually used it as his primary residence, but monarchs from Béla IV, in the 13th century, through Matthias Corvinus, in the late 15th century, spent time in Visegrád and contributed to its development, the latter expanding the palace into a great Renaissance center known throughout Europe.

## ESSENTIALS

**Visegrád Tours** (☎ **26/398-160**) is located across the road from the RÉV ferry boat landing. It is open April through October daily, 9am to 6pm; November through March weekdays, 10am to 4pm.

## AN ANNUAL FESTIVAL

Each summer on the second weekend in July, Visegrád hosts the International Palace Tournament, an authentic medieval festival replete with dueling knights on horseback, early music, and dance. For more information, contact Visegrád Tours.

## EXPLORING THE PALACE & THE CITADEL

The **Royal Palace** covered much of the area where the boat landing and Fő utca (Main Street) are now found. Indeed, the entrance to its ruins, called the **King Matthias Museum,** is at Fő u. 27. The buried ruins of the palace, having achieved a near-mythical status, were not discovered until this century. Almost all of what you see is the result of reconstruction. Aside from the general atmosphere of ruined grandeur, the main attractions are the red-marble base of the Hercules Fountain in the Ornamental Courtyard and the reconstructed Gothic arcaded hallway behind it.

The **Citadel** (Salamon Torony) on the hilltop above Visegrád affords one of the finest views you'll find over the Danube. Off to your left you can see the site of the controversial Nagymaros Dam, an abandoned Hungarian-Czechoslovak hydroelectric project (more information on this dam dispute, see "Esztergom," below). There are buses to the Citadel; it's more than a casual walk, ideal for a day-hike.

## WHERE TO DINE

Your best bet in Visegrád is the recently opened **Renaissance Restaurant,** at Fő út 11. It's open daily, 11:30am to 10pm. In keeping with its name and its location, at the foot of the Citadel, the restaurant specializes in authentic medieval cuisine. Food is served in clay crockery without silverware (only a wooden spoon). The decor and the lyra music enhance the fun, openly kitsch atmosphere. This is perhaps the only restaurant in the whole country where you won't find something on the menu spiced with paprika. All for the sake of authenticity; paprika wasn't around in medieval Hungary. If you're big on the medieval theme, come for dinner on a Thursday (June through August), when a six-course "Royal Feast" is celebrated following a 45-minute duel between knights. No vegetarians, please! Tickets for this special evening are handled by Visegrád Tours. The price is DM 20 ($11.40). The duel gets underway at 5:15pm sharp.

## 4  Esztergom

46km (29 miles) NW of Budapest

Formerly a Roman settlement, Esztergom (pronounced *Ess*-tair-gome) was the seat of the Hungarian kingdom for 300 years. Prince Géza and his son Vajk, who was crowned by the pope in A.D. 1000 as Hungary's first king, István I (Stephen I), were the first rulers to call Esztergom home. István converted Hungary to Catholicism, and Esztergom became the country's center of the early church. Though its glory days are far behind it, the quiet town remains today the seat of the archbishop-primate—the "Hungarian Rome."

From Esztergom west all the way to the Austrian border, the Danube marks the border between Hungary and Slovakia. There's an international ferry crossing at Esztergom.

## ESSENTIALS

**Gran Tours,** centrally located at Széchenyi tér 25 (☎ 33/413-756), is the best source of information in Esztergom. The office is open Monday through Friday from 8am to 4pm and on Saturday from 8am to noon. You can get city maps and concert information, and book private rooms here.

# EXPLORING THE TOWN
## ESZTERGOM'S CATHEDRAL & MUSEUMS

### Esztergom Cathedral

Szent István tér. ☎ **33/315-260.** Treasury, 130 Ft (60¢); cupola, 50 Ft (20¢). Cathedral, summer, daily 8am–8pm; winter, daily 9am–3pm. Treasury, Crypt, Cupola, summer, daily 9am–5pm; winter, daily 10am–3pm.

This massive, neoclassical cathedral on Castle Hill, Esztergom's most popular attraction and one of Hungary's most impressive buildings, was built in the last century to replace the cathedral ruined during the Turkish occupation. The intricately carved red-marble, Renaissance-style **Bakócz Chapel** inside the cathedral (to the left) dates from the early 16th century. The chapel survived the Turkish destruction of the former cathedral; when the present structure was being built the chapel was dismantled (into 1,600 numbered pieces) to be reincorporated into the new cathedral. The cathedral **Treasury** (*Kincstár*) contains a stunning array of ecclesiastical jewels and gold works. Since Cardinal Mindszenty's body was moved to the **crypt** in 1991 (he died in exile in 1975), it has been a place of pilgrimage for Hungarians; they come to see the final resting place of the uncompromisingly anti-Communist cleric who spent a good portion of the Cold War living inside the American Embassy in Budapest. The **cupola,** has, as far as church towers go, one of the scarier and more cramped ascents. If you venture up, though, you're rewarded at the top with unparalleled views of Esztergom and the surrounding Hungarian and Slovak countryside.

If you happen to be in town during the first week of August, don't miss out on one of the classical guitar concerts performed in the cathedral. The acoustics are sublime. The concerts are part of Esztergom's annual International Guitar Festival, now in its 11th year.

### Castle Museum

Szent István tér. ☎ **33/315-986.** Admission 150 Ft (40¢); special exhibits, 250–400 Ft (90¢–$1.90). Apr–Sept, Tues–Sun 9am–4:30pm; Oct–Mar, Tues–Sun 10am–3:30pm.

This museum is next door to the cathedral, in the reconstructed Royal Palace. The palace, vacated by Hungarian royalty in the 13th century, was used thereafter by the archbishop. Though it was one of only two fortresses in Hungary able to withstand the Mongol onslaught in 1241–42, it fell into decay under the Turkish occupation. The museum has an extensive collection of weapons, coins, pottery, stove tiles, and fragments of old stone columns; unfortunately, the descriptions are only in Hungarian. Outside the palace, sections of the fortified walls have been reconstructed.

### Keresztény Múzeum (Christian Museum)

Mindszenty tér 2. ☎ **33/313-880.** Admission 150 Ft (55¢) adults. Tues–Sun 10am–5:30pm; closed Jan–Mar.

This museum, in the neoclassical former primate's palace, houses Hungary's largest collection of religious art and the largest collection of medieval art outside the National Gallery. The Lord's Coffin of Garamszentbenedek is probably the museum's most famous piece; the ornately carved, gilded coffin on wheels was originally used in Easter celebrations.

To get to the museum, continue past the Watertown Parish Church on Berényi Zsigmond utca. Even if you don't plan on visiting this museum, it's definitely worth taking a break from the crowds at the cathedral and taking a stroll through the quiet, cobblestoned streets of Esztergom's Víziváros (Watertown).

## A BRIDGE IN RUINS

### Prímás-sziget

Across the Danube from Esztergom is the Slovak town of Sturovo. The two towns were once connected by Mária Valéria Bridge, a wrought-iron construction, blown up by the Germans in World War II. All that remains is a curious stump, along with four unconnected pylons in the river. Trapped in the middle of a diplomatic dispute between Hungary and Slovakia, this is the only Danube bridge destroyed by the Germans in World War II that has not yet been rebuilt. To fully appreciate this strange sight you should walk along the riverbank and pass underneath the "bridge."

There is a grassroots movement in Hungary favoring reconstruction of the bridge, as travel between the two countries in this region is still primarily dependent on boats. But the Slovak government, under the bellicose Prime Minister Vladimir Meciar, has taken the official position that the Hungarians should resume construction of the nearby Negymaros Dam, a joint Slovak-Hungarian project abandoned a decade ago by Hungary, which was to include a roadway across the Danube. The Slovaks believe that reconstruction of the bridge would be unnecessary if the dam were completed. In 1997, the International Court of Justice in the Hague (the World Court) ruled that Hungary was at fault for abandoning the dam project, but that Hungary had no obligation to resume construction. The court urged the two countries to come to a formal resolution of the crisis. As yet, the stalemate remains, and the bridge still lies in ruins, a forlorn pawn in a diplomatic rift.

The site of the ruins is halfway between the Hotel Esztergom and Szalma Csárda (see "Where to Dine," below). To get here, walk straight out Táncsics Mihály utca until you hit the river.

## WHERE TO STAY

### Alabárdos Panzió

Bajcsy-Zsilinszky út 49, 2500 Esztergom. ☎ **33/312-640.** 21 rms. TV. 5,000–6,000 Ft ($25–$30) double. Rates include breakfast. No credit cards. Free parking. Bus: 1, 5, or 6 from the train station.

This lime-green pension is located in the heart of Esztergom, just minutes from Castle Hill. Although situated on the town's main thoroughfare, the pension is set back off the road and is much quieter than you'd expect. A restaurant of the same name is in the front of the building. The Alabárdos is far more modern than its rival the Plátán Panzió, a fact amply reflected in the higher prices. Pension rooms are small but clean and cheery. A cross hangs over every bed, and every room has a toilet and shower. To find the reception, go up the steep cobblestoned driveway to the left of the building.

### ✪ Plátán Panzió

Kis-Duna sétány 11, 2500 Esztergom. ☎ **33/311-355.** 16 rms, all with bath. 2,500 Ft ($12.50) double. No credit cards. Free parking. Bus: 1, 5, or 6 from the train station to Rákóczi tér; then walk west on Lörincz utca to Kis-Duna sétány and turn right.

The prices in this nondescript, old-style pension make it the great budget-travel bargain of Esztergom. The pension is located in one wing of a large institutional neobaroque building. The rooms are worn and bare, but clean. The shared facilities are also clean. It's located on a quiet street just minutes from the city center. If the building's outer door is locked, ring the bell on your right. Once you've been buzzed into the courtyard, turn right and go up the stairs to find the reception.

## WHERE TO DINE

The food at the recently remodeled and enlarged ✪ **Szalma Csárda,** located at Nagy-Duna sétány 2 (☎ 33/315-336), is absolutely first-rate, with everything made to order and served piping hot. The excellent house soups (200 to 340 Ft/$1 to $1.70)—fish soup (halászlé), goulash (gulyásleves), and bean soup (babgulyás)—are all large enough to constitute meals in themselves. For main courses, which cost 600 to 800 Ft ($3 to $4), the stuffed cabbage (töltött kaposzta) and the stuffed pepper (töltött paprika) are both outstanding, though not always offered on the menu. Finish off your meal with a dish of sweet chestnut purée (gesztenyepuüré), a Hungarian specialty prepared here to perfection. There are outdoor tables as well as seating in two dining rooms.

## 5 Vác

34km (21 miles) N of Budapest

Overlooked by most tourists, who neglect the flatter east bank of the Danube Bend, Vác (pronounced *Vahts*), halfway between Szentendre and Visegrád, is a quietly charming baroque town. Though King Stephen established a bishopric here when he set up the Hungarian church, Vác's golden age was the late 15th century, when Miklós Báthori, the bishop, oversaw the town's blossoming. Most sights in the historic core, however, date from the early 18th century (Vác was destroyed by the late 17th-century battles to recapture it from Turkish occupation and it was rebuilt in the baroque style of the time). The town's elegant, well-maintained squares and its sleepy Danube-side parks exude an unmistakable charm.

### ESSENTIALS

The best source of information is **Tourinform,** at Dr. Csányi László krt. 45 (☎ 27/316-160). They have free city maps as well as a useful little guidebook on Vác monuments. The office is open April through September Monday through Friday, 8am to 5pm and Sat, 9am to 1pm; October through March weekdays only.

If you arrive in Vác by train it might make sense to use the **Ibusz** office, at Széchenyi u. 46, for your information-gathering purposes. You can also change money here.

### EXPLORING THE HISTORIC INNER CITY

The best thing to do in Vác is to wander around the historic Inner City and its four main squares and admire the baroque architecture. **Március 15 tér** is the town's central square. Here you'll find the Town Hall (Városház), with its intricate wrought-iron gate; the Fehérek Church, with its elegant facade dominating the square's southern end; and a row of baroque houses across from the Town Hall. Nearby **Szentháromság tér** features an elaborate Plague Column and the Piarist Church, whose church bell is the favorite of locals. Lush beds of roses ring large, empty **Konstantin tér.** Old-fashioned street lamps line the walkways. The Bishop's Cathedral, one of Hungary's earliest (1765–77) examples of neoclassical architecture, dominates Konstantin tér. **Géza király tér,** the center of medieval Vác, was the site of the former fortress and cathedral. Now you can see the baroque Franciscan church here.

There's a pleasant breezy park along the Danube bank and a public swimming pool complex (*strand*) just off Szentháromság tér on Fürdő utca. Near the northern end of the Inner City, on Köztársaság tér, you'll find Hungary's only triumphal arch, built to celebrate the 1764 visit of Habsburg empress Maria Theresa. It stands near Vác's infamous prison, where political prisoners were held under both the interwar Horthy regime and the early Communist regime.

Vác has a few museums of note. Exhibits on the town's history from the **Ignác Tragor Museum** are currently being housed in the building of the **Gyula Hincz Collection,** at Káptalan u. 16 (☎ **27/313-463**). A new **Ignác Tragor Museum** is under construction. The **Gyula Hincz Collection** is open Tuesday through Sunday from 10am to 6pm in summer and 9am to 5pm in winter; admission is 60 Ft (30¢). The tiny **Medieval Cellar Exhibition** (Középkori pince kiállítás), at Széchenyi u. 3–7, features a 15th-century winepress in an excavated cellar. It's open Tuesday through Sunday from 10am to 4pm; admission is 50 Ft (25¢).

## WHERE TO DINE

**Halászkert Étterem,** at Liszt Ferenc sétány 9 (☎ **27/315-985**), a large outdoor garden restaurant set right on the Danube Promenade at the northern end of the Inner City, is the best choice in Vác for a Hungarian meal. The extensive menu features a number of fish specialties (the restaurant's name means "fish garden"). Lavender cloth napkins and porcelain china give the tables a festive appearance. Main courses are priced 650 to 1,000 Ft ($3.50 to $5). The restaurant is open daily from noon to 10pm.

**Barlang Pizza and Disco,** on Március 15 tér (☎ **27/315-584**), serves mediocre pizza and pasta, but the restaurant, doubling as Vác's hottest disco at night, has a certain subterranean appeal. Located as it is, deep in an original medieval cellar (*barlang* means cave) in the center of Március 15 tér (reached by stairs; the sign is not visible at street level), the temperature is always cool. If you ignore the vaguely tacky decor, it's a pleasant place to dine. The simplest and most pizza-like pizza is the "Margareta"; use the ketchup freely. Pizzas cost 300 to 600 Ft ($1.50 to $3). Barlang is open on Sunday through Thursday from noon to 11pm, and on Friday and Saturday from noon to 1am.

**Margaréta Kávéház,** Széchenyi u. 19, offers scrumptious pastries, Italian ice cream, and specialty coffees in an upbeat atmosphere on the town's most bustling street. Sit outside in the summertime. It's open Monday through Friday from 6am to 10pm and on Saturday and Sunday from 6am to 11pm.

# 11

# The Lake Balaton Region

Lake Balaton may not be the Mediterranean, but don't tell that to Hungarians. Somehow over the years they have managed to create their own Central European variety of a Mediterranean culture along the shores of their long, shallow, milky white lake. Throughout the long summer, swimmers, windsurfers, sailboats, kayaks, and cruisers fill the warm and silky smooth lake, Europe's largest at 80 kilometers (50 miles) long and 15 kilometers (10 miles) wide at its broadest stretch. Around the lake's 197 kilometers (315 miles) of shoreline, people cast their reels for pike, play tennis, ride horses, and hike in the hills.

First settled in the Iron Age, the Balaton region has been a recreation spot since at least Roman times. From the 18th century onward, the upper classes erected spas and villas along the shoreline. Not until the post-World War II Communist era did the lake open up for a wider tourist base. Many large hotels along the lake are former trade union resorts built under the previous regime.

Lake Balaton, it seems, has something for everyone. Teenagers, students, and young travelers tend to congregate in the hedonistic towns of the south shore. Here, huge 1970s-style beachside hotels are filled to capacity all summer long, and disco music pulsates into the early morning hours. The south-shore towns are as flat as Pest; walk 10 minutes from the lake and you're in farm country. The air here is still and quiet; in summer, the sun hangs heavily in the sky.

Older travelers and families tend to spend more time on the hillier, more graceful north shore. There, little villages are neatly tucked away in the rolling countryside, where the grapes of the popular Balaton wines ripen in the strong southern sun. However, if you're coming from Budapest, the northern shore of the lake at first appears every bit as built up and crowded as the southern shore. Beyond Balatonfüred, this impression begins to fade. You'll discover the Tihany Peninsula, a protected area whose 12 square kilometers ($4^3/_4$ square miles) jut out into the lake like a knob. Moving westward along the coast, passing from one lakeside settlement to the next, you can make forays inland into the rolling hills of the Balaton wine country. Stop for a swim—or the night—in a small town like Szigliget. The city of Keszthély, sitting at the lake's western edge, marks the end of its northern shore. All towns on the lake are within $1^1/_2$ to 4 hours from Budapest by a *gyors* (fast) train, but the trip takes much longer on a *sebes* (local) train.

## 1 Exploring the Lake Balaton Region

### GETTING THERE & GETTING AROUND

**BY TRAIN**    From Budapest, trains to the various towns along the lake depart from Déli Station. The local (*sebes*) trains are interminably slow, stopping at each village along the lake. Unless you're going to one of these little villages (sometimes a good idea), try to get on an express (*gyors*). To Keszthély, the trip takes about 4 hours and costs 1,084 Ft. ($5.40). To Tihany, travel time is 2 hours, and a single ticket will run 700 Ft ($3.50).

**BY CAR**    From Budapest, take the M7 motorway south through Székesfehérvár until you hit the lake. Route 71 circles the lake.

If you're planning a trip to Lake Balaton for more than a day or two, you should consider renting a car, which will give you much greater mobility. The various towns differ enough from one another that you may want to keep driving until you find the place that's right for you. Without a car, this is obviously more difficult. Also, wherever you go in the region, you'll find private rooms to be both cheaper and easier to get if you travel a few miles off the lake. Driving directly to the lake from Budapest will take about an hour and 15 minutes.

**BY BOAT & FERRY**    Passenger boat travel on Lake Balaton lets you travel across the lake as well as between towns on the same shore. It's both extensive and cheap, but considerably slower than surface transportation. All major towns have a dock with departures and arrivals. Children 3 and under travel free, and those 13 and under get half-price tickets. A single ferry (*komp*) running between Tihany and Szántód lets you transport a car across the width of the lake.

All boat and ferry information is available from the **MAHART** office in Siófok (☎ **84/310-050** or 84/312-907). Local tourist offices all along the lake (several listed below) also have schedules and other information.

**BY BUS**    Once at the lake, you might find buses to be the best way of getting around locally. Buses will be indispensable, of course, if you take private-room lodging a few miles away from the lake.

### WHERE TO STAY IN THE AREA

Since hotel prices are unusually high in the Balaton region, and since just about every local family rents out a room or two in summer, we especially recommend **private rooms** as the lodging of choice in this area. You can reserve a room through a local tourist office (addresses listed below by town) or you can just look for the ubiquitous SZOBA KIADÓ (or ZIMMER FREI) signs that decorate most front gates in the region. When you take a room without using a tourist agency as the intermediary, prices are generally negotiable. In the height of the season, you shouldn't have to pay more than 8,000 Ft. ($40) for a double room within reasonable proximity of the lake.

In addition to staying in private rooms, many budget travelers pitch their tents in **lakeside campgrounds** all around the lake. Campgrounds are generally quite inexpensive, and their locations are well marked on maps.

# Lake Balaton Region

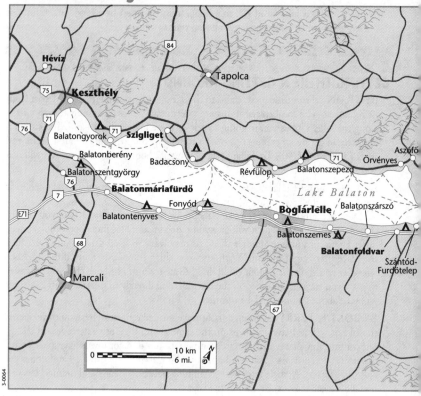

All the campgrounds have working facilities, but are probably not as clean as most Americans are accustomed to.

## 2 En Route to Lake Balaton: Veszprém

116km (72 miles) SW of Budapest

Just 10 miles from Lake Balaton, Veszprém (pronounced *Vess*-praym) surely ranks as one of Hungary's most charming and vibrant small cities. It often serves as a starting point for trips to that popular resort area. In Veszprém you'll find a harmonious mix of old and new: A delightfully self-contained and well-preserved, 18th-century baroque Castle District spills effortlessly into a typically modern city center, itself distinguished by lively wide-open pedestrian-only plazas.

The history of Veszprém, like the scenic Bakony countryside that surrounds it, is full of peaks and valleys. The city was first established as an episcopal see in the time of King Stephen I, Hungary's first Christian king, but was completely destroyed during the course of the long Turkish occupation, the Habsburg-Turkish battles, and the subsequent Hungarian-Austrian independence skirmishes. The reconstruction of Veszprém commenced in the early 18th century, though the castle itself, blown up by the Austrians in 1702, was never rebuilt. The baroque character of that era today attracts thousands of visitors who pass through each year.

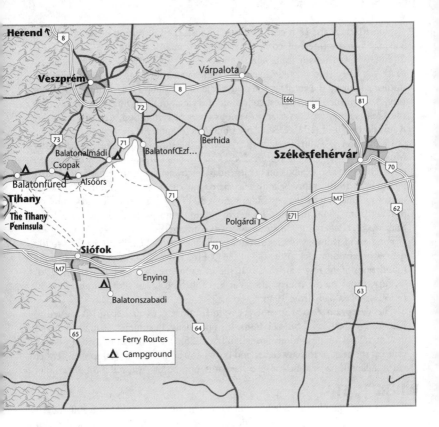

Herend
Veszprém
Várpalota
Balatonalmádi
Csopak
Balatonfüred
Alsóörs
Tihany
The Tihany Peninsula
Berhida
BalatonfŒzf...
Székesfehérvár
Polgárdi
Siófok
Enying
Balatonszabadi

- - - Ferry Routes
△ Campground

## ESSENTIALS

**GETTING THERE**   Six daily trains depart Budapest's Déli Station for Veszprém, a 1³/₄-hour trip. Tickets cost 600 Ft ($3).

If you're driving from Budapest, take the M7 motorway to Székesfehérvár, and then Route 8 to Veszprém.

**VISITOR INFORMATION**   **Balatontourist,** Kossuth u. 21 (☎ **88/429-630;** fax 88/427-062), is open Monday through Friday from 8:30am to 5pm (to 4pm off-season) and on Saturday from 9am to noon; and **Ibusz,** Kossuth u. 10 (opposite Balaton Tourist in the odd modern structure marked "KINIZSI ÜZLETHÁZ"), (☎ **88/ 426-492** or 88/427-604), is open Monday through Friday from 9am to 5:30pm (to 5pm off-season) and on Saturday from 9am to noon. Both offices provide informa-tion, sell city maps, and help with hotel or private-room bookings.

**LAUNDRY**   If you happen to arrive with dirty laundry, have it done while you tour the city at **Mosoda,** a launderette and dry cleaner located next to Hotel Veszprém (the depressing, mammoth-sized hotel overlooking Kossuth utca). Mosoda is open Monday through Friday, 7:30am to 6pm, and Saturday, 8am to 1pm.

## EXPLORING THE CITY

Most of Veszprém's main sights are clustered along Vár utca, the street that runs the length of the city's small but lovely Castle District. The Bakony Museum, though, is located in the new (low) part of the town.

Housed inside the 18th-century canon's house, the **Exhibition of Religious Art,** Vár u. 35, has a fine collection of religious (Roman Catholic) art. Admission is 20 Ft (10¢). Open daily from 9am to 5pm.

At Vár u. 16, the vaulted **Gizella Chapel,** named for King Stephen's wife, was unearthed during the construction of the adjoining Bishop's Palace in the 18th century. Today it houses a modest collection of ecclesiastical art, but is best known for the 13th-century frescoes that, in various states of restoration, decorate its walls. Admission is 20 Ft (10¢). Open daily from 9am to 5pm.

In addition to Roman relics uncovered in the surrounding area, the **Bakony Museum,** on Megyház tér, features local folk exhibits (art, costumes, tools, utensils, etc.). There are also exhibits on the legendary highwaymen of the region, celebrated figures from 19th-century Bakony who share some characteristics with the Wild West outlaw of American mythology. Admission is 80 Ft (40¢). It's open Tuesday through Sunday from 10am to 6pm. To get to the museum, walk directly south from Szabadsag tér, where the old and new towns converge.

For a wonderful view of the surrounding Bakony region, climb up the steps to the narrow observation deck at the top of the ✪ **Fire Tower,** at Óváros tér. Though the foundations of the tower are medieval, the structure itself was built in the early 19th century. Enter via the courtyard of Vár u. 17, behind Óváros tér. Admission is 80 Ft (40¢). Open daily from 10am to 6pm.

The **Veszprém Zoo** (Kittenberger Kálmán Növény és Vadaspark) is located at Kittenberger u. 17 (☎ **88/421-088**). It's open daily, in summer, 9am to 6pm and in winter, 9am to 3pm. Admission is 250 Ft ($1.25). The zoo is set in a small wooded valley at the edge of the city center and boasts 450 animals from 120 species. Rather sad and depressing by American zoo standards, but the kids will still learn something.

## WHERE TO STAY

For a double room in a private home in Veszprém you pay 2,000 Ft to 2,500 Ft ($10 to $12.50). The room price usually does not include breakfast. You can book a **private room** through either of the tourist offices mentioned above.

**Péter-Pál Panzió** (☎ **88/324-091**) is conveniently located on Dózsa György u. 3; it's only a 5-minute walk from the center. Don't be put off by the grungy building facade. Inside are 12 tidy but very small rooms, all with twin beds, toilet, shower, and television. Insist on a room in the rear of the building, as the pension sits close to the busy road. Rates are 3,200 Ft ($16) single, 4,200 Ft ($21) double, and 5,500 Ft ($27.50) triple. Breakfast is included and is served in the garden in summer. Call ahead for reservations.

**Hotel Villa Medici** (☎ and fax **88/406-685**), at Kittenberger K. u. 11, is a brand-new, full-service hotel set in a small gorge on the edge of the city, next to Veszprém's zoo-park. There are 24 double rooms and 2 suites; each has a bathroom with shower, telephone, and TV. Rates are $55 to $65 for a double room; $90 for a suite. Breakfast is included. The hotel also features a sauna, a small indoor swimming pool, and a beauty salon. Credit cards are accepted. Buses 3, 5, and 10 take you as far as the bridge overlooking the gorge. You can walk from there.

## WHERE TO DINE

Veszprém does not have plentiful dining options, but at the following places you should be able to find a satisfying meal.

For fast food, try **Mackó Cukrászda,** at Kossuth u. 6 (a few doors down from Ibusz). Open daily 7am to 8pm (opening and closing an hour earlier on Sunday), this quick-stop, no-frills eatery is always bustling. Pizza, hot dogs, French fries, fried

## Herend: Home of Hungary's Finest Porcelain

About 10 miles west of Veszprém lies the sleepy village of Herend. What distinguishes this village from other villages in the area is the presence of the Herend Porcelain factory, where Hungary's finest porcelain has been made since 1826.

Herend Porcelain began to establish its international reputation as far back as 1851, when a dinner set was displayed at the Great Exhibition in London. Artists hand paint every piece, from tableware to decorative accessories. Patterns include delicate flowers, butterflies, and birds.

Although the factory is not open for tours, the **Herend Museum** (☎ **88/ 261-144,** ext. 197) displays a dazzling collection of Herend porcelain and features a porcelain-making demonstration. The museum is open Tuesday through Saturday, 8:30am to 4pm; Sunday, 9am to 4:30pm. At the **factory store** (☎ **88/ 261-489**), which accepts credit cards, you might find patterns that are unavailable in Budapest's Herend Shop (see chapter 8). Prices will be comparable to those in Budapest, but much less than what Herend costs in the United States. The factory store is open Monday through Friday, 9am to 5pm and Saturday 9am to 2pm. In winter, the store closes an hour early. Herend is easily accessible via bus from Veszprém.

chicken, and various sweets are served. There's also a salad counter (heavy on the mayonnaise dressings); salads are sold by the decagram. A meal here will put you back about 500 Ft ($2.50).

**Cserhát Étterem** (☎ **88/425-441**), also housed in the huge structure that is Kossuth u. 6, is an authentic *önkiszólgáló* (self-service cafeteria). You'll find the restaurant behind the Nike store; go up the winding staircase inside the building. Cserhát serves up extremely cheap traditional fare. Hearty meals are available for less than 300 Ft ($1.50). The menu changes daily; it's posted on a bulletin board at the bottom of the stairs. Open Monday through Friday from 11am to 4pm and Saturday 11am to 3pm.

You can get lunch or dinner at **Óváros Vendéglő (Old City Guest House),** at Szabadság tér 14, a traditional Hungarian restaurant with a large outdoor terrace and a number of smaller indoor dining rooms. The food is fine; prices are reasonable. Main courses run 500 to 900 Ft ($2.50 to $4.50). Steer clear of the salad bar—the vegetables are all pickled.

For something more upscale, ✪ **Villa Medici Étterem** (owned by the same people who own the hotel), at Kittenberger u. 11 (☎ **88/321-273**), is *the* place. Our American friend who first told us about this place, claiming at the time that it was one of Hungary's best restaurants, liked it enough to have his wedding reception there. It's expensive but worth it. Main courses here are between 1,200 and 2,000 Ft ($6 to $10). Villa Medici serves Hungarian/continental cuisine. Open daily from 11am to 3pm.

## 3 The Tihany Peninsula

The Tihany (pronounced *Tee*-hine) Peninsula, a national park since 1952, has several towns on it, the most notable of which is called, appropriately, **Tihany** (or Tihany Village). Because the peninsula is a protected area, building is heavily restricted; consequently, it maintains a rustic charm that's unusual in the Balaton region.

The Tihany Peninsula also features a lush, protected interior, accessible by a trail from Tihany Village, with several little inland lakes—the aptly named **Inner Lake** and **Outer Lake**—as well as a lookout tower offering views out over the Balaton. Give yourself at least an hour or two to explore the interior.

As you travel west from the Tihany Peninsula, the landscape begins to get hillier.

## ESSENTIALS

**GETTING THERE**    The rail line that circles Lake Balaton does not serve the Tihany Peninsula. The nearest railway station is in Aszófő, about 3 miles from Tihany Village. If you don't have your own car, you can get here by land or by water. A local bus comes to Tihany from the nearby town of Balatonfüred. You can also go by ferry from Szántód or Balatonföldvár, or by boat from Balatonfüred.

**VISITOR INFORMATION**    Visitor information and private-room bookings for the Tihany Peninsula are available in Tihany Village at **Balatontourist,** Kossuth u. 20 (☎ and fax **87/448-519**). The office is open March through October only, Monday through Friday from 8:30am to 4:30pm and on Saturday from 8:30am to 12:30pm.

## EXPLORING TIHANY VILLAGE

The 18th-century baroque ✪ **Abbey Church** is, undoubtedly, Tihany Village's main attraction. The church stands on the site of an earlier 11th-century Romanesque church, around whose remains the crypt of the current church was built. These remains include the marble gravestone of King Andrew, who died in 1060; this is the sole Hungarian royal tomb that remains in its original location. A resident Austrian-born monk carved the exquisite wooden altar and pulpit in the 18th century. The frescoes in the church are by three of Hungary's better-known 19th-century painters, whose work can be viewed throughout the country: Károly Lotz, Bertalan Székely, and Lajos Deák-Ébner.

Next door to the Abbey Church is the **Tihany Museum** (☎ **87/448-650**), housed in an 18th-century baroque structure, like the church. The museum features exhibitions on the surrounding region's history and culture. You pay a single entry fee of 150 Ft (75¢) for both church and museum. Both are open daily: from 9am to 5:30pm in summer and 10am to 3pm off-season.

Tihany Village is also the site of the legendary **Echo Hill,** a scenic spot overlooking the lake (near the Echo Restaurant), which is reached via a winding path that starts from the left side of the Abbey Church. Legend has it that voices on Echo Hill reverberated back from the side of the church.

## 4  Szigliget

Halfway between Tihany and Keszthély is the lovely village of Szigliget (pronounced *Sig*-lee-get). If you are as taken as we were by the thatched roof houses, the lush vineyards, and sunny Mediterranean quality of Szigliget, you might consider spending the night. **Natur Tourist,** in the village center, can help in booking private rooms. There are also plenty of ZIMMER FREI signs along the roads. **Szőlőskert Pánzio,** on Vadrózsa utca, might be the best option, given its close proximity to the beach. Situated on the hillside amidst terraces of grapes, the pension is open only in summer.

## EXPLORING THE VILLAGE

Szigliget is marked by the fantastic ruins of the 13th-century **Szigliget Castle,** which stand above it on **Várhegy (Castle Hill).** In the days of the Turkish invasions, the Hungarian Balaton fleet, protected by the high castle, called Szigliget its home. You can hike up to the ruins for a splendid view of the lake and the surrounding countryside; look for the path behind the white 18th-century church, which stands on the highest spot in the village.

A good place to fortify yourself for the hike is the **Vár Vendéglő,** on the road up to the castle. It's a casual restaurant with plenty of outdoor seating, serving traditional Hungarian fare.

If you really enjoy hiking, you might take a local bus from Szigliget to the nondescript nearby village of **Hegymagas,** about 3 miles to the north along the Szigliget-Tapolca bus route. The town's name means "Tall Hill," and from here you can hike up onto **Szent György-hegy (St. George Hill).** This marvelous vineyard-covered hill has several hiking trails, the most strenuous of which goes up and over the rocky summit.

The lively **beach** at Szigliget provides a striking contrast to the quiet village. In summer, buses from neighboring towns drop off hordes of beachgoers. The beach area is crowded with fried food and beer stands, ice cream vendors, a swing set, and a volleyball net. Admission to the beach is 100 Ft (50¢).

Szigliget is also home to the **Eszterházy Wine Cellar,** the largest wine cellar in the region. After a hike in the hills or a day in the sun, a little wine tasting just might be in order. Natur Tourist can provide you with the best directions.

## 5  Keszthély

117 miles SW of Budapest

Keszthély (pronounced *Kest*-hay), which sits at the western edge of Lake Balaton, is one of the largest towns on the lake. Though Keszthély was largely destroyed during the Turkish wars, the town was rebuilt in the 18th century by the Festetics family, an aristocratic family who made Keszthély their home through World War II. The town's main sites all date from the days of the wealthy Festetics clan.

### ESSENTIALS

For information about Keszthély, stop in at **Tourinform,** at Kossuth u. 28 (☎ and fax **83/314-144**). It's open in summer, Monday through Friday from 9am to 6pm and on Saturday from 9am to 1pm; off-season, Monday through Friday from 8am to 4pm and on Saturday from 9am to 1pm. For private-room bookings, try **Zalatours,** at Kossuth u. 1 (☎ **83/312-560**), or **Ibusz,** at Kossuth u. 27 (☎ **83/314-320**).

### EXPLORING THE TOWN

The highlight of a visit to Keszthély is the splendid ✪ **Festetics Mansion,** at Szabadsag u. 1 (☎ **83/312-190** or 83/312-191), the baroque 18th-century home (with 19th-century additions) for generations of the Festetics family. Part of the mansion is now open as a museum. The main attraction is the ornate Helikon library, which features floor-to-ceiling oak bookcases—hand-carved by a local master, János Kerbl. The museum also features hunting gear and trophies of a bygone era. The museum is open in summer, daily from 9am to 6pm; in winter, it closes at 5pm and is closed on Monday. Admission for foreigners is 550 Ft ($2.75). Hungarians pay only 200 Ft ($1) to enter; this museum appears to be the last in Hungary to maintain this petty and discriminatory Communist-era policy.

The mansion's lovely concert hall is the site of **classical music concerts** almost every night throughout the summer (just two or three times a month from September through May). Concerts usually start at 8pm; tickets, at 400 Ft ($2) apiece, are available at the door or earlier in the day at the museum cashier. Another part of the mansion has in the past—and, we are informed, may again—serve as a hotel.

## An Excursion to the Thermal Lake in Hévíz

If you think the water of Lake Balaton is warm, just wait until you jump into the lake at Hévíz (pronounced *Hay*-veez), a resort town about 5 miles northwest of Keszthély. Here you'll find the largest thermal lake in Europe and the second largest in the world (the largest being in New Zealand)), covering 50,000 square meters (60,000 square yards).

The lake's water temperature seldom dips below 85° to 90°F—even in the most bitter spell of winter. Consequently, people swim in the lake year-round. You are bound to notice the huge numbers of German tourists taking advantage of the waters. Hévíz has been one of Hungary's leading spa resorts for over 100 years, and it retains a distinct 19th-century atmosphere.

While the lakeside area is suitable for ambling, no visit to Hévíz would be complete without a swim. An enclosed causeway leads out into the center of the lake where locker rooms and the requisite services, including massage, float rental, and a *palacsinta* (crêpe) bar are housed.

You can easily reach Hévíz by bus from Keszthély. Buses depart every half hour or so from the bus station (conveniently stopping to pick up passengers in front of the church on Fő tér). The entrance to the lake is just opposite the bus station. You'll see a whimsical wooden facade and the words TÓ FÜRDŐ (Bathing Lake). Tickets cost 340 Ft ($1.70) for up to 3 hours or 680 Ft ($3.40) for a day pass. Your ticket entitles you to a locker; insert the ticket into the slot in the locker and the key will come out of the lock. Keep the ticket until exiting, as the attendant needs to see it to determine whether you've stayed a half day or a full day.

Incidentally, there is no shallow water in the lake, so use discretion when bringing children. There is a nice small playground on the grounds that they will enjoy, however.

---

Not far from the Festetics Mansion is the **Georgikon Farm Museum** (☎ 83/311-563), at Bercsényi u. 67, on the site of Europe's first agricultural college, built by György Festetics in 1797. The museum is devoted to an exhibit of the area's agricultural history. Open April through October only, Tuesday through Sunday from 10am to 6pm. Admission is 40 Ft (20¢).

Another Keszthély museum worth a visit is the **Balaton Museum,** on the opposite side of the town center from the Festetics Mansion, at Múzeum u. 2 (☎ 83/312-351). This museum features exhibits on the geological, archaeological, and natural history of the Balaton region. It's open Tuesday through Sunday from 10am to 6pm. Admission is 120 Ft (60¢).

Located down the hill from Fő tér (Main Square), is Keszthély's **open-air market.** Vendors line the street. You'll find fruit and vegetables, spices, preserves, honey, as well as household appliances, handmade baskets, and children's clothing. It's a lively, bustling place, particularly in the morning. Open daily. Dawn to mid-afternoon is the busiest time. Some vendors stay open into early evening.

The center of Keszthély's summer scene, just like that of every other settlement on Lake Balaton, is down by the water on the "strand." Keszthély's **beachfront** is dominated by several large hotels. Regardless of whether or not you're a guest, you can rent windsurfers, boats, and other water-related equipment from these hotels.

## WHERE TO STAY

As elsewhere in the Lake Balaton region, private rooms are the recommended budget accommodations in Keszthély. Tourinform, Zalatours, or Ibusz can help in booking you a private room. Rates are from 1,500 Ft to 2,500 Ft ($7.50 to $12.50) per person.

You can also stay at one of several large German-tourist oriented hotels on the beach. Try **Danubius Hotel Helikon,** ☎ **83/311-330.** Rates are DM 118 ($67) for a double room with bath. Breakfast is included. The hotel has a good size indoor swimming pool, a sauna, massage parlor, and outdoor sundeck.

## WHERE TO EAT

**Oázis Reform Restaurant,** ☎ **83/311-023,** at Rákóczi tér 3, is a self-serve salad bar featuring adequate (if uninspired) vegetarian fare. Cold and hot options. Go at lunch time, when the food is freshest. Oázis is open daily, 11am to 8pm.

**Csiga Kisvendéglő** (Little Snail Guest House), at Tessedik u. 30, a good 15-minute walk from the center, is a small neighborhood eatery serving a variety of meat and fish dishes. At 400 to 900 Ft ($2 to $4.50) for main dishes, prices are more than reasonable. Csiga is open Monday through Saturday, 11am to 9pm.

## 6  On Lake Balaton's Southern Shore

If you're looking for long days at the beach followed by long nights out on the town, the southern shore of Lake Balaton may be the place for you. After all, a million Hungarian students can't be wrong!

**Siófok,** the largest resort town on Lake Balaton, is at the lake's southeastern end. Its growth dates back to the 1860s, when Budapest was first connected to the southern shore of the lake by rail. Thus, we suppose, nobody alive can remember a time (other than the war years) when Siófok was not overrun by summertime revelers. Today bustling Siófok caters to a young, active crowd of students and teenagers who fill every inch of the town's beaches all day long and then pack their sunburned bodies into the town's discos until the early morning hours. Large, modern, expensive hotels line the shore in Siófok. You'll find no empty stretches of beach here, but you will find windsurfing, tennis, and boating.

Other popular spots on the southern shore include **Balatonföldvar, Boglarlelle,** and **Balatonmáriafürdő.**

For **information on the southern shore,** contact the **Tourinform** office in Siófok, at Fő u. 41 (☎ and fax **84/310-117**).

# Northeastern Hungary: Traveling into the Hills

**N**ortheast of the Danube Bend is Hungary's hilliest region, where its highest peak—Matra Hill at 3,327 feet—can be found. Here you can visit the preserved medieval village of Hollókő; see remnants of the country's Turkish heritage in Eger, also known for its regional wines; or explore the 14-mile cave system in Aggtelek.

## 1 Hollókő: A Preserved Palóc Village

64 miles NE of Budapest

The village of Hollókő (pronounced *Ho*-low-koo) is one of the most charming spots in Hungary. This UNESCO World Heritage site is a perfectly preserved but still vibrant Palóc village. The rural Palóc people speak an unusual Hungarian dialect, and they have some of the more colorful folk customs and costumes in Hungary. If you're in Hungary at Easter time, by all means consider spending the holiday in Hollókő. Hollókő's traditional Easter Celebration features townspeople in traditional dress and Masses in the town church.

### ESSENTIALS

**GETTING THERE**   The easiest way to get to Hollókő is by bus. From Budapest's Népstadion bus station (☎ **1/252-4496**), take a bus to Szécseny; there, switch to a local bus to Hollókő. Six daily buses ply the Budapest-Szécseny route, departing at 7am and 12:25, 2:25, 3:35, 4:25, and 5:25pm. The 2¹/₂-hour ride costs 586 Ft ($2.95). Eight daily buses connect Szécseny with Hollókő, departing Szécseny at 9:50am and 1:30, 2:30, 3:20, 4:10, 5:20, 6:40, and 8:30pm. That ride takes about half an hour and costs 113 Ft (55¢).

If you're driving from Budapest, take the M3 motorway to Hatvan, the M21 from Hatvan to Paszto, and local roads from Paszto to Hollókő.

**VISITOR INFORMATION**   The best **information office** is the Foundation of Hollókő, at Kossuth Lajos út 68 (☎ **32/379-266**). You can also get information through **Nograd Tourist** in Salgótarján (☎ **32/310-660**) or through **Tourinform** in Szécseny, at Ady Endre u. 12 (☎ **32/370-777**).

### SEASONAL EVENTS

At Eastertime, villagers wear national costumes and participate in a folklife festival. Traditional song, dance, and foods are featured.

Every August, the Palóc Szőttes festival is held in Hollókő. Folk dance troupes of Nógrád county as well as foreign dance companies perform on an open air stage. Folk art by local craftsmen is also on display. In the winter, groups visiting Hollókő can participate in a wild pig hunt and subsequent roast.

## EXPLORING THE VILLAGE

A one-street town, Hollókő is idyllically set in a quiet, green valley, with hiking trails all around. A recently restored 14th-century castle is perched on a hilltop over the village.

In the village itself, admire the 14th-century wooden towered church and the sturdy, traditional peasant architecture (normally seen only in stylized *skanzens,* such as the one near Szentendre), and observe the elderly women at work on their embroidery (samples are for sale). You can also visit the **Village Museum** at Kossuth Lajos u. 82, where exhibits detail everyday Palóc life from the turn of the century. Official hours are Tuesday through Saturday from 10am to 4pm. Like everything else in town, though, the museum's opening times are flexible. Entry is 60 Ft (30¢).

## WHERE TO STAY

In Hollókő, traditionally furnished thatch-roofed **peasant houses** are available to rent on a nightly or longer basis. You can rent a **room in a shared house** (with shared facilities), or rent an entire **house.** The prices vary depending on the size of the room or house and the number of people in your party (2,500 Ft/$12.50 for a double room is average). Standard **private rooms** are also available in Hollókő. All accommodations can be booked in advance through the tourist office in Hollókő or Salgótarján (see "Essentials," above). If you arrive without reservations (which is not advised), knock on the door of villager Erika Terékne, at Kossuth 14. She works at the Foundation of Hollókő and can assist in finding you a bed for the night.

## WHERE TO DINE

Dining options are limited in tiny Hollókő. The **Vár Étterem,** at Kossuth Lajos u. 95, serves decent Hungarian food at very low prices. There is indoor and outdoor seating. The menu is not in English, but the waiters are patient. The restaurant is open daily, 12am to 8pm.

## 2 Eger

79 miles NE of Budapest

Eger (pronounced *Egg*-air), a small city lying in a valley between the Matra and Bükk mountains, is best known for three things: its castle, its wine, and its women—the women of the 16th century, that is. In that dark era of Turkish invasions, the women of Eger claimed their place in the Hungarian national consciousness by bravely fighting alongside István Dobó's army in defense of Eger's castle. Greatly outnumbered by the invaders, the defenders of Eger fought off the Turks for 38 grueling days, achieving a momentous victory that would stall the Turkish advance into Hungary for nearly half a century. Forty-four years later, in 1596, the sultan's forces attacked Eger again, this time taking the castle without great difficulty. Dobó's initial victory, though, and particularly the role of the women defenders, is memorialized in numerous paintings and poems, as well as monuments throughout Hungary.

As for the wine, the area around Eger is known for producing some fine vintages. Most famous among the regional potions is undoubtedly the heavily marketed Egri bikavér (Eger Bull's Blood), a strong dark-red wine, but there are many others worth sampling as well—and no shortage of places in Eger to sample them.

Today Eger's landscape presents a harmonious blend of old and new. The ruined castle, one of Hungary's proudest symbols, dominates the skyline; throughout the summer huge groups of Hungarian children visit the castle. Eger is also home to one of Hungary's most impressive Turkish ruins: a single, tall, slender minaret. The view from the minaret affords a wonderful vista of the town's surroundings. If you wander beyond the confines of the old section, you'll find a small modern city.

## ESSENTIALS

**GETTING THERE**   Eger is a 2-hour direct **train** ride from Budapest. Five daily trains depart Budapest's Keleti Station. Tickets cost 800 Ft ($4).

If you're **driving from Budapest,** take the M3 motorway east to Kerecsend, where you pick up Route 25 north to Eger.

**VISITOR INFORMATION**   For information, contact **Tourinform,** at Dobó tér 2 (☎ **36/321-807;** fax 36/321-304). The office is open in summer, Monday through Friday from 9am to 6:30pm and on Saturday from 10am to 2pm; off-season, the office closes an hour early. For private-room booking, try **Egertourist,** at Bajcsy-Zsilinszky u. 9 (☎ **36/411-724**). The office is open in summer, Monday through Saturday from 10am to 6pm; off-season, closed Saturday.

## EXPLORING OLD EGER

All of Eger's main sites are within easy walking distance of **Dobó István tér,** the lovely, dignified square that's the center of old Eger. Dobó István tér is home to the Minorite Church, a fine 18th-century baroque church. You'll also find a statue of Dobó, flanked by a knight and a woman, by Alajos Strobl, one of the country's leading turn-of-the-century sculptors. Strobl's work includes the statues of King Stephen on Buda's Castle Hill and the poet János Arany in front of the National Museum in Pest. The larger statue in the square, erected in the 1960s, is a more recent—and less subtle—rendition of the fight against the Turks.

The ruined **Eger Castle,** visible from just about anywhere in Eger, can be reached by walking northeast out of the square; enter it via the path out of Dózsa György tér. You can just wander around the grounds or explore two museums on the premises. The **István Dobó Castle Museum** displays a history of the castle and some Turkish artifacts. The **Eger Picture Gallery** is particularly worth a visit for those who have not yet seen the Hungarian National Gallery in Buda; the same fine 19th-century Hungarian artists are featured in both museums. The museums are open Tuesday through Sunday from 9am to 5pm. Admission to both is 200 Ft ($1).

Just to the west of the castle, on Harangöntó utca, is Eger's most visible reminder of the Turkish period, its ✪ **Minaret.** Though the mosque of which it was once a constituent part was destroyed in 1841, the 14-sided 110-foot-tall minaret survives to this day in remarkably good condition. For just 40 Ft (20¢), you can ascend its narrow height. It's a terrifying journey up a steep, cramped spiral staircase; because the space is so narrow, you can't turn back if anyone is behind you. Consequently, the ascent is not recommended for the weak-kneed or weak-hearted. Those who do make the climb, however, are justly rewarded with a spectacular view. Officially, the Minaret is open daily from 10am to 6pm, but the ticket taker in the little booth at the Minaret's base is not always faithful to these hours. If no one is there, you might ask at the nearby Minaret Hotel.

Moving from the graceful to the overpowering, you'll find the massive **Basilica**—the second-largest church in Hungary (after Esztergom's Basilica)—a few blocks to the south on Eszterhazy tér. József Hild, who was one of the architects of St. Stephen's

# Eger

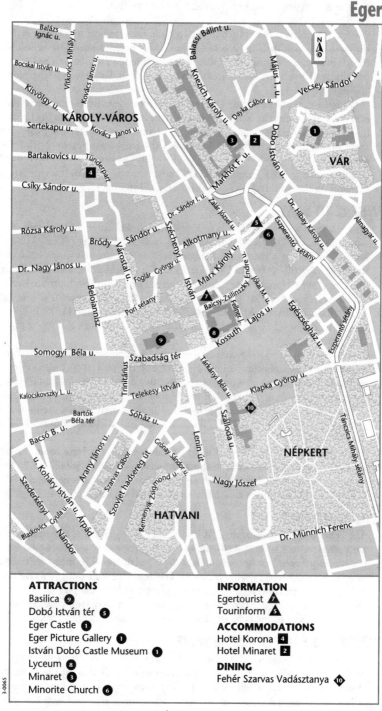

## ATTRACTIONS
Basilica **9**
Dobó István tér **5**
Eger Castle **1**
Eger Picture Gallery **1**
István Dobó Castle Museum **1**
Lyceum **8**
Minaret **3**
Minorite Church **6**

## INFORMATION
Egertourist **7**
Tourinform **5**

## ACCOMMODATIONS
Hotel Korona **4**
Hotel Minaret **2**

## DINING
Fehér Szarvas Vadásztanya **10**

3-0065

Basilica in Pest, built this church in the 1830s in the grandiose neoclassical style of the time. It's open daily from 6am to 7pm. Daily organ concerts are held in the church in summer, starting at 11:30am Monday through Saturday and at 12:30pm on Sunday. These times are subject to change; check at Tourinform. Admission is 200 Ft ($1).

Opposite the cathedral is the ✪ **Lyceum,** perhaps Eger's finest example of 18th-century architecture. The library (*könyvtár*) is the highlight of a visit to the Lyceum; the ceiling fresco of the Council of Trent by Johann Lukas Kracker and József Zach ranks among the greatest pieces of Hungarian art. The baroque carved bookshelves are awe inspiring. The library is open to the public, in summer Tuesday through Sunday from 9am to 3:30pm; in winter, Tuesday through Friday from 9:30am to 12:30pm and on weekends to noon. Admission is 150 Ft (75¢).

## WHERE TO STAY

Eger is blessed with several fine little hotels right in the center of town. Two stand out in particular. The **Hotel Korona,** Tündérpart 5, 3300 Eger (☎ **36/310-287;** fax 36/310-261), is a clean, cozy establishment on an extremely quiet, residential street just a few blocks west of Dobó István tér. The hotel has a shaded patio, where breakfast is served, and a wine cellar. There are 21 rooms, all with private bath. A double room goes for DM 70 to 80 ($40 to $46), with prices about 20% lower off-season. Rates include breakfast. Credit cards are accepted. Bus no. 11, 12, or 14 will get you there from the train station; get off at Csiky Sándor utca and you're practically at the doorstep.

On a par with the Hotel Korona is the **Hotel Minaret,** directly adjacent to Eger's Minaret, at Harangöntó u. 5, 3300 Eger (☎ and fax **36/410-473**). Just minutes north of Dobó István tér, this hotel offers spare, tidy double rooms for DM 65 ($37). Rates include breakfast. All but 3 of the 17 rooms are equipped with private bath. Credit cards are accepted. Take bus no. 11, 12, or 14 from the train station; after getting off at the Main Post Office (Főposta), you have to walk 5 minutes or so to the northeast.

Travelers on a tighter budget should consider renting a **private room** through **Egertourist** (see above) or through **Ibusz,** at Szécseny u. 28 (☎ **36/427-757**). Rates in Eger are as low as at 1,800 Ft ($9) for a bed with a shared bathroom and as high as 3,500 Ft ($17.50) for an apartment with bath and kitchen.

## WHERE TO DINE

The **Fehér Szarvas Vadásztanya (White Stag Hunting Inn),** located next door to the Park Hotel at Klapka u. 8 (☎ **36/411-129**), a few blocks south of Dobó István tér, is one of Eger's best-known and best-loved restaurants. The menu offers a full range of Hungarian wild-game specialties. The hearty, paprika-laced stews are especially good. Regional wines are featured. A piano and bass duet play nightly, amid the kitschy hunting lodge decor. The restaurant is open daily for dinner only (6pm to midnight), and reservations are recommended. Credit cards are accepted.

## WHERE TO SAMPLE LOCAL WINE

The best place to sample well-known local wines is in the vineyard country just west of Eger, in the wine cellars of the **Szépasszony-völgy (Valley of the Beautiful Women).** More than 50 wine cellars are here, each offering its own vintage. Some cellars have live music. Although the wine cellars don't serve food, you can grab a meal at a few local restaurants. Generally, the cellars open at 10am and close by 9 or 10pm.

## An Excursion to Bükk National Park

Just to the northeast of Eger lies the Bükk mountain range, a lush, rugged terrain of cliffs and forest land. Since 1976 a large part of this region has comprised the **Bükki Nemzeti Park** (Bükk National Park). In addition to numerous hiking trails, area highlights include a visit to the Lippizaner horse-breeding stables in the village of Szilvásvárad and a ride on the narrow-gauge railroad from Szilvásvárad to Szalajka-völgy. This train ride takes you through a serene landscape of mountain streams and waterfalls.

This mountainous national park is best visited in the spring, when countless wild-flowers color the landscape. The area has several pensions and hotels, as well as accommodations in private rooms. Egertourist or Tourinform (in Eger) should be able to help you book a room. Carografia publishes the best area map; called *Bükk hegyseg* (Bükk Hills), it shows all the area hiking trails in fairly good detail.

The easiest way to get to the Szépasszony-völgy is by taxi, though you can also walk there from the center in 30 or 40 minutes. You could also take bus no. 3 or 4 to the Hatvani Temető (Hatvan Cemetery) and walk from there; it's a 10- to 15-minute walk.

## 3 Aggtelek: An Entrance to the Caves

140 miles NE of Budapest

Tucked away beneath the Slovak border in northernmost Hungary, about 50 miles north of Eger, Aggtelek National Park (Aggteleki Nemzeti Park) is home to the extensive **Baradla cave network,** one of Europe's most spectacular cave systems. Although the remote and sparsely populated Aggtelek region is also suitable for hiking, people travel to Aggtelek primarily to explore the caves.

You can enter the Baradla cave system on guided tours from either of two villages: Aggtelek or Jósvafő, which is on the other side of the mountain. The tours are good fun. If this is your first time in a cave, you'll be astounded by the magical subterranean world of stalactites, stalagmites, and other bizarre formations. Three different guided tours—appropriately called short (*rövid*), medium (*közép*), and long (*hosszú*)—depart at different times throughout the day. Remember, no matter how hot it is outside, the caves are always damp and chilly (a constant 50° to 52°F), so dress appropriately.

The **Hotel Cseppkő** (☎ **48/343-075**), in the village of Aggtelek, is a popular place to crash after a day in the caves. Time-worn double rooms start at 2,500 Ft ($12.50). Though it's nothing to write home about, the Cseppkő is clean and conveniently located. Camping is also popular in the area.

Travelers without cars can get to Aggtelek by bus from Eger. The trip takes three hours. From Miskolc, the trip takes two hours. Ask about transportation at the local tourist office (such as Eger's Tourinform or Egertourist), where you can also ask for help booking a room in the Hotel Cseppkő (off-season there is no need to book in advance).

# 13 Southern Hungary: Traveling into the Great Plain and the Mecsek Hills

The mainly agricultural region of the Alföld (Great Plain), including the last remnants of the Puszta, Hungary's prairie, lies south and east of the Danube River. The main cities here are Kecskemét and Szeged. The Great Plain comprises approximately 20,000 square miles. On the other side of the river, in southwestern Hungary, are the verdant Mecsek Hills. The city of Pécs is the centerpiece of this hilly region.

## 1 The 2,000-Year-Old City of Pécs

123 miles SW of Budapest

Pécs (pronounced *Paych*) is a delightful, exuberant city, the largest and loveliest city in the Mecsek Hill region. Situated 20 miles or so from the Croatian border, in the scenic, rolling Mecsek Hills, the city enjoys a particularly warm and arid climate; the region around Pécs is the source of some of Hungary's finest fresh fruit. Few places in Hungary possess a more Mediterranean quality than Pécs.

Known as the "2,000-year-old city," Pécs was a major settlement in Roman times, when it was called Sopianae. It was later the site of Hungary's first university, founded in 1367. While that university no longer exists, Pécs remains one of the country's more important centers of learning. The city's present university, Janus Pannonius University (named for a local ecclesiastical poet of the 15th century) was moved here from Bratislava after that city (known as Pozsóny to Hungarians) was given to Czechoslovakia when Czechoslovakia was created after World War I.

Pécs thrived during the almost 150-year Turkish occupation as well, and reminders of this period fill the city. Although Pécs (like much of Hungary) was almost completely destroyed during the bloody liberation battles between the Ottoman and Christian armies, what did survive—particularly the Mosque of Pasha Gazi Kassim—may well be the best examples of Turkish architecture in the country.

The people of Pécs are proud of their city. If you travel just a block or two outside the historic core, you'll see that the place is thriving: Shops and streets throng with people; buses thunder past in every direction. Pécs is a city on the move. It exhibits none of the torpor you might notice on a hot summer afternoon in a Great Plains town like Kecskemét or Szeged.

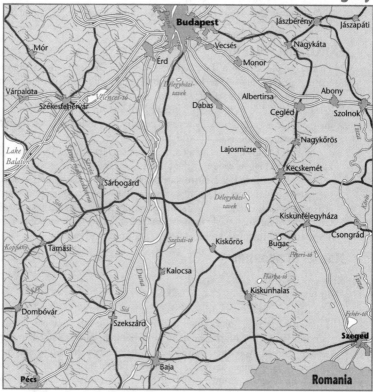

And if you walk up Janus Pannonius utca toward Széchenyi tér, about a block up the street, you'll notice on your left a small metal fence covered with padlocks. Young lovers visiting Pécs have left these locks as a token of their desire to live in this beautiful city.

A more recent development in Pécs (since 1996) is the presence of NATO troops, including a sizable American contingent, who are based just outside the city as part of the peacekeeping mission in Bosnia and Croatia.

## ESSENTIALS

**GETTING THERE**   Nine **trains** depart daily from Budapest's Déli Station; five of these are Intercity trains. On an Intercity train, the journey takes 2¹/₂ hours, costing 1,168 Ft ($5.85) plus the 250 Ft ($1.25) compulsory reservation. On a fast train (*gyors*), the trip is 3 hours, and you don't need a reservation.

**VISITOR INFORMATION**   The best source of information in Pécs is **Tourinform,** at Széchenyi tér 9 (☎ **72/213-315;** fax 72/212-632). The office is open April through October, Monday through Friday from 8am to 6pm (to 6pm in July and August) and on Saturday from 9am to 2pm; in winter, Monday through Friday from 8am to 4pm. Tourinform can provide a list of local private-room accommodations, but you'll have to reserve the room yourself.

If you want to have a room reserved for you or are specifically interested in finding accommodations, visit **Mecsek Tourist,** at Széchenyi tér 1 (☎ **72/213-300;** fax

72/212-044). The office is open Monday through Friday from 9am to 5pm and on Saturday from 9am to 1pm.

# EXPLORING OLD PÉCS

Today, the old section of Pécs captivates visitors. One of Hungary's most pleasing central squares is here—**Széchenyi tér,** set on an incline with the mosque at the top and the powerful equestrian statue of János Hunyadi at the bottom. Hunyadi defeated the Turks in the 1456 Battle of Nandorfehérvár (Belgrade), thus forestalling their northward advance by nearly a century. Grand pastel-colored buildings line the cobblestoned streets that border the square.

Old Pécs is known for its many museums and galleries; after Budapest, Pécs is perhaps the next biggest center of the arts in Hungary. The large student population contributes greatly to this creative state of affairs. We list several museums below, but there are many more as well, some containing the work of contemporary and student artists. Pécs is also home to the Zsolnay ceramics factory; Zsolnay porcelain, though lesser known internationally than its rival Herend, may be more popular nationally. The Zsolnay Museum, also listed below, is a "must see" in Pécs.

## HOUSES OF WORSHIP

### Mosque of Pasha Gazi Kassim
At the top of Széchenyi tér. ☎ **72/321-976.**

The largest Turkish structure still standing in Hungary today, this former mosque is now used as a Catholic church. It was built in the late 16th century, during the Turkish occupation, on the site of an earlier church. The mix of religious traditions is oddly evident everywhere you look, but the effect is rather pleasing. An English-language description of the church's history is posted on a bulletin board on the left-hand wall. Open in summer, daily 10am to 4pm; winter, Monday through Friday from 10am to noon.

### Pécs Cathedral
On Dom tér. ☎ **72/315-538.**

Dating back to the 11th century, this four-towered cathedral has been destroyed and rebuilt on several occasions. During the Turkish occupation it was used as a mosque, sporting a minaret. The neoclassical exterior is the work of the early–19th-century architect Mihály Pollack. The interior remains primarily Gothic, with some baroque additions and furnishings. Various paintings and murals by leading 19th-century artists Károly Lotz and Bertalan Székely are inside the church.

The square in front of the cathedral—as well as the little park beneath it—is a popular gathering place, and occasionally the site of folk concerts or dances. Admission to the cathedral is 160 Ft (80¢) and includes entrance to the treasury and the ancient crypt. For 500 Ft ($2.50) you can have the lights turned on. Open summer, daily from 9am to 5pm; winter, Monday through Friday, 10am to 4pm.

### Pécs Synagogue
Pécs's grand old synagogue is incongruously situated in what is now one of the city's busiest shopping squares, Kossuth tér (home of the Konsum Department Store). Nevertheless, once inside you'll find it to be a quiet, cool place far removed from the bustle outside. The synagogue was built in 1869, and the original rich oak interior survives to this day. Next door is the former Jewish school of Pécs, now a Croatian school.

Prior to World War II, the synagogue had over 4,000 members, of whom only 464 survived the Holocaust. Every year, Pécs's small Jewish community commemorates the 1944 deportations to Auschwitz on the first Sunday after July 4.

# Pécs

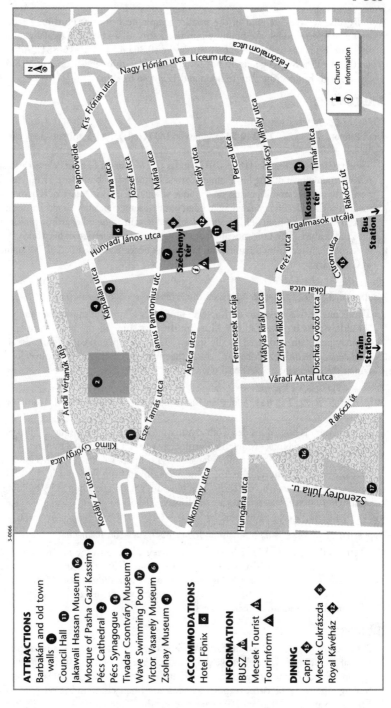

**ATTRACTIONS**
Barbakán and old town walls ❶
Council Hall ⓫
Jakawali Hassan Museum ⓰
Mosque of Pasha Gazi Kassim ❼
Pécs Cathedral ❷
Pécs Synagogue ⓮
Tivadar Csontváry Museum ❹
Wave Swimming Pool ⓱
Victor Vasarely Museum ❻
Zsolnay Museum ❹

**ACCOMMODATIONS**
Hotel Fönix ❻

**INFORMATION**
IBUSZ ⓯
Mecsek Tourist ⓭
Tourinform ❾

**DINING**
Capri ⓯
Mecsek Cukrászda ❽
Royal Kávéház ⓬

3-0066

205

Regular services are held in the smaller temple next door at Fürdőu. 1 (there isn't a sign; go through the building into the courtyard and cross diagonally to the right) on Friday at 6:30pm and on Saturday at 10:30am (☎ **72/315-881**). Admission to the Pécs Synagogue is 40 Ft (20¢). Open May through October only, Sunday through Friday from 9am to noon and 12:30pm to 4pm.

## MUSEUMS

### Tivadar Csontváry Museum

Janus Pannonius u. 11. ☎ **72/310-544.** Admission 160 Ft (80¢). Tues–Sun 10am–6pm; closes at 4pm in winter.

Tivadar Csontváry Kosztka (1853–1919), today one of Hungary's most beloved artists, remained unknown during his lifetime, scorned by the art establishment. His mystical post-impressionist landscapes suggest a unique vision of the world, one that is both tormented and idyllic. Hungarians like to point out that some time after Csontváry's death Picasso saw an exhibition of his work and referred to him as the other artistic genius of the 20th century. This little museum houses an impressive collection of his work.

Across the street from the museum, in the park beneath Pécs Cathedral, is a statue of Csontváry.

### ✪ Zsolnay Museum

Kaptalan u. 2. ☎ **72/324-822.** Admission 160 Ft (80¢). Tues–Sun 10am–6pm.

This is one of five museums on Kaptalan utca, Pécs's "street of museums," and you shouldn't miss it. The Zsolnay Museum displays some of the best examples of Zsolnay porcelain, produced locally since 1852—vases, plates, cups, figurines, and even ceramic paintings. Once you've seen the museum, check out the Zsolnay fountain at the lower end of Széchenyi tér.

### Jakawali Hassan Museum

Rákóczi út 2. ☎ **72/313-853.** Admission 100 Ft (50¢). Everyday except Wed, 10am–6pm. Closed Oct–Mar.

This museum is housed inside a 16th-century mosque, the only mosque in Hungary with a minaret still intact (though unfortunately you can't ascend the minaret as you can Eger's Minaret). Like the much larger mosque up in Széchenyi tér, this mosque was converted to a church after the Turks were driven from Pécs, but in the 1950s it was restored to its original form. The museum's main attraction is its building, although some religious artifacts are on display.

### Victor Vasarely Museum

Kaptalan u. 3. ☎ **72/334-822.** Admission 160 Ft (80¢). Tues–Sun 10am–6pm.

The recently deceased Victor Vasarely, internationally known founder of "op art," was born in the house where this museum now stands. This is one of two museums in the country devoted solely to his work (the other is in Óbuda; see "More Museums & Sights," in chapter 6). While Vasarely's fame was achieved abroad, Hungarians proudly consider him their native son.

## SHOPPING

A short stroll through the center of town is enough to see that Pécs is prospering. Several pedestrian-only streets make shopping in Pécs extra pleasant. If you find yourself on Ferencesek utca, stop in at **Kreativ,** at Ferencesek u. 22. It's a great place for buying gifts: ceramic cups, teapots, wooden toys, hair clips, and jewelry. It's all handmade and very affordable. For a more exotic shopping experience, visit the **Pécsi Vásár** (Pécs Flea Market). At this crowded, bustling open air market you can find everything from antique china and silver to Turkish T-shirts and Chinese baby booties. Tables of homemade preserves and honey stand alongside boxes of used car parts. The main attraction, however, is the animal market. People sell puppies and kittens out of the trunks of their cars. Also chickens, rabbits, and sometimes pigs and horses. It's open every day, though Sunday is the biggest and best day (particularly as concerns the animal market). A special bus (marked "Vásár") departs the Konsum shopping center in the center of downtown Pécs regularly. You need two standard city bus tickets for this bus (available for 65 Ft [$.33] each at newsstands and kiosks). You can also take the no. 3 bus from the Konsum (only one ticket required), but you'll have to walk some distance from the stop to the entrance of the flea market.

## SWIMMING POOLS & A PLAYGROUND

If you are visiting Pécs in the summer, you are bound to feel the heat. Cool off in the waves at **Hullám uszoda** (Wave Swimming Pool) on Szendrey Julia utca. Admission is 150 Ft (75¢). Another swimming pool complex is on Rókusalja utca. There is a wading pool for kids, as well as a 25-meter lap pool. Admission is 100 Ft (50¢). After swimming, treat yourself to some of the best ice cream in town, right down the street at **Egerszegi Cukraszda.**

Pécs is home to perhaps one of the nicest playgrounds in all of Hungary. **Napsugár Játszókert** (Sunshine Playground) is on Vadász utca, a short bus ride from the city center. Built in 1997 by a foundation and with donations from the community, this small grassy playground has a quaint friendly appeal. There are chunky wooden climbing structures, slides, seesaws, swings (including a real infant swing), a sandbox, and picnic tables. To get there, take bus 27 from the Konsum to "Ledina" stop.

## WHERE TO STAY

You can book a **private room** through Mecsek Tourist (see "Essentials," above) or Ibusz, across Széchenyi tér at no. 8 (☎ 72/312-176).

If you're in the mood for a funky little hotel right in the center, try the popular ✪ **Hotel Fönix,** at Hunyadi út 2 (☎ **72/311-680;** fax 72/324-113). This unique hotel, just off the top of Széchenyi tér, has 14 rooms, each one with oddly angled walls and sloped ceilings. The rooms are a bit cramped, but all are clean and have refrigerators and TVs. Each room has a shower, but only eight have toilets; the common facilities, however, are well maintained. One apartment, with full facilities and its own entrance off the street, is also available. A double room costs 4,690 Ft ($23.45), a room with a private toilet is 5,190 Ft ($25.95), and the apartment goes for 9,390 Ft ($46.95). Rates include breakfast. Call several days ahead to reserve a room. Credit cards are accepted.

If the Hotel Fönix is full, the management can book a room for you at a pension they operate, **Kertész Panzió,** at Sáfrány u. 42 (☎ **72/210-087;** fax 72/311-680). If you'd prefer a smaller, quieter accommodation in the hills anyway, this pension might be just the place for you. A double room is 5,990 Ft ($29.95); a suite is 7,990 Ft ($39.95). Bus no. 32, which stops in front of the Hotel Fönix, will take you to Kertész Panzió.

## WHERE TO DINE

### Bagolyvár Étterem

Felsőhavi Dülő 6/1. ☎ **72/211-333.** Bus: 33 from in front of the Konsum shopping center to the last stop.

This large, classy restaurant serves delicious food in a fabulous setting, high in the hills overlooking the city. The view is excellent, and the service equally good. Bagolyvár features a well-stocked wine cellar, from which patrons can make their selection.

Reservations are a good idea for dinner in the summer. The same owner operates a second restaurant, Dóm Vendéglő, in the city center, at Király u. 3 (☎ 72/210-088).

## COFFEEHOUSES & ICE-CREAM PARLORS

Pécs offers numerous places to enjoy coffee and sweets. Try **Mecsek Cukrászda,** on Széchenyi tér, for a quick jolt of espresso and any number of sinfully good and inexpensive pastries. For a more leisurely coffeehouse experience, try the **Royal Kávéház,** at the corner of Király utca and Széchenyi tér. There's outdoor seating, but the recently renovated art deco interior makes sitting inside worthwhile. You can also order a more substantial meal here; soups cost 190 to 390 Ft (95¢ to $1.95), while main courses cost 350 to 800 Ft ($1.75 to $4).

For ice cream, **Capri,** at Citrom u. 7, 3 blocks south of Széchenyi tér, serves up various sundaes as well as cones. The original recipe for *somloi galuska* is reputedly in use at Capri. Some locals, however, claim that the ice cream at Capri is inferior to that of the **Egerszegi Fagylaltozó,** on Rókusalja utca, a 15-minute walk from the center. The owners of Egerszegi recently opened a second, easier-to-reach place at Bajcsy-Zsilinzsky u. 5 (☎ 72/327-540). Our current favorite place for sweets and ice cream in Pécs is **Magda Cukrászda,** at Kandó Kálmán u. 4. Open daily from 10am to 10pm, this is a bright, bustling neighborhood cukrászda, where the selection and quality of cakes is superb. The slightly out-of-the-way location (near the train station) apparently hasn't deterred customers at all.

## 2 Kecskemét

53 miles SE of Budapest

Kecskemét (pronounced *Ketch*-keh-mate), a city of over 100,000 inhabitants in the western portion of the Great Hungarian Plain, has a decidedly small-town feel to it. A quiet city with wide, open squares and broad avenues, Kecskemét is blessed with some of the most interesting architecture in the Great Plain. The town's dizzyingly colorful art nouveau buildings may be the equal of any in the country outside the capital.

Kecskemét was the birthplace of Zoltán Kodály, the musicologist, teacher, and composer who, along with his friend and colleague Béla Bartók, achieved worldwide renown earlier this century. Today, a music school in town bears his name. Kecskemét is also famous throughout the country for its many varieties of apricot brandy (*barack palinka*).

## ESSENTIALS

**GETTING THERE**   Twelve daily **trains** depart Budapest's Nyugati Station. The trip is just over one hour by Intercity train and costs 500 Ft ($2.50), plus 250 Ft ($1.25) for the compulsory reservation. Fast trains (*gyors*) make the trip in just less than 1½ hours, and you don't have to pay for a reservation.

If you're **driving from Budapest,** take the M5 motorway south. You will have to pay a 1,600 Ft ($8) highway toll each way.

**VISITOR INFORMATION**   The best source of information is **Tourinform,** at Kossuth tér 1 (☎ and fax 76/481-065). The office is open Monday through Friday from 8am to 5pm and on Saturday and Sunday from 9am to 1pm. **Pusztatourist,** at Szabadság tér 2 (☎ 76/483-493; fax 76/321-215), will be useful if you're planning a side trip to Bugac. It's open summer, Monday through Friday from 8am to 6pm; winter, 8am to 4:30pm.

## EXPLORING KECSKEMÉT'S MAIN SQUARE

The museums mentioned here are in the immediate vicinity of **Kossuth tér,** Kecskemét's main square.

Photography lovers will not want to miss the excellent **Hungarian Photography Museum,** Katona József tér 12 (☎ **76/483-221**), featuring the works of contemporary Hungarian photographers, including foreign photographers of Hungarian origin. Admission is 100 Ft (50¢). Open Tuesday through Sunday from 10am to 5pm.

Located inside the Cifra Palace, the city's other art nouveau gem, the **Kecskemét Gallery (Kecskeméti Galéria),** Rákóczi u. 1 (☎ **76/480-776**), features Hungarian art of the 19th and 20th centuries. Even if you don't go inside, make sure you check out this incredible building. Admission is 100 Ft (50¢). It's open Tuesday through Sunday from 10am to 5pm.

The ✪ **Museum of Hungarian Naîve Artists (Naív Művészeti Galéria),** Gáspár András u. 11 (☎ **76/324-767**), houses the works of local folk artists from the early 20th century to the present. In one gallery, artworks are available for purchase. Admission is 150 Ft (75¢). Open Tuesday through Sunday from 10am to 5pm.

Hungary's largest toy collection can be found at the **Toy Museum (Játék-műhély és Múzeum),** at the corner of Gáspár András utca and Hosszú utca (☎ **76/481-469**). This quaint museum has exhibits on toy design and manufacturing. Families with children should try to come on the weekend, when youngsters are allowed to play with some of the toys. Admission is 50 Ft (25¢) for adults, 30 Ft (15¢) for students and children. Open Tuesday through Sunday from 10am to 5pm.

### ✪ Town Hall

Kossuth tér 1. ☎ **76/483-683.** Admission 50 Ft (25¢). Weekdays 9am–5pm.

Built in 1893 by Ödön Lechner and Gyula Pártos, this delightful art nouveau structure is a "must see" for aficionados of Lechner's later Budapest buildings, the former Post Office Savings Bank (see "Leopold Town & Theresa Town," in chapter 7) and the Applied Arts Museum (see "More Museums & Sights in Pest, Buda & Óbuda," in chapter 6). Like those buildings in the capital, Lechner's Kecskemét masterpiece is generously decorated with colorful Zsolnay majolica tiles. The council chamber (*dísz terem*) contains ceiling frescoes by the artist Bertalan Székely, whose work is also on exhibit in Buda's National Gallery. If the building is closed when you arrive, admire it from the outside while you listen to the bells that play music by Kodály and others throughout the day (usually on the hour).

Just in front of the Town Hall is an odd monument: a stone broken in two to symbolize the heart attack suffered on that spot by József Katona, the beloved playwright and native son, who is recognized as the father of modern Hungarian drama. A figure of the Enlightenment, in the first half of the 18th century, Katona is best known for *Bánkbán,* a play that was later put to music by Ferenc Erkel, becoming the first Hungarian opera.

## WHERE TO STAY

**Private rooms** can be booked through Pusztatourist (see "Essentials," above) or the nearby Ibusz office, at Széchenyi tér 1–3 (☎ **76/322-955**). Both offices are open Monday through Friday from 8am to 4pm. Tourinform also has local pension and hotel listings.

**Hotel Három Gúnár,** at Batthyány u. 7, 6000 Kecskemét (☎ **76/483-611;** fax 76/481-253), is a well-maintained, clean, comfortable hotel, just minutes from central Kossuth tér. The hotel has 45 rooms and 4 suites, all with private bath. A double room costs 6,900 Ft ($34.50); suites start at 9,500 Ft ($47.50). All rooms have minibar, telephone, and TV. Insist on a room above the ground floor to avoid the noise from the bowling alley in the hotel basement. There's a restaurant on the premises and free parking. Credit and charge cards are accepted.

✪ **Caissa Panzió,** at Gyenes tér 18, 6000 Kecskemét (☎ and fax **76/481-685**), is another centrally located and reasonably priced option; the Caissa, named for the goddess of chess, is also *the* choice for enthusiasts of the game. A family-owned and -operated pension, Caissa hosts official grandmaster tournaments every year. Recent guests have included the Polgar family and Péter Lékó. Bobby Fischer, having chosen Budapest as his place of self-imposed exile, is said to order books regularly from the Caissa chess book shop. The hotel reception is on the fifth floor, where the kitchen and common room are also located. There are 11 rooms; two have private toilet and shower, and four have TVs. The small rooms are clean and bright; many overlook the quiet residential park on the front side of the building. Prices for a double range from 2,700 to 4,200 Ft ($13.50 to $21). Breakfast, served from 7 to 11am, costs 400 Ft ($2) extra. Laundry facilities are available for guests' use.

## WHERE TO DINE

We recommend the ✪ **Görög Udvar Étterem,** a Greek restaurant, housed inside the Greek culture museum, at Hornyik János krt. 1 (☎ **76/492-513**). The authentic Greek fare is delicious. Main courses cost 500 to 1,300 Ft ($2.50 to $6.50). Alcohol is served, including Greek specialty liquors. Open daily from 11am to 11pm.

Another good dining option is **Italia,** just down the street at Hornyik János krt. 4 (☎ **76/484-627**). Italia serves great tasting pizza that costs 300 to 610 Ft ($1.50 to $3.05), as well as pasta, priced at 300 to 500 Ft ($1.50 to $2.50), in a bright, busy atmosphere. There's outdoor seating in summer. Open daily from 11:30am to 11pm.

**HBH,** Csányi u. 4 (☎ **76/481-945**), is the best choice for traditional Hungarian and Bavarian fare at reasonable prices: Soups cost 250 Ft ($1.25), while main courses run 700 to 1,500 Ft ($3.50 to $7.50). HBH also brews its own beer; a halfliter mug, *korsó,* is 180 Ft (90¢). Open daily from 11am to midnight.

## 3 Bugac & the Puszta

Much of the Great Hungarian Plain was once comprised of open, rugged puszta (prairie) country, home to a fondly remembered culture of nomadic shepherds and fierce horsemen. The vast wilderness of grasslands and marshes has long since given way to the modern era of agricultural reclamation, but pieces of the native terrain— and the puszta way of life—are preserved in national parks in the Great Plain.

**Kiskunság National Park,** ☎ **76/321-777,** and especially the village of **Bugac,** about 25 miles south of Kecskemét, are well worth a visit. If you're lucky enough to be in Hungary in late spring, you can see one of the region's finest sights: endless fields ablaze with wild red poppies.

You can book a tour to Bugac from Budapest through Ibusz. The scheduled tour includes a traditional horse-riding show featuring Hungarian cowboys (*csikós*), horseback riding on the trails, and a traditional puszta dinner of bogrács gulyás, a hearty stew cooked over an open fire.

You can also travel to Bugac on your own by train from Kecskemét; three trains depart and return daily. A local bus also departs Kecskemét for Bugac Monday through Friday at 11am daily. The bus leaves from the main bus station (next to the train station); the trip takes 30 minutes. You can still see the riding show; tickets are 700 Ft ($3.50), or 1,400 Ft ($7) for a combined ticket which includes an hourlong horse-drawn carriage ride. Of course, you can always skip the show and hike out into the wilderness, too.

If you want to spend a night on the puszta, you can book a room through **Pusztatourist,** in Kecskemét at Szabadság tér 2 (☎ **76/483-493**). (Ask them for riding and trail information as well.) Try the **Gedeon Tanya Panzió** (Gedeon Farm Boarding House), a traditional old farmhouse with three double rooms. An adjoining new building has five double rooms, a large dining room, and a wine cellar. A double room costs 6,900 Ft ($34.50). Gedeon Tanya also has its own stables. You're welcome to visit just for the horseback riding. **Táltos Lovaspanzió** (Táltos Equestrian Pension) (☎ **76/372-633**) is another accommodation in Bugac for horse lovers. The pension operates a large stable. There are double rooms with private shower (5,500 Ft/$27.50) and double rooms with shared facilities (4,400 Ft/ $22). There are also bungalows (10,900 Ft/$54.50). Each bungalow sleeps about six people.

No trip to Bugac would be complete without a meal at the **Bugaci Csárda,** ☎ **76/372-522,** locally famous for "authentic" Puszta meals: rich, hearty paprika stews. Meals cost between 600 and 1,020 Ft ($3 to $5.10).

## 4 Szeged: Hungary's Spice Capital

**105 miles SE of Budapest**

World famous for its paprika and salami (Pick Salami), Szeged (pronounced *Seh*-ged) is also home to one of Hungary's major universities, named after Attila József, the brilliant but disturbed interwar poet who rose to artistic heights from a childhood of desperate poverty. As a young man, he was expelled from the Szeged university that would later change its name to honor him. Driven by private demons, Hungary's great "proletarian poet" committed suicide at the age of 32 by hurling himself under a train at Balaton-szárszo, near Lake Balaton. Like Van Gogh, József failed to achieve wide recognition during his lifetime; today, though, he is universally adored in Hungary, particularly by teenagers and students who find his rebellious, nonconformist, irreverent spirit deeply appealing. An unassuming statue of the poet stands in front of the university's main building on Dugonics tér.

In addition to its status as a center of learning and culture, Szeged is the industrial capital of the Great Plain (Alföld), though you wouldn't know it by spending a day or two in the city center. The Tisza River splits the city in two, with the historic center lying, Pest-style, within a series of concentric ring boulevards on the left bank. Indeed, the river looms large in Szeged's history: The city was almost completely destroyed by an 1879 Tisza flood, but with financial assistance from a number of European cities— Brussels, Berlin, Rome, London, and Paris—was rebuilt in the characteristic ring style of the time. The post-flood reconstruction explains why Szeged's finest architecture is of the *fin-de-siècle* art nouveau style. Don't miss the synagogue (see below) and the newly restored Reök Building (now a bank) on the corner of Kölcsey utca and Bajcsy-Zsilinszky utca.

Szeged, the proud capital of the Great Plain, is a hot and dusty but hospitable town. Its people, many of whom are students, love to stroll along the riverside, sit in the cafes, and window-shop on Karász utca, the town's main pedestrian street. Dom tér, a beautiful wide open square, is home to the **Szeged Summer Festival,** a popular summer-long series of cultural events. Ask about this at Tourinform or Szeged Tourist. On hot days, the line at the most popular ice-cream shop, Palank (on the corner of Tömörkény utca and Oskola utca), snakes out the door and down the street. By all means, join the queue.

## ESSENTIALS

**GETTING THERE**    Twelve daily **trains** depart Budapest's Nyugati Station. By Intercity train, the trip is just over 2 hours and costs 1,250 Ft ($6.25), plus the 250 Ft ($1.25) compulsory reservation. Fast trains (*gyors*) make the trip in 2¹/₂ hours, and you don't need a reservation.

If you're **driving from Budapest,** take the M5 motorway south through Kecskemét and Kiskunfélegyháza. You will have to pay a 1,600 Ft ($8) highway toll each way.

**VISITOR INFORMATION**    The best source of information, as usual, is **Tourinform,** at Victor Hugo u. 1 (☎ **62/311-966**). The office is open Monday through Friday from 9am to 5pm.

If you arrive on a weekend or wish to book a private room, try **Szeged Tourist,** at Klauzal tér 7 (☎ **62/321-800**), open Monday through Friday from 9am to 5pm and on Saturday from 9am to 1pm.

**MAHART,** the Hungarian ferry line company, organizes boat tours up and down the Tisza river from the first of April through mid-October. For information, contact the MAHART boat station in Szeged at ☎ **62/313-834.**

## EXPLORING THE HISTORIC CENTER

### ✪ Synagogue
Jósika utca. ☎ **62/311-402.** Admission 100 Ft (50¢).

A relic of Szeged's once-thriving Jewish community, this grandiose art nouveau synagogue was completed in 1903. It occupies a full block in a quiet, tree-lined residential neighborhood just west of the city center on Jósika utca, between Gutenberg utca and Hajnóczy utca. From Dugonics tér, walk right on Tisza Lajos körút, and turn left on Gutenberg utca.

Inside the vestibule is a series of marble plaques, listing by name the local victims of the Holocaust. Behind the synagogue, at Hajnoczy u. 12, stands the Old Synagogue, built in 1843 and badly damaged by the flood of 1879. It is currently under reconstruction, scheduled for completion in 1998. It will serve as a cultural center, the venue for alternative theater groups and chamber music concerts.

The synagogue is open to the public Sunday through Friday from 9am to noon and 1 to 6pm. If you find the synagogue closed during these hours, you might go to the address that's sometimes posted near the entrance, and the caretaker will open the synagogue for you.

### Votive Church
On Dom tér.

The symbol of Szeged's postflood revitalization, this church with its two tall, slender clock towers was built in 1912. Its elaborately painted neo-Renaissance interior suggests a much older structure. Inside the church is one of Europe's largest organs, with over 9,000 pipes. Ask at Tourinform or Szeged Tourist about organ recitals.

In front of the church is the Broken Tower, a remnant of an earlier church that stood on the same spot. The church is open Monday through Saturday from 9am to 6pm and on Sunday from 9:30 to 10am, 11 to 11:30am, and 12:30 to 6pm.

### Móra Ferenc Museum
Roosevelt tér 1–3. ☎ **62/470-370.** Admission 70 Ft (35¢). Tues 10am–3pm.

This imposing structure by the river's edge houses a varied collection devoted to local history. Of particular note is the display of local folk costumes.

# Szeged

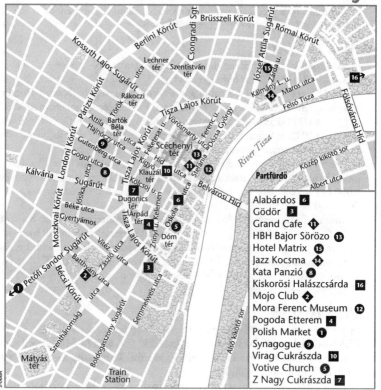

Alabárdos **6**
Gödör **3**
Grand Cafe **11**
HBH Bajor Sörözo **13**
Hotel Matrix **15**
Jazz Kocsma **14**
Kata Panzió **8**
Kiskorösi Halászcsárda **16**
Mojo Club **2**
Mora Ferenc Museum **12**
Pogoda Etterem **4**
Polish Market **1**
Synagogue **9**
Virag Cukrászda **10**
Votive Church **5**
Z Nagy Cukrászda **7**

## OPEN-AIR MARKETS

Szeged, a city situated within 20 miles of two international borders (Romanian and Serbian), has long attracted shoppers and vendors from a variety of countries. If this kind of open-air market interests you, check out the **Polish Market (Lengyel Piac)** at the southwestern edge of town. Once filled with Polish smugglers, this dusty flea market is now home to Vietnamese, Chinese, Romanians, Serbs, Uzbekis, and others. The Poles are gone, but the name has stuck. You never know what kind of junk you might find here—it all depends on what's "in season." Unfortunately, the Cold War souvenirs that once attracted Westerners to markets like this are seldom displayed. The market is open Monday through Saturday from dawn to midafternoon. To get to the Polish Market, located in a dusty field at the corner of Petőfi Sándor utca and Rákóczi utca, walk straight out Petőfi Sándor utca from the center of town or take tram no. 4.

Szeged's ✪ main **fruit and vegetable market** is located behind the bus station on Mars tér (formerly Marx tér, and still known to many as such). The vendors are local Hungarian farmers. If you haven't tried any Hungarian produce yet, you're definitely missing out on something wonderful. You won't be disappointed with the peaches, apricots, watermelons, cherries, strawberries, plums, or pears. The market is open daily from dawn until midafternoon—arrive early for the best selection. Fresh flowers and dried paprika wreathes are also sold here.

You can buy Szeged's signature paprika and salami anywhere food is sold. See chapter 1 for descriptions of types of paprika.

## WHERE TO STAY

**Private rooms** can be booked through Szeged Tourist (see "Essentials," above) or Ibusz (☎ **62/471-177**), at Somogyi u. 11.

The ✿ **Kata Panzió** is located in a quiet residential neighborhood, a 10-minute walk from central Klauzál tér at Bolyai János u. 15, between Gogol utca and Kálvária sgt. (☎ **62/311-258**). We highly recommended this lovely little pension, which opened in 1995. It features plenty of common space, sunny balconies on each floor, an enchanting terrace garden, and a friendly German shepherd named Ivan. Four double rooms, one triple, and one quad are available. All rooms have TVs. Half the rooms have private bath facilities; the others share. A double with private bath costs 5,000 Ft ($25); a double with shower costs 4,000 Ft ($20). Breakfast costs an additional 300 Ft ($1.50).

Another fairly new establishment is the **Hotel Matrix,** Zárda u. 8 (☎ **62/313-666;** fax 62/313-827), about 10 minutes from central Széchenyi tér by tram no. 1 or trolleybus no. 9. This tasteful small hotel is clean and pleasant, with a friendly and professional management. Its 10 double rooms all have showers, TVs, and telephones. A double costs 5,100 Ft ($25.50). Breakfast is an additional 510 Ft ($2.55). Laundry service is available.

## WHERE TO DINE

In Szeged, you'd do well to sample the local fish fare at the authentic, riverside **Kiskőrösi Halászcsárda,** at Felső Tisza-part 336 (☎ **62/328-410**). Paprika is the spice of choice for hearty fish stews and bisques alike. Reservations are recommended. Open daily from noon to midnight.

The **Gödör,** at Tisza Lajos krt. 103 (next to the Hero's Gate), is the local university's restaurant; faculty members pack it at lunchtime. The extensive menu of Hungarian specialties (including many vegetarian options) is extremely reasonably priced. Open daily from 11am to 10pm.

**HBH Bajor Söröző,** ☎ **62/313-934,** is another good option for Hungarian and Bavarian fare. Located at Deák Ferenc u. 4, the HBH brews its own beer and is a popular nighttime gathering place. Soups cost 100 to 140 Ft (50¢ to 70¢); main courses, 420 to 1,600 Ft ($2.10 to $8). A half liter of beer will set you back 190 Ft (95¢).

Our favorite Chinese restaurant in all Hungary is ✿ **Pagoda Étterem,** at Zrinyi u. 5. Main courses start at 550 Ft ($2.75). The Chinese lanterns, dragon-red tablecloths, and service staff in silk kimonos add to the appeal. Open daily from noon to midnight.

**Alabárdos,** at Oskola u. 13 (☎ **62/312-914**), is *the* choice for an elegant, upscale dining experience. Hungarian cuisine is served on Herend porcelain; the cutlery is sterling. Reservations are necessary. Locals consider it the town's finest restaurant. Main courses are 700 to 1,200 Ft ($3.50 to $6). Open Monday through Saturday from 11:30am to 3pm and 6pm to midnight. Alabárdos has recently opened a pub right next door. The menu is small but wholesome: salads and cheese-based dishes. Draft beer is available. A popular place with Szeged's large foreign student population.

### COFFEEHOUSES & ICE-CREAM PARLORS

No trip to Szeged would be complete without a stop at the ✿ **Virág Cukrászda,** an old-world coffeehouse sprawled on Klauzál tér. A local petition drive in the early 1990s prevented this Szeged institution from being turned into a car showroom.

Antique espresso machines press out tiny cupfuls of rich, aromatic coffee. The pastries are sinfully good and inexpensive. The adjoining "Green Room" is a nonsmoking section. The whole place is open daily from 9am to 8pm.

Across the square is the **Kis Virág (Little Flower),** where a variety of pastries and the best ice cream in town are available for take-out. Rivaling (and some say surpassing) the Kis Virág for take-out pastries and cakes is tiny **Z. Nagy Cukrászda,** located on Somogyi utca, just off Karász utca (the central pedestrian street). Z. Nagy is the only pastry shop we found in Hungary that sells macaroons. Z. Nagy also dispenses a lovely *Erzsi kocka,* a treat consisting of walnut paste sandwiched between two shortbread cookies, with hard chocolate frosting on top.

## SZEGED AFTER DARK

**Jazz Kocsma,** at Kálmány L. u. 14 (☎ **62/327-420**), is reputedly *the* place for live jazz. Different local bands play nightly. It's a groovy, smoky scene. The kitchen serves Mexican food. Reservations are highly recommended. Open daily, 11am to 2am. While Jazz Kocsma is the hottest venue for the university crowd, **Mojo Club** serves a slightly older, less hip clientele. Reservations are highly recommended at both. Located at Batthyány u. 30, on the corner of Alföldi utca. The sunken rooms have a distinctly bohemian appeal. Local blues bands perform once a week. There's a full bar, and decent pizza and pasta. Open Monday through Saturday from 11am to 11pm. No cover.

A brand new and extremely popular nighttime spot is the **Grand Cafe,** at Deák Ferenc u. 18, ☎ **62/313-578.** Part cafe, part movie theater, the Grand Cafe is owned and run by graduates of Szeged's Attila József university. Three features play each day, beginning at 6pm, 8pm, and 10pm. You won't find any dubbed movies here. If the features don't interest you, stop in for a coffee and the artsy atmosphere. The Grand Cafe is open Monday through Friday 2pm to midnight; Saturday 5pm to midnight; Sunday 9:30am to noon and 5pm to midnight. No cover. Reservations are not accepted; a table can be hard to find.

# Appendix

Our transcription of Hungarian pronunciations is of necessity approximate. Stress is always on the first syllable, and all letters are pronounced (there are no diphthongs in Hungarian).

| | | | |
|---|---|---|---|
| a | t*au*t | ö | sub*u*rb, minus the r |
| á | b*ahh* | ő | same as above but held |
| e | *e*ver | | longer |
| é | d*ay* | u | l*oo*k |
| I | m*i*t | ú | b*oo*t |
| í | t*ee*n | ü | like the French fl*eu*ve |
| o | b*o*ne | ű | same as above but held |
| ó | same as above but held longer | | longer |

Most Hungarian consonants are pronounced approximately as they are in English, including the following: *b, d, f, h, k, l, m, n, p, t, v,* and *y.* There are some differences, however, particularly in the consonant combinations, as follows:

| | | | |
|---|---|---|---|
| c | ge*ts* | r | slightly rolled |
| cs | *ch*ill | s | *sh*eet |
| g | *g*ill | sz | *s*ix |
| gy | he*dge* | z | *z*ero |
| j | *y*outh | zs | a*z*ure, plea*s*ure |
| ny | as in Russian *ny*et | | |

## A  Menu Terms

### GENERAL TERMS

**Bors**  black pepper
**Főételek**  main courses
**Főzelék**  vegetable purée
**Gyümölcs**  fruits
**Halak**  fish
**Húsételek**  meat dishes
**Italok**  beverages
**Kenyér**  bread
**Levesek**  soups

**paprika**  red pepper/paprika
**Sajt**  cheese
**Saláták**  salads
**Só**  salt
**Tészták**  pasta/dessert
**Tojás**  eggs
**Vaj**  butter
**Zöldség**  vegetables

## COOKING TERMS

**Csípos** hot (peppery)
**Forró** hot (in temperature)
**Főzött** boiled
**Friss** fresh
**Fuszerezve** spiced
**Hideg** cold

**Párolt** steamed
**Pirított** toasted
**Pörkölt** stew
**Sútve** baked/fried
**Töltött** stuffed

## SOUPS (Levesek)

**Gombaleves** mushroom soup
**Gulyásleves** goulash soup
**Húsleves** bouillon
**Karfioleves** cauliflower soup
**Lencseleves** lentil soup

**Paradicsomkrémleves** cream of tomato soup
**Zöldborsöleves** pea soup
**Zöldségleves** vegetable soup

## EGGS (TOJÁS)

**Kolbásszal** with sausage
**Rántotta** scrambled eggs
**Sonkával** with ham

**Szalonnával** with bacon
**Tükörtojás** fried eggs

## MEAT & POULTRY (Hús és Baromfi)

**Bárány** lamb
**Bécsi szelet** Wiener schnitzel
**Borjú** veal
**Csirke** chicken
**Gulyás** goulash
**Kacsa** duck
**Kotlett** cutlet
**Liba** goose

**Marha** beef
**Sertés** pork
**Tokány** ragoût
**Pulyka** turkey
**Agyonsütve** well done
**Félig nyersen** rare
**Közepesen kisütve** medium

## FISH (Hal)

**Csuka** pike
**Fogas Balaton** pike-perch
**Halászlé** fish stew

**Pisztráng** trout
**Ponty** carp
**Tonhal** tuna

## VEGETABLES (Zöldség)

**Bab** beans
**Burgonya** potato
**Fokhagyma** garlic
**Gomba** mushrooms
**Hagyma** onion
**Káposzta** cabbage

**Paradicsom** tomato
**Sóska** sorrel
**Spenót** spinach
**Tök** squash
**Zöldbab** green beans

## SALADS (Saláta)

**Fejes saláta** green salad
**Paprikasaláta** pickled-pepper salad
**Uborkasaláta** cucumber salad

**Vegyes saláta** mixed salad
**Lecsó** stewed pepper, tomatoes, and onion

## FRUITS *(Gyümöcs)*

**Alma**  apple
**Barack**  apricot
**Cseresznye**  cherry
**Dinnye**  watermelon
**Körte**  pear
**Meggy**  sour cherry

**Narancs**  orange
**Őszibarack**  peach
**Sargadinnye**  cantaloupe
**Szilva**  plum
**Szőlő**  grapes

## DESSERTS

**Almás rétes**  apple strudel
**Dobos torta**  layer cake with caramel
candied frosting
**Fagylalt**  ice cream
**Ischler**  chocolate-dipped,
shortbread cookie sandwich

**Lekváros palacsinta**  crêpe filled
with preserves
**Meggyes rétes**  sour-cherry strudel
**Túrós rétes**  cheese strudel

## BEVERAGES

**Barna sör**  dark beer
**Fehér bor**  white wine
**Kávé**  coffee
**Koktél**  cocktail
**Narancslé**  orange juice

**Sör**  beer
**Tej**  milk
**Víz**  water
**Vörös bor**  red wine

# B  Basic Phrases & Vocabulary

## QUESTION WORDS (IN THE NOMINATIVE)

| English | Hungarian | Pronunciation |
|---|---|---|
| Where | **Hol** | hole |
| When | **Mikor** | *mee*-kor |
| What | **Mi** | mee |
| Why | **Miert** | *mee*-ayrt |
| Who | **Ki** | kee |
| How | **Hogy** | hohdge |

## USEFUL PHRASES

| | | |
|---|---|---|
| Good day/Hello | **Jó napot** | *yoh* napoht |
| Good morning | **Jó reggelt** | *yoh* reg-gelt |
| Good evening | **Jó estét** | *yoh* esh-tayt |
| Good-bye | **Viszontlátásra** | *vee*-sont-lah-tahsh-ra |
| My name is . . . | . . . **vagyok** | . . . *vodge*-yohk |
| Thank you | **Köszönöm** | *kuh*-suh-nuhm |
| You're welcome | **Kérem** | *kay*-rem |
| Please | **Legyen szíves** | *ledge*-yen *see*-vesh |
| Yes | **Igen** | *ee*-gen |
| No | **Nem** | *nem* |
| Good/Okay | **Jó** | *yo* |
| Excuse me | **Bocsánat** | *boh*-chahnat |
| How much does it cost? | **Mennyi bekerül?** | *men*-yee *beh*-keh-roohl? |

| **English** | **Hungarian** | **Pronunciation** |
|---|---|---|
| I don't understand | **Nem értem** | *nem* ayr-tem |
| I don't know | **Nem tudom** | *nem too*-dum |
| Where is the . . . ? | **Hol van a . . . ?** | *hohl* von a . . . ? |
| bus station | **busz állomás** | *boos ahh*-loh-mahsh |
| train station | **vonatállomás** | *vah*-not *ahh*-loh-mahsh |
| bank | **bank** | *bahnk* |
| museum | **múzeum** | *moo*-zeh-oom |
| pharmacy | **patiká** | *paw*-tee-kah |
| theater | **színház** | *seen*-hahz |
| tourist office | **turista iroda** | *too*-reesh-ta *eer*-ohda |
| embassy | **nagykövetség** | *nahdge koo*-vet-shayg |
| restaurant | **étterem** | *ayt*-teh-rehm |
| rest room | **wc** | *vayt*-say |

## RESTAURANT SERVICE

| | | |
|---|---|---|
| Breakfast | **Reggeli** | *rehg*-geh-lee |
| Lunch | **Ebéd** | *eh*-bayd |
| Dinner | **Vacsora** | *vah*-choh-rah |
| I would like . . . | **Kérnék . . .** | *kayr*-nayk . . . |
| a table | **Egy asztalot** | Edge *ah*-stah-lot |
| a menu | **egy étlapot** | edge *ayt*-lah-poht |
| a glass (of water) | **egy pohár (vizet)** | edge poh-har (*vee*-zet) |
| to pay | **fizetni** | *ee*-zeht-nee |
| I have a reservation | **Foglaltam már** | *fohg*-lawl-tahm mahr |

## TRAIN TRAVEL

| | | |
|---|---|---|
| A ticket, please | **Egy jegyet kérek** | *Edge ye*-dget *kay*-rek |
| Seat reservation | **helyjegy** | *heyh*-yedge |
| One way only | **csak oda** | *chalk oh*-da |
| Round-trip | **oda-vissza** | *oh*-dah-*vees*-sah |
| First class | **első osztály** | *ell*-shooh *oh*-stahy |
| Arrive | **érkezik** | *ayr*-kez-eek |
| Depart | **indul** | *inn*-doohl |
| Track | **Vagány** | *vah*-ghine |

## POST OFFICE

| | | |
|---|---|---|
| Airmail | **Légiposta** | *lay*-ghee-posh-ta |
| A stamp, please | **Egy bélyeget kérek** | Edge *bay*-yeh-get *kay*-rek |
| A postcard . . . | **Egy képeslapot . . .** | Edge *kay*-pesh law-poht |
| An envelope . . . | **Egy borítéket . . .** | Edge *bohr*-ree-tay-ket |

## USEFUL WORDS

| | | |
|---|---|---|
| map | **térkép** | *tayr*-kayp |
| police | **rendőrség** | *ren*-du(r)r-shayg |
| hospital | **korház** | *kohr*-hahhz |
| emergency | **szükséghelyzet** | *soohk*-shayg-hey-zet |
| theft | **lopás** | *loh*-pahsh |
| passport | **útlevél** | *oot*-leh-vayhl |

## SIGNS

| | | | |
|---|---|---|---|
| **Bejárat** | Entrance | **Tilos a dohányzás** | No Smoking |
| **Érkezések** | Arrivals | **Toalettek** | Toilets |
| **Indulások** | Departures | **Veszélyes** | Danger |
| **Informácio** | Information | **Vigyázat** | Beware |
| **Kijárat** | Exit | | |

## NUMBERS

| | | | |
|---|---|---|---|
| 1 | **egy** (*edge*) | 16 | **tizenhat** (*teez*-en-hawt) |
| 2 | **kettó** (*ket*-tu(r)) | 17 | **tizenhét** (*teez*-en-hayt) |
| 3 | **három** (*hahh*-rohm) | 18 | **tizennyolc** (*teez*-en-nyohlts) |
| 4 | **négy** (*naydge*) | 19 | **tizenkilenc** (*teez*-en-kee-lents) |
| 5 | **öt** (*u(r)t*) | 20 | **húsz** (*hoos*) |
| 6 | **hat** (*hawt*) | 30 | **harminc** (*hahr*-mints) |
| 7 | **hét** (*hayt*) | 40 | **negyven** (*nedge*-vehn) |
| 8 | **nyolc** (*nyohlts*) | 50 | **ötven** (*u(r)t*-vehn) |
| 9 | **kilenc** (*kee*-lents) | 60 | **hatvan** (*hawt*-vahn) |
| 10 | **tíz** (*teez*) | 70 | **hetven** (*het*-vehn) |
| 11 | **tizenegy** (*teez*-en-edge) | 80 | **nyolcvan** (*nyohlts*-vahn) |
| 12 | **tizenkettó** (*teez*-en-ket-tu(r)) | 90 | **kilencven** (*kee*-lents-vehn) |
| 13 | **tizenhárom** (*teez*-en-hahh-rohm) | 100 | **száz** (*sahhz*) |
| 14 | **tizennégy** (*teez*-en-naydge) | 500 | **ötszáz** (*u(r)t*-sahhz) |
| 15 | **tizenöt** (*teez*-en-u(r)t) | 1,000 | **ezer** (*eh*-zayr) |

# C  Useful Toll-Free Numbers & Web Sites

## AIRLINES

### Air Canada
☎ 800/776-3000
www.aircanada.ca

### American Airlines
☎ 800/433-7300
www.americanair.com

### British Airways
☎ 800/247-9297
☎ 0345/222-111 in Britain
www.british-airways.com

### Canadian Airlines International
☎ 800/426-7000
www.cdair.ca

### Continental Airlines
☎ 800/525-0280
www.flycontinental.com

### Delta Air Lines
☎ 800/221-1212
www.delta-air.com

### Trans World Airlines (TWA)
☎ 800/221-2000
www2.twa.com

### United Airlines
☎ 800/241-6522
www.ual.com

### US Airways
☎ 800/428-4322
www.usairways.com

### Virgin Atlantic Airways
☎ 800/862-8621 in
Continental U.S.
☎ 0293/747-747 in Britain
www.fly.virgin.com

## CAR-RENTAL AGENCIES

**Advantage**
☎ 800/777-5500
www.arac.com

**Avis**
☎ 800/331-1212 in the
Continental U.S.
☎ 800/TRY-AVIS in Canada
www.avis.com

**Budget**
☎ 800/527-0700
www.budgetrentacar.com

**Dollar**
☎ 800/800-4000

**Enterprise**
☎ 800/325-8007

**Hertz**
☎ 800/654-3131
www.hertz.com

**National**
☎ 800/CAR-RENT
www.nationalcar.com

**Payless**
☎ 800/PAYLESS
www.paylesscar.com

**Thrifty**
☎ 800/367-2277
www.thrifty.com

**Value**
☎ 800/327-2501
www.go-value.com

## MAJOR HOTEL & MOTEL CHAINS

**Best Western International**
☎ 800/528-1234
www.bestwestern.com

**Clarion Hotels**
☎ 800/CLARION
www.hotelchoice.com/cgi-bin/res/
webres?clarion.html

**Hilton Hotels**
☎ 800/HILTONS
www.hilton.com

**Holiday Inn**
☎ 800/HOLIDAY
www.holiday-inn.com

**Hyatt Hotels & Resorts**
☎ 800/228-9000
www.hyatt.com

**ITT Sheraton**
☎ 800/325-3535
www.sheraton.com

**Marriott Hotels**
800/228-9290
www.marriott.com

**Radisson Hotels International**
☎ 800/333-3333
www.radisson.com

**Ramada Inns**
☎ 800/2-RAMADA
www.ramada.com

# Index

See also separate Accommodations and Restaurants indexes, below.

## FROMMER'S® PORTABLE GUIDES

*(Pocket-size guides for travelers who want everything in a nutshell)*

Bahamas
California Wine Country
Charleston & Savannah
Chicago

Dublin
Las Vegas
London
Maine Coast
New Orleans

Puerto Vallarta, Manzanillo
  & Guadalajara
San Francisco
Venice
Washington, D.C.

## FROMMER'S® NATIONAL PARK GUIDES

*(Everything you need for the perfect park vacation)*

Grand Canyon
National Parks of the American West
Yellowstone & Grand Teton

Yosemite & Sequoia/
  Kings Canyon
Zion & Bryce Canyon

## FROMMER'S® IRREVERENT GUIDES

*(Wickedly honest guides for sophisticated travelers)*

Amsterdam
Chicago
London

Manhattan
New Orleans
Paris

San Francisco
Santa Fe

Walt Disney World
Washington, D.C.

## FROMMER'S® BY NIGHT GUIDES

*(The series for those who know that life begins after dark)*

Amsterdam
Chicago
Las Vegas
London

Los Angeles
Madrid
  & Barcelona
Manhattan

Miami
New Orleans
Paris

Prague
San Francisco
Washington, D.C.

## THE COMPLETE IDIOT'S TRAVEL GUIDES

*(The ultimate user-friendly trip planners)*

Cruise Vacations
Las Vegas
New Orleans

New York City
Planning Your Trip
  to Europe

San Francisco
Walt Disney World

## SPECIAL-INTEREST TITLES

Arthur Fommer's New World of Travel
The Civil War Trust's Official Guide to
  the Civil War Discovery Trail
Frommer's Caribbean Hideaways
Frommer's Complete Hostel Vacation
  Guide to England, Scotland & Wales
Frommer's Europe's Greatest
  Driving Tours
Frommer's Food Lover's Companion
  to France
Frommer's Food Lover's Companion to
  Italy
Israel Past & Present
New York City with Kids
New York Times Weekends

Outside Magazine's Adventure Guide
  to New England
Outside Magazine's Adventure Guide
  to Northern California
Outside Magazine's Adventure Guide
  to the Pacific Northwest
Outside Magazine's Adventure Guide
  to Southern California & Baja
Outside Magazine's Guide to Family Vacations
Places Rated Almanac
Retirement Places Rated
Washington, D.C., with Kids
Wonderful Weekends from New York City
Wonderful Weekends from San Francisco
Wonderful Weekends from Los Angeles

# WHEREVER YOU TRAVEL, *H*ELP IS NEVER FAR AWAY.

From planning your trip to providing travel assistance along the way, American Express® Travel Service Offices are always there to help you do more.

| *Hungary* |
| --- |

American Express Travel Service
Deak Ferenc U 10
Budapest
36-1-2668680

do more®  AMERICAN EXPRESS
Travel

http://www.americanexpress.com/travel
**American Express Travel Service Offices
are found in central locations
throughout Eastern Europe.**